International specification for developing and continuously improving preventive maintenance

S4000P-B6865-04000-00

Issue No. 2.1

S-Series IPS specifications
Block release 2021

Publisher:

Applicable to: All

S4000P-A-00-00-0000-00A-001A-A

This specification has been developed by the following organizations:

–	AIRBUS Defence & Space	Germany & Spain
–	AIRBUS Helicopters	Germany
–	Babcock International Group (LSC Group)	United Kingdom
–	BAE Systems	United Kingdom
–	DBM Engineering Solutions Ltd	United Kingdom
–	Fox Flight Systems	Germany
–	HICO-ICS GmbH t/a HICO Technology Austria (HICO-AT)	Austria
–	Isselnord S.R.L.	Italy
–	Logistikkommando der Bundeswehr (LogKdoBw)	Germany
–	Saab AB	Sweden
–	Sopra Steria	France/Germany
–	Thyssenkrupp Marine Systems (tkMS)	United Kingdom
–	UK MoD	United Kingdom

Editor:

–	O'Neil & Associates, Inc.	United States of America

Copyright and user agreement

1 Copyright

Copyright© 2021 AeroSpace and Defence Industries Association of Europe - ASD

All rights reserved. No part of this document may be reproduced or transmitted in any form or by any means, electronic or mechanical, including photocopying and recording, or by any information storage or retrieval system, except as may be expressly permitted by the Copyright Act or in writing by the Publisher.

S4000P™ is a trademark owned by ASD.

S1000D® is an in EU registered trademark owned by ASD.

All correspondence and queries should be directed to:

ASD
Rue du Trône
1050 Brussels
Belgium

2 Agreement for use of the specification S4000P™ suite of information

2.1 Definitions

S4000P™ suite of information means, but is not limited to:

- the "International specification for developing and continuously improving preventive maintenance" - ASD S4000P
- examples (e.g., XML instances, PDF files, style sheets) and schemas
- any other software or information under the heading "**S4000P™ suite of information**" available for download from www.s4000p.org

Copyright Holder means AeroSpace and Defence Industries Association of Europe (ASD).

2.2 Notice to user

By using all or any portion of **S4000P™ suite of information** you accept the terms and conditions of this User Agreement.

This User Agreement is enforceable against you and any legal entity that has obtained **S4000P™** or any portion thereof and on whose behalf it is used.

2.3 License to use

As long as you comply with the terms of this User Agreement, the Copyright Holder grant to you a non-exclusive license to use **S4000P™ suite of information**.

2.4 Intellectual property rights

S4000P™ suite of information is the intellectual property of and is owned by the Copyright Holder. Except as expressly stated herein, this User Agreement does not grant you any intellectual property right in the **S4000P™ suite of information** and all rights not expressly granted are reserved by the Copyright Holder.

2.5 No modifications

You shall not modify, adapt or translate, in whole or in part, **S4000P™ suite of information**. You may however add business rules.

Applicable to: All   **S4000P-A-00-00-0000-00A-021A-A**

2.6 No warranty

S4000P™ suite of information is being delivered to you "as is". The Copyright Holder does not warrant the performance or result you may obtain by using **S4000P™ suite of information**. The Copyright Holders make no warranties, representations or indemnities, express or implied, whether by statute, common law, custom, usage or otherwise as to any matter including without limitation merchantability, integration, satisfactory quality, fitness for any particular purpose, or non-infringement of third parties rights.

2.7 Limitation of liability

In no event will the Copyright Holders be liable to you for any damages, claims or costs whatsoever or any consequential, indirect or incidental damages, or any lost profits or lost savings or for any claim by a third party, even if the Copyright Holder has been advised of the possibility of such damages, claims, costs, lost profits or lost savings.

2.8 Indemnity

You agree to defend, indemnify, and hold harmless the Copyright Holder and its parents and affiliates and all of their employees, agents, directors, officers, proprietors, partners, representatives, shareholders, servants, attorneys, predecessors, successors, assigns, and those who have worked on the preparation, publication or distribution of the **S4000P™ suite of information** from and against any and all claims, proceedings, damages, injuries, liabilities, losses, costs, and expenses (including reasonable attorneys' fees and litigation expenses), relating to or arising from your use of **S4000P™ suite of information** or any breach by you of this User Agreement.

2.9 Governing law and arbitration

This User Agreement will be governed by and construed in accordance with the laws of the Kingdom of Belgium.

In the event of any dispute, controversy or claim arising out of or in connection with this User Agreement, or the breach, termination or invalidity thereof, the parties agree to submit the matter to settlement proceedings under the ICC (International Chamber of Commerce) ADR (Alternative Dispute Resolution) Rules. If the dispute has not been settled pursuant to the said Rules within 45 days following the filing of a Request for ADR or within such other period as the parties may agree in writing, such dispute shall be finally settled under the Rules of Arbitration of the International Chamber of Commerce by three arbitrators appointed in accordance with the said Rules of Arbitration. All related proceedings should be at the place of the ICC in Paris, France.

The language to be used in the arbitral proceedings shall be English.

Note

The following letter from the Secretary General of ASD extends the special usage rights of this specification and has been included for information, without affecting the technical contents. The content of this letter will be included in the copyright information as part of the S-Series 2024 block release.

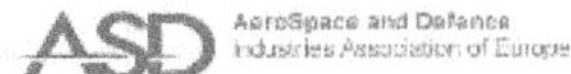

Special Usage Rights for the S-Series Specifications

To whom it may concern,

This letter seeks to clarify the special usage rights for the suite of documents known as the S-Series Specifications, for which the Aerospace and Defence Industries Association of Europe (ASD) holds the copyright and trademark.

The special usage rights are described as follows:

Permission to use or deliver training from the information contained in the S-Series Specifications, and the right to reproduce or publish the S-Series Specifications, in whole or in part, is hereby given to the following:

1. National Associations who are members of ASD and all their member companies;

2. Members of Aerospace Industries Association of America;

3. Members of the ATA e-Business Program;

4. Members of International Coordinating Council of Aerospace Industries Associations (ICCAIA) not included in categories 1 through 2 inclusively;

5. Airlines and Armed Forces that are customers of Companies included in Categories 1 through 3 inclusively;

6. Ministries of Defence of the member countries of ASD, of NATO and NATO Partners[1];

7. The Department of Defense of the USA;

8. NATO bodies, organizations & agencies;

9. Universities;

10. Technologies and Research Institutes.

Any further requirement for clarification, should in the first instance be directed to the Service Commission of the ASD.

Yours Sincerely,

Jan Pie

Secretary General of ASD

---

[1] as per: https://www.nato.int/cps/en/natohq/51288.htm);

Page intentionally blank.

Highlights

Table of contents

Page

Highlights 1

References..1

1   General 1

2   Editorial changes 1

3   Content 2

List of tables

1   References 1

2   Chap 1 2

3   Chap 2 2

5   Chap 4 3

4   Chap 6 4

References

Table 1 References

Chapter/Document No.	Title
Chap 1	Introduction to the specification
Chap 2	Developing PMTR
Chap 4	S4000P Interfaces
Chap 6	Terms, abbreviations and acronyms

1 General

Changes that are included in this Issue are 2.1 are limited to changes and updates in Chap 1, Chap 2, Chap 4 and Chap 6. Issue 2.1 is mainly driven by necessary updates in Chap 2.3 (System Analysis)

2 Editorial changes

Editorial changes are not changed marked in this Issue 2.1. Similarly, editorial changes are not described in detail is these highlights pages.

3 Content

Highlights of changes to chapters 2, 4 and 6 (and their subchapters), are provided.

Note

The main table of contents, in the front matter, has been updated to include the change of the chapter 4.2 title to replace "ILS" with "IPS".

For:

- chapter 1, refer to Table 2
- chapter 2, refer to Table 3
- chapter 4, refer to Table 4
- chapter 6, refer to Table 5

Table 2 Chap 1

Chapter	Summary of changes from Issue 2.0 to Issue 2.1
Chap 1.1	– Change of the wording of the NOTE before the new Para 1.3.
	– Introduction of the additional Para Harmonization as Para 1.3 between Para S4000P ASD approval (Para 1,2) and Para S4000P future revisions (before Para 1.3, now Para 1.4)
	– Update of the wording in the last text section of the new Para 1.4
Chap 1.2	– Editorial changes
Chap 1.3	– Editorial changes
Chap 1.4	– Editorial change

Table 3 Chap 2

Chapter	Summary of changes from Issue 2.0 to Issue 2.1
Chap 2.1	– Editorial change
Chap 2.2	– Update of Para 1.1 (Purpose) in the second half of the text
Chap 2.3	– Supplement S3000L in Table 1 (References)
	– Update of the header line and wording in Para 2.3
	– Update of the wording in the first text segment before the 4 questions in Para 2.4.
	– Update of the wording in the NOTE after the 4 questions in Para 2.4.
	– Deletion of "customers or" before "users" in Para 3.1
	– Update of Para 3.5 after Fig 6: Modified explanation, how fault tolerant systems are defined and covered by the system analysis methodology in chapter 2.3
	– Minor updates of the explanation of Fig 8 in Para 4.1.2
	– Modification of the text segment after Fig 18 in Para 4.2.2 by introduction of bullet points
	– Update of the explanations related to Fig 26 thru Fig 29 in Para 4.2.3
	– Replacement of "maintenance task type" by "PMTRI task type" in Para 4.2.4 Table 2
	– Deletion of "/user" in Para 4.2.5, Table 3, at column FFEC 3 and FFEC 7

Chapter	Summary of changes from Issue 2.0 to Issue 2.1
	– Replacement of "maintenance task type" by "PMTRI task type" and "maintenance task" by "PMTRI" in Para 4.2.6 including Table 4
	– Update of the PMTRI task type selection criteria for the PMTRI task type "Restoration/Overhaul" in combination with "economic effect" (FFEC 4 & 8) in Table 4 in Para 4.2.6
	– Update of the PMTRI task type selection criteria for the PMTRI task type "TCI" in combination with "Economic effect" (FFEC 4 & 8) in Table 4 in Para 4.2.6
	– Update of the sentence before the last sentence and further minor wording updates in Para 5.1
	– Minor wording updates in Para 5.2
	– Modification of Fig 30 and Fig 31: Replacement of "deterioration" by "deterioration/degradation"
	– Update of the header line of Para 5.2.2
	– Correction of the numbering of the referenced Fig from Fig 32 to Fig 31
	– Replacement of "scheduled maintenance task" by PMTRI and "maintenance task type" by "PMTRI task type" and update of last sentence in Para 5.3.2
	– Update of the wording in Para 6
	– Minor wording updates in Para 7

Table 4 Chap 4

Chapter	Summary of changes from Issue 2.0 to Issue 2.1
Chap 4.0	– Title of chapter 4.2 changed to replace "ILS" with "IPS"
Chap 4.1	– Title of chapter 4.2 in Table 1, changed to replace "ILS" with "IPS"
Chap 4.2	– Title changed to replace "ILS" with "IPS"
	– Supplement of "Product maintenance program" before abbreviations OMP
	– Update of header lines of Para 2, 2.1, 3 and 3.1,
	– Update of the wording of the last two sentences in Para 2
	– Update of the wording of the last sentence in Para 3
	– Update of Fig 1 thru Fig 4
Chap 4.6	– Update of Fig 1 (replace "ILS" with "IPS")

Table 5 Chap 6

Chapter	Summary of changes from Issue 2.0 to Issue 2.1
Chap 6.2	– Shift definition for "acceptable corrosion level" according to correct alphabetical sequence
	– Supplement definition for "failure"
	– Update definition for "General Visual Inspection (GVI)"
	– Supplement definition for "Life Cycle (LC)"
	– Update definition for "maintenance relevant structure" in line with Chapter 2.4
	– Update definition for "non-critical structure"
	– Update definition for "Product"
	– Update definition for "Structure Significant Item (SSI)" in line with Chapter 2.4
	– Update definition for "uncritical structure" in line with Chapter 2.4
Chap 6.3	– Update abbreviation for DEF-STAN
	– Supplement AFRP, CFRP, EIS, F, GFRP, ILS, IPS, LC, LSA, MTA, OMR, PMRB, PMTL, P/N, UV
	– Update abbreviations for PMTRE and PMTRI

Applicable to: All

End of data module

DMC-S4000P-A-00-00-0000-00A-0UA-A_002-00_EN-US.docx

Table of contents

The listed documents are included in Issue 2.1, dated 2021-04-30, of this publication.

Chapter	Data module title	Data module code	Applic
Chap 1	Introduction to the specification	S4000P-A-01-00-0000-00A-009A-A	All
Chap 1.1	Purpose	S4000P-A-01-01-0000-00A-040A-A	All
Chap 1.2	Scope	S4000P-A-01-02-0000-00A-040A-A	All
Chap 1.3	How to use the specification	S4000P-A-01-03-0000-00A-040A-A	All
Chap 1.4	Changes to the specification	S4000P-A-01-04-0000-00A-040A-A	All
Chap 2	Developing PMTR	S4000P-A-02-00-0000-00A-009A-A	All
Chap 2.1	Developing PMTR - General	S4000P-A-02-01-0000-00A-040A-A	All
Chap 2.2	Developing PMTR - Development of preventive maintenance task requirements (PMTR)	S4000P-A-02-02-0000-00A-040A-A	All
Chap 2.3	Developing PMTR - System analysis	S4000P-A-02-03-0000-00A-040A-A	All
Chap 2.4	Developing PMTR - Structure analysis	S4000P-A-02-04-0000-00A-040A-A	All
Chap 2.5	Developing PMTR - Zonal analysis	S4000P-A-02-05-0000-00A-040A-A	All
Chap 2.6	Developing PMTR - Consolidation of analysis results, harmonization with other preventive maintenance task requirement sources for traceability	S4000P-A-02-06-0000-00A-040A-A	All
Chap 2.7	Developing PMTR - Special event analysis	S4000P-A-02-07-0000-00A-040A-A	All
Chap 3	Optimizing PMTR	S4000P-A-03-00-0000-00A-009A-A	All
Chap 3.1	Optimizing PMTR - General	S4000P-A-03-01-0000-00A-040A-A	All
Chap 3.2	Optimizing PMTR - ISMO preparation phase	S4000P-A-03-02-0000-00A-040A-A	All
Chap 3.3	Optimizing PMTR - ISMO analysis phase	S4000P-A-03-03-0000-00A-040A-A	All
Chap 3.4	Optimizing PMTR - ISMO follow-up phase	S4000P-A-03-04-0000-00A-040A-A	All
Chap 3.5	Optimizing PMTR - Review of PMTRE for special events	S4000P-A-03-05-0000-00A-040A-A	All
Chap 4	S4000P Interfaces	S4000P-A-04-00-0000-00A-009A-A	All
Chap 4.1	S4000P Interfaces - General	S4000P-A-04-01-0000-00A-040A-A	All

Chapter	Data module title	Data module code	Applic
Chap 4.2	S4000P Interfaces - S4000P interfaces outside the S-Series IPS specifications	S4000P-A-04-02-0000-00A-040A-A	All
Chap 4.3	S4000P Interfaces - S1000D	S4000P-A-04-03-0000-00A-040A-A	All
Chap 4.4	S4000P Interfaces - S3000L	S4000P-A-04-04-0000-00A-040A-A	All
Chap 4.5	S4000P Interfaces - S5000F	S4000P-A-04-05-0000-00A-040A-A	All
Chap 4.6	S4000P Interfaces - SX000i	S4000P-A-04-06-0000-00A-040A-A	All
Chap 5	Data model and data exchange	S4000P-A-05-00-0000-00A-009A-A	All
Chap 5.1	Data model and data exchange - General	S4000P-A-05-01-0000-00A-040A-A	All
Chap 5.2	Data model and data exchange - Data model	S4000P-A-05-02-0000-00A-040A-A	All
Chap 5.3	Data model and data exchange - Data exchange	S4000P-A-05-03-0000-00A-040A-A	All
Chap 6	Terms, abbreviations and acronyms	S4000P-A-06-00-0000-00A-009A-A	All
Chap 6.1	Terms, abbreviations and acronyms - General	S4000P-A-06-01-0000-00A-040A-A	All
Chap 6.2	Terms, abbreviations and acronyms - Glossary of terms	S4000P-A-06-02-0000-00A-040A-A	All
Chap 6.3	Terms, abbreviations and acronyms - Abbreviations and acronyms	S4000P-A-06-03-0000-00A-040A-A	All
Chap 7	Examples	S4000P-A-07-00-0000-00A-009A-A	All
Chap 7.1	Examples - General	S4000P-A-07-01-0000-00A-040A-A	All
Chap 7.2	Examples - Product system analysis	S4000P-A-07-02-0000-00A-040A-A	All
Chap 7.3	Examples - Policy and Procedure Handbook content	S4000P-A-07-03-0000-00A-040A-A	All

Chapter 1

Introduction to the specification

Chapter	Data module title	Data module code	Applic
Chap 1	Introduction to the specification	S4000P-A-01-00-0000-00A-009A-A	All
Chap 1.1	Purpose	S4000P-A-01-01-0000-00A-040A-A	All
Chap 1.2	Scope	S4000P-A-01-02-0000-00A-040A-A	All
Chap 1.3	How to use the specification	S4000P-A-01-03-0000-00A-040A-A	All
Chap 1.4	Maintenance of the specification	S4000P-A-01-04-0000-00A-040A-A	All

Page intentionally blank.

Chapter 1.1

Purpose

Table of contents

Page

Purpose 1

References..1

1 Preface 2
1.1 History and feasibility...2
1.2 S4000P ASD approval...2
1.3 Harmonization...3
1.4 S4000P future revisions 3
2 Objective...4

List of tables

1 References 1

List of figures

1 S-Series of IPS specifications 3

References

Table 1 References

Chap No./Document No.	Title
Chap 1.4	Changes to the specification
Chap 2.7	Developing PMTR - Special event analysis
Chap 3.1	Optimizing PMTR - General
Chap 3.2	Optimizing PMTR - ISMO preparation phase
Chap 3.3	Optimizing PMTR - ISMO analysis phase
Chap 3.4	Optimizing PMTR - ISMO follow-up phase
Chap 3.5	Optimizing PMTR - Review of PMTRE for special events
Chap 4	S4000P Interfaces
Chap 5	Data model and data exchange
S3000L	International procedure specification for Logistic Support Analysis - LSA
SX000i	International guide for the use of the S-Series Integrated Product Support (IPS) specifications
SX000H	Harmonized Suite of the S-Series Integrated Product Support (IPS) Specifications

Chap No./Document No.	Title
www.s4000p.org	Internet homepage of the international specification ASD S4000P

1 Preface

1.1 History and feasibility

In 2004, the Customer Product Support Committee (CPSC) of AECMA (Association européenne des constructeurs de matériel aérospatial) decided to conduct a feasibility study for a new specification/handbook for "developing scheduled maintenance programs for military aircraft". A task was allocated to a group of maintenance specialists from different European aircraft/components manufacturers with direction to perform that feasibility study. The results of the feasibility study were approved by the CPSC of AECMA and the task for developing that specification/handbook was officially launched.

Since 2005 AECMA is named Aerospace and Defense Industries association of Europe (ASD) and CPSC is now named Product Services Specification Group (PSSG).

A new specification S4000M was developed taking into account existing and approved analysis procedures/specifications available. In addition, the S4000M development team took into consideration the experience of analysts from European and world-wide industry in using different analytical methodologies specifically at military and civil aeronautics industries.

Due to an updated scope of ASD based on market needs, the S4000M specification was neither published nor applied for Product analytical purposes.

The following points led to the development of a new specification S4000P Issue 1.0 that replaced S4000M in May 2014:

- Applicability of the described analysis methodologies on all complex technical Product types
- Implementation of innovations and new analysis methodologies in Product system analysis, structure analysis and zonal analysis for developing Preventive Maintenance Task Requirements with repetitive scheduled Intervals (PMTRI)
- Necessity of information about consolidation, harmonization and traceability of analysis results from system-, structure- and zonal analysis and in between
- Extension of the applicability of the specification on the whole life cycle of a Product by introduction of an In-Service Maintenance Optimization (ISMO) process for preventive maintenance tasks with intervals (PMTRI)
- Description and clarification of interfaces between S4000P and other specifications of the S-Series IPS specifications and further interfaces outside the S-Series
- Introduction of examples to support Product analysis eg, for developing a Policy and Procedure Handbook (PPH))

1.2 S4000P ASD approval

The content of each issue of S4000P has been prepared by experts from various European industries and Product customers. After a final editorial check of every document issue according to the S1000D rules, ASD decides to publish the specification.

S4000P is an integrated part of the S-Series IPS specifications. Relevant interfaces to and from this specification are described in Chap 4. Refer to Fig 1.

Interfaces of S4000P with the focus on the data model and data exchange for the purpose of Information Technology (IT) are described in Chap 5 of this document.

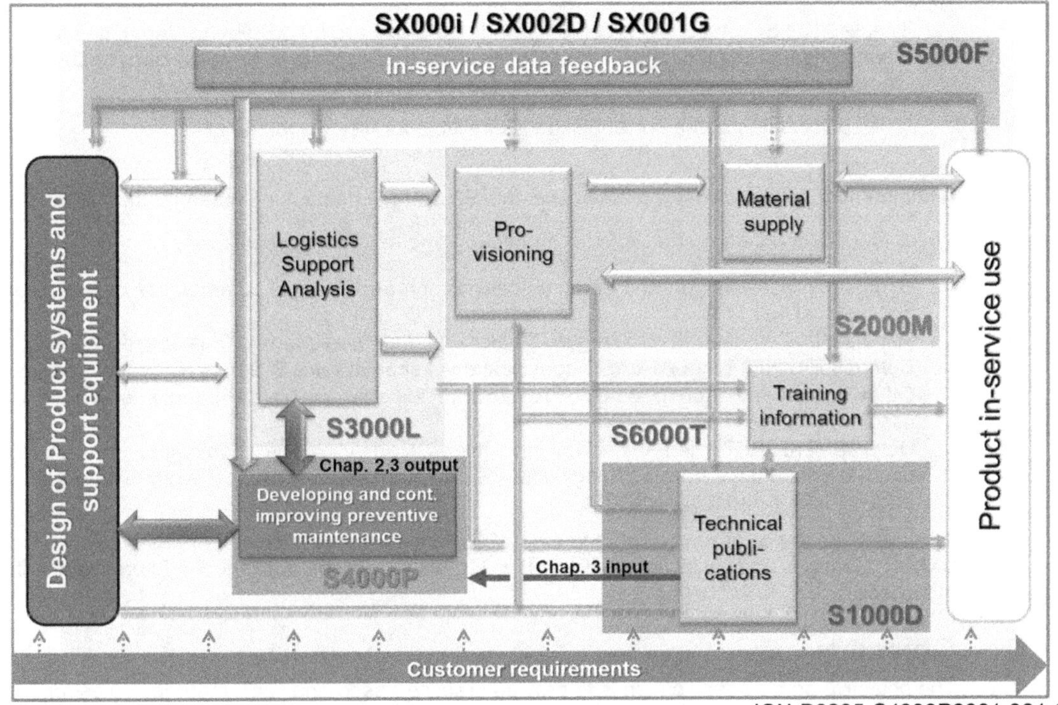

Fig 1 S - Series IPS specifications

In <u>Fig 1</u> the main interrelations between the specifications S1000D, S2000M, S3000L, S4000P, S5000F and S6000T with the focus on the integration of S4000P into the S-Series IPS specifications are shown. SX000i and the subordinated specifications SX002D and SX001G cover overall information and regulations related to interfaces, interrelations and data exchange within the S-Series IPS specifications.

Note

The S-Series of IPS specifications shown in <u>Fig 1</u> do not cover all IPS elements described in SX000i. A future extension of the specification suite on further IPS elements is expected.

1.3   Harmonization

In 2021, the S-Series IPS Council decided to publish the S-Series of IPS specifications together in a so-called "block release". To achieve this, an overarching handbook has been developed that brings all the specifications together, in an integrated manner. The issue date for SX000H in common with all the S-Series IPS specifications is 2021-04-30. Refer to SX000H.

1.4   S4000P future revisions

An international Steering Committee (SC) was already established for S4000M in January 2013. This SC switched the responsibility from S4000M to S4000P in December 2013. The future update/development of this specification is intended to be done in cooperation with experts from national and international industry organizations and in addition with customers' contribution.

The S4000P SC is responsible for maintaining the specification.

Note

The S4000P SC must not be confused with the project-related Steering Committee for developing and continuously improving preventive maintenance for a specific Product as described in Chap ¡**Error! No se encuentra el origen de la referencia.**.

This specification at the current issue is available for free download at: www.s4000p.org.

A comment/question form is available and an ASD point of contact is named on this website.

The S4000P SC will be responsible for monitoring and reviewing the following:

- Comments received from the aeronautical and non-aeronautical communities or any other body associated to ASD
- Modifications as a result of changes in other documents relevant for this specification
- Compatibility with other AIA/ASD specifications especially the S-Series IPS specifications
- Other inputs (new or changed laws, regulations, experiences from Product in-service usages, etc.)
- Development and implementation of innovations in analytical methodologies, incl. coverage of up-to-date analysis methodology aspects and/or implementation of "lessons learned" from S4000P project applications

Comments and/or questions related to the S4000P content must follow the rules published in SX000i. Changes and updates agreed by the S4000P SC will be published in future issues of this specification. Refer to Chap 1.4.

2 Objective

The objective of this specification is to provide practice-based analytical methodologies for developing PMTR with repetitive scheduled intervals (PMTRI) as the basis for elaboration of initial preventive maintenance programs for Products. In addition, preventive maintenance programs must comprise sets of preventive maintenance tasks without repetitive scheduled intervals that are applicable, effective and performed after the confirmed entry or after the assumed entry of special events (PMTRE). Refer to Chap 2.6 and S3000L.

In addition, processes for continuously improving preventive maintenance during the Product in-service phase are provided. Refer to Chap 3.1 thru Chap 3.5.

Project regulatory requirements, if any, must be met and the specified processes and methodologies must be acceptable to customers and manufacturers. This specification can be applied to any Product that needs to meet continued Product safety, law conformity, environmental integrity and mission/operational requirements at maximum availability and minimum cost. These aspects justify the costs and effort of applying S4000P analysis and methodologies to a project.

This specification concentrates on covering in-service Product usage under specified usage conditions (eg, those defined in a Product use study). If an analysis is partially or completely based on design solutions that are not completely frozen, it should be recorded in the respective analysis for confirming and/or updating the analysis results.

In order to meet the requirements of the project it is essential that, with customer support, the analysis results from the S4000P analysis be interchanged with other specifications of the S-Series IPS specifications. An S4000P data model and the data exchange can be used for that. Refer to Chap 5. For information on the complete suite of the S-Series IPS specification's data exchange in between the specifications, Refer to SX000i.

Chapter 1.2

Scope

Table of contents

Page

Scope   1

References...1

1   Scope..2

2   Analysis methods..3

List of tables

1   References 1

References

Table 1 References

Chap No./Document No.	Title
Chap 2.1	Developing PMTR - General
Chap 2.2	Developing PMTR - Development of preventive maintenance task requirements (PMTR)
Chap 2.3	Developing PMTR - System analysis
Chap 2.4	Developing PMTR - Structure analysis
Chap 2.5	Developing PMTR - Zonal analysis
Chap 2.6	Developing PMTR - Consolidation of analysis results, harmonization with other preventive maintenance task requirement sources for traceability
Chap 2.7	Developing PMTR - Special event analysis
Chap 3.1	Optimizing PMTR - General
Chap 3.2	Optimizing PMTR - ISMO preparation phase
Chap 3.3	Optimizing PMTR - ISMO analysis phase
Chap 3.4	Optimizing PMTR - ISMO follow-up phase
Chap 3.5	Optimizing PMTR - Review of PMTRE for special events
Chap 4.2	S4000P Interfaces - Outside the S-Series IPS specifications
Chap 4.3	S4000P Interfaces - S1000D
Chap 4.4	S4000P Interfaces - S3000L
Chap 4.5	S4000P Interfaces - S5000F
Chap 4.6	S4000P Interfaces - SX000i

Chap No./Document No.	Title
Chap 5	Data model and data exchange
Chap 7	Examples

1 Scope

In line with the other S-Series IPS specifications, the terms "the Product" and "project" are introduced as follows:

- **Product** - Any technical platform, system, equipment, vehicle, facility, etc, be it air, sea, land, space, civil or military eg, aerial ropeway systems, trains, ships, submarines, wind energy production plants, etc.

- **project** - The task spectrum to develop, maintain and dispose of the Product

As well as aspects covered by existing, valid analysis procedures/specifications, this specification also takes into account the following requirements/aspects which are recommended to be articulated in a Product-specific PPH:

- Operation of the Product in both normal and adverse conditions
- Extension of applicability from the aeronautical industry on other technical Product groups
- Introduction of "mission" next to "operation" as a Functional Failure Effect (FFE) in system analysis
- Introduction of FFE related to environmental integrity or other aspects eg, confliction with law in system analysis
- Standardization of the preventive maintenance task type selection
- Introduction of an interface between the logic-based preventive maintenance analysis and the concept for Product Health and Condition Monitoring (PHCM) for Product systems and between the concept for Structure Health and Condition Monitoring (SHCM) and Product structure analysis
- Provision of selection logics for determining technically correct interval type(s) and applicable numerical interval value(s) for PMTRI
- Analysis of accidental damage on Product structure (for civil and military Product usage)
- Analysis of environmental deterioration impact on Product structure (for civil and military Product usage)
- Introduction of the category "maintenance relevant structure" in structure analysis
- Introduction of Significant Details (SD) to be defined within an SSI (if necessary) in structure analysis
- Modularity and flexibility for adaptations of the zonal analysis methodology to allow the analysis of aeronautical and non-aeronautical technical Products
- Harmonization of PMTRI in between the single analysis sources (system, structure and zonal analysis) and with additional, S4000P-external PMTRI sources (eg, Certification Maintenance Requirements (CMR), national law(s))
- Integration of the special event analysis developing PMTRE
- Introduction of processes to optimize PMTRI and/or PMTRE. For PMTRI the In-Service Maintenance Optimization (ISMO) process must be applied during the Product in-service phase
- Interconnection of the initial analysis results from developing PMTR (refer to Chap 2.1 thru Chap 2.7) with the Optimization of PMTR (refer to Chap 3.1 thru Chap 3.5) for continuously improving preventive maintenance
- Description of S4000P interfaces within the S-Series IPS specifications. Refer to Chap 4.3 thru Chap 4.6.
- Description of S4000P interfaces outside the S-Series IPS specifications. Refer to Chap 4.2.

- Modifications in definitions and processes to meet requirements from individual Product types
- Definition of a data model and provision of information on data exchange(s). Refer to Chap 5.
- Provision of examples supporting the understanding of this specification and its application for various projects. Refer to Chap 7.

2 Analysis methods

S4000P provides analysis methods in the following chapters:

- Development of PMTR. Refer to Chap 2.
- System analysis. Refer to Chap 2.3.
- Structure analysis. Refer to Chap 2.4.
- Zonal analysis, including enhanced zonal analysis, L/HIRF analysis and other analysis modules. Refer to Chap 2.5.
- Special event analysis and PMTRE development. Refer to Chap 2.7.
- Optimizing PMTR - General. Refer to Chap 3.1.
- ISMO preparation phase. Refer to Chap 3.2.
- ISMO analysis phase. Refer to Chap 3.3.
- ISMO follow-up phase. Refer to Chap 3.4.
- Review of PMTRE for special events. Refer to Chap 3.5.

Each chapter in S4000P contains its own explanatory process on basis of traceable decision logic diagram(s), as appropriate.

S4000P chapters can be used independently for Product analysis, without other S4000P chapters.

Page intentionally blank.

Chapter 1.3

How to use the specification

Table of contents

Page

How to use the specification 1

References 1

1   Project organization 2
1.1   Program steering committee 2
1.2   Working groups 2
2   Preparation of a Product-specific PPH 3
2.1   Maintenance program/OMP development 4
2.2   Maintenance program/OMP optimization during a Product in-service phase 5

List of tables

1   References 1

References

Table 1 References

Chap No./Document No.	Title
Chap 2.1	Developing PMTR - General
Chap 2.2	Developing PMTR – Development of preventive maintenance task requirements (PMTR)
Chap 2.3	Developing PMTR - System analysis
Chap 2.4	Developing PMTR - Structure analysis
Chap 2.5	Developing PMTR - Zonal analysis
Chap 2.6	Developing PMTR - Consolidation of analysis results, harmonization with other preventive maintenance task requirement sources for traceability
Chap 2.7	Developing PMTR - Special event analysis
Chap 3.1	Optimizing PMTR - General
Chap 3.2	Optimizing PMTR - ISMO preparation phase
Chap 3.3	Optimizing PMTR - ISMO analysis phase
Chap 3.4	Optimizing PMTR - ISMO follow-up phase
Chap 3.5	Optimizing PMTR - Review of PMTRE for special events
Chap 4	S4000P Interfaces
Chap 5	Data model and data exchange
Chap 7	Examples

Chap No./Document No.	Title
S1000D	International specification for technical publications using a common source database
S3000L	International procedure specification for Logistics Support Analysis LSA

1 Project organization

To ensure the effective management and conduct of:

- the development of PMTRI during the Product design and development phase
- the correct application of the ISMO methodology for PMTRI during the Product in-service phase
- the development and review (during the Product in-service phase, if necessary) of PMTRE sets applicable for special events

the project organization should consist of appropriate stakeholders as representatives of the Product.

The final decision process, including the specialist involvement, will be decided by the Product manufacturer in accordance with the program objectives, contract and certification requirements. This means that it is up to the Product manufacturer to decide the organization required, support documentation and the involvement of operators, authorities, equipment manufacturers, etc, into the process. Details must be described in a PPH.

1.1 Program steering committee

A program Steering Committee (SC) should be established and be responsible for managing preventive maintenance development and improvement activities. The program SC should comprise members from representative stakeholders including, but not limited to, operator(s), the prime manufacturer, the main equipment manufacturers/suppliers and regulatory authorities (if involved).

The responsibilities of the project SC include, but are not limited to:

- overall governance and establishing of both policy and initial goals for the preventive maintenance of a Product
- providing directions to analysis working group activities
- liaising with manufacturers and operators, as required
- establishing contact(s) to research- and/or test institution(s)
- preparing the final recommendations
- ensuring that a Product specification for developing PMTR and/or for optimizing PMTR is applied on the complete Product (systems, structure and zones)
- coordinating inputs related to Product preventive maintenance
- perform top-level program decisions

Where applicable, the program SC will advise working groups to account for vendor requirements, accepting them only if they are both applicable and effective according to the criteria of S4000P.

1.2 Working groups

Specialist working groups should be formed as necessary to perform the analytical work. Members of these working groups should be suitably qualified and experienced specialists from the appropriate stakeholders.

To ensure the correct application of this specification, all personnel involved in the analysis, must be trained before starting any analytical work.

In parallel, the program SC will explore all possible avenues to obtain the detailed technical information necessary to enable the working groups to:

- determine applicable and effective PMTRI
- highlight and justify identified redesign requirements and/or recommendations based on analytical results
- evaluate the effectiveness and applicability of preventive maintenance tasks with repetitive scheduled intervals defined in the Product technical publication on basis of the ISMO process using in-service data/task background information (eg, PMTRI)
- determine PMTRE sets applicable for special events
- review PMTRE sets during the Product in-service phase

In all cases, it is essential that a documented audit trail be kept to support the recommendations from the working groups to the SC. Once these recommendations have been approved by the SC all supporting evidence and analyses should, when required, be consolidated into one or more report(s) or dataset(s) for submission to the appropriate regulatory authorities and/or to respective manufacturer quality control departments. After acceptance and after release of the analysis results, the PMTR data transfer for further Product support activities take place. Refer to Chap 4 and Chap 5. Depending on the project, a continuous review and update process of the PMTR must be established if, for example, the Product becomes subject to numerous design changes.

2 Preparation of a Product-specific PPH

It is essential that this specification must be tailored or extended in a PPH or analysis guideline to the specific requirements of the Product under analysis, thus ensuring that all basic requirements of this specification are met.

All assumptions, guidelines and information applying to the Product analysis project (which is not limited to a single S4000P analytical methodology) must be documented in a PPH, in business rules and in a User's Guideline or in a similar document.

Depending on the project, one or more PPH can be required during a Product's life cycle to cover the different analytical methodologies. For the complete Product life cycle, it is strongly recommended that the following PPH variants are used:

- PPH specific for developing PMTRI and PMTRE on basis of Chap 2. This PPH-type must be available and applied during the initial Product design and development process, and applied to limited new developments/modifications, selected during the Product in-service phase.
- PPH specific for optimizing PMTRI and/or PMTRE during the in-service phase in accordance with Chap 3. This PPH-type must be available and applied during the Product in-service phase.
- PPH for a combined application of developing and optimizing PMTR for Products with a limited share of new development(s) in Product systems, on Product structure and/or in Product zones. Refer to Chap 2 and Chap 3.

During development of a PPH, special attention must be paid to the following aspects:

- For international projects, having a split of Product design and development responsibilities, the responsibilities and work shares for the analysis of systems, structure and zones must be clearly allocated and defined
- The allocation of analysis responsibilities must cover the complete hardware and software of the Product under analysis

- Customer/user inputs or specifications are required to support analysts in making decisions for PMTR applicability and effectiveness during the analysis. This applies to intended or specified Product usage, different usage scenarios, overall maintenance strategy, etc.
- It is recommended to define and document the following information in an overview list of the Product with systems, structure and zones in the PPH including justifications:

  - Systems that must be analyzed or excluded. Refer to Chap 2.3.
  - Structure that must be analyzed or excluded. Refer to Chap 2.4.
  - Systems that must be analyzed or excluded for both system and structure analysis
  - Zones that must be analyzed or excluded. Refer to Chap 2.5. A project specific zonal analysis must be defined in the PPH for all selected Zonal Analysis Modules (ZAM)
  - ZAM which have been allocated and justified for a specific Product type
  - Rating of Product systems, structure and zones in terms of in-service impact on the different maintenance levels (eg, high/medium/low impact)
  - Special events and their expected impacts on one or more Product systems, structures and/or on zone(s) and therefore, must be analyzed. Refer to Chap 2.7.

- Each PPH should contain exhaustive information and details required by the analysts to correctly perform the analysis. This includes a detailed description of every anticipated Product usage scenario (if more than one). If a customer usage exceeds or does not meet the design usage scenario, this must be recorded in the PPH.
- The initial Product usage scenario that was the basis for both the Product design and the development of the maintenance concept for the Product must be compared with:

  - the individual customer/user Product usage scenario(s) foreseen for the future in-service phase and with
  - potential changes/variations in the individual customer/user Product usage scenario throughout the future in-service phase.

In addition, a PPH defines analysis workshares, responsibilities, points of contact, project milestones, deliverables and further administrative and organizational topics.

Prior to beginning the analytical activities, the PPH should be prepared, harmonized and signed by involved stakeholders and accepted by responsible authorities.

Note

Examples for PPH content variants are provided in Chap 7.

Note

Each PPH must be reviewed during the Product life cycle. Necessary updates/supplements must be implemented to keep analysis methodologies and the PMTR background information up to date. Depending on these updates additional analytical work can be decided (eg, analysis compensation).

2.1 Maintenance program/OMP development

All PMTRI resulting from a S4000P analysis will initially be consolidated and harmonized with additional S4000P-external PMTRI sources such as Certification Maintenance Requirements (CMR) and/or requirements from national law (refer to Chap 2.6). In subsequent work steps, analysis results must be transferred to an applicable data storage device for a subsequent Product support analysis. Refer to S3000L.

Packaging of PMTRI is a prerequisite for the later optimized in-service phase performance of Product maintenance. Rules and processes for PMTRI packaging resulting from S4000P analysis must be defined and applied on basis of S3000L. Selected maintenance task interval types and the numerical interval values of PMTRI must be adjusted so that an effective Product maintenance program/Operators' Maintenance Program (OMP) can be produced and provided to the customer.

Among others the S3000L processes cover the following aspects:

- Performance of a Maintenance Task Analysis (MTA) for PMTRI and PMTRE transferred from S4000P analysis to the S3000L database
- PMTRI must be decided to be packaging candidates or not
- PMTRI and PMTRE must be reviewed and checked regularly to ensure they still conform to individual customer Product usage requirements, which are the basis for both the design and the analysis for developing PMTR. If the customer changes the Product usage, the impact on PMTR must be identified and assessed
- Definition of preventive maintenance task packages/groups either calendar based (eg, yearly) or based on Product usage data (eg, every 1000 operating hours of the Product)
- Performance of a further Maintenance Task Analysis (MTA) for the preventive maintenance task packages/groups

Accepted and released single maintenance tasks with repetitive scheduled intervals, scheduled maintenance task packages/groups with repetitive master intervals and prepared sets of preventive maintenance tasks applicable for identified special events drive the Product maintenance program/OMP. This is to be delivered as technical publications for the Product. Refer to S1000D.

2.2 Maintenance program/OMP optimization during a Product in-service phase

The In-Service Maintenance Optimization (ISMO) process and logic define the rules and methodologies for correctly optimizing the scheduled maintenance during the Product in-service phase. Refer to Chap 3.1 thru Chap 3.4.

The accepted and authorized output of each ISMO analysis loop requires an updated packaging of the reviewed set of all PMTRI prior to produce the next issue of the Product maintenance program/OMP, which are delivered as updated technical publications. Refer to S1000D.

For the special event analysis during the Product in-service phase, when a System FMEA, the structural analysis and/or a zonal analysis was updated or if in-service experience has accumulated due to the occurrence of special event(s), the previous selection of the respective PMTRE sets must be reviewed. Refer to Chap 2.7.

Page intentionally blank.

Chapter 1.4

Changes to the specification

Table of contents

Page

Changes to the specification 1

References 1

1   General 1

2   Change process..1

3   Records of change 1

List of tables

1   References 1

References

Table 1 References

Chap No./Document No.	Title
SX000i	International guide for the use of the S-Series Integrated Product Support (IPS) specifications

1   General

To allow the traceability of updates and changes implemented in every new issue of the specification S4000P the following rules are applied:

- Only updates/changes to the specification that deviate from the previous issue are recorded
- All updates/changes having a direct influence on extant analysis methodologies are recorded
- All new and/or additional or modified analysis methodologies are recorded
- Editorial changes are not recorded

2   Change process

Requests for change, their assessment and incorporation follow the processes given in SX000i.

3   Records of change

The records of changes are given in the highlights pages, of the front matter of every issue of the specification.

Page intentionally blank.

Chapter 2

Developing PMTR

Chapter	Data module title	Data module code	Applic
Chap 2.1	Developing PMTR - General	S4000P-A-02-01-0000-00A-040A-A	All
Chap 2.2	Developing PMTR - Development of preventive maintenance task requirements (PMTR)	S4000P-A-02-02-0000-00A-040A-A	All
Chap 2.3	Developing PMTR - System analysis	S4000P-A-02-03-0000-00A-040A-A	All
Chap 2.4	Developing PMTR - Structure analysis	S4000P-A-02-04-0000-00A-040A-A	All
Chap 2.5	Developing PMTR - Zonal analysis	S4000P-A-02-05-0000-00A-040A-A	All
Chap 2.6	Developing PMTR - Consolidation of analysis results, harmonization with other preventive maintenance task requirement sources for traceability	S4000P-A-02-06-0000-00A-040A-A	All
Chap 2.7	Developing PMTR - Special event analysis	S4000P-A-02-07-0000-00A-040A-A	All

Page intentionally blank.

Chapter 2.1

Developing PMTR - General

Table of contents

Page

Developing PMTR - General...1

References...1

1   General 1

List of tables

1   References 1

References

Table 1 References

Chap No./Document No.	Title
Chap 2.2	Developing PMTR - Development of preventive maintenance task requirements (PMTR)
Chap 2.3	Developing PMTR - System analysis
Chap 2.4	Developing PMTR - Structure analysis
Chap 2.5	Developing PMTR - Zonal analysis
Chap 2.6	Developing PMTR - Consolidation of analysis results, harmonization with other preventive maintenance task requirement sources, traceability
Chap 2.7	Developing PMTR - Special event analysis

1   General

To effectively develop the Preventive Maintenance Task Requirements (PMTR) for a Product, various analyses must be carried out. These are described, in general terms in Chap 2.2.

The Product system analysis according to Chap 2.3 identifies applicable and effective PMTRI to identify and/or to mitigate Failure Causes (FC) for Functional Failures (FF) in due time and/or provides feedback to the responsible design department(s) (at Product manufacturer and/or for suppliers/Original Equipment Manufacturers (OEM)).

Additional analysis is applied to identify and/or to mitigate potential impacts on Product structure in due time such as impacts caused by Accidental Damage (AD), by Environmental Deterioration (ED) impacts, by Structure Fatigue Failures (SFF), etc. Refer to Chap 2.4.

Further analysis is applied to identify and/or to mitigate potential FC in Product zones and/or damage impacts on Product's zones in due time which can't be allocated to the analysis of one Product system or the Product structure only. Refer to Chap 2.5.

PMTRI resulting from these analysis methodologies are initially consolidated at their own level (eg, systems analysis consolidation of PMTRI results) and again at the Product level. Refer to Chap 2.6.

In addition, the Product's systems, structures and zones are subject to analysis that identifies PMTRE or sets of PMTRE applicable for special events. Refer to Chap 2.7.

Chapter 2.2

Developing PMTR - Development of preventive maintenance task requirements (PMTR)

Table of contents

Page

Developing PMTR - Development of preventive maintenance task requirements (PMTR) 1

References...1

1   Introduction 1
1.1   Purpose 2
1.2   Preventive maintenance objectives 3
1.3   Preventive maintenance content 3
1.4   Methodologies for preventive maintenance development..3
1.5   Selection of system and/or structure analysis methodology 4

List of tables

1   References 1

References

Table 1 References

Chap No./Document No.	Title
Chap 1	Introduction to the specification
Chap 2.1	Developing PMTR - General
Chap 2.3	Developing PMTR - System analysis
Chap 2.4	Developing PMTR - Structure analysis
Chap 2.5	Developing PMTR - Zonal analysis
Chap 2.6	Developing PMTR - Consolidation of analysis results, harmonization with other preventive maintenance task requirement sources for traceability
Chap 2.7	Developing PMTR - Special event analysis
Chap 3	Optimization of Preventive Maintenance Task Requirements (PMTR)
Chap 7	Examples
S3000L	International procedure specification for Logistics Support Analysis - LSA

1   Introduction

Each new Product or Product variant must have an applicable and effective set of Preventive Maintenance Task Requirements (PMTR) developed prior to its introduction into service,

preferably in accordance with analysis methodologies of this chapter. They also support the later review and optimization of these PMTR during the Product in-service phase. Refer to Chap 3). Experience shows that for complex technical Products preventive maintenance can't completely be covered by Product-integrated health and condition monitoring and evaluation systems. Therefore, it is essential to define a balanced relationship between Product-integrated technology and the preventive maintenance performed by personnel.

This chapter is applicable for being applied both during the Product design and development phase and in the frame of limited developments/modifications of Product systems/equipment/items during the Product in-service phase.

If the review and optimization of PMTR according to Chap 3 can identify the necessity of analysis compensations (eg, due to new analysis aspects having been implemented in the latest S4000P issue), the analysis methodologies in this chapter become relevant again.

In addition to the development of PMTRI with repetitive scheduled intervals, applicable and effective PMTRE are to be defined, which are initiated by special events (refer to Chap 2.6) and not by any repetitive scheduled intervals.

If a new Product is planned to be composed of already existing systems, subsystems and equipment (eg, already used in former Product generations) and of others being newly developed, a combination of this chapter with Chap 3 should be applied in a project-specific Policy and Procedure Handbook (PPH).

1.1 Purpose

The purpose of this chapter is to assist the prime Product manufacturer, suppliers and involved regulatory authorities (if any) in developing initial PMTRI and PMTRE for new Products under development.

The analytical processes according to the subchapters Chap 2.3, Chap 2.4 and Chap 2.5 determine applicable and effective PMTRI to keep the inherent safety and reliability levels and the law conformity including environmental integrity of the Product from the beginning of the in-service phase. In addition, further PMTRI can be selected to meet Product operational/mission availability and/or economical operator requirements (to achieve specified or predicted Product's Life Cycle Costs (LCC)).

The PMTR evaluation comprises optional reviews of the Product-integrated Product Health and Condition Monitoring (PHCM) technology for Product systems in Chap 2.3 and of the Structure Health and Condition Monitoring (SHCM) technology for Product Structure in Chap 2.4 (if installed or intended to be installed). These reviews of the Product testability support the effective cooperation of S4000P analysts with responsible design departments and Product testability experts. The scope of these reviews is to merge technology from PHCM and SHCM with the preventive maintenance effort to achieve economic on-condition maintenance for the Product. If preventive maintenance is not applicable and/or not effective for the Product design under analysis, redesign must be required or recommended, depending on the Functional Failure Effect Criticality (FFEC) of the analyzed Failure Cause (FC) under analysis.

Due to the involvement of PHCM and SHCM, design changes are not limited to a redesign of the Product system, structure or zone under analysis and not limited to improve access to allow PMTR execution. The integration of additional sensors, cameras, etc. for PHCM/SHCM are also (re)design options to be evaluated.

PMTR resulting from this analytical methodology belong to the minimum set of preventive maintenance tasks to be performed during the Product in-service phase. The summary of all user-relevant PMTRI and of other preventive maintenance-relevant requirements or limitations like Certification Maintenance Requirements (CMR), Preventive Maintenance Task Limitations (PMTL) are eg known as Operators' Maintenance Program (OMP).

Different to an OMP, the processes in the specification suite of the S-Series Integrated Product Support (IPS) Specifications can elaborate an efficient Product maintenance program that supports the Product maintainer in scheduling packaging-relevant PMTRI and the other relevant inputs in appropriate master task packages. Refer to S3000L.

Before any special event, real or expected, that can impact a Product occurs, the analysis for one or more applicable and effective PMTRE must be carried out and the task(s) defined and allocated accordingly. PMTRE must also be described in an OMP and/or Product maintenance program. The selection of PMTRE for special events must be linked to the results from the analysis methodologies described from Chap 2.3 thru Chap 2.5. The results from the PMTRI consolidation and harmonization of PMTRI and other relevant inputs must also be taken into account for PMTRE selection. Refer to Chap 2.6.

The preventive maintenance documented tasks in an OMP or Product maintenance program, developed on basis of original (analysis-based) PMTRI other relevant inputs like CMR/PMTL and PMTRE applicable after special events can be revised considering actual experience that is accumulated throughout the Product use during the in-service phase. Refer to Chap 3.

1.2 Preventive maintenance objectives

The primary objectives related to efficient preventive Product maintenance are:

- to keep the inherent Product safety level, conformity with law (covering the environmental integrity), mission/operation accomplishment and reliability levels of the Product
- to maintain inherent Product safety, mission/operation accomplishment and reliability levels when deterioration has occurred
- to achieve these objectives at minimum costs
- to provide the information required for design changes/improvements and where necessary to exclude a confliction with law and exclude or minimize any impact on the environmental integrity
- to enable maintenance responsible personnel to evaluate the status of the technical Product as quick as possible after an entry or after an assumed entry of a special event

Note

Preventive maintenance cannot correct deficiencies in the inherent safety and reliability levels of the Product. Should an inherent level be found to be unsatisfactory, design change or modification will be necessary to obtain Product improvement.

1.3 Preventive maintenance content

The guidance to determine and select PMTRI and PMTRE is defined in this specification.

The definition of a Product maintenance program or OMP for preventive Product maintenance is based on the PMTRI and PMTRE development. The concept and process how to select PMTRI candidates for packaging/grouping into master intervals, how to package or group selected PMTRI and how to adapt single intervals in an appropriate way. Refer to S3000L.

1.4 Methodologies for preventive maintenance development

A Product's design and development evolves until its completion. Therefore, the planning for the scope, content and depth of the analytical processes for developing PMTR must take this evolution into account.

To effectively support the Product design departments from an early stage, engineering support departments (reliability, maintainability, testability and safety) must provide and interchange the results from their analytical work and from maintenance in-service experience from other Products.

This is because:

- Mandatory redesign requirements must be identified during the Product design and development phase as early as possible
- If no PMTR is identified to be applicable and/or effective, a feedback to the responsible engineering departments is essential latest before the Critical Design Review (CDR) takes place

Note:

The CDR is an important project milestone during the Product/equipment development phase, where the design status is fixed for the subsequent production phase.

- After a first analytical approach, identified PMTR must be checked in parallel to subsequent design-updates (if any). Analytical completion work and/or updates of analysis results must ensure conformity with the latest (serial) Product design status.

Product design and development activities are not limited to the design and development phase. Selected modifications or retrofits of the original Product design become necessary during a Product in-service phase. For those cases this analytical methodology of developing preventive maintenance applies, too.

The development of applicable and effective PMTRI for a Product is based on three analytical methods provided within this specification:

- System analysis (refer to Chap 2.3)
- Structure analysis (refer to Chap 2.4)
- Zonal analysis (refer to Chap 2.5)

Results from each of these analytical methods must be consolidated and harmonized in accordance with Chap 2.6.

The definition of applicable and effective PMTRE which must be performed after the entry of a special event is covered by Chap 2.7.

1.5 Selection of system and/or structure analysis methodology

The determination of Analysis Relevant Candidates (ARC) according to the system analysis (refer to Chap 2.3) must not be confused with the selection of Structure Significant Items (SSI) that is part of the structure analysis in Chap 2.4.

To avoid confusion and to ensure that all ARC and/or SSI of a Product are analyzed, an overview on analysis methodologies to be applied is recommended in the PPH. Refer to Chap 1.

Examples for the applicability of both the system and the structure analysis methodologies in parallel (from aviation technology):

- A landing gear system on a fixed wing aircraft
- The main rotor assembly on a rotary wing aircraft (helicopters)

Chapter 2.3

Developing PMTR - System analysis

Table of contents

Page

Developing PMTR - System analysis 1

References...3

1   System analysis procedure 3
2   ARC and non-ARC determination process...4
2.1 Scope of ARC and non-ARC determination 4
2.2 Establishment of a Product breakdown structure......................................5
2.2.1 Product Type 1 5
2.2.2 Product Type 2 5
2.3 Preparation of the ARC/non-ARC determination..6
2.4 Determination of ARC/non-ARC..6
2.5 Presentation and approval of ARC/non-ARC results 8
2.6 Ongoing control of ARC/non-ARC determination......................................8
3   ARC System Failure Mode and Effects Analysis 8
3.1 ARC Functions..10
3.2 Functional failures..10
3.3 ARC Functional failure effects 11
3.4 ARC Failure causes..11
3.5 Documentation of ARC System-FMEA..12
4   Application of system analysis logics 13
4.1 FF categorization logic 13
4.1.1 FF categorization logic diagram 13
4.1.2 FF categorization procedure...15
4.1.3 Overview of FFEC in FF categorization analysis 22
4.2 FC assessment and PHCM analysis 24
4.2.1 FC assessment and PHCM analysis logic diagrams.................................24
4.2.2 FC assessment and PHCM analysis procedure..25
4.2.3 Explanation of FC assessment and PHCM analysis decisions.................26
4.2.4 PMTRI selection criteria for FC assessment and PHCM analysis 38
4.2.5 Redesign requirement assessment...38
4.2.6 PMTRI task type selection criteria 39
5   Interval determination for PMTRI...40
5.1 General 40
5.2 Traceable selection of PMTRI interval types..42
5.2.1 Example for a PMTRI interval type selection logic....................................42
5.2.2 Explanation of the example for interval type selection logics...................43
5.3 Determination of numerical interval values for PMTRI...............................43
5.3.1 Example for a PMTRI interval value determination logic 44
5.3.2 Explanation of the example for a PMTRI interval value determination logic...............44
6   Certification maintenance requirements 46
7   Trend-leader selection 46

List of tables

1   References 3
2   PMTRI selection criteria 38
3   Redesign requirement assessment 38
4   Maintenance task type selection criteria 39

List of figures

1   System analysis process overview 4
2   Product Type 1 breakdown principle 5
3   Product Type 2 breakdown principle 6
4   Example ARC/non-ARC list/table 8
5   Top-down and bottom-up FMEA principles 9
6   ARC System FMEA table - Example 12
7   FF categorization logic diagram .... **¡Error! Marcador no definido.**
8   FF categorization - Decision 1 15
9   FF categorization - Decision 2 16
10   FF categorization - Decision 3 17
11   FF categorization - Decision 4 18
12   FF categorization - Decision 5 19
13   FF categorization - Decision 6 20
14   FF categorization - Decision 7 21
15   FF categorization - Decision 8 22
16   FC assessment and PHCM analysis logic diagram (Sheet 1 of 2) 24
17   FC assessment and PHCM analysis logic diagram (Sheet 2 of 2) 25
18   Preventive maintenance task type hierarchy 26
19   FC assessment Decision A 27
20   FC assessment Decision B 28
21   FC assessment Decision C 29
22   FC assessment Decision D 30
23   FC assessment Decision E 31
24   FC assessment Decision F 32
25   FC assessment Decision G 33
26   FC assessment Decision H 34
27   PHCM review - Decision I 35
28   PHCM review – Decision J 36
29   PHCM review - Decision K 37
30   Example for a decision logic for PMTRI interval types (Sheet 1 of 2) 42
31   Example for a decision logic for PMTRI interval types (Sheet 2 of 2) 43
32   Example for a PMTRI interval value determination logic 44

References

Table 1 References

Chap No./Document No.	Title
Chap 1	Introduction to the specification
Chap 2.6	Developing PMTR - Consolidation of analysis results, harmonization with other preventive maintenance task requirement sources for traceability
Chap 2.7	Developing PMTR - Special event analysis
Chap 3	Optimizing PMTR
Chap 6	Terms, abbreviations and acronyms
S1000D	International specification for technical publications using a common source database
S3000L	International procedure specification for Logistic Support Analysis - LSA
S5000F	International specification for operational and maintenance data feedback
AC 25-19	Advisory Circular from US department of transportation dated 11/28/94
DIN Norm 31 051/(DIN/EN 13306)	Maintenance Terminology
SAE ARP 5580	Recommended Failure Modes and Effects Analysis (FMEA) Practices for Non-Automobile Applications
	Engineering Society For Advancing Mobility Land Sea Air and Space International (SAE), Issue 2001

1 System analysis procedure

The determination of Preventive Maintenance Task Requirements with repetitive scheduled Intervals (PMTRI) for Product systems, including installed components and equipment must follow a clear and traceable process sequence using logic diagrams to support all analytical decisions.

The Product System Analysis follows the sequence of four major work steps as shown in Fig 1.

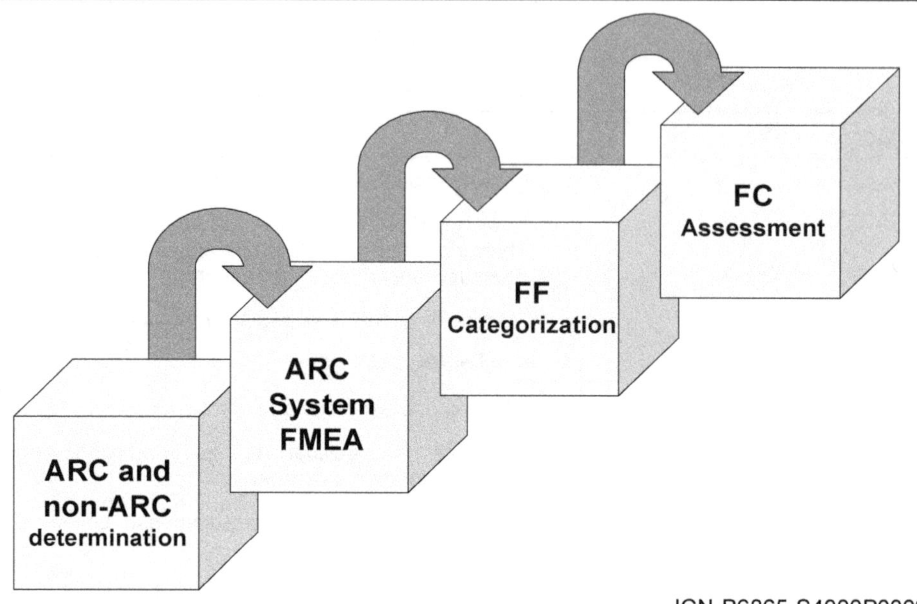

ICN-B6865-S4000P0002-001-01

Fig 1 System analysis process overview

The determination of Analysis Relevant Candidates (ARC) and the identification of candidates not being relevant for analysis (non-ARC) is followed by a system Failure Mode and Effects Analysis (FMEA).

Principally, the FMEA evaluations of this analytical methodology are based on the Functions (F), Functional Failure Effects (FFE), and the respective Failure Causes (FC) identified for selected ARC.

Based on the FMEA results the criticality of each Functional Failure (FF) must be categorized based on a logic diagram. Another logic diagram is used to determine applicable and effective PMTRI or to give redesign feedback to the design responsible department for each identified FC.

The determination of the ARC/non-ARC and all further analysis steps must be checked and adapted accordingly (if necessary) if a crisis/war scenario of military Products and/or if specific civil Product usage conditions must be covered by a system analysis.

All terms, abbreviations and acronyms are listed in Chap 6.

2 ARC and non-ARC determination process

2.1 Scope of ARC and non-ARC determination

The main scope of this analysis work step 1 must identify all ARC and non-ARC for the systems/components of the Product under analysis.

Product items not relevant for a further/deeper system analysis (categorized as non-ARC) are also identified and must be documented in a project-specific Policy and Procedure Handbook (PPH) or analysis guideline prior to starting this system FMEA.

The determination of ARC and non-ARC identifies the number of candidates for analysis and supports the reduction of the system analytical effort.

2.2 Establishment of a Product breakdown structure

Prior to determining ARC and non-ARC, the Product design departments usually provide a Product design approach that is intended to fulfill the functional requirements specified for the Product under analysis.

In very early project phases, it is possible that a suitable Product Breakdown Structure (PBS) is not always available to start this system analysis. In this scenario an initial PBS must be elaborated following the rules described in S1000D and taking into account the following aspects:

Two main types of Products must be taken into account when determining the PBS:

- Product Type 1
- Product Type 2

2.2.1 Product Type 1

Product Type 1 as a unit comprises all technical systems installed within and/or directly on a common Product structure (eg, a manned aircraft, train or ship). The common Product structure can be subdivided into dedicated zonal areas. For Product Type 1 the analysis relevant usage data and assumptions are valid for the whole Product under analysis.

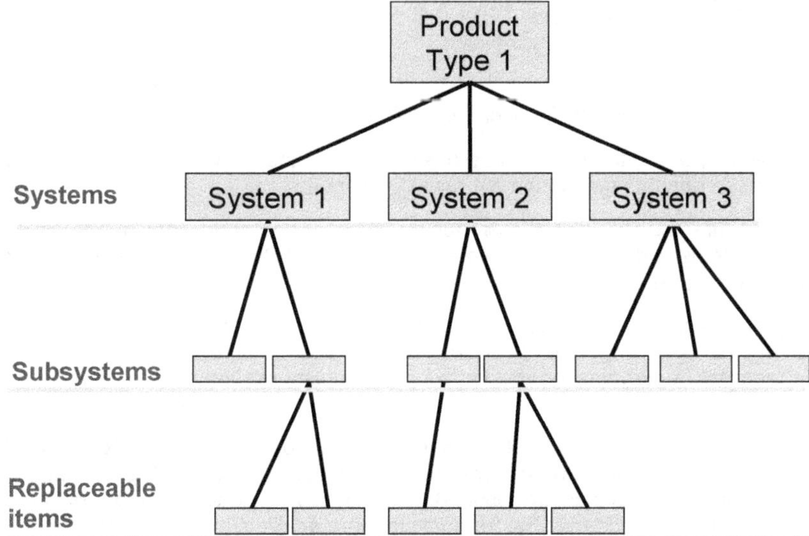

ICN-B6865-S4000P0003-001-01

Fig 2 Product Type 1 breakdown principle

2.2.2 Product Type 2

Product Type 2 has a higher Product complexity level in comparison to Product Type 1. A Product Type 2 is a System of systems (eg, Unmanned Air Vehicle (UAV) systems that can comprise different types of ground stations and components as well as airborne components). Product Type 2 must first be subdivided into its major Product components. Each component of this Product type must be subdivided into its technical systems, structure and zonal areas. Analysis relevant data and assumptions must be defined for each Product component. The data/assumptions can be significantly different between individual Product components.

Note

It is recommended to prepare the PPH for the analysis of each Product component of Product Type 2.

S4000P-A-02-03-0000-00A-040A-A

Chap 2.3

2021-04-30 Page 5

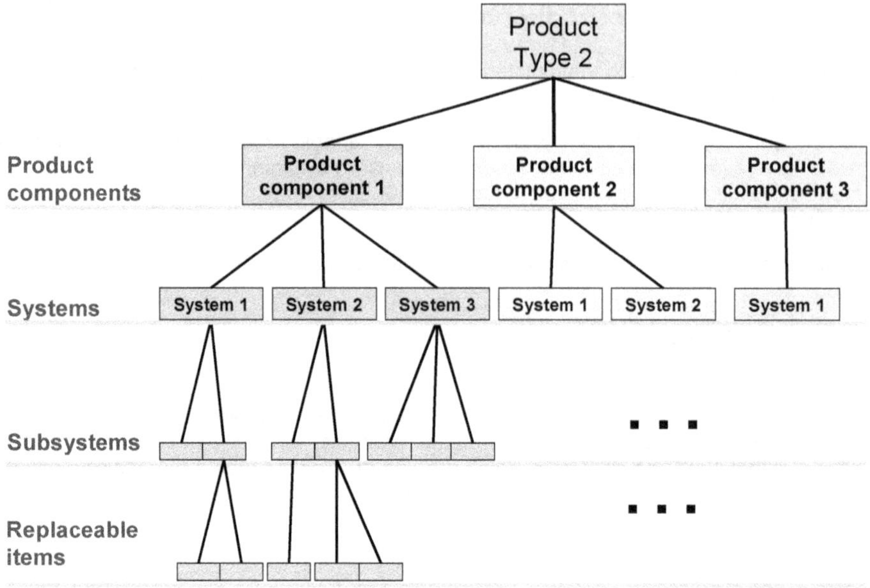

ICN-B6865-S4000P0004-001-01

Fig 3 Product Type 2 breakdown principle

For example, Unmanned Air Vehicle (UAV) Systems that can comprise different types of ground stations/components next to the airborne components

The hardware and software of a Product must be divided and arranged into major functional areas, systems and subsystems. Refer to S1000D. All Product items/equipment must be covered within the overall PBS.

The system analyst determines ARC and non-ARC on a highest selectable level in the Product system breakdown structure to concentrate and reduce the resulting analysis effort. The ARC/non-ARC determination must cover the complete system under analysis.

Note

Product structures that are broken down in accordance with S1000D can contain subsystems, equipment or items that are functionally relevant (eg, fuselage drains, door mechanisms, electrical systems, etc) that must be included in the Product system analysis and must be included in the Product structure analysis in parallel. For safety/emergency systems or similar equipment, appropriate information must be obtained for the analyst(s) if preventive maintenance analysis is required.

2.3   Preparation of the ARC/non-ARC determination

Based on the selection of analysis-relevant systems in the PBS of the PPH, the analyst subdivides the selected analysis-relevant system on a highest manageable PBS level to determine a list or table of items to which the ARC/non-ARC determination will be applied.

If portions of the analysis-relevant system can be excluded from the ARC/non-ARC determination both the appropriate justification and the indication of those impacted portions of the PBS must be documented by the analyst.

2.4   Determination of ARC/non-ARC

The ARC/non-ARC determination for selected systems/sub-systems of a Product comprises a set of decisions on potential FFE in case the item function fails.

Answering questions as defined in the PPH will identify all ARC/non-ARC.

The analyst for the ARC/non-ARC determination must apply all the following questions or selected questions to the analysis-relevant Product systems identified in the PPH:

- **Question 1**: Could an FF affect Product safety, including safety/emergency systems and/or emergency equipment?
- **Question 2**: Could an FF conflict with law and/or have a significant impact on environmental integrity (ecological damage)?
- **Question 3**: Could an FF have an impact on mission/operational capability?
- **Question 4**: Could an FF of the selected item have significant economic impact?

Note

Questions 1 and 2 are recommended to answer for all complex technical Products. For questions 3 and 4, it is recommended that the criteria of significance are agreed with the customer and documented in the PPH. The decision documented in the PPH can for example, exclude question 3 and/or 4 if decided and accepted by the project.

Question 1 and Question 2 are related to Product safety and Product conformity with law/environmental integrity. If one of these questions is answered YES, the full system analysis must be conducted. Therefore, a YES answer to Question 1 and/or Question 2 identifies the item under analysis as an ARC irrespective of the answers to Questions 3 and 4.

If both Question 1 and Question 2 are answered NO and one or both answers to Question 3 and Question 4 are answered YES, the decision for a full system analysis must be evaluated. For example, a full system analysis is required to meet specific contractual requirements (eg, performance-based Product support requirements). In this case the item under analysis becomes an ARC.

Items that are declared as non-ARC items will not be subject to further system analysis. PMTRI can also be decided to be analyzed and/or optimized during the later Product in-service phase. Refer to Chap 3.

If the answer to Question 1 thru Question 4 is NO or the answer to Question 1 and Question 2 is answered NO and the answers Question 3 and/or Question 4 are not relevant to select ARC, then no further system analysis is required and the item under analysis is classified as a non-ARC.

Note 1

A System analysis for a selected ARC will not necessarily result in PMTRI.

Note 2

In complex technical Products comprising of several components which can be located and operated in different places (eg, UAV system components), Product components which have been identified as ARC can be handled/operated by different crews/personnel. Therefore, FFE must be analyzed and judged separately for the ARC of different Product components. For example, FF for UAV cannot endanger human beings on board during flight for obvious reasons. However, human beings on the ground or in another manned aircraft flying in a common airspace can be endangered by a FF of a UAV air segment.

UAV ground components directly linked to UAV guidance and control can be allocated to the same categories of criticality such as the UAV air segment.

In addition, UAV ground components must be analyzed for FF of items, equipment or subsystems which are safety relevant for the ground crew/operating crew. FF can have FFE during ground component handling (disassembly, packaging, transporting, unpackaging, assembly, test) and/or during their operating or mission periods.

The results out of the ARC/non-ARC determination (refer to Para 2) must be recorded in the ARC/non-ARC overview list/table. An example is shown in Fig 4.

Sequence indicator or no.	Design Identi-fication, (drawing-no. part-no. Etc.)	S1000D SNS DMC S3000L BEI / LCN / etc …	ITEM NAME	DETERMINATION QUESTIONS				ARC selected ?	REMARKS
Product System Analysis ARC / non-ARC determination				Could a Functional Failure (FF) affect Product safety, including safety/ emergency systems and/or emergency equipment ?	Could a FF conflict with law and/or could the FF have a significant impact on environmental integrity (ecological damage) ?	Could a FF have an impact on mission/ operational capability ?	Could a FF of the selected item have significant economic impact ?		
A	TBD	TBD	PRODUCT ITEM A	Yes	Yes	Yes	Yes	Yes	
B	TBD	TBD	SUBSYSTEM 1	Yes	No	No	No	Yes	
C	TBD	TBD	SUBSYSTEM 2	No	Yes	No	No	Yes	
D	TBD	TBD	SUBSYSTEM 3	No	No	Yes	Yes	To be evaluated	Decision depending on contract etc.
E	TBD	TBD	SUBSYSTEM 4	No	No	Yes	No	To be evaluated	Decision depending on contract etc.
F	TBD	TBD	SUBSYSTEM 5	No	No	No	Yes	To be evaluated	Decision depending on contract etc.
G	TBD	TBD	SUBSYSTEM 6	No	No	No	No	No	Non-ARC; the System Analysis stops

ICN-B6865-S4000P0005-001-01

Fig 4 Example ARC/non-ARC list/table

2.5 Presentation and approval of ARC/non-ARC results

The results from Para 2 must be documented in the Product ARC/non-ARC overview list/table and presented to the project Steering Committee (SC), which must check and approve the list/table for subsequent allocation and distribution to analysts.

2.6 Ongoing control of ARC/non-ARC determination

Each analyst must:

- Monitor the completeness of selected ARC/non-ARC throughout the application of analysis activities
- Validate and control the correct selection of the highest manageable item level
- Propose modifications/supplements with justifications of the ARC/non-ARC list/table to the project SC

The primary aim of ARC/non-ARC determination must verify that no ARC has been overlooked, and that the correct level for the analysis has been chosen, taking into account the current Product configuration and it is configuration variants. The manufacturer must ensure that analysts are included in established engineering change processes to ensure impact analysis.

3 ARC System Failure Mode and Effects Analysis

Analysis work step 2 is a top-down Failure Mode and Effects Analysis (FMEA) method as opposed to a bottom-up analytical method. Refer to Fig 5.

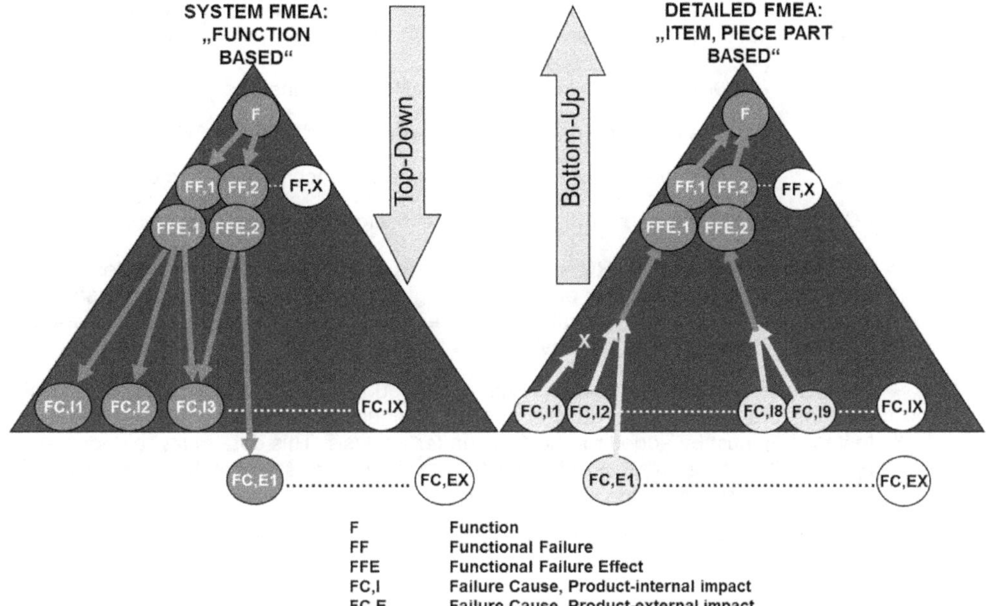

ICN-B6865-S4000P0006-001-01

Fig 5 Top-down and bottom-up FMEA principles

SAE ARP 5580 subdivides FMEA into different variants. Fig 5 shows the principle of a System FMEA (ie, top-down analysis methodology, see Fig 5 left side) in comparison to a detailed Equipment FMEA (ie, bottom-up analysis methodology, see Fig 5 right side):

As shown in Fig 5, a system FMEA approach identifies the relevant FC impacting Product system functions. Other FC that do not impact on an FF are not selected. Direct FC can be either inherent parts or equipment of the Product hardware/software (ie, internal to the Product) or not part of a Product hardware/software (ie, external to the Product. FC in a system FMEA can be technical failures, environmental damage impacts and/or accidental damage impacts.

The Failure Mode and Effects Criticality Analysis (FMECA) is a detailed technical FMEA. It is applied on Product equipment extended by an assessment of technical failure mode severities and the probabilities of failure mode occurrence. The FMECA applies the bottom-up analytical approach for Product equipment that is involved at least in safety-relevant Product functions. The output of the FMECA leads to functional relevant FC impacting the Product system under analysis and forms the interface between system FMEA and equipment FMECA.

Combinations of FC must also be performed by system safety analysts with a bottom-up analysis methodology (using the Fault Tree Analysis (FTA)) to prevent safety relevant FFE on Product level. If not already eliminated by the Product design, identified FC combinations must be taken into account in the system FMEA to develop applicable and effective PMTRI for each FC.

After ARC has been selected and prior to applying further system analysis activities, a top-down System-FMEA must be prepared for each ARC listing:

Function: One or more Functions of the ARC under analysis

FF: One or more Functional Failures identified for each ARC Function

FFE: The potential worst-case end effect of each FF resulting on Product level

FC: One or more Failure Causes allocated to each FF with its FFE

As a prerequisite for the ARC analysis, a brief system, subsystem or item description must be prepared or be available (eg, provided by engineering). For all involved analysts it is essential to know about the specified Product usage scenario and about foreseen usage parameters. Related information must be provided in a Product-specific PPH.

Additionally, any analysis relevant data (eg, S1000D system reference, Product applicability, manufacturer/supplier part numbers, reliability figures, design principles (eg, redundancy, testability)) must be added for the ARC under analysis. This data must be documented as the prerequisite for the further Product system analysis and as part of the total preventive maintenance analysis data set of a Product.

A detailed understanding of the ARC under analysis is essential to produce the ARC System FMEA.

The analyst must start with listing the ARC functions and not with the analysis of an individual FC. The list of functions must be complete and not be restricted to the main functions. Also, secondary or minor functions must be included in the analysis in order to provide a complete view of the ARC functions.

3.1 ARC Functions

When defining an ARC function, the analyst must not only consider the function as defined but also include:

- Drawing the attention of the users to abnormal conditions
- Shutting down equipment in the event of an FF
- Eliminating or relieving abnormal conditions following an FF
- Taking over from a failed function
- Prevent dangerous occurrences from arising

Functions of protective devices, emergency equipment and false operation (eg, untimely, unwanted exercising of the function) must also be taken into account. For example, the function of both paths of system components with dual design redundancy, such as concentric tubes, must be analyzed individually. It is possible that the degradation and/or fault of one path is not always evident.

3.2 Functional failures

Each ARC Function can have one or more FF. In all cases the ARC fails to perform its intended function within its specified limits.

For redundant systems or components, the loss of redundancy must be covered as an FF even if there is no direct impact on the normal operation of the Product.

Dormant FF of emergency equipment must be categorized as safety relevant during a normal Product operation or mission. For analysis purposes the prerequisites and/or circumstances must be explained (eg, emergency of a helicopter rescue hoist cable, emergency fuel shut-off valves, emergency power supply battery, etc).

3.3   ARC Functional failure effects

For each FF the worst-case criticality of the FFE at the Product level must be evaluated. FFE on the performance of the Product must be defined for both evident and hidden FF.

3.4   ARC Failure causes

Each FC documented in the ARC System FMEA is a potential source for one or more FF of the system under analysis that can appear or has already appeared during Product in-service phase.

Each FC, identified by ARC System FMEA, can be initiated by one or more of the following FC origins:

1   An inherent technical defect of equipment or items of the Product during specified Product operation or mission.

2   Damage or malfunction of one or more equipment or items of the Product induced by deterioration due to accidental damage(s) which are expected during specified Product operation or mission.

3   Damage or malfunction of one or more equipment or items of the Product induced by deterioration due to environmental impacts which are expected during specified Product operation or mission.

4   Special events or one-time events which are not expected to contribute to regular Product deterioration process(es) but which can take place unscheduled with different probabilities (eg, impact on a flying aircraft by: bird strike, lightning strike, particles/substances on air due to volcano eruption, etc.)

Positions from 1 thru 3 are subject to this analysis methodology. Refer to Chap 2.3. The process and the analysis methodology applicable for special events (Position 4) are described in Chap 2.7.

One FC can lead to one or more FF. More than one FC can contribute to one FF with different probabilities. It is possible that an individual FC associated with several FF is allocated to identical or to different FFE categories.

Each FC must be defined in such a way that an effective FC assessment and Product Health and Condition Monitoring (PHCM) analysis (refer to Para 4.2) can be made during subsequent analytical steps. The description of an FC must not only identify eg, a component and how it fails (eg, mechanical or electrical defect, failing in open or closed switch position, open or short circuit, jammed linkage, contaminated orifice, broken housing) but also provide additional information about the maintenance analysis-relevant technical background.

Equipment, items or parts, which are not a direct part of the system under analysis, can also be identified as a probable FC in the System FMEA for the ARC under analysis.

Selected FC for FF of the ARC under analysis are items or interfaces, which are not covered by the system breakdown structure of the ARC under analysis. These items or interfaces include:

—   Wires transferring electrical signals
—   Wires transferring electrical power
—   Tubes and/or pipes with or without pressurized fluids (eg, from hydraulic system)
—   Other Product subsystems or individual items being connected to the system under analysis to ensure system functions

To cover items and/or parts of other Product systems, the information about the related FC must be documented by the ARC analyst and transferred to the analyst of the respective item and/or other system of the PBS. The analyst of the respective system, subsystem or sub-subsystem must define applicable and effective PMTRI for those FC. Refer to S1000D.

Attention must be paid to all probable safety relevant FFEC of other systems that are linked to safety relevant FFE of the ARC under analysis.

The integrity of data and information must be ensured across multi-national development programs or where programs share design responsibilities within different organizations.

3.5 Documentation of ARC System-FMEA

A complete and correct ARC System FMEA is the important prerequisite in performing subsequent system analysis steps 3 and 4.

The content of the ARC System-FMEA is recommended to be reviewed and accepted by the responsible system design engineering and/or safety departments for the Product.

For a traceable overview on all analysis results of the ARC System-FMEA, a tabular form must be selected as it is shown in Fig 6.

ASD S4000P **SYSTEM ANALYSIS**				ARC identification data (BEI, configuration data)	...				
ARC FUNCTION AND FAILURE **DATA SHEET / TABLE**				ARC nomenclature	...				
Issue Date	...	Company name	...	Analyst name	...	Notes: ...			
REF. no. for F	FUNCTION(S) (F) Description of Function(s) provided by the ARC under analysis	REF. no. for FF	FUNCTIONAL FAILURE(S) (FF) Description of Functional Failure(s) identified for each listed ARC Function	REF. no. for FFE	FUNCTIONAL FAILURE EFFECT(S) (FFE) Description of the potential "worst-case" end effect of each Functional Failure on Product level	REF. no. for FC	FAILURE CAUSE(S) (FC) Identification of Failure Cause(s) which can cause a Functional Failure	Additional information (e.g. probability ranking of single FC) Estimation of a probability of each FC occurence in relation to the other identified FC per FF	Remarks, update information, etc.

ICN-B6865-S4000P0007-001-01

Fig 6 ARC System FMEA table - Example

Where applicable, the SC must advise its working groups to fully account for vendor requirements, accepting them only if they are both applicable and effective according to the criteria of the system analysis.

The ARC System FMEA must cover the latest and/or final configuration status and all variants of the Product (if any). Any modification of a Product system during the in-service phase or the decision for Product variants following other build standards requires a review of the ARC System FMEA.

This analysis also covers the so-called fault tolerant systems or sub-systems being designed with redundant items to ensure functionality. Based on a single or even multiple item redundancy, single items of those systems can fail without a direct impact on Product safety, on its law/environmental integrity. It is possible that these faults are not apparent and are therefore hidden to the operating crew and/or to the maintainer(s) of the Product. In spite of at least one of the redundant items fails, the fault tolerant design ensures a safe and law conform (including environmental integrity) Product in-service phase and provides required mission/operation capabilities without any negative impact on specified system functions.

Consequently, a manufacturer's fault-tolerant system design enhances the system reliability and availability.

The results from the ARC System FMEA must be continuously reviewed and updated (if necessary) based on the in-service experience. Refer to Chap 3. An updated ARC System FMEA becomes an important basis for the later review and optimization of PMTR during the Product in-service phase. FC that have been identified on a theoretical basis for individual ARC the FF can be compared with real data from in-service experience (ie, missing FC can be added in the System FMEA and analyzed in subsequent analysis steps). Relevant FC for each FF can be evaluated in terms of the probability of occurrence during Product usage. Bringing them into an FC sequence of probabilities (ie, highest probability down to lowest probability), the content and the efficiency of failure trouble shooting procedures will be supported. Refer to S1000D.

4   Application of system analysis logics

Based on the results of the ARC System FMEA (refer to Para 3.5), the analyst categorizes each FF, and assesses and reviews all corresponding FC using:

- FF categorization logic. Decisions 1 thru 8 must be applied as system analysis work step 3 prior to the FC assessment and PHCM logic. It requires the evaluation of the overall effect of each FF on the Product level to determine the Functional Failure Effect Code (FFEC) (eg, evident or hidden, related to safety, mission, operation, law/environmental integrity, economy).
- FC assessment and PHCM logic. Decisions A thru K must be applied as system analysis work step 4. The relevant logic starts with an approval of whether preventive maintenance for the FC under analysis can be avoided by justification. Relevant decision criteria depend on the FFEC defined for that FC. If preventive maintenance is required, a selection of one or more applicable and effective PMTRI follows.

If more than one PMTRI are identified, selection criteria given in Table 2 must be applied. A review of the expected PMTRI maintenance effort together with a review of the Product-integrated PHCM system can then be performed.

If no PMTRI is identified as applicable and/or effective, redesign must be assessed using the criteria given in Table 3.

4.1   FF categorization logic
4.1.1   FF categorization logic diagram

In system analysis work step 3, the decision logic shown in ¡Error! No se encuentra el origen de la referencia. is used for the analysis of each identified FF. The logic flow is designed in this way so that the analyst begins the analysis at the top of the diagram and answers the YES or NO to each question which dictates the direction of the analysis flow. Having answered the logic questions, the most critical FFEC out of eight selectable FFEC is allocated to the FF under analysis.

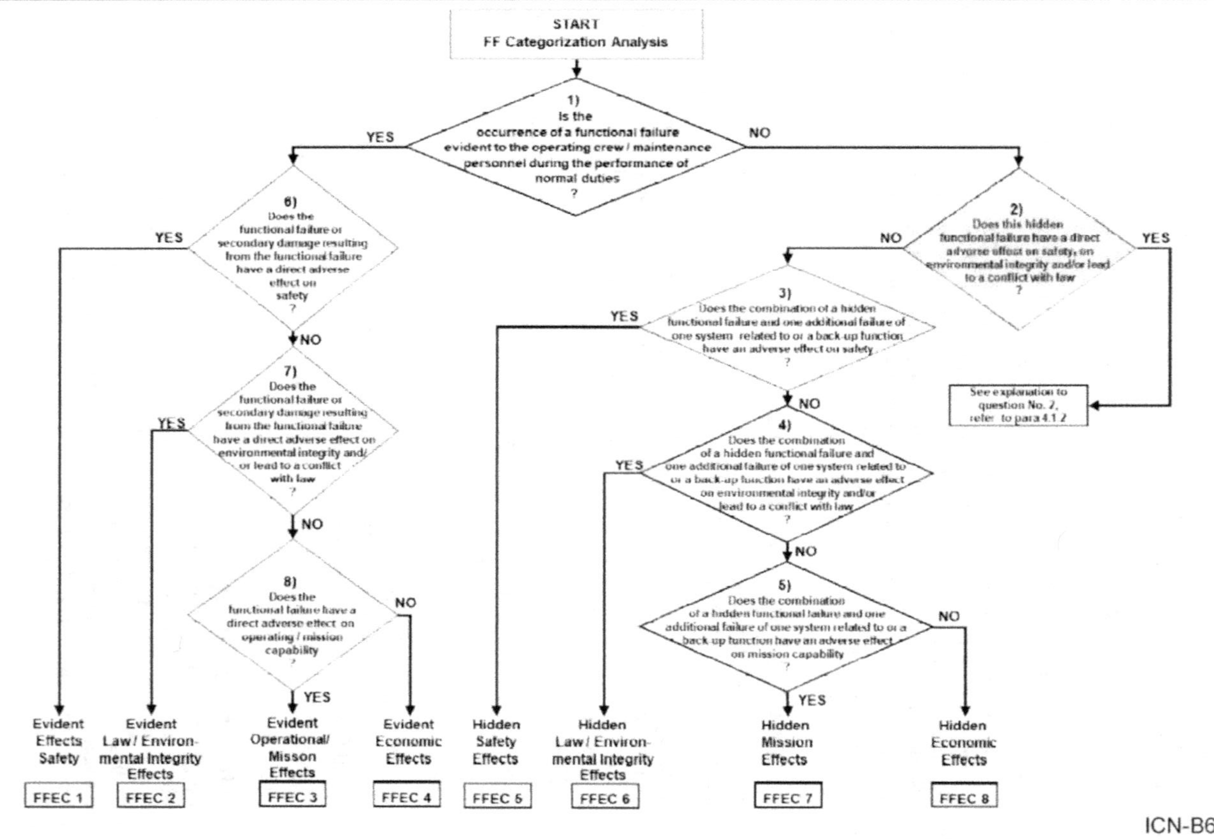

ICN-B6865-S4000P0008-001-01

Fig 7 FF categorization logic diagram

4.1.2 FF categorization procedure

Each FF identified in system analysis step 2 processed through the logic will be directed into one of the eight FFE criticality categories that is most analysis relevant.

Decision 1

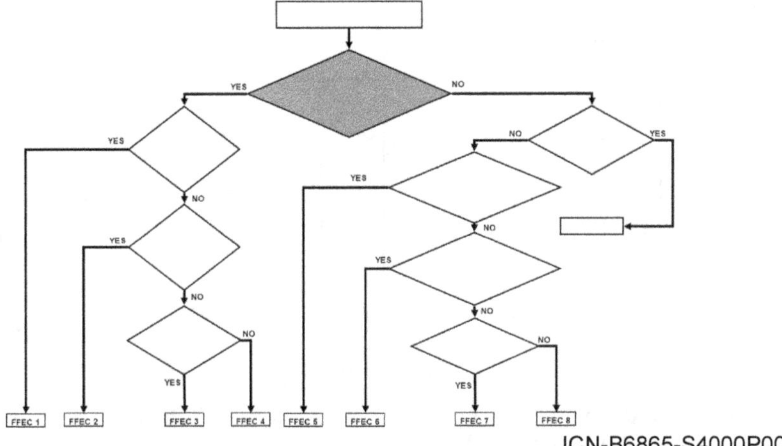

ICN-B6865-S4000P0009-001-01

Fig 7 FF categorization - Decision 1

Is the occurrence of an FF evident to the operating crew/ maintenance personnel during the performance of normal duties?

Decision 1 is related to each FF of the item under analysis. The intent is to segregate the evident and hidden FF.

The FF is classified as evident if the loss of function caused by its occurrence alone will eventually become apparent to the operating crew and/or maintenance personnel during normal duties or routine operation of the Product.

Where uncertainty exists with respect to the frequency of activation of certain systems of the Product, assumptions can be made in addition to the prerequisites given in the PPH. All assumptions must be documented by the analyst.

For example, an Aircraft Flight Manual (AFM) is not available during the initial preventive maintenance analysis performed in parallel to the Product design and development phase. Such an AFM will contain flight crew normal duties and must be accomplished by the flight crew.

Based on the PPH, Working Groups (WG) can consider flight crew tasks as part of the operating crew/personnel's normal duties in advance. The detection of respective FF and FC covered by future flight crew tasks must be categorized as evident. Every system analyst must document when such flight crew tasks are taken into account.

Once the AFM is available, all above mentioned assumptions made by the analysts must be verified to ensure that documented flight crew tasks are included in the AFM. The FF categorization and the coverage of allocated FC must be updated in case of the identified flight crew task cannot be included into the AFM.

Taking into account both the activities of the operating crew and of the maintenance-responsible personnel, the question of the initial Decision 1 must be answered.

- If the answer is YES, the FF is defined as evident - proceed to Decision 6.

- If the answer is NO, the FF is defined as hidden - proceed to Decision 2.

Decision 2

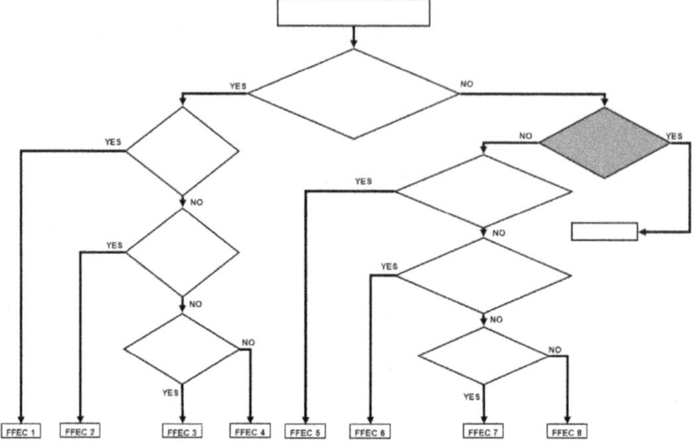

ICN-B6865-S4000P0010-001-01

Fig 8 FF categorization - Decision 2

Does this hidden FF have a direct adverse effect on safety, on environmental integrity and/or lead to a conflict with law?

For additional design evaluation, this decision excludes single hidden FF that might have a potential impact on safety, on environmental integrity and/or might lead to a conflict with law that should have been prevented already by initial Product design.

Note
> In general, this decision is applicable for none aircraft analysis, since aircraft certification rules excludes an individual hidden FF affecting safety, confliction with law or impacting environmental integrity.

–   If the answer is YES, then a mandatory redesign is required to avoid safety related FF.

For FF which can affect environmental integrity and/or lead to a conflict with law, redesign must be evaluated in accordance with applicable national or international laws and protocols.

–   If the answer is NO, a fault tolerant system design (redundancy) is required and leads to Decision 3.

Decision 3

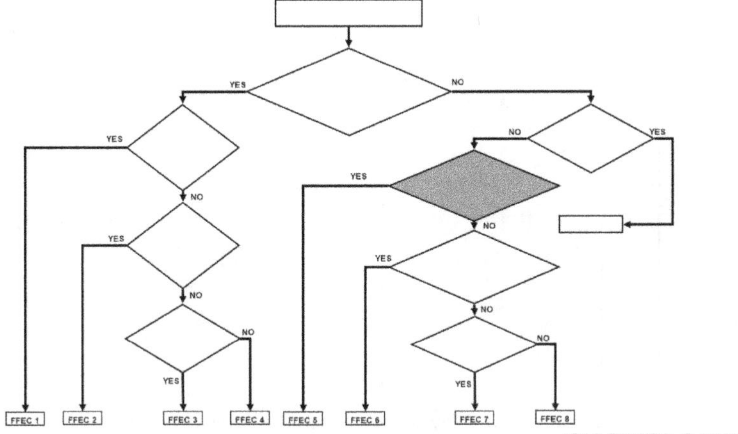

ICN-B6865-S4000P0011-001-01

Fig 9 FF categorization - Decision 3

Does the combination of a hidden FF and one additional failure of a system-related or back-up function have an adverse effect on safety?

This decision is related of each hidden FF that has been identified in Decision 1.

The decision takes into account failures in which the loss of the one hidden function (whose failure is unknown to the operating crew/ maintenance personnel) does not by itself affect safety. However, in combination with additional FF, whether system related or intended to serve as a back-up this FF has a direct or indirect adverse effect on safety.

For hidden functions of safety and/or emergency systems or equipment, the additional technical failure is the event for which this function of the system or equipment is designed (eg, failure of fire extinguisher in combination with the event fire). In these cases, a FFEC 5 (hidden safety effect) must be selected.

- If the answer is YES, there is a hidden safety effect (FFEC 5).

- If the answer is NO, there is a hidden non-safety effect and Decision 4 must be answered.

Decision 4

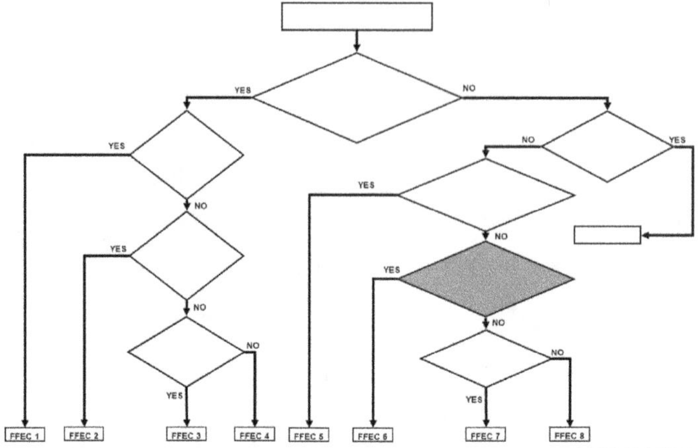

ICN-B6865-S4000P0012-001-01

Fig 10 FF categorization - Decision 4

Does the combination of a hidden FF and one additional failure of a system-related or a back-up function have an adverse effect on environmental integrity and/or lead to a conflict with law?

This decision considers the impact of hidden FF on environmental integrity and/or a conflict with law. Refer to Fig 10.

- If the answer is YES, there is a hidden effect on environmental integrity and/or a conflict with law (FFEC 6).

- If the answer is NO, Decision 5 must be answered.

Decision 5

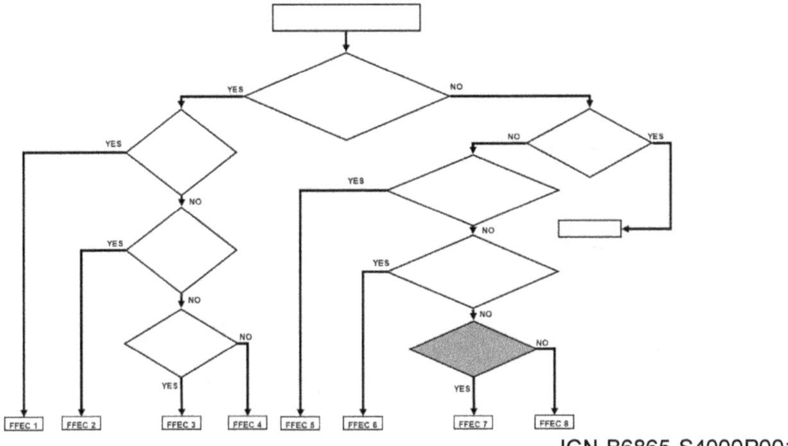

ICN-B6865-S4000P0013-001-01

Fig 11 FF categorization - Decision 5

Does the hidden FF have an adverse effect on mission capability?

This decision is related to each hidden FF not having an adverse effect on safety but can require use of abnormal mission procedures or limitation/cancellation of the mission. Refer to Fig 11.

The assessment of whether a failure has an effect on mission capability can require consultation of documentation with mission procedures and/or manuals. FF affecting the performance of specific missions can also deteriorate operating capability.

- If the answer is YES, there is a hidden mission effect (FFEC 7).

- If the answer is NO there is a hidden economic effect (FFEC 8).

Decision 6

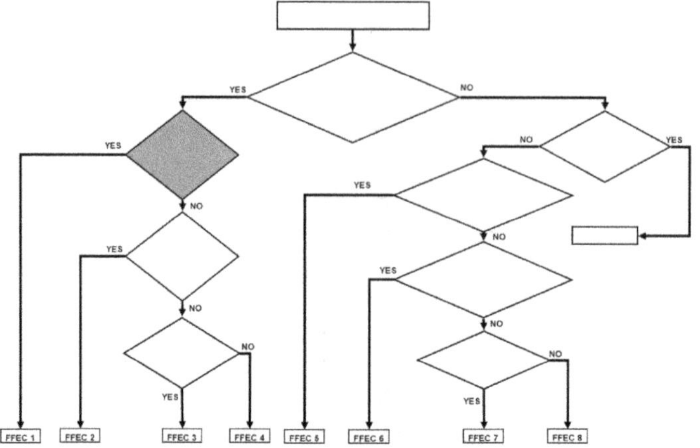

ICN-B6865-S4000P0014-001-01

Fig 12 FF categorization - Decision 6

Does the FF or secondary damage resulting from the FF have a direct adverse effect on safety?

This decision is related to each FF to evaluate its direct adverse effect on safety. Refer to Fig 12.

For a YES answer the FF must have a direct adverse effect on safety.

To have a direct adverse effect on safety, the FF or resulting secondary damage must achieve its effect by itself, not in combination with other FF (ie, no redundancy exists).

Safety must be considered as adversely affected, if the consequences of the FF prevent the continued safe operation of the Product could cause serious or fatal human injury.

–   If the answer is YES, this FF must be treated within the evident safety effect category (FFEC 1)

–   If the answer is NO, the evident FF is non-safety and Decision 7 must be answered.

Decision 7

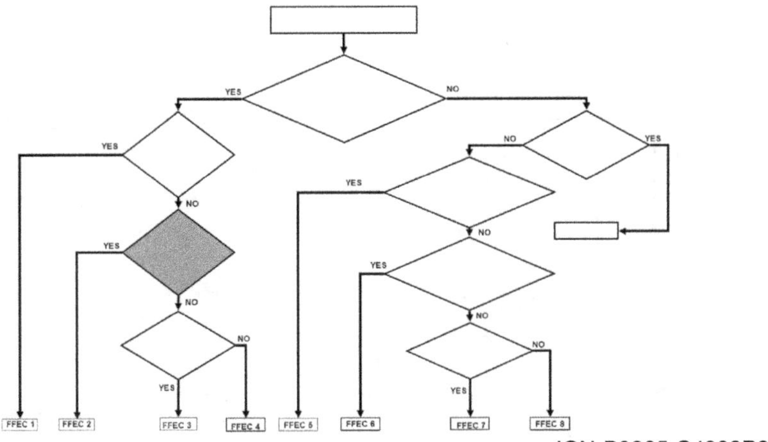

ICN-B6865-S4000P0015-001-01

Fig 13 FF categorization - Decision 7

Does the FF or secondary damage resulting from the FF have a direct adverse effect on environmental integrity and/or lead to a conflict with law?

This decision must take into account the influence of potential evident FF on law/environmental integrity. Refer to Fig 13.

–   If the answer is YES, there is an evident effect on environmental integrity and/or a conflict with law (FFEC 2).

–   If the answer is NO, the effect is either operational/mission related or economic and Decision 8 must be answered.

Decision 8

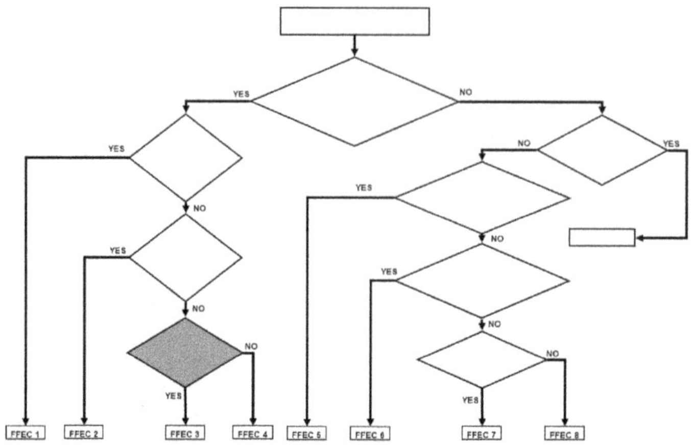

ICN-B6865-S4000P0016-001-01

Fig 14 FF categorization - Decision 8

Does the FF have a direct adverse effect on operating/mission capability?

This decision is related to each evident FF not having a direct adverse effect on safety, law or environmental integrity. The answers can depend on the type of mission/operation. Refer to Fig 14.

Civil operations as well as the accomplishment of military missions must be considered.

The assessment of whether an FF has an effect on mission/operating capability can require consultation of documentation with operational or mission procedures and/or manuals and can therefore require customer/user involvement.

As the documents necessary to assess the effect on operating or mission capability are often not available during the initial system analysis, all assumptions made for FF categorization analyses must be documented. Once the documents become available, all FF categorization analyses based on such assumptions must be reviewed and verified.

–   If the answer is YES, answer is determined: There is an evident operational and/or mission effect (FFEC 3).

–   If the answer is NO, answer indicates that there is an evident economic effect (FFEC 4).

4.1.3   Overview of FFEC in FF categorization analysis

Once the analyst has decided on the applicable FF categorization, the FF of the system under analysis are first separated into evident or hidden attributes.

With further assessment they are directed to the following eight criticality categories represented by FFEC:

–   **Evident safety (FFEC 1).** Evident FF with an impact on safety
–   **Evident law/environmental integrity (FFEC 2).** Evident FF with an impact on environmental integrity and/or leading to a conflict with law
–   **Evident operation or mission (FFEC 3).** Evident FF with an impact on operation or mission
–   **Evident economic (FFEC 4).** Evident FF with an impact on economy
–   **Hidden safety (FFEC 5).** Hidden FF with an impact on safety

- **Hidden law/environmental integrity (FFEC 6).** Hidden FF with an impact on environmental integrity and/or leading to a conflict with law
- **Hidden mission (FFEC 7).** Hidden FF with an impact on mission capability
- **Hidden economic (FFEC 8).** Hidden FF with an impact on economy

4.2 FC assessment and PHCM analysis

4.2.1 FC assessment and PHCM analysis logic diagrams

START System Analysis FC + PHCM Assessment

Is probability of occurrence of identified Failure Cause (FC) below a numerical threshold value (to be defined) ? — **A** — YES

NO

C — Is the condition and/or degradation trend of an identified Failure Cause (FC) under analysis fully detectable by Product-BIT and/or evaluated via health monitoring equipment ? — **B** — YES

- Perform on-condition maintenance for FC
- Evaluate scheduled functional test of PHCM system for FC with critical FFEC

NO

Is a SERVICING task applicable and effective ? — **C**

YES → Select SERVICING task

NO

Is an OPERATIONAL CHECK / SIMPLE INSPECTION applicable and effective ? — **D**

YES → Select OPERATIONAL CHECK / SIMPLE INSPECTION

NO

Is an INSPECTION or FUNCTIONAL TEST applicable and effective ? — **E**

YES → Select INSPECTION / FUNCTIONAL TEST

NO

Is a RESTORATION / OVERHAUL task applicable and effective ? — **F**

YES → Select RESTORATION / OVERHAUL task

NO

Is a TCI task applicable and effective ? — **G**

YES → Select TCI task

NO

Is a single PMTRI or a combination of PMTRI applicable and effective ? — **H**

YES → Select PMTRI/ PMTRI combination most effective and applicable in accordance with TABLE 2

NO

Assessment of REDESIGN in accordance with TABLE 3

(A) (B)

END System Analysis FC + PHCM Assessment

No PMTRI for FC under analysis

ICN-B6865-S4000P0017-001-01

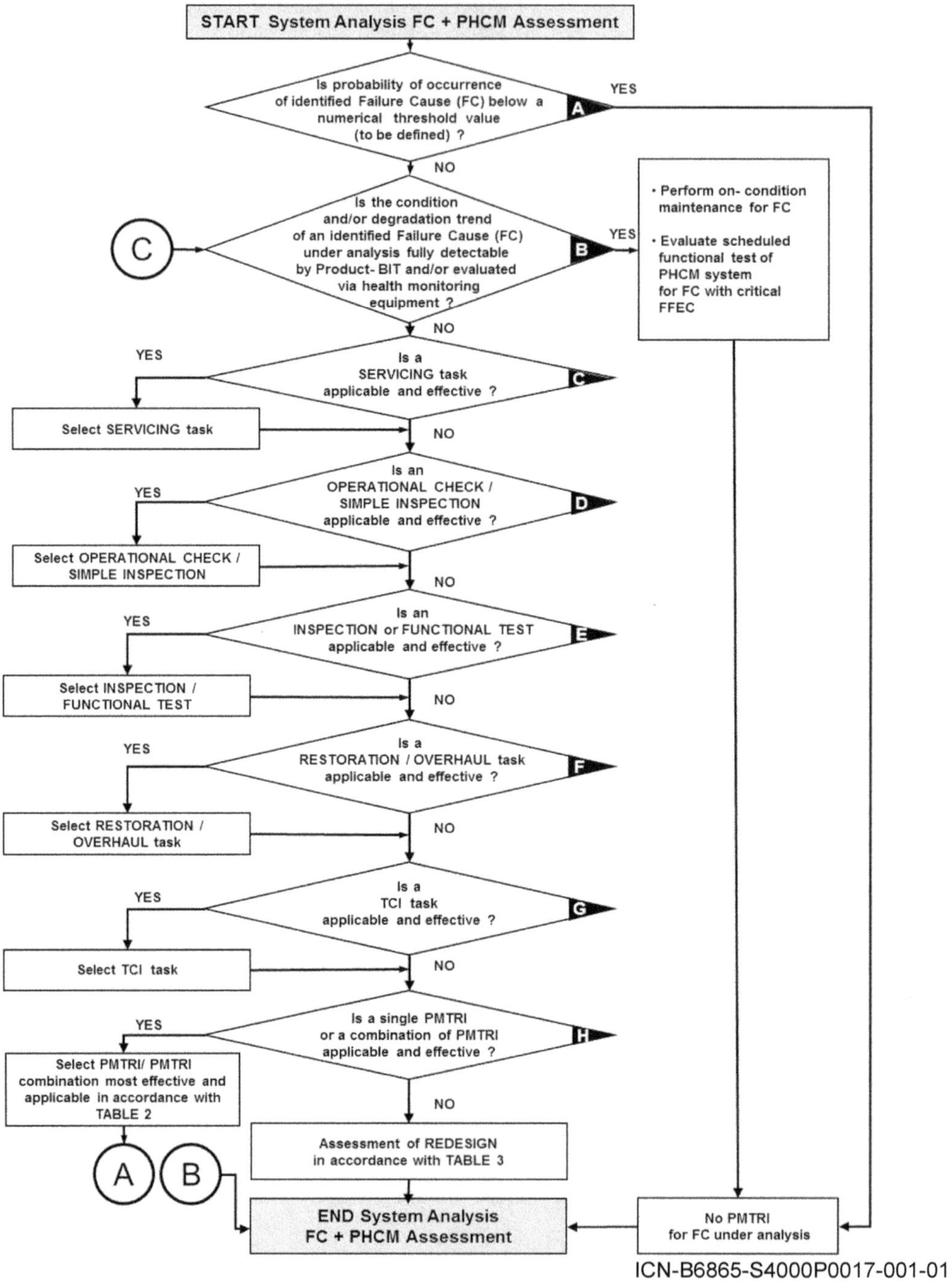

Fig 15 FC assessment and PHCM analysis logic diagram (Sheet 1 of 2)

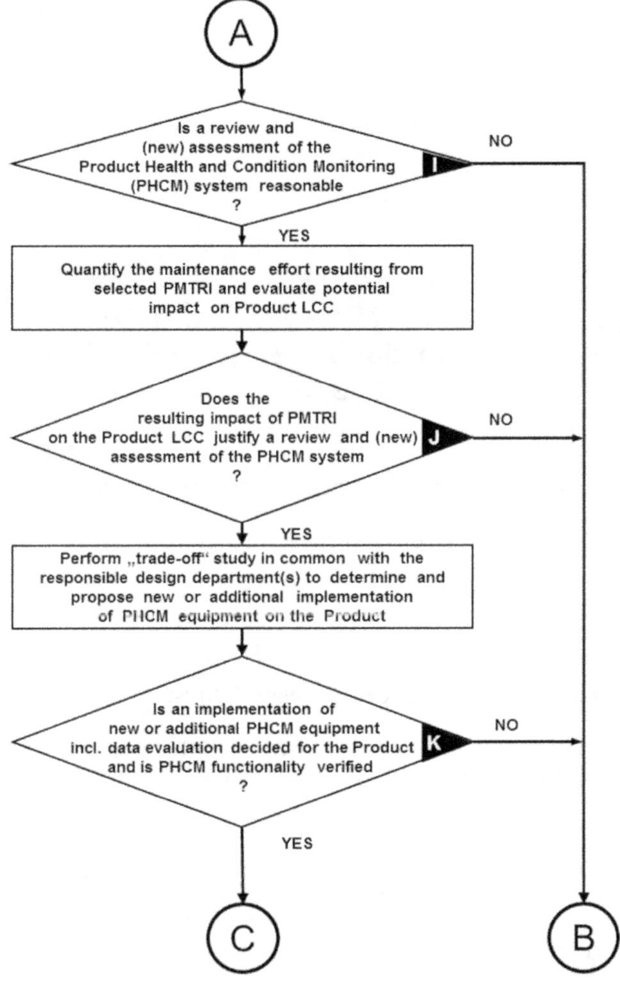

ICN-B6865-S4000P0018-001-01

Fig 16 FC assessment and PHCM analysis logic diagram (Sheet 2 of 2)

4.2.2   FC assessment and PHCM analysis procedure

In this system analysis work step 4, it is necessary to apply each FC, identified in the ARC System FMEA (refer to system analysis step 3), to the FC assessment and PHCM analysis logic diagrams. Refer to <u>Fig 15</u> and <u>Fig 16</u>.

Having completed the decisions of the FC assessment and PHCM logic, the selected FFEC for the FC under analysis has either influence on the PMTRI selection, initiates a review of the Product-integrated PHCM system or leads to redesign assessment of design aspects of the system under analysis and/or of SSI/SD accessibility aspects.

Assumptions made during the analysis must be recorded for later traceability and validation. For example, if an analysis is (partially or as a whole) based on design solutions that are not completely frozen, particularly during early Product design phases, this must clearly be recorded in the documentation of analysis results. All assumptions made during the analysis must be checked and validated once the information required for this analysis work has become available.

Fig 17 shows the hierarchy of preventive maintenance task clusters eases the understanding of the PMTRI selection in the analytical processes described in this specification:

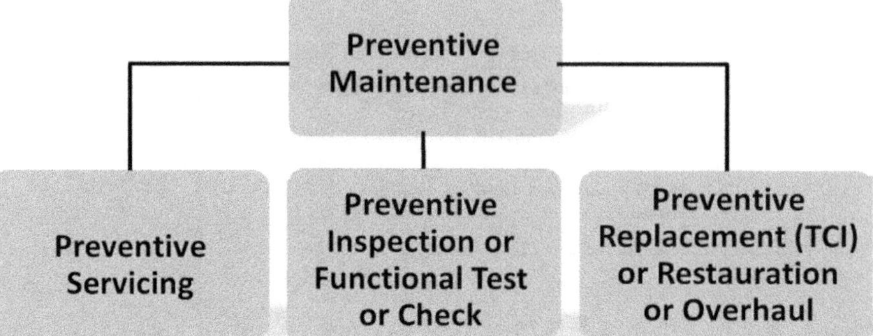

ICN-B6865-S4000P0019-001-01

Fig 17 Preventive maintenance task type hierarchy

The main maintenance task type clusters are:

- Preventive servicing
- Preventive inspection
- Functional test
- Check
- Preventive replacement, Time Change Item (TCI) restauration or overhaul

Each of these clusters can contain further detailed PMTRI task types. For example, both a preventive lubrication and a preventive replenishment belongs to the same task type cluster preventive servicing.

Note 1

The FC assessment and PHCM analysis logic sequence assumes of an increasing maintenance effort from one logic decision to the following. The decision sequence starts with servicing task types, followed by inspection or test task types and concludes with restoration, overhaul or TCI tasks.

Note 2

After having determined one or more applicable and effective PMTRI, a review of the PHCM system can be performed as an integrated part of the FC assessment analysis logic. The review takes the PMTRI impacts on the Product Life Cycle Costs (LCC) into account. An evaluation of the potential PMTRI maintenance effort is the prerequisite to enabling a subsequent trade-off study resulting in a decision on PHCM integration or a PHCM redesign.

4.2.3   **Explanation of FC assessment and PHCM analysis decisions**

Prior to the decisions on applicable and effective PMTRI, Decision A and Decision B clarify if a PMTRI must be selected.

Having concluded the initial Decision A and Decision B in this analysis logic guide through the whole spectrum of possible PMTRI (refer to DIN/EN Norm 31 051/DIN/EN 13306)

All decisions and work steps of the FC assessment and PHCM analysis decisions are explained and background information is provided.

Decision A:

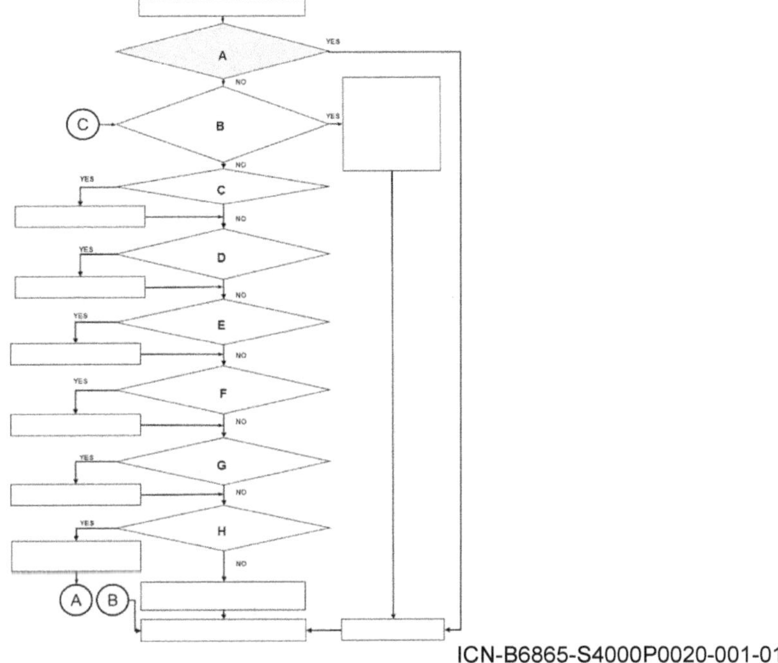

ICN-B6865-S4000P0020-001-01

Fig 18 FC assessment Decision A

Is probability of occurrence of identified Failure Cause (FC) below a numerical threshold value (to be defined)?

Numerical values for a FC probability threshold are recommended to be defined in a Product-specific PPH at least for FFEC allocated to the FC which are focused by responsible authorities.

The definitions of threshold values are subject to project risk management.

Threshold values should be adapted to the criticality of FFEC. The lowest numerical value of a threshold or a project-specific exclusion of a threshold is to be assigned to FFEC 1 and 5.

–　If the answer is YES, an FC occurrence is below the predicted threshold , no PMTRI must be selected.

–　If the answer is NO, the threshold, relevant for the criticality of the FC under analysis, is exceeded or the thresholds are to be excluded for a certain Product according to the PPH proceed with Decision B.

Decision B:

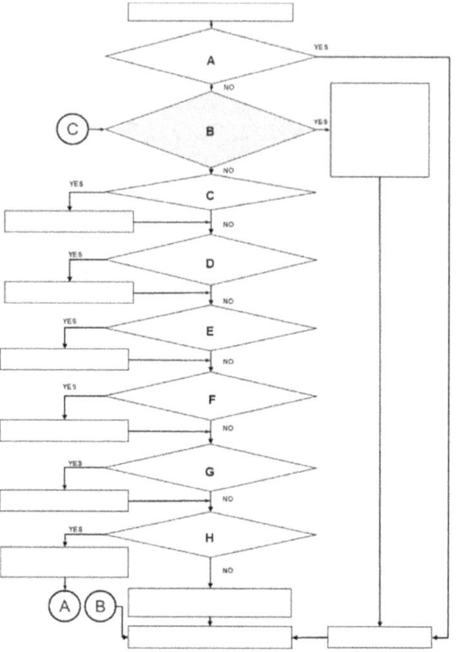

ICN-B6865-S4000P0021-001-01

Fig 19 FC assessment Decision B

Is the condition and/or degradation trend of an identified Failure Cause (FC) under analysis fully detectable by Product BIT and/or evaluated via health monitoring equipment?

- If the answer is YES, the Product-integrated Built-In-Test (BIT) system and/or health monitoring equipment/system delivers sufficient and useable data for technical interpretation necessary to clearly evaluate the FC condition, the degradation status and/or the trend of the degradation of the item that causes the FF is defined as known and therefore additional preventive maintenance is not required.

For a FC in combination with a critical FFEC (specific FFEC 1 and 5) evaluate preventive functional test tasks for the Product BIT and/or health monitoring system.

- If the answer is NO, a BIT/health monitoring system is not installed for the FC or if it does not deliver required condition-based information, continue with Decision C.

Decision C:

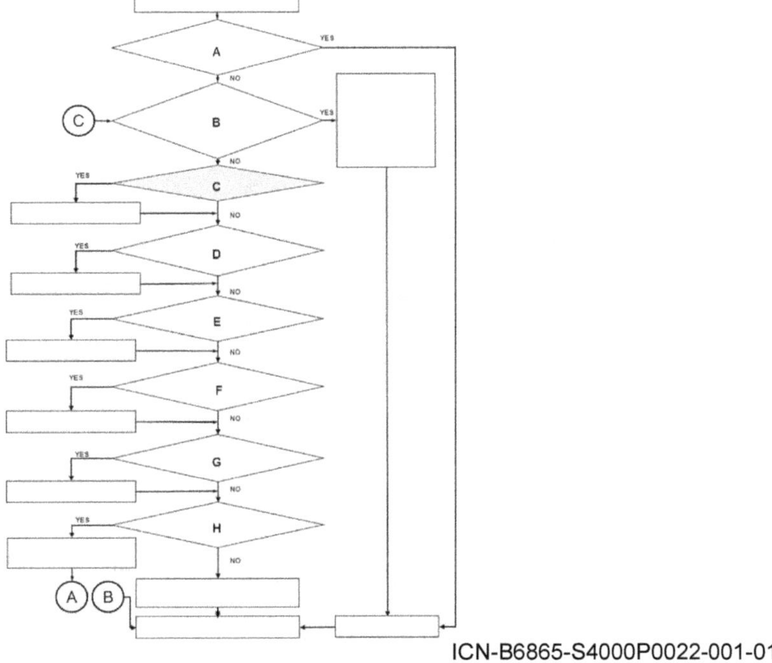

ICN-B6865-S4000P0022-001-01

Fig 20 FC assessment Decision C

Is a servicing task applicable and effective?

A servicing task must maintain inherent design capabilities to avoid the FC of the item under analysis. Servicing comprises, but is not limited to, the following PMTRI task types:

– Lubrication
– Adjustment
– Cleaning/washing
– Replenishment

Applicability and effectiveness criteria for the selected PMTRI task type or a combination of them are listed in Table 4.

– If the answer is YES, select PMTRI.

– If the answer is NO, continue with Decision D.

Decision D:

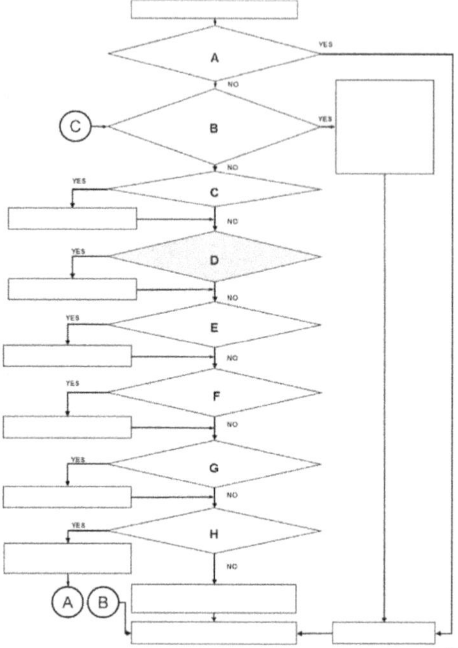

ICN-B6865-S4000P0023-001-01

Fig 21 FC assessment Decision D

Is an operational check/simple inspection applicable and effective?

The scope of this PMTRI task type is to verify functional operation of the FC.

Operational checks/simple inspections are PMTRI task types to verify that an item is fulfilling its intended purpose. The check does not require quantitative tolerances. Both are failure finding PMTRI task types.

In the assessment of this decision the selected PMTRI task types must be seen as independent from additional/external support equipment. The use of standard maintenance tools is allowed (eg, lamp, mirror).

Operational checks/simple inspections comprise the following PMTRI task types:

– Operational test directly on the Product with or without BIT
– General Visual Inspection (GVI)
– Detailed Inspection (DET)

Applicability and effectiveness criteria for the selected PMTRI task type or a combination of them are listed in Table 4.

Note:
A GVI resulting from the analysis can be transferred either into routine inspections or into the zonal inspection program as long as the FFEC for the FC is not allocated to FFEC 1, FFEC 2, FFEC 5 and FFEC 6.

– If the answer is YES, select PMTRI.

– If the answer is NO, continue with Decision E.

Decision E:

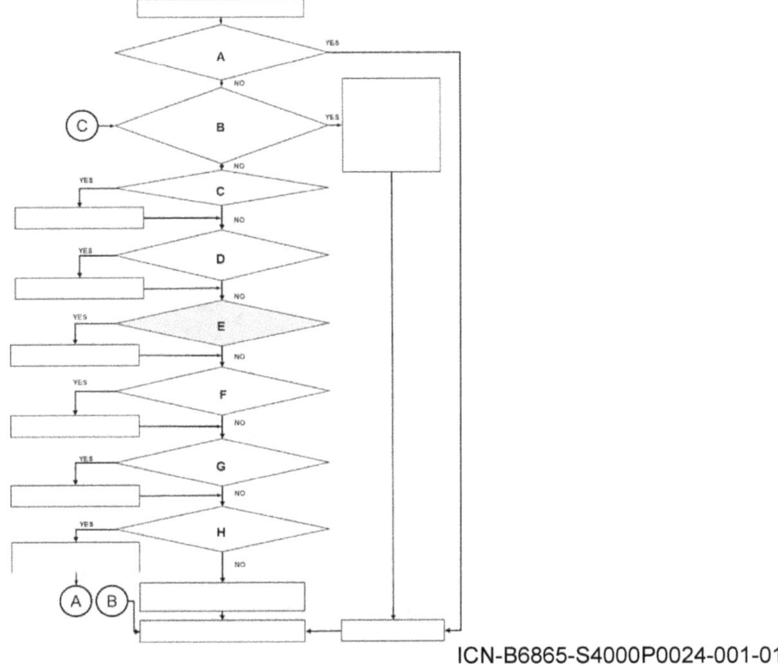

ICN-B6865-S4000P0024-001-01

Fig 22 FC assessment Decision E

Is an inspection or functional test applicable and effective?

The scope of this PMTRI task type is to detect the degradation of function caused by the FC under analysis. When deciding an answer to this question the analyst must consider whether the effort and/or training to accomplish the selected PMTRI task type causes a higher maintenance effort than the maintenance task type determined through Decision D.

A functional test is a quantitative test carried out directly on the Product system, item or assembly level. The scope must verify that one or more functions of an item or assembly perform within specified limits. Therefore, the following inspections or functional tests can require additional and/or Product external support equipment:

– Special Detailed Inspection (SDI)
– Non-Destructive Testing (NDT)
– Functional testing including evaluation of BIT/health monitoring data

Applicability and effectiveness criteria for the selected PMTRI task type or a combination of them are listed in Table 4.

– If the answer is YES, select PMTRI.

– If the answer is NO, continue with Decision F.

Decision F:

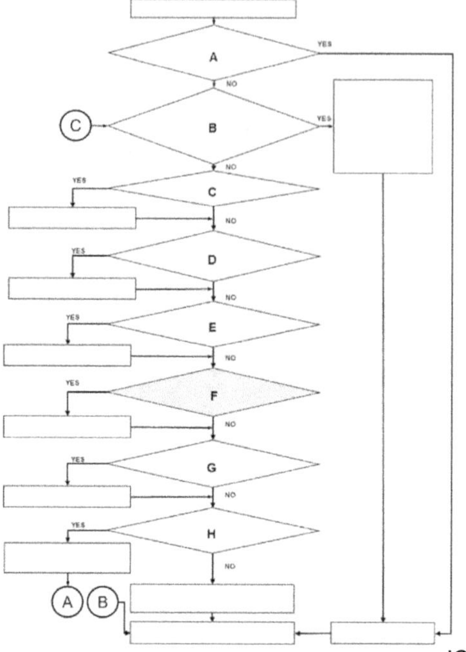

ICN-B6865-S4000P0025-001-01

Fig 23 FC assessment Decision F

Is a restoration / overhaul task applicable and effective?

The scope of this PMTRI task type is to avoid failures or reduce the failure rate related to the FC under analysis.

A restoration or overhaul task is the work carried out on the Product or on its equipment so that its resistance to failure can be restored to an acceptable level. It is usually a sequence of various PMTRI task types. However, the focused maintenance task types are:

– Part replacement
– Overhaul (partial or complete)

During the restoration or overhaul process these PMTRI task types are normally accompanied by servicing and test task types (eg, cleaning individual parts, adjustments, final acceptance test).

Applicability and effectiveness criteria for the selected PMTRI task type or a combination of them are listed in Table 4.

– If the answer is YES, select PMTRI.

– If the answer is NO, continue with Decision G.

Decision G:

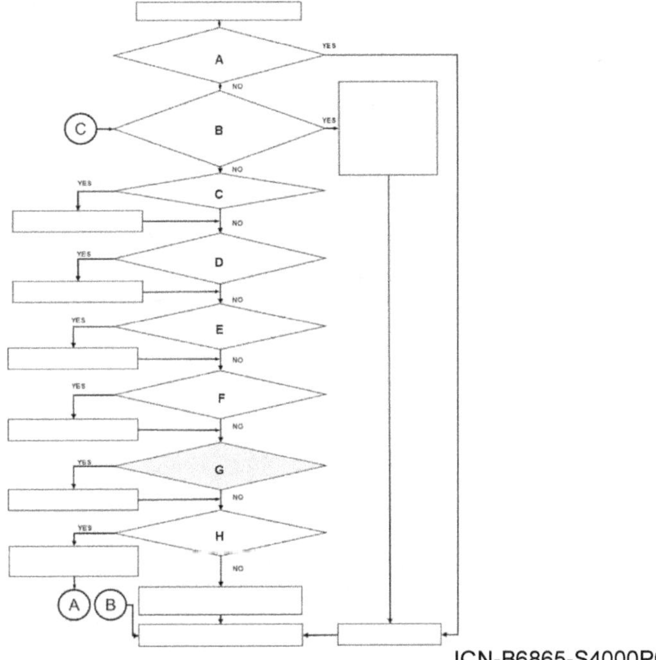

ICN-B6865-S4000P0026-001-01

Fig 24 FC assessment Decision G

Is a TCI task applicable and effective?

The scope of this PMTRI task type is to avoid failures or reduce the failure rate related to the FC under analysis.

The pre-requisites for selecting a TCI task are:

- When a specified life limit is defined for the item
- When a restoration task is not applicable and effective

TCI tasks are normally applied to items such as cartridges, canisters, cylinders, engine components (eg, compressor or turbine disks).

Applicability and effectiveness criteria for the selected PMTRI task type or a combination of them are listed in Table 4.

- If the answer is YES, select PMTRI.

- If the answer is NO, continue with Decision H.

Decision H:

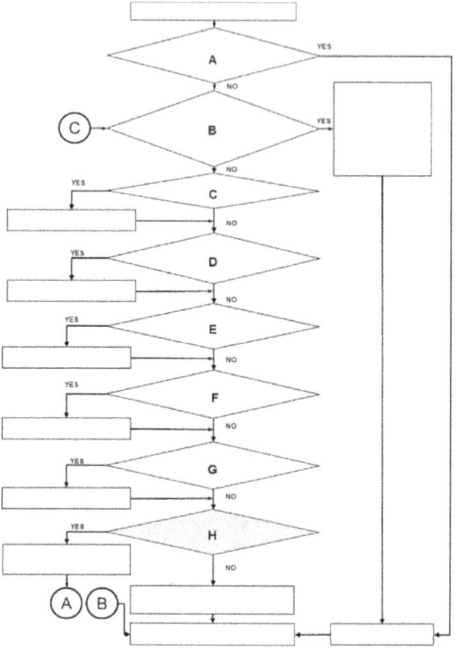

ICN-B6865-S4000P0027-001-01

Fig 25 FC assessment Decision H

Is a single PMTRI or a combination of PMTRI applicable and effective?

–   If the answer is YES, a review of all selected PMTRI identified as applicable and effective is necessary. For this review the FFEC, resulting from the FF categorization analysis, must be taken into account. Refer to Table 2. After having performed the PMTRI selection, continue with Decision I in Fig 26.

–   If the answer is NO, a redesign must be assessed in accordance with Table 3.

Decision I:

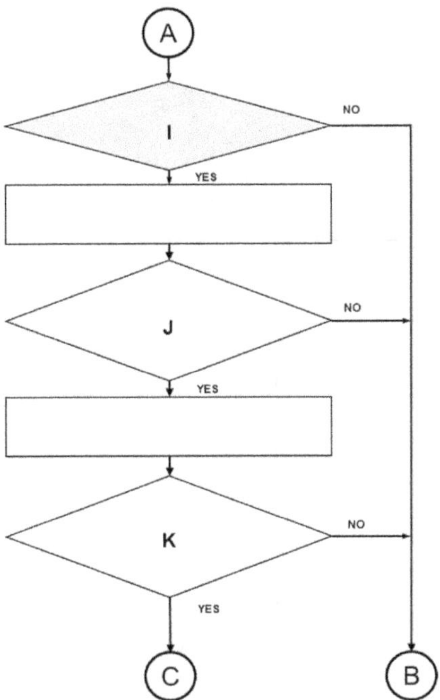

ICN-B6865-S4000P0028-001-01

Fig 26 PHCM review - Decision I

Is a review and (new) assessment of the Product Health and Condition Monitoring (PHCM) system reasonable?

The result from Decision H is the selection of one or more applicable and effective based on the current Product design (including the PHCM design approach).

If a PHCM system is to be implemented into the Product and if the selected system with the FC under analysis will be/is monitored by that PHCM system, a review of the PHCM system can be performed.

Because the answer on Decision B was NO, the detection or avoidance of the FC is either covered or not sufficiently covered by the present PHCM system.

–   If the answer is YES, the decision to perform a PHCM system review requires a quantification of the expected maintenance effort resulting from the selected PMTRI and an evaluation of the potential impact on the Product LCC. Continue with Decision H.

–   If the answer is NO, the assessment of the PHCM is to be excluded (justification is required). The FC and PHCM assessment ends.

Decision J:

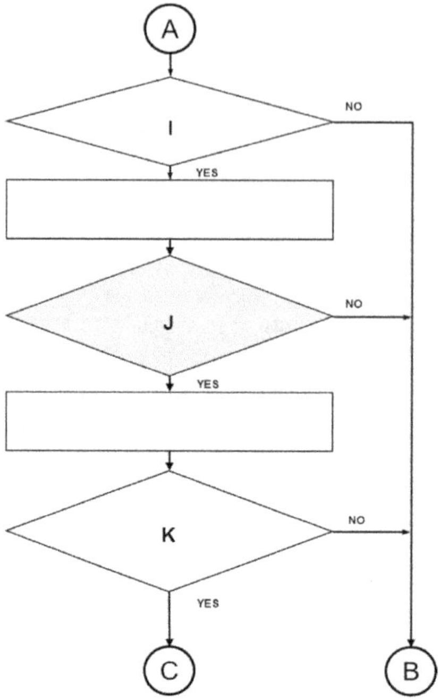

ICN-B6865-S4000P0029-001-01

Fig 27 PHCM review – Decision J

Does the resulting impact of on the Product LCC justify a review and (new) assessment of the PHCM system?

With a first pass of the maintenance effort resulting from the selected PMTRI, taking into account the planned Product fleet size and the expected/specified usage profiles, the potential impact on Product LCC can be quantified.

Depending on these results the analyst decides, if the PHCM system design must become the subject of an assessment of the PHCM system. This assessment should be performed prior to the CDR date of the PHCM system.

–   If the answer is YES, on this Decision H leads to a trade-off study in common with the responsible design department(s) to determine and propose new or additional implementation of PHCM equipment into the Product. Continue with Decision B.

–   If the answer is NO, an assessment of the PHCM system is excluded The FC and PHCM assessment ends.

Decision K:

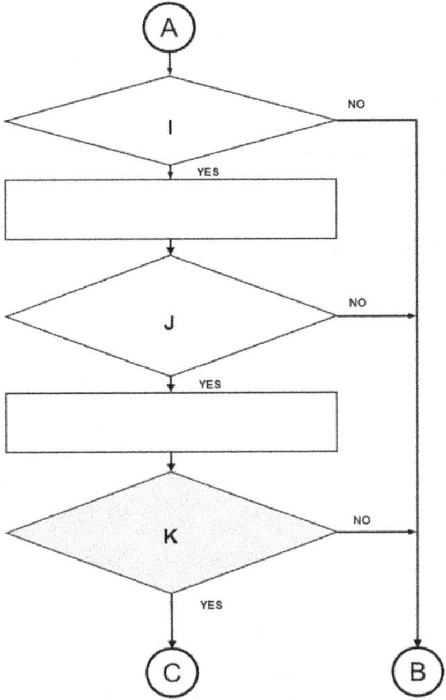

ICN-B6865-S4000P0030-001-01

Fig 28 PHCM review - Decision K

Is an implementation of new or additional PHCM equipment incl. data evaluation decided for the Product and is PHCM functionality verified?

Based on the outcome of the trade-off-study (see Decision H), the Product manufacturer decides if updating the PHCM system should be considered in order to reduce the Product maintenance effort by implementing further equipment and/or functionalities for integrated testing and/or data collection of the PHCM system.

- If the answer is YES, a degree of confidence must be established for each new PHCM functionality. Test bench results etc, must support the analyst to justify the answer YES and to return to Decision B.

- If the answer is NO, the result of the trade-off study is either the PHCM system can't be integrated or that it can't be improved, The FC and PHCM assessment ends.

Note:

PMTRI resulting from this system analysis work step 4 are developed when the system under analysis is operated as described in the PPH. If the PPH contains, for example, a second scenario that a system will not be used/activated for longer period (eg, in between two deployments to a test/operating range), the analyst must decide about PMTRI covering that scenario, too.

4.2.4 PMTRI selection criteria for FC assessment and PHCM analysis

Table 2 PMTRI selection criteria

FFEC	Selection of PMTRI task type or a combination of them	Remark
1 Evident - Safety	Select the applicable and effective PMTRI or an appropriate combination of them	PMTRI interval to be defined for each PMTRI task type. Refer to Para ¡**Error! No se encuentra el origen de la referencia.**.
2 Evident - Law/ Environmental integrity	Select the most effective PMTRI or a combination of them	Harmonization of PMTRI intervals is recommended
3 Evident - Operation or mission	Select a maximum of two applicable and effective PMTRI	PMTRI interval to be defined for each PMTRI task type. Refer to Para ¡**Error! No se encuentra el origen de la referencia.**. Harmonization of PMTRI intervals is recommended
4 Evident - Economic	Select the most applicable and effective PMTRI	None
5 Hidden - Safety	Select the applicable and effective PMTRI or an appropriate combination of them	PMTRI interval to be defined for each PMTRI task type. Refer to Para ¡**Error! No se encuentra el origen de la referencia.**. Harmonization of PMTRI intervals is recommended
6 Hidden - Law/ Environmental integrity	Select the most effective PMTRI or a combination of them	Harmonization of PMTRI intervals is recommended
7 Hidden - Mission	Select a maximum of two applicable and effective PMTRI	PMTRI interval to be defined for each PMTRI task type. Refer to Para ¡**Error! No se encuentra el origen de la referencia.**. Harmonization of PMTRI intervals is recommended
8 Hidden - Economic	Select the most applicable and effective PMTRI	None

Note

A servicing task type for a FC must be selected as a PMTRI in all cases if considered applicable and effective.

4.2.5 Redesign requirement assessment

When no PMTRI is applicable and effective, a redesign requirement must be assessed in accordance with Table 3.

Table 3 Redesign requirement assessment

FFEC	Redesign requirement	Remark
1 Evident - Safety	Redesign is mandatory	FC and resulting FF cannot be avoided by preventive maintenance and is not detectable by the PHCM system
2 Evident - Law/ Environmental integrity	Redesign must be evaluated	National/international laws and protocols must be taken into account
3 Evident - Operation or mission	Redesign must be evaluated	Customer requirements/contract must be taken into account
4 Evident - Economic	No redesign requirement necessary	Cost benefit analysis can be appropriate
5 Hidden - Safety	Redesign is mandatory	FC and resulting FF cannot be avoided by preventive maintenance and is not detectable by the PHCM system
6 Hidden - Law/ Environmental integrity	Redesign must be evaluated	National/international laws and protocols must be taken into account
7 Hidden - Mission	Redesign must be evaluated	Customer requirements/contract must be taken into account
8 Hidden - Economic	No redesign requirement necessary	Cost benefit analysis can be appropriate

4.2.6 PMTRI task type selection criteria

<u>Table</u> 4 gives the criteria for the selection of applicable and effective PMTRI task types with respect to the FFEC.

Table 4 PMTRI task type selection criteria

PMTRI task type	Applicability	Safety effect	Law/Environmental integrity effect	Operational /mission effect	Economic effect
		FFEC 1 & 5	**FFEC 2 & 6**	**FFEC 3 & 7**	**FFEC 4 & 8**
Servicing	The PMTRI task restores the item to a specific status to enable its intended use	The PMTRI task must reduce the risk that a FC could lead to a safety relevant FF	The PMTRI task must reduce the risk that a FC could lead to a FF that causes a conflict with law /or have a negative impact on environmental integrity	The PMTRI task must reduce the risk that a FC could lead to a FF that potentially reduces the operational availability and/or impacts the mission performance	The PMTRI task must be cost effective.
Operational test or simple inspection	Identification if the FC has occurred	The PMTRI task must ensure availability of the function to assure safety	The PMTRI task must ensure availability of the function to assure that there is no conflict with law or negative impact on environmental integrity	The PMTRI task must ensure availability of the function to ensure operational availability or mission performance is not negatively impacted	The PMTRI task must be cost effective
Inspection or functional test	Reduced resistance to failure must be detectable on the FC and there must be a reasonable consistent interval between the potential to failure and actual failure (P to F interval)	The PMTRI task must be able to measure an items functional performance level against a specific value to ensure availability of the function assuring safety	The PMTRI task must ensure availability of the function to reduce the risk of resulting in a conflict with law or in a negative impact on environmental integrity	The PMTRI task must ensure availability of the function to reduce the risk of resulting in a reduction of operational availability or negatively impacting mission performance	The PMTRI task must be cost effective
Restoration / Overhaul	The FC must show functional degradation characteristics at an identifiable age, and a large proportion of units must survive to that age. It must be possible to restore the item to a specific standard of failure resistance	The PMTRI task must prevent or reduce the probability of a FF to assure safety	The PMTRI task must prevent or reduce the probability of a FF that results in a conflict with law or in a negative impact upon environmental integrity	The PMTRI task must prevent or reduce the probability of a FF to an acceptable level to enable operational availability or mission performance to meet the requirements	This PMTRI must be more cost effective than a TCI
TCI	The FC must show functional degradation characteristics at an identifiable age and a large proportion of units must survive to that age	The TCI task must reduce the risk that a FC could lead to a safety relevant FF	The TCI task must prevent or reduce the probability of a FF that results in a conflict with law and/or in a negative impact upon environmental integrity	The TCI task must prevent or reduce the probability of a FF to an acceptable level to enable operational availability or mission performance to meet the requirements	An economic life limit including discard must be cost effective

5 Interval determination for PMTRI

5.1 General

As part of the system analysis, the analyst must determine and justify one or more appropriate repetitive scheduled intervals for each consolidated PMTRI in a traceable way. These intervals

must satisfy the applicability and effectiveness criteria as specified for the Product including the maintainability requirements in general.

Every PMTRI is composed of at least four elements:

- Effected subsystem, equipment or item with configuration data
- PMTRI task type
- Numerical interval value
- Appropriate interval type

For example:

- The part number X of an air filter of the engine on Product Y, location of installation Z (if more than one location)
- Replace filter
- 5 Years

If several degradations and/or deterioration processes can impact the equipment and/or item of the system under analysis, the analyst can select more than one numerical interval values in combination with different interval types for one PMTRI.

Para 5.2 and Para 5.3 support a traceable selection of applicable and effective maintenance interval types and numerical interval values based on selection logics.

A PMTRI interval type belongs either to the category calendar time or to the category usage parameter.

Typical measurement bases for the PMTRI interval type calendar time include, but are not limited to:

- Daily
- Weekly
- Monthly
- Yearly

Typical measurement bases for the PMTRI interval type usage parameter include, but are not limited to:

- Before every Product usage
- After every Product usage
- Before the accumulation of a predefined amount of a Product operating parameter (eg, flight hours for aircraft, driving distance for lorries/trains)
- Before the accumulation of a predefined amount of Product operating cycles (eg, start cycles for an engine)
- After every expected event which is Product usage-related (eg, number of role changes, loadings/de-loadings)

The determination of applicable and effective numerical interval values must take into account available technical data, maintenance experience and/or best engineering judgement.

The analyst must consider aspects or data that include, but are not limited to:

- Product manufacturer's data including test results and technical analyses
- User - specific usage scenario (information about one or more scenarios)
- Other/different user requirements
- Vendor/equipment manufacturer recommendations/requirements
- Certification authorities and/or law-based requirements (if existing)
- Experience gained from identical or from comparable Products

Where specific data on FF rates and technical failure characteristics are not available for the equipment or item under analysis, then the intervals for PMTRI must be based on results from either engineering/safety analysis and/or experience with similar systems, equipment or items.

For a newly developed Product or selected equipment or items of it, sufficient experience and information is not available in many cases. This makes the determination of optimum numerical interval values for PMTRI more difficult.

In order to lower potential risks during the Product in-service phase, it is known that numerical interval values for PMTRI are defined conservatively with small interval values at the initial in-service phase. This will result in higher PMTRI task frequencies.

The review and optimization of Product maintenance programs including all PMTRI on basis of in-service data and feedback is subject Chap 3.

In Para 5.2 and Para 5.3 the selection of the correct and traceable interval types and the determination of effective numerical interval values for PMTRI are supported.

5.2 Traceable selection of PMTRI interval types

A selection logic for correct PMTRI interval types must be documented in a PPH and applied during the system analysis. This selection logic enables traceability of all analyst decisions made and any follow-up analyst considerations when performing later optimizations of an OMP or the Product maintenance program. Refer to Chap 3.

Depending on the deterioration processes impacting the individual FC, one or more interval types can be selected in parallel to be applicable for an individual PMTRI.

5.2.1 Example for a PMTRI interval type selection logic

Fig 29 and Fig 30 show PMTRI interval type selection logics:

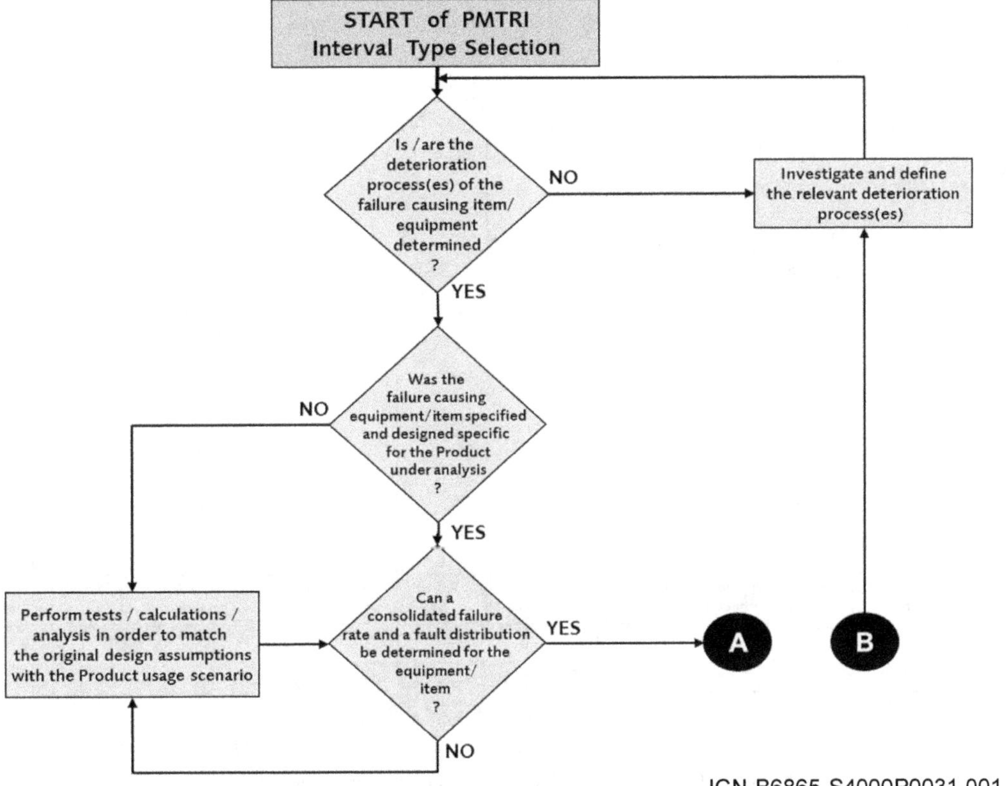

ICN-B6865-S4000P0031-001-01

Fig 29 Example for a decision logic for PMTRI interval types (Sheet 1 of 2)

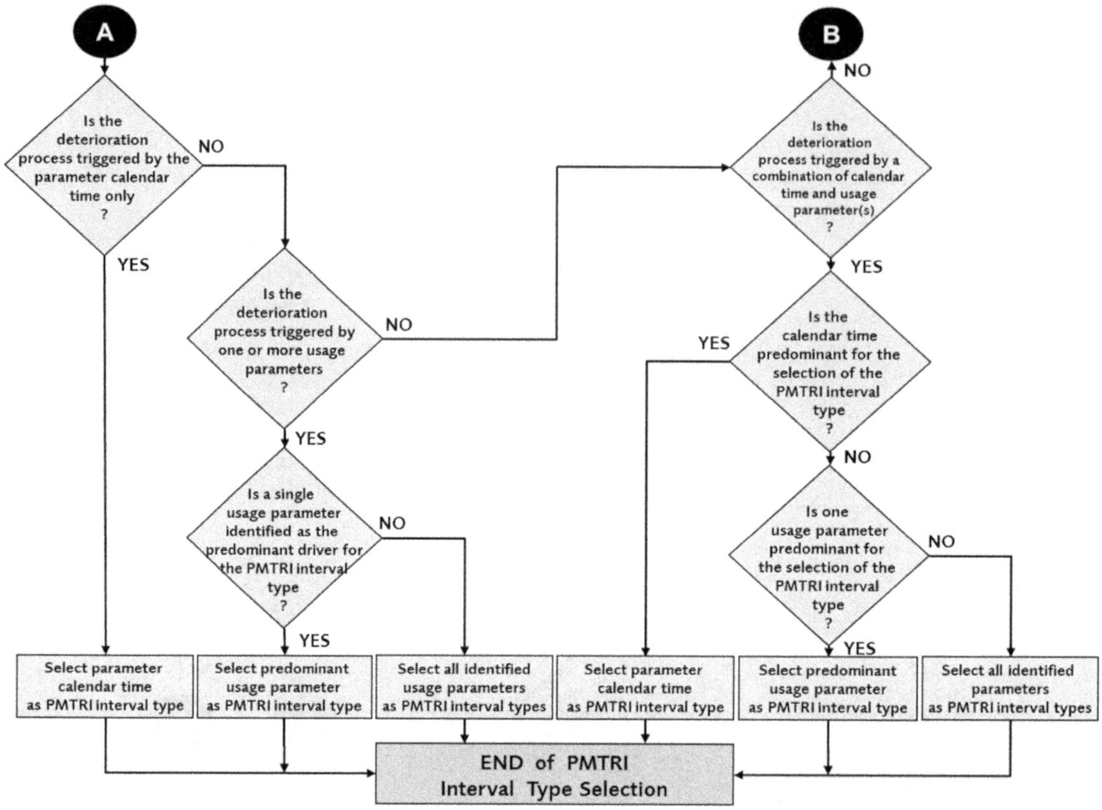

ICN-B6865-S4000P0032-001-01

Fig 30 Example for a decision logic for PMTRI interval types (Sheet 2 of 2)

5.2.2 Explanation of the example for interval type selection logics

With the PMTRI interval type selection logic Part 1 as shown in Fig 29, the FC deterioration processes for an identified FF are taken into account to allow traceability at a later project stage.

In addition, the analyst must check, to confirm that the system, equipment or item for which the PMTRI has been defined was specifically designed or selected for realistic Product usage parameters. In addition, the analyst must be aware, if the system, equipment or item will be installed on a location with FC impact parameters as specified for the Product or on another location with deviating FC impact parameters.

Based on the evaluation steps, a realistic failure rate with statistical distribution of the expected defects or malfunctions must be determined for each FC under analysis. Reliable in-service data and other useful feedback or experience must be taken into account. Refer to S5000F.

Fig 30 shows Part 2 of the PMTRI interval selection logic based on the knowledge and/or estimation about deterioration processes from decision logic Part 1. Following the answers on the individual logic decisions, a calendar-based interval type, a usage parameter-based interval type, or a combination of both interval types can be selected for an individual PMTRI.

5.3 Determination of numerical interval values for PMTRI

To complete a scheduled PMTRI interval, one effective numerical interval value must be determined in Para 5.2 for each interval type. To support the analysis and to ensure a

harmonized and traceable determination of PMTRI interval values by different analysts, a determination support logic is recommended to be provided in the project-specific analysis PPH.

5.3.1 Example for a PMTRI interval value determination logic

Fig 31 shows an example for an PMTRI interval value determination logic that allows to take predefined interval values into account for the Product (if any) prior to perform subsequent PMTRI harmonization activities.

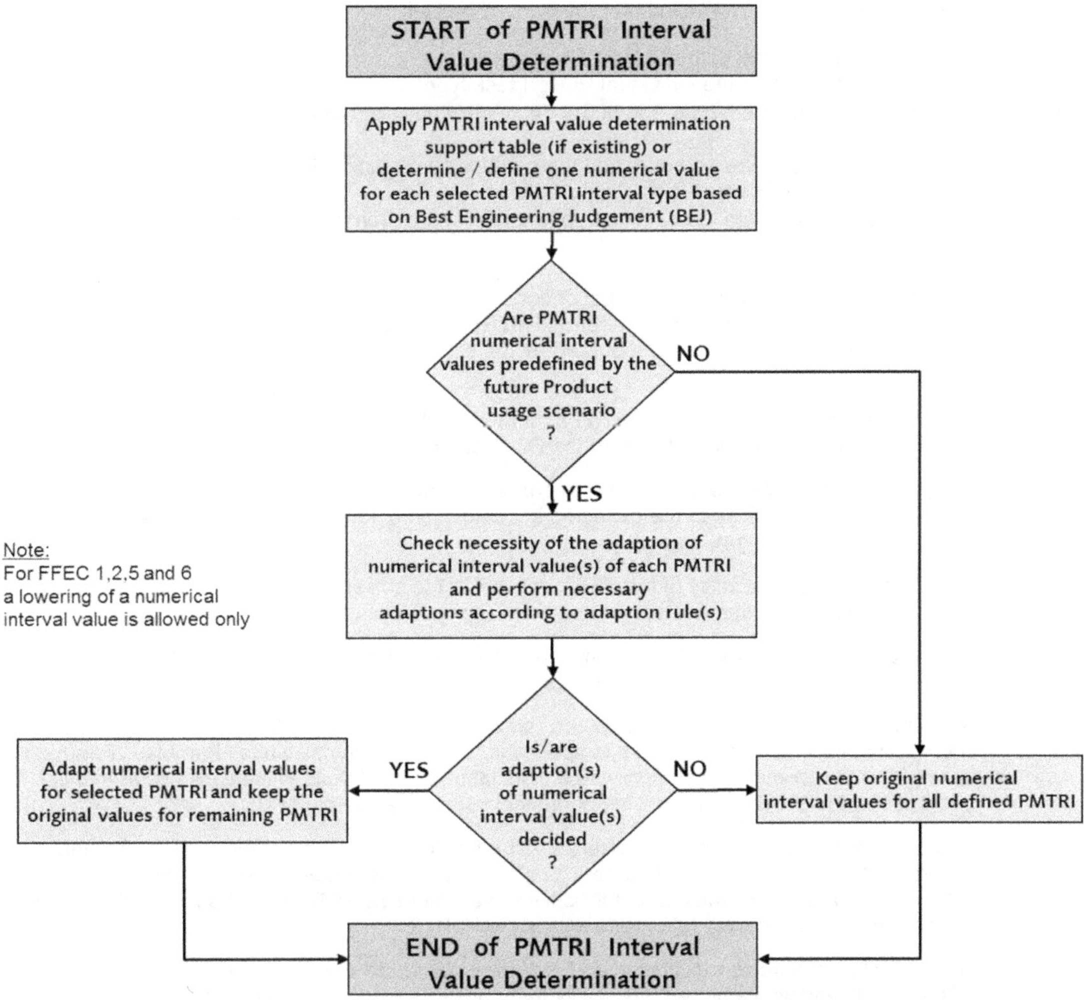

ICN-B6865-S4000P0033-001-01

Fig 31 Example for a PMTRI interval value determination logic

5.3.2 Explanation of the example for a PMTRI interval value determination logic

Each repetitive scheduled interval of a PMTRI is defined as a combination of one numerical value plus an applicable interval type, such as:

- 10.000 Miles
- 500 Start Cycles
- 5 Years

A numerical interval value defines an upper limit of the maturity to perform the PMTRI task on a system, on an equipment or item, on a structure or on a zone of a Product.

Depending on the criticality category of a potential FFE that was caused by the identified failure or malfunction of the FC, the numerical interval value can be adapted for FC with uncritical FFE or it can be strictly limited as an upper limit (eg, for FC with safety critical FFEC).

To determine a correct numerical value for a scheduled PMTRI interval, the analyst must take into account aspects that include, but are not limited to:

– Selected task type of the PMTRI
– FFEC selected for the individual PMTRI task type
– Expected average failure rate of the FC under analysis during a future Product in-service phase
– The probable or known curve and the peak of the statistical failure distribution of the FC during a future Product in-service phase
– Deviation risks from the expected failure rate and/or from the expected statistical failure distribution

PMTRI task types servicing or inspection/functional test, must be performed frequently before the FC is expected to fail. The number of PMTRI events prior to an accumulation of failures or malfunctions of the FC must be triggered by the selected criticality of the allocated FFEC. The following rule applies:

The higher the criticality of the FFEC of the FC, the more frequent a PMTRI of these task types must be performed prior to the FC accumulation is expected.

Numerical interval values of PMTRI task types scheduled replacement or scheduled overhaul must be defined as close to the expected accumulation of failures or malfunctions of the FC as possible. The following rule applies:

The lower the criticality of the FFEC of the FC, the closer the numerical value of the selected PMTRI interval to the expected FC accumulation.

For safety-critical FC the PMTRI must clearly be performed prior to the expected FC accumulation due to a given safety-margin.

Deviation risks on assumptions on failure rates and/or on statistical failure distribution can be compensated by correction factors in applicable interval value calculation formulas. To support analysts, it is recommended to provide a calculation support table in the PPH covering the impact parameters when calculating numerical interval values of PMTRI.

Having determined the numerical interval value for the interval type of the PMTRI, the analyst must finally take into account if numerical all interval values are predicted as documented in the PPH. If yes, a harmonization of numerical interval values for PMTRI can be required. If not, the original numerical interval value remains for the PMTRI.

Some technical defects resulting in an FF can be caused by damage impacts with a limited detectability and with a higher probability than those defects resulting from the regular deterioration processes. In these cases, the numerical interval value of the PMTRI must be less than the shortest likely interval between the point at which a potential technical defect becomes detectable and the point at which it degrades into a FF. If failure data is available, this interval is referred to as the P to F interval. The shortest time between the discovery of a potential FC and the occurrence of the FF must be long enough for an appropriate action to be taken to avoid, eliminate or minimize the consequences of the FF.

A high damage probability can therefore mean the smallest numerical interval value is selected. For example, the value 1 in combination with the interval type day, engine start means the PMTRI must be performed every day, before each engine start etc. For some PMTRI, it can be

appropriate for the analyst to consider specifying an initial scheduled interval or threshold that is different from the smaller repeat interval.

The original PMTRI interval values must be determined on the basis of the harmonized Product usage scenario for a standard Product in-service utilization.

Where different usage scenarios deviate from the standard usage scenario with other operating or mission, environments and/or climatic conditions, deterioration characteristics and external impacts on the Product under analysis, the PMTRI interval values must be reassessed based on information provided in the PPH. Refer to Chap 1. Consequently, selected PMTRI interval values must be adjusted accordingly. The justification for these changes or adjustments of PMTRI interval values must be noted in the respective analysis reports.

If the maintenance effort to perform a PMTRI is low, this must not automatically lead to selecting a high task frequency. This is because the risk of maintenance induced errors increase the probability of a negative impact on safety and/or reliability.

Scheduled interval packages, (eg, expected), in a Product development specification (if any) must not drive any initial PMTRI interval value determination. The interval determination in the frame of this analysis methodology must be based on the technical evaluation performed by each analyst.

6   Certification maintenance requirements

In addition to those PMTRI with repetitive scheduled intervals established through this system analysis methodology, further preventive maintenance-related requirements and/or limitations can arise within a Product certification process (eg, Certification Maintenance Requirements (CMR) known from civil aviation, Preventive Maintenance Task Limitations (PMTL), Other Maintenance Requirements (OMR)).

For example, in a civil aircraft certification process, a CMR is comparable to a PMTL for other Products, established during the design certification of the Product. CMR usually results from a formal, numerical analysis conducted to show compliance with potential catastrophic and hazardous FFE. For civil aircraft systems a CMR is intended to detect and/or eliminate safety significant latent FC that would, in combination with one or more other specific Product-internal FC or Product-external FC, result in a hazardous or catastrophic FFE. In addition, all FFE with an impact on environmental integrity and/or FFE that can conflict with law are also assumed to be a CMR.

Note

    CMR/PMTL can be derived from relevant law or from a fundamentally different analytical process than the PMTRI development that results from this system analysis.

The harmonization of PMTRI resulting sources from this analysis methodology with CMR or other relevant sources is described in Chap 2.6. This takes place prior to the data exchange/transfer from S4000P to S3000L for subsequent analysis activities.

7   Trend-leader selection

PMTRI for systems, equipment or items defined in the system analysis procedure can be selected for a trend-leader concept.

A trend-leader selection is a process to evaluate and determine a sample of systems, equipment or items under analysis for inspection or testing at defined intervals for any unexpected degradation and/or external impact (eg, caused by the environment, or by accidental impacts).

The performance of preventive Product maintenance on basis of identified PMTRI will be limited on selected trend-leaders only. The selected locations of item installation, the number of trend-leader items per individual Product and/or the number of selected Product serial numbers must

---

statistically represent the technical status of the Product fleet. The selection-strategy of trend leaders increases the technical knowledge on the Product and reduces the total maintenance effort of the complete Product fleet.

Trend-leader selection and sampling are part of the PMTRI optimization process to be established during a Product in-service phase. Refer to Chap 3.

Chapter 2.4

Developing PMTR - Structure analysis

Table of contents

Page

Developing PMTR - Structure analysis 1

References 2

1 Product structure 3
2 Damage and failure sources on Product structure 3
2.1 Accidental Damage 3
2.2 Environmental Deterioration 4
2.3 Structure Fatigue Failure 4
3 Objectives of structural preventive maintenance..5
4 Structure analysis procedure..6
4.1 Structural analysis logic 6
4.2 Description of the structural analysis logic 8
4.2.1 Corrosion prevention 14
4.2.2 Corrosion control 15
4.2.3 Maintenance relevant Product structure...20
4.2.4 Non-critical Product structure 21
5 PMTRI assessment and SHCM analysis for SSI/SD 22
5.1 General 22
5.2 PMTRI assessment and SHCM analysis logic diagrams 23
5.3 PMTRI assessment and SHCM analysis procedure 25
5.3.1 Explanation of the PMTRI assessment and SHCM analysis decisions 26
6 Rating systems for SSI/SD 35
6.1 Rating structure fatigue failure..36
6.2 Rating accidental damage 36
6.2.1 Susceptibility to minor accidental damage 37
6.2.2 Residual strength after damage occurrence 37
6.2.3 Timely detection of damage 37
6.3 Rating environmental deterioration of metallic structure 37
6.4 Rating environmental deterioration of non-metallic structure................................38
6.5 Rating of metallic and non-metallic structure material combinations 38
7 Definition of interval thresholds 38
8 Definition of repeat inspection intervals..38
9 Documenting preventive scheduled maintenance tasks with intervals during Product in-
service phase..39

List of tables

1 References 2

List of figures

1 Product structure analysis - Main logic diagram...7
2 Product structure analysis - Fatigue analysis for SSI/SD.......................................11
3 Product structure analysis - AD/ED/CPCP Analysis for metallic SSI/SD....................13
4 Product structure analysis - AD/ED Analysis for non-metallic SSI/SD........................16
5 Product structure analysis - Analysis of SSI/SD material combinations 18

6	SSI/SD PMTRI Selection including SHCM Assessment (Part 1)	23
7	SSI/SD PMTRI Selection including SHCM Assessment (Part 2)	24
8	Detailed selection Logic for Inspections or Functional Tests for SSI/SD - Example	25
9	Decision A	27
10	Decision B	28
11	Decision C	29
12	Decision D	30
13	Decision E	31
14	Decision F	32
15	Decision G	33
16	Decision H	34
17	Decision I	35
18	Structure analysis summary sheet (to be defined and filled with rating data specific for a Product under analysis), example	40
19	AD analysis sheet Part 1, example	41
20	Combined interval rating sheet for metallic SSI/SD covering both AD Part 2 and ED, example	42
21	AD analysis sheet, Part 2 for composite SSI/SD, example	43
22	ED analysis sheet for composite SSI/SD, example	44

References

Table 1 References

Chap No./Document No.	Title
Chap 1	Introduction to the specification
Chap 2.	Developing PMTR
Chap 2.1	Developing PMTR - General
Chap 2.3	Developing PMTR - System analysis
Chap 2.5	Developing PMTR - Zonal analysis
Chap 2.6	Developing PMTR - Consolidation of analysis results, harmonization with other preventive maintenance task requirement sources for traceability
Chap 2.7	Developing PMTR - Special event analysis
Chap 3	Optimizing PMTR
Chap 3.3	Optimizing PMTR - ISMO analysis phase
Chap 3.5	Optimizing PMTR - Review of PMTRE for special events
Chap 4.5	S4000P Interfaces - S5000F
Chap 6	Terms, abbreviations and acronyms
S1000D	International specification for technical publications using a common source database
S3000L	International procedure specification for Logistic Support Analysis - LSA
S5000F	International specification for operational and maintenance data feedback

Chap No./Document No.	Title
DIN Norm 31 051/(DIN/EN 13306)	Maintenance Terminology

1   Product structure

A Product structure consists of all load carrying and/or load bearing members (eg, body of a submarine, engine/motor mountings of a land vehicle, wings on an aircraft, aircraft landing gear, flight control surfaces and related points of attachment, ship hull, etc).

The actuating portions of Product items or equipment such as a wheel axle of a land vehicle, aircraft landing gear or aircraft wing flaps will be treated as Product systems and must be analyzed as Analysis Relevant Candidates (ARC) as described in Chap 2.3. Attachments of system actuators or other power-generating equipment to the Product structure including hinges must be analyzed as Product structure.

Note:

Refer to Chap 1 and Chap 2.3 for more information and clarification regarding the selection of ARC and/or Structure Significant Item (SSI).

Product structure can be subdivided according to the consequences of their loss of function as follows:

- Necessary for continued Product safety during the in-service phase
- Necessary to avoid conflicts with law and/or environmental integrity)
- With significant impact on Product maintenance and/or Product availability
- Without significant impact on Life Cycle Cost (LCC) during the Product in-service phase

Consequently, Product structure can be allocated to the following categories:

- Structure Significant Item (SSI) with or without Significant Details (SD). When loss of item function can impact Product safety and/or can lead to a conflict with law and/or environmental integrity.
- Maintenance relevant structure. When loss of item function can cause high maintenance effort and/or can have significant impact on the Product availability.
- Non-critical structure. When loss of item function has no significant impact on in-service Product usage.

2   Damage and failure sources on Product structure

The assessment of Product structure for the selection of Preventive Maintenance Task Requirements with repetitive scheduled intervals (PMTRI) must consider the following damage and failure sources impacting the Product structure during the specified usage conditions during the in-service phase:

2.1   Accidental Damage

Accidental Damage (AD) is the physical alteration of an item, normally caused by:

- any impact that occurs as standard event with an expected probability during the in-service Product usage. For example (from aircraft technology), rain, hail, weapons release, cargo air delivery, role changes, air to air refueling, debris or spillage etc.
- human error during Product manufacturing, assembly, operation or maintenance
- less obvious AD parameters such as those arising from operator, passenger or maintainer activities. These AD types can manifest themselves as distortion, overheating, torn, punctured, delamination, separation of individual material layers, etc.

Potential sources of AD must be considered for all material variants of the Product structure (ie, metallic, non-metallic or a combination of both).

Note:

> Unexpected accidental impacts on Product structure must be covered by the special event analysis. Refer to Chap 2.7. During the Product in-service phase, the review and optimization process for special event based PMTR (PMTRE) must be applied in accordance with Chap 3.5.

2.2 Environmental Deterioration

Environmental Deterioration (ED) is the gradual physical degradation of structural material properties because of their interaction with the climate or the localized environmental conditions assumed during the Product in-service phase.

Causes of ED can include, but not be limited to:

- chemical interaction
- erosion
- fluid or gas absorption
- thermal cycling
- electromagnetic radiation

Evidence of ED can manifest itself on the Product structure can include, but not be limited to:

- corrosion
- stress corrosion
- cracking
- loss of surface finish
- softening of composite material matrices (including adhesives used in laminated composites)
- delamination
- degradation of static strength
- degradation of dynamic/fatigue strength

A local interface of different material types including material combinations of metallic and non-metallic structural components can cause electrochemical processes that can degrade the structural materials. All identified ED impacts must be analyzed for each selected SSI/SD.

Note:

> Unexpected environmental impacts on Product structure must be covered by the special event analysis. Refer to Chap 2.7. During the Product in-service phase, the review process for PMTRE must be applied in accordance with Chap 3.5.

2.3 Structure Fatigue Failure

Structure Fatigue Failure (SFF) is based on a process of progressive, permanent structural change occurring inside structural material. An SFF usually begins and grows on a microscopic scale until it manifests itself as visible material cracking.

The crack propagation depends on:

- material properties and its geometry
- the level, amplitude and frequency of fluctuating stresses
- the number of load cycles applied

SFF culminates in material cracks that reduce the residual strength of the structural item and causes fractures if the residual strength of the structural material falls below the applied load.

3   Objectives of structural preventive maintenance

During the Product in-service phase, structural failures and/or structural damages of the Product structure under analysis must be identified as soon as possible before a potential loss of the structural function can lead to critical or other unacceptable consequences.

Identified PMTRI cover all parameters from both AD and ED impact parameters.

Further sets of PMTRE without scheduled intervals follow the same objectives. These PMTRE must be performed after an assumption or occurrence of unscheduled special events in accordance with Chap 2.7.

The primary objectives of the preventive structural maintenance of a Product are to:

− maintain the inherent Product safety level
− avoid a potential conflict with law and/or environmental integrity throughout the operational or usage life cycle of the Product
− ensure and/or optimize the Product availability for operations or missions
− optimize the Product LCC in an economical manner without neglecting the previous listed objectives

PMTRI for SSI/SD selected on basis of this analysis methodology must be aligned with at least:

− Product type Certification Maintenance Requirements (CMR)
− National and/or international legal publications and/or changes

   Note:

   Regulatory authorities can require or predict safety limitations, replacement times for structural safe-life parts or items to ensure continued Product safety. These Time Change Items (TCI), must be aligned with corresponding PMTRI that have been developed on the basis of this analytical process or in subsequent processes if information becomes available at a later stage in the project. Refer to S3000L.

− Additional PMTRI or PMTRI changes raised by the Maintenance Review Board (MRB) or a comparable organization or team

This analytical process for Product structure analysis must take the following into account:

− Structural design philosophy and characteristics
− Fatigue evaluations and calculations dependent on safe life or damage tolerance design principles
− In-service experience from similar structural items on other Products
− Structural fatigue tests, results and experience
− Item susceptibility to failure and/or damage (AD, ED and SFF)
− PMTRI from Corrosion Prevention and Control Program (CPCP) for metallic parts or items, based on in-service experience
− Consequences of structural deterioration to continuing safe Product operation including:

  • The effect on the Product (eg, loss of function or reduction of residual strength)
  • The effect on Product usage or response characteristics caused by the interaction of structural damage or failure with associated Product systems
  • Loss of structural items during mission or operation

− Applicability and effectiveness of all selectable maintenance task types to detect, delay, prevent or stop structural deterioration
− Inspection or test interval thresholds and repeat intervals
− Sampling and/or trend or fleet leader program or other methods

To achieve an optimized maintenance regime on Product structure, applicable and effective inspections or tests must meet the detection requirements from each of the AD, ED, CPCP and

SFF assessments. Current and available support equipment technology must be taken into account when selecting inspection or test tasks. Newest testability technology should be the baseline for making decisions on Structure Health and Condition Monitoring (SHCM) of the Product structure.

Developments in Product-integrated inspection and test technology enable an extended integration of SHCM systems and equipment to support Product structural maintenance. For SS/SD, potential failure causes, and different damage causes must be detected on time during the Product in-service phase. Experience shows that it is not applicable and/or effective to cover all relevant failure causes and/or damage causes for a selected SSI/SD by integrated SHCM systems or equipment alone.

Selected failures or damages causing a high maintenance effort and consequent high LCC on SSI/SD should preferably be covered by SHCM system or equipment. For the remaining failures or damages on SSI/SD, PMTRI performed by trained personnel are more effective.

New structure materials and material combinations are already selected by Product designers. Additional new types can be developed for future Product structures. Therefore, the analysis must also include the analysis of all possible material combinations (eg, metallic material combined with non-metallic material). Generally, the individual structural materials of such combinations remain inseparable after the production process.

This structural analysis methodology leads to harmonized PMTRI with analysis-based interval types and numerical interval values for structural items. The determination of preventive maintenance tasks with scheduled intervals for the Product maintenance program or Operators' Maintenance Program (OMP) are based on the PMTRI. The original PMTRI intervals can be adapted for packaging or grouping into master intervals following the process and rules given in S3000L.

PMTRI selected for Product structure can also be applicable and effective when performed as PMTRE after an expectation or occurrence of a special event. The PMTRE selection, applicable for special events on Product structure, is defined in Chap 2.7.

To review and optimize PMTRI and/or PMTRE for Product structure that are documented in a maintenance program or OMP, optimization processes must be applied during the Product in-service phase. Refer to Chap 3.

4   Structure analysis procedure

A structural analysis procedure follows logic, guidelines and explanations for developing applicable and effective PMTRI for the structure of a Product. These logic, guidelines and explanations must be supplemented and extended with information necessary to support the analytical work to prepare the Product-specific PPH. Refer to Chap 1.

If additional information is necessary to cover specific structural impacts, (eg, for military Products due to crisis, a war scenario and/or specific usage conditions), it must be included in the PPH for the project.

It is recommended that the PPH be approved by all stake holders prior to commencing the analytical work.

4.1   Structural analysis logic

The procedure for developing and harmonizing structural PMTRI for a Product structure must follow the main structural analysis logic diagram according to Fig 1.

The process steps Step S8, Step S9, Step S10 and Step S11 in the main logic diagram comprise a set of Decisions (D) and work Steps (S) necessary to analyze each SSI or each SD on individual SSI.

More detailed logics ([Fig] 2 thru [Fig] 5) are integrated in the descriptions of selected work Steps (S) of the main logic diagram.

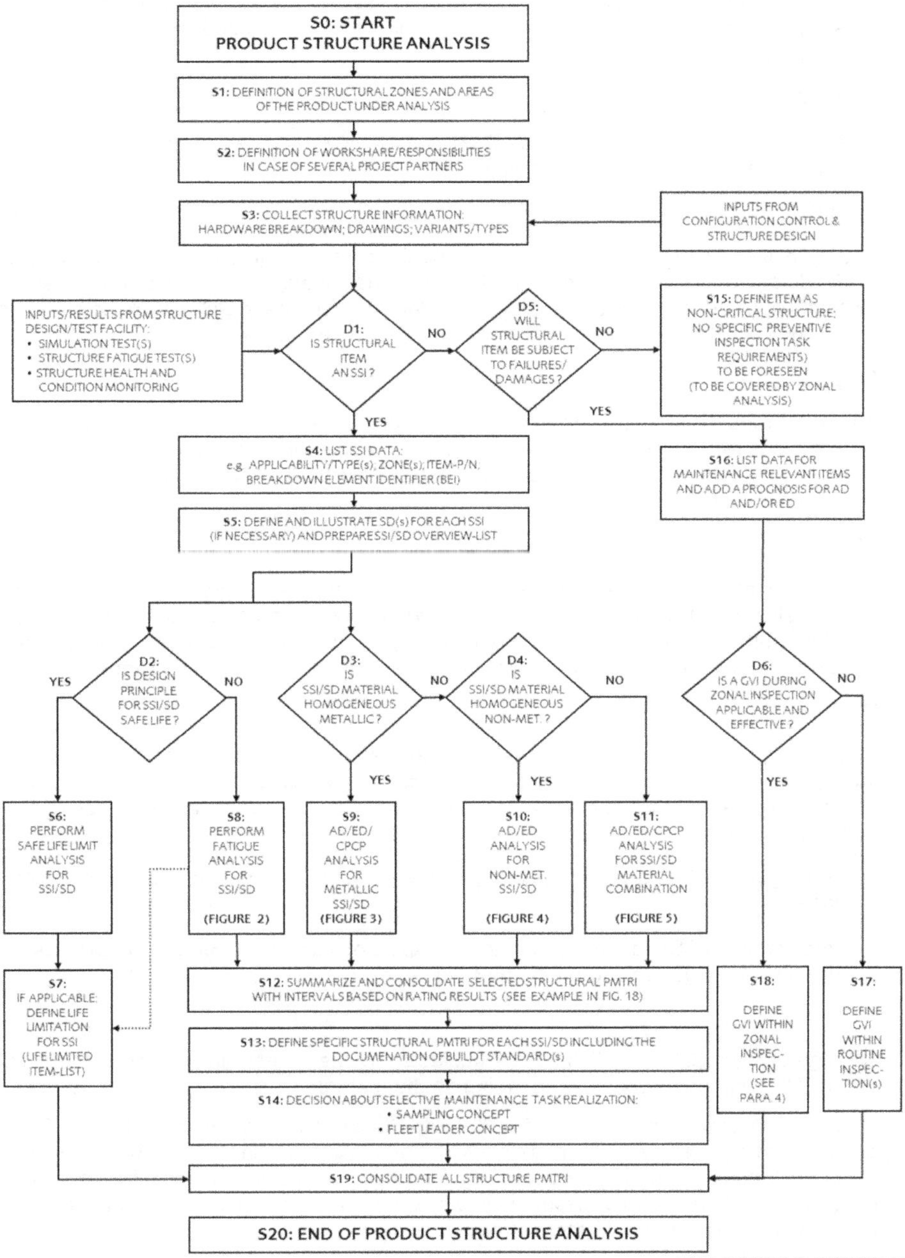

ICN-B6865-S4000P0034-001-01

Fig 1 Product structure analysis - Main logic diagram

4.2 Description of the structural analysis logic

The process steps (Step S1, Step S2, Step S3, etc.) and decisions (Decision D1, Decision D2, Decision D3, etc) of the structural analysis logic diagram are described and explained. For some process steps of the logic diagram (eg, for Step S8), detailed sub-logic diagrams are described and explained.

Step S0:

After preparation and approval of the Product-specific PPH by all involved stakeholders, the structure analysis of a Product can begin.

Step S1:

The definition of both zones and areas for the Product structure under analysis is a prerequisite for Product overview and for documenting the results of analyses. If several Partner Companies (PC) are involved in a Products' design and development, each PC is responsible for their own structural work share of the analyses according to the PPH.

Step S2:

Where a Products' structural development is shared over several PC. SSI/SD as well as maintenance-relevant structure must be defined for the complete Product structure. Interface problems must be solved, and solutions must be defined in the PPH. One or more analysts must be nominated from each PC.

Step S3:

As an initial activity, each analyst must collect basic information about the structural items of the Product structure allocated to their analytical work share (eg, structural items drawing tree, structure part numbers, specification data, design status and categorization of the individual structural items and information about Product variants and design deviations).

Decision D1:

As a prerequisite for structural analysis, the build standard of each SSI for all Product structure variants must be clearly defined by design departments (eg, by drawing number, part number, modification status). This is a prerequisite for correct maintenance task type selection and for scheduled interval rating of PMTRI.

Depending on the SSI design data and parameters, the SSI location and the expected failure or damage:

— the complete SSI can be subject to an inspection or test task and/or CPCP task requirements depending on the material type

or

— one or more SD on an SSI can be subjected to one or more inspection or test task and/or CPCP task requirements, depending on the material type

Only the structural items that fulfill the SSI and SD criteria, must be selected for a further detailed structural analysis on the basis of interval rating systems. Each SSI decision is based on inputs from the design department (eg, from calculations, simulations, fatigue test results, etc), safety hazard analysis, experience with other Products (eg, data evaluation from health monitoring) and/or on requirements from authorities.

Note:

The SSI selection must not be confused with the ARC selection that is part of the system analysis explained in Chap 2.3. Both the SSI and the ARC selection can become relevant on Products (eg, main rotor assembly and tail rotor assembly of helicopters). Clarification of the selected types of analysis candidates must be given in the PPH. Refer to Chap 1 and Chap 2.2.

If the structural item is judged to be an SSI/SD (Answer YES), continue with Step S4.

If not (Answer NO), continue with Decision D5.

Step S4:

Document all selected SSI with drawing and item data in an SSI overview list. The analyst must evaluate the installation of each SSI and must create an overview sketch for later analysis.

Step S5:

In accordance with Para 1, an SD is defined as a limited area of an SSI or a local spot on the SSI. In general, the SD has no part number apart from the identification data from the SSI. Therefore, every SD and its geometrical dimensions must be defined and documented on the drawing of the SSI under analysis.

The SD definition on an SSI is based on:

- results from Product and/or item fatigue tests
- simulation results from manufacturers

or on

- operator experience with similar structural items based on comparable usage conditions

Each SD on an SSI must be selected on the basis of the:

- highest fatigue-related criticality (eg, those areas, where initial cracks are to be expected first)
- highest probability for accidental damage and/or environmental deterioration impact

Depending on the SSI location, different failure causes, impacts from the environment and/or accidental damage can influence the selection of one or more SD on an SSI. The analyst must allocate and document relevant failures and relevant impact parameters to each selected SD for the later analysis work steps.

If an SHCM system does not make a PMTRI obsolete, applicable and effective PMTRI must be selected to cover the identified failure or damage causes impacting the SSI/SD.

The determination of the location and the geometrical size of an SSI/SD is a prerequisite to correctly define PMTRI for each SD. Location and surroundings of each SS/SD has an influence on the PMTRI selection.

For PMTRI, the numerical size of the interval and the interval type must be determined based on a traceable interval rating system for SSI/SD. Different SD on one SSI can therefore lead to different PMTRI task types with different intervals. For each SSI/SD Decision D2 and Decision D3 must be answered in parallel.

Decision D2:

Input from the design department is necessary to make a decision about the design principle safe life or damage tolerant for each SSI/SD. The result must be added in the SSI/SD overview list. Refer to Step S4.

If the SSI/SD design principle is safe life (Answer YES), continue with Step S6.

If not (Answer NO), continue with Step S8.

Step S6:

For SSI/SD with a safe life design principle, the design department must deliver information or data about the respective SSI. Depending on the specified Product life cycle the individual SSI life limit:

–   ends within the Product life cycle and this type of SSI must be replaced and discarded before reaching its predicted life limit at a predefined interval
–   is equal to or exceeds the Product life cycle. In which case, this type of SSI must not be replaced and discarded in a scheduled manner. In the case of a future extension of the Product life cycle, these SSI must be analyzed again.

Step S7:

All life-limited SSI must be listed in the Product life-limited item list for the approval of authorities.

Step S8:

In <u>Fig</u> 2, further process steps and decisions for Fatigue analysis are described:

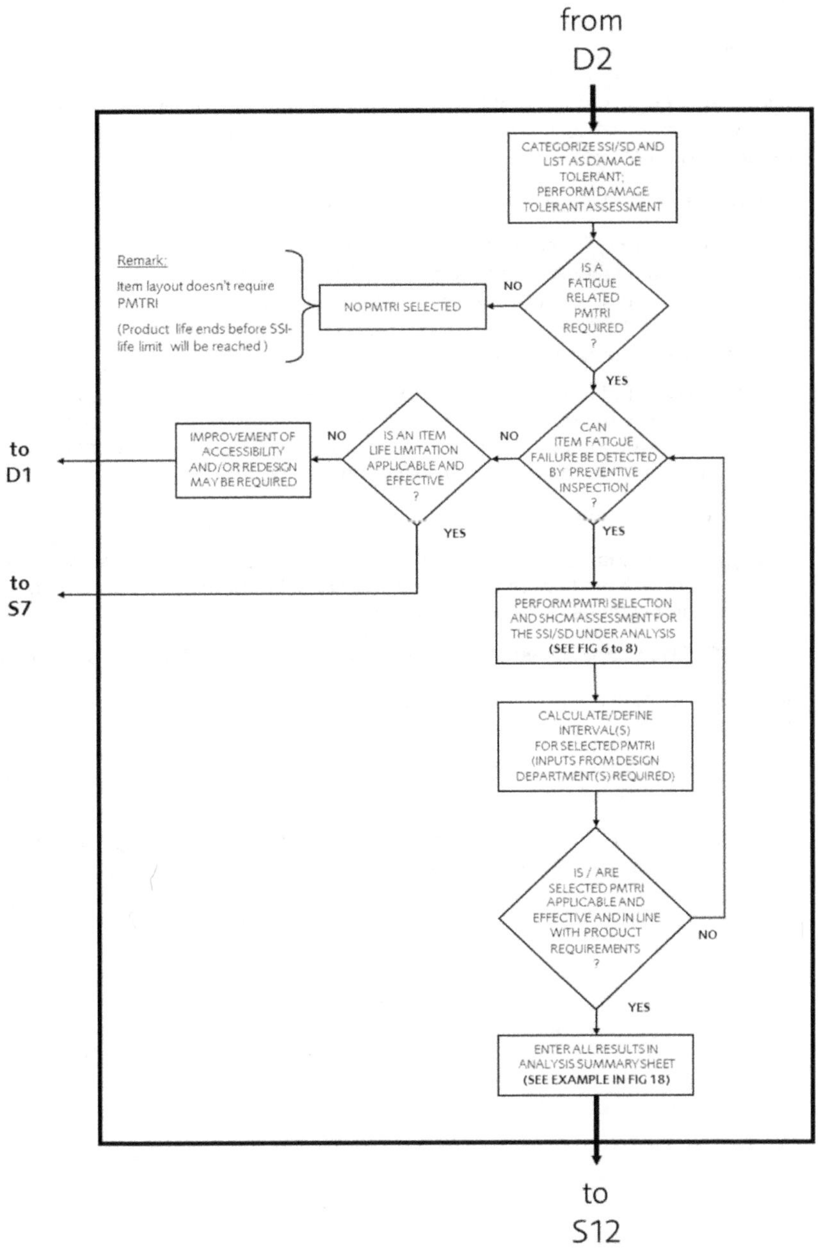

ICN-B6865-S4000P0035-001-01

Fig 2 Product structure analysis - Fatigue analysis for SSI/SD

For metallic SSI with a damage tolerant design principle, the applicable and effective inspection or test must be defined by the analyst, taking into account maintainability experience.

A PMTRI assessment and SHCM analysis detailed in the PPH must be performed. Refer to Fig 6 thru Fig 8.

The structural design department determines the preventive inspection interval for a timely detection of an SFF. This depends on manufacturers' calculations and/or simulation data. If either a PMTRI is not applicable and/or effective, or the SHCM system is inadequate, or the SSI/SD accessibility is improved, a scheduled replacement of the SSI/SD or item redesign must be taken into account.

The fatigue related inspections can be influenced by:

- manufacturers' damage tolerance evaluations
- results from fatigue data simulation at the manufacturer
- manufacturers' hardware tests including destructive test results
- significant changes of usage parameters at the operator documented in an approved analysis procedure (PPH)

Inspections related to the detection of SFF in non-metallic SSI are assumed not to be required if the SSI design is based on a no-damage growth design philosophy, substantiated by test results. Where no in-service experience exists with similar structure material, structural PMTRI must be based on manufacturers' recommendations only.

Decision D3/Decision D4:

The type of material of the SSI/SD under analysis leads to the subsequent decision sheets or files and logics. Next to homogeneous metallic SSI or homogeneous non-metallic SSI, SSI material combinations must be analyzed separately.

If the SSI/SD material is homogeneous metallic (Answer to D3 is YES), continue with Step S9.

If the SSI/SD material is not homogeneous metallic (Answer to D3 is NO), continue with Decision D4.

If the SSI/SD material is homogeneous non-metallic (Answer to D3 is NO, Answer to D4 is YES), continue with Step S10.

If the SSI/SD material is neither homogeneous metallic nor homogeneous non-metallic (Answer to both D3 and D4 are NO), continue with Step S11.

Step S9:

The homogeneous metallic SSI/SD analysis is described in <u>Fig</u> 3.

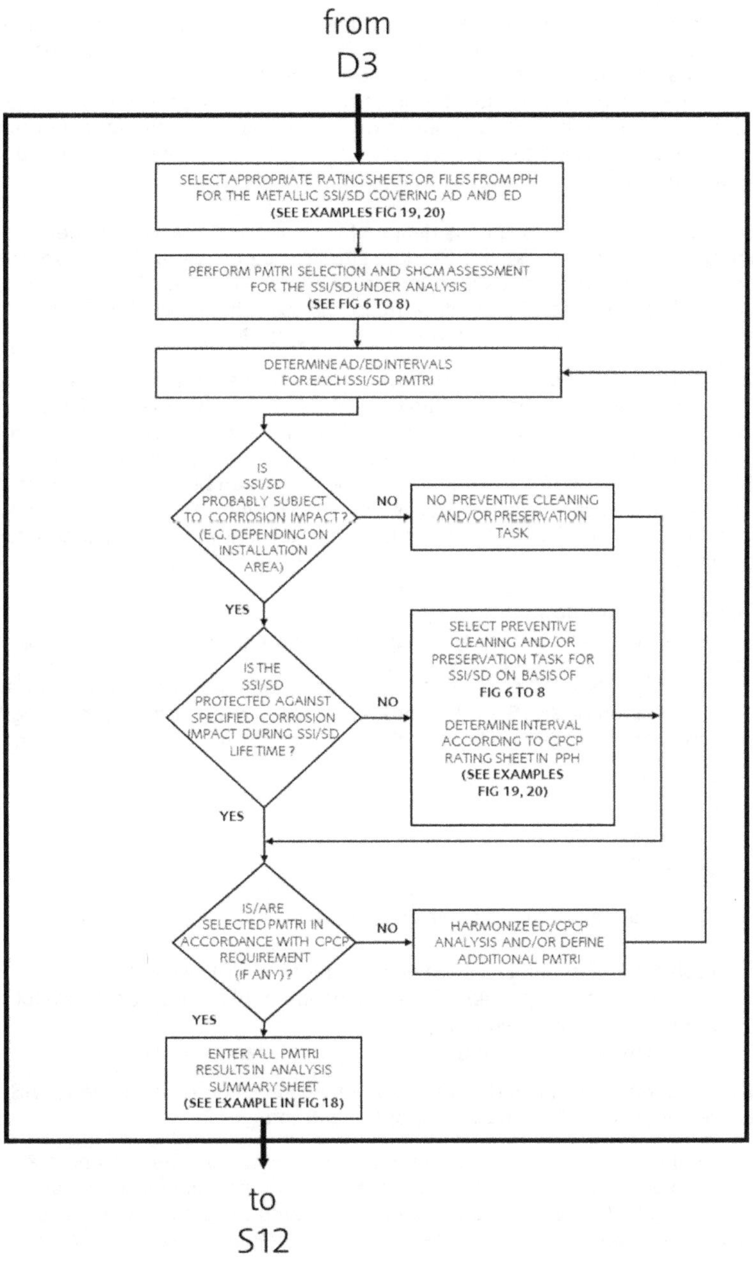

ICN-B6865-S4000P0036-001-01

Fig 3 Product structure analysis - AD/ED/CPCP Analysis for metallic SSI/SD

<u>Fig</u> 3 shows the individual analytical steps and decisions on how to determine and combine scheduled inspections or tests based on AD/ED analysis and PMTRI from CPCP. PMTRI based on CPCP can include Temporary Protection Systems (TPS) for SSI/SD.

AD, together with stress corrosion and other forms of corrosion, can occur at any time during a Product's service or usage life; because these are random in nature. Inspection or test requirements pertaining to these conditions must apply to each Product throughout its operational life. However, most forms of corrosion depend on time or usage and are more likely to occur as the Product ages. In these cases, operator and manufacturer experience on similar structures can be used to establish appropriate PMTRI (including PMTRI based on CPCP) for the control of ED.

Where environmental conditions deviate from specified operating conditions for the Product, expected corrosion on metallic Product structure can deviate. To prevent the Product from corroding or from a not to exceed corrosion process limit, the CPCP contains PMTRI for metallic SSI/SD. The objective of preventive maintenance is the early identification of the beginning and the continuous monitoring of corrosion process on Product structure.

Depending on the Product structure materials and the specified operational environments, a CPCP can be established to maintain the resistance of the metallic Product structure to corrosion because of systematic structural deterioration through chemical and/or environmental interactions. The CPCP is an integral part of this analytical step for metallic SSI/SD. Therefore PMTRI (eg, scheduled cleaning, preservation, etc) can be selected so that predicted corrosion processes which can have a negative influence on the SSI fatigue can be avoided or delayed. Scheduled intervals for PMTRI must take into account the main impact parameters on probable corrosion.

4.2.1 Corrosion prevention

Preventive maintenance task types applicable for corrosion prevention are:

- Cleaning of SSI/SD from substances, which can otherwise support or accelerate corrosion,
- Preservation of SSI/SD with a protective coating temporarily protecting the SSI/SD surface from corrosion (TPS). These protective coatings must neither impact any of the Products'

  - material
  - paint
  - equipment
  - functions

  nor the performance of other PMTRI.

- Replacement of paint that protects the metallic SSI/SD surface
- Installation and a later scheduled replacement of an additional item for an SSI/SD surface protection (eg, by design modification)
- Reduction of moisture or humidity on the relevant SSI/SD

All PMTRI must be selected based on the task selection sheet or file for SSI/SD. For PMTRI assessment and SHCM analysis refer to <u>Fig</u> 6 thru <u>Fig</u> 8.

With regards to CPCP, a servicing task combination (eg, washing and preservation) must be taken into account in addition to inspection tasks. Servicing tasks can also be applied to the surrounding structure of the SSI/SD or in the complete zone of the SSI/SD. The treatment of the whole area or zone might be more effective in comparison to a limited spot treatment. Details about the treatment process must be decided by the analyst in cooperation with design departments.

TPS of Product structure are recommended for the whole Product fleet, which operates under the same comparable environmental conditions.

The determination of effective intervals for PMTRI based on CPCP is affected by:

- Estimated or known effectiveness from comparable SSI/SD material surfaces already operated with or without corrosion protection
- Applicability of washing- and/or preservation task requirement for the selected SSI/SD
- Effectiveness of washing and/or preservation task requirement for the selected SSI/SD
- Changes of corrosion impact parameters on SSI/SD due to different Product usage or operation parameters and the basic corrosion protection does not withstand the new environmental scenario

When a PMTRI will neither be applicable nor effective and the SHCM doesn't cover failure or damage detection, an SSI/SD redesign or accessibility improvement by redesign of other items or equipment must be assessed and taken into account (eg, modification of the SSI/SD surface by material coating).

4.2.2   **Corrosion control**
The objective of the CPCP program is to monitor corrosion on the metallic Product structure up to an acceptable level. PMTRI can be based on the ED analysis, assuming a Product is operated in a specified and typical environment. If corrosion is found to exceed the specified corrosion limit, at any inspection or SHCM data, the PMTRI based on CPCP for the affected area must be reviewed by the operator or manufacturer. To monitor the corrosion level of metallic material, PMTRI related to ED are usually applicable at an interval threshold that is established during the Product type certification process. The definition of those interval thresholds can be based on manufacturer and/or operator in-service experience with similar Product structures, taking into account differences in relevant design features such as choice of material, assembly process and/or corrosion protection systems.

The analyst must determine inspection repeat intervals based on separate interval rating sheets or files for AD and ED. Applicable rating sheets or files must be provided in a PPH as the basis for efficient analytical work.

For the individual SSI/SD metallic material, the Product usage and operational scenario, the most important AD and ED impact parameters causing material damages as well as the forecast of the future deterioration process, must be taken into account and documented in interval rating sheets or files. Refer to Fig 19 and Fig 20. The intervals for repetition of identified PMTRI must also be defined in accordance with applied interval rating sheets or files.

Note 1
> A Product structure age exploration program can verify the Product structure's resistance to corrosion deterioration prior to defining PMTRI interval thresholds for CPCP. The age exploration program can be established and submitted to the program SC for approval and inclusion into the preventive structural maintenance concept.

Note 2
> Susceptibility to a long-term deterioration of Product structure is assessed with regard to the operating or mission environment. Areas such as major attachments, joints of non-metallic parts with metallic parts and areas of high stress levels are likely candidates for PMTRI. This also includes direct interfaces between metallic material and non-metallic materials. These interfaces must be analyzed for potential electrochemical interaction and/or wear damage and/or deterioration.

Step S 10:

The homogeneous non-metallic SSI/SD analysis is described in <u>Fig 4 Product structure analysis - AD/ED Analysis for</u> non-metallic SSI/SD

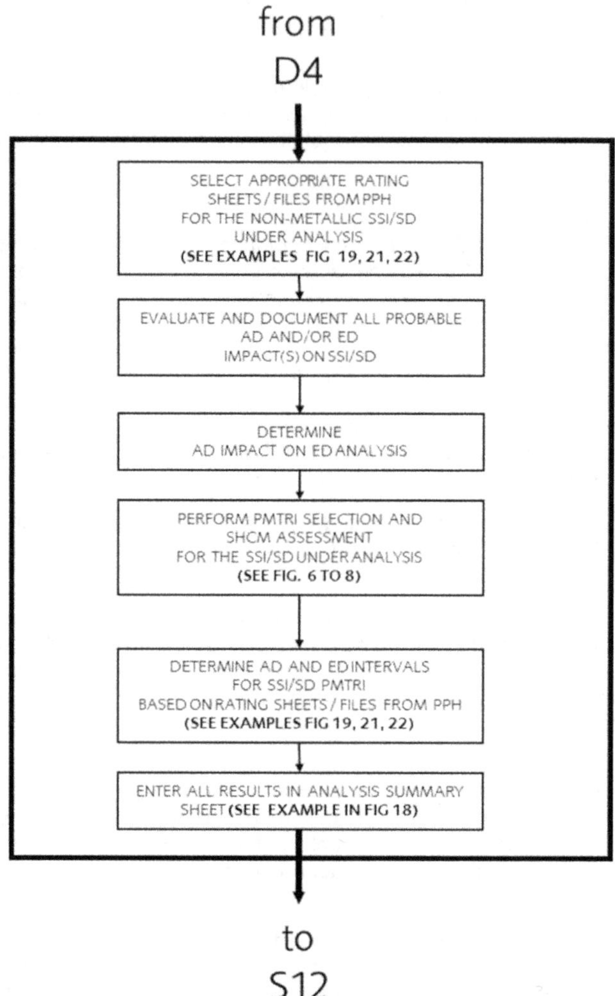

ICN-B6865-S4000P0037-001-01

Fig 4 Product structure analysis - AD/ED Analysis for non-metallic SSI/SD

Non-metallic SSI/SD structure materials are also susceptible to damage and/or deterioration (eg, delamination, dissolution). When a Product structure is classified as an SSI comprising one or more SD, preventive inspections and/or test PMTRI are required to verify adequate structural strength throughout the in-service phase of the Product.

Following the sequence of the work steps shown in <u>Fig 4 Product structure analysis - AD/ED Analysis for</u> non-metallic SSI/SD

, the applicable and effective SSI/SD inspection or test task requirements must be selected prior to the determination of a PMTRI interval. A PMTRI selection sheet or file must be available in the PPH for the analysts. Refer to Fig 6 thru Fig 8.

Having defined the task type of the PMTRI, the analyst determines intervals for all PMTRI selected for each SSI/SD based on the rating sheets or files. Specific to the SSI/SD structure material, AD and ED interval rating sheets or files must be completed and the different interval results must be harmonized by the analyst. For the individual SSI/SD material, an estimation of future AD and ED impact parameters, the Product usage or operational scenario and the forecast of the future deterioration process, must be taken into account and documented on the interval rating sheets or files. Refer to Fig 18 and Fig 19.

Note:
A CPCP analysis is not applicable for non-metallic SSI/SD. An age exploration program can support the verification of the rate of structural deterioration of non-metallic SSI/SD. Results can support the improvement on the PMTRI interval rating for non-metallic SSI/SD.

Step S11:

The SSI/SD material-combination analysis is described in <u>Fig</u> 5.

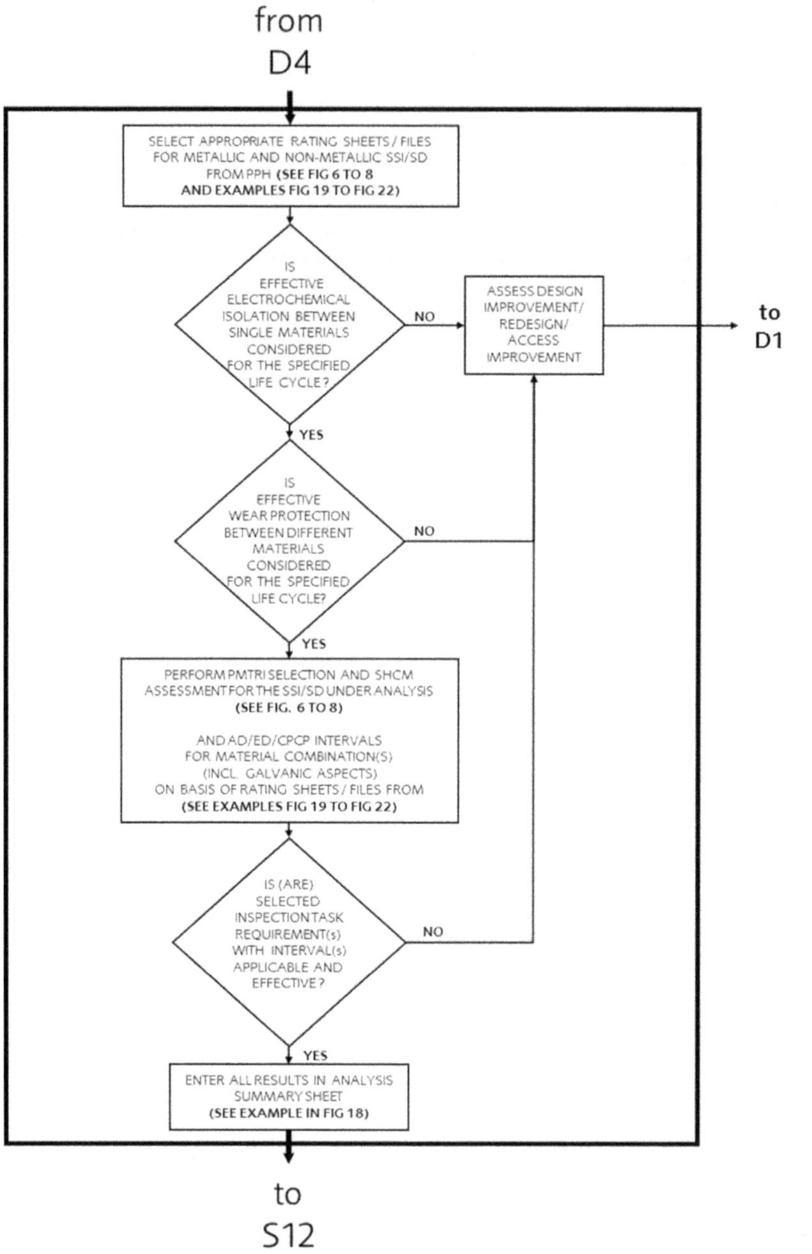

from
D4

to
S12

ICN-B6865-S4000P0038-001-01

Fig 5 Product structure analysis - Analysis of SSI/SD material combinations

Material combinations of SSI/SD are not limited to a local interface between two or more different materials that can be separated from each other. The material combinations in this Product structure analysis cannot be separated from each other without destroying the SSI/SD. For example, a non-metallic structure material that is reinforced with metallic layers and/or wires permanently fixed inside a common resin matrix.

After checking technical preventive measures implemented by design (eg, electro-chemical isolation between different material types, protection against water ingress), the structural analysis continues with the analysis of both the metallic components and the non-metallic components of the material combination. Depending on the design combination and location of the individual SSI/SD material components, the analysis based on AD and ED interval rating sheets lead to different severities of AD/ED impacts in comparison to a homogeneous material component rating. SSI/SD material layers that are located close to the item surface have a higher impact severity to ED. The AD impacts on the individual SSI/SD material components depend on the design of the SSI/SD, the overall location and the installation of the SSI/SD on the Product.

The process steps described in the PPH and the interval rating sheets for the individual material components, both metallic and non-metallic, are also applicable for the analysis of an SSI/SD material combination.

Step S12:

All process steps from Step S8 thru Step S11 determine PMTRI for the selected SSI/SD. Depending on the location of SSI/SD relative to each other, PMTRI can be combined or harmonized from the technical point of view in order to reduce the total maintenance effort in a Product in-service phase.

Having established an interval harmonization process, the maintenance effort can increase for the individual PMTRI with a higher numerical interval value. However, this effect is compensated, if the total maintenance effort for both PMTRI with a common interval can be reduced significantly.

For example, two SD on an SSI are located very close to each other on a Product. According to the structural analysis results they must be inspected at different intervals. For each detailed inspection, a high accessibility effort is necessary (ie, Product disassembly or assembly). The combination of both detailed inspections at a common lowest interval is most effective.

Step S13:

After a first harmonization of PMTRI for SSI/SD on the rating sheets or files, all analysis results must be documented including references to the valid build standard of each SSI (eg, drawing number, part number, etc). This is to follow-up decisions for future configuration changes after completing the initial Product structural analysis.

Step S14:

Products in a fleet with the highest rate of usage, operation or mission cycles in combination with excessive usage stress parameters, are most susceptible to initial SFF and cracking. Differences of Product usage enable the selection of a sampling methodology to perform preventive inspection or test tasks on selected Products of the fleet.

For example, an aircraft with highest number of hard landings should become preferred candidates for inspections or tests on structural items of the landing gear structure. Inspections or tests of structural items on pre-selected Products, provide the highest probability for a detection of failures and/or damage. Sampling and/or a trend or fleet leader strategy must be based on in-service data feedback (refer to S5000F) and be defined on the basis of confirmed statistical data, including, but not limited to:

–   the number of Products inspected with a build standard representative for the SSI/SD

- the inspection or test methods and PMTRI repeat intervals
- in-service or usage experience and data resulting from inspections and/or tests
- the operational surroundings and conditions in which the Product will be operated within the life cycle period (eg, preferable in cold weather, sea-water, desert conditions)

Selected SSI with SD can be suitable for a fatigue related inspection on several selected Product trend or fleet leaders. Justification for the selection criteria for those trend or fleet leader inspections or tests must be documented and submitted to the program Steering Committee (SC) for approval and acceptance.

Notes:

The sampling objective is to select Products with the highest amount of accumulated operating age or usage parameters so that the first evidence of deterioration in the structural condition can be identified. That information supports the development of master interval packages for a later scheduled maintenance program or OMP for the Product. Refer to S3000L.

Every reduction of the preventive maintenance effort for the Product fleet achieved by the introduction of a trend or fleet leader concept, must be agreed by the Product authorities and/or the Product manufacturer.

The trend or fleet leader concept is also subject to the ISMO analysis phase performed during the Product in-service phase. Refer to Chap 3.3. Here one or more analysis loops of the ISMO process are recommended to be performed in order to update the OMP of a Product. For both the development of the initial OMP and OMP updates by the ISMO process during the in-service phase, regulatory authorities must be involved.

Decision D5:

In addition to the SSI/SD, remaining structural items are defined as non-SSI.

Non-SSI according to this specification consists of two structural item categories:

- Maintenance relevant Product structure
- Non-critical Product structure

4.2.3 Maintenance relevant Product structure

Potential failures or damage to non-SSI are not as critical as failures or damage to SSI/SD. However, failures or damage on maintenance relevant structures can lead to a significant reduction of Product availability for mission or operation, and/or can cause high repair costs.

Within geometric zonal boundaries defined in a Product zonal plan, maintenance relevant structures can be located both externally and internally in the Product structure. Zonal areas which do not require specific accessibility will either be inspected during routine inspections based on a higher task frequency (eg, daily, preflight, turnaround, transit, post flight inspections on an aircraft) or by zonal inspections with a lower task frequency.

For maintenance relevant structures, the most effective inspection or test method is not limited to a General Visual Inspection (GVI). Failures or damage to maintenance relevant structure must be detected by an appropriate inspection or test method with applicable intervals during the Product life cycle. The objective is a timely detection of failures and/or damages to the selected structural item or the item deterioration status.

For maintenance relevant structures, two types of PMTRI must be preferred:

- Scheduled inspection and/or test during routine inspections
- Scheduled inspection and/or test during an applicable preventive maintenance task package that will be defined later based on S3000L (eg, every 6 months)

The decision on whether the PMTRI interval for a maintenance relevant structure can be based on individual operator and/or manufacturer experience with similar Product structure. For

---

structures containing new materials and/or Product design concepts, selected intervals can be based on an assessment of the manufacturers' structural material test results, experience and/or recommendations from structural material suppliers.

4.2.4 Non-critical Product structure

Non-critical structures are neither SSI/SD nor maintenance relevant structures. The inspection of non-critical structures must be covered by a GVI performed during zonal inspections.

Structural items categorized as non-critical Product structure do not require specific PMTRI. This Product structure is covered by a GVI performed during zonal inspections. If experience shows that damage and/or environmental impact leads to time-consuming and/or cost-intensive repair or modification, non-SSI can be switched to the category maintenance relevant structure when applying processes to optimize PMTRI in accordance with Chap 3.

If the structural item is judged to become maintenance relevant during the Product in-service phase (Answer YES), continue with Step S16.

If not (Answer NO), continue with Step S15.

Step S15:

Non-critical structures do not require the definition of specific PMTRI. Potential failures or damage on this Product structure are covered by the GVI and its interval defined in the standard zonal analysis. Refer to Chap 2.4. Non-critical structures are recommended to be identified in the structural item list for future control and overview purposes. Based on the structural item list, the correct categorization of criticalities of all structural items can be verified.

Step S16:

The analyst collects information, data and drawings about selected maintenance relevant items and evaluates the item susceptibility to AD and/or ED.

Note:
The selection of maintenance relevant items can be used by the Product design departments, for example, to develop standard structure repair procedures prior to the Product in-service phase.

Decision D6:

The GVI on a maintenance relevant structural item must identify potential SFF and/or damage which are visible and accessible. Maintenance personnel must have access to the structural item without removing LRU, wiring, tubes etc, and without the use of support equipment or tools.

If the GVI interval is judged to be frequent enough during the standard zonal inspection (Answer YES), continue with Step S17.

If not (Answer NO), continue with Step S18.

Step S17:

Depending on the estimated SFF or damage cause, the analyst defines a preventive GVI task requirement (eg, GVI to be performed during routine inspections where routine inspection intervals are lower than zonal inspection intervals).

Step S18:

A low probability of SFF, damage events or a slow deterioration process on maintenance relevant structure can be covered by the GVI performed during the zonal inspection. A GVI must detect all obvious and visible SFF, damage, loose items and/or foreign objects inside the zone under inspection. The selection of the numerical value of the interval for the GVI in the zone results from the zonal interval rating. Refer to Chap 2.5.

Step S19:

Consolidate all PMTRI identified during Product structure analysis. Include the different analysis relevant work shares of the Product structure including the selection background.

To allow a better traceability of the analytical work and to optimize the correlation of analysis results, it is recommended that selected PMTRI be described in more detail on the analysis summary sheets (however a description on technical publication level is not required).

Step S20:

End of the Product structure analysis for a defined Product configuration or state of construction.

If the design changes on the Product structure, the manufacturer must establish an approval process. The structural analysis process must be performed again for the impacted structure. The structure analysis results must be reviewed, confirmed and updated accordingly.

5 PMTRI assessment and SHCM analysis for SSI/SD

5.1 General

The PMTRI assessment and SHCM analysis for SSI/SD follows the analysis principle that is applied for the Failure Cause (FC) Assessment in the system analysis. Refer to Chap 2.2.

However, project-specific adaptions are required in the analysis logic and sequence for SSI/SD. Selectable PMTRI are adapted specific for SSI/SD maintenance. The adapted PMTRI selection spectrum should be limited for a Product structure analysis project. All limitations must be documented in the project-specific PPH.

5.2 PMTRI assessment and SHCM analysis logic diagrams

Fig 6 thru Fig 8 show the detailed selection logic for inspections.

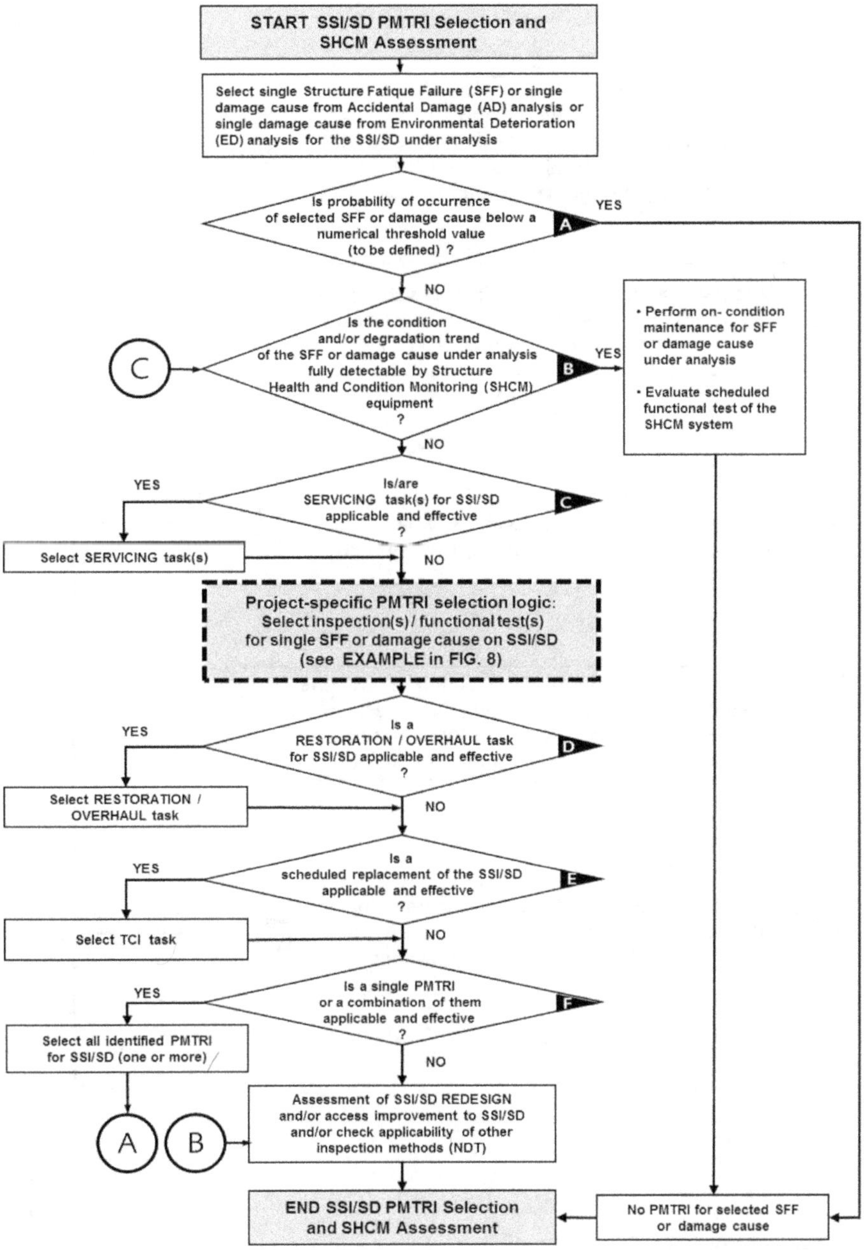

Fig 6 SSI/SD PMTRI Selection including SHCM Assessment (Part 1)

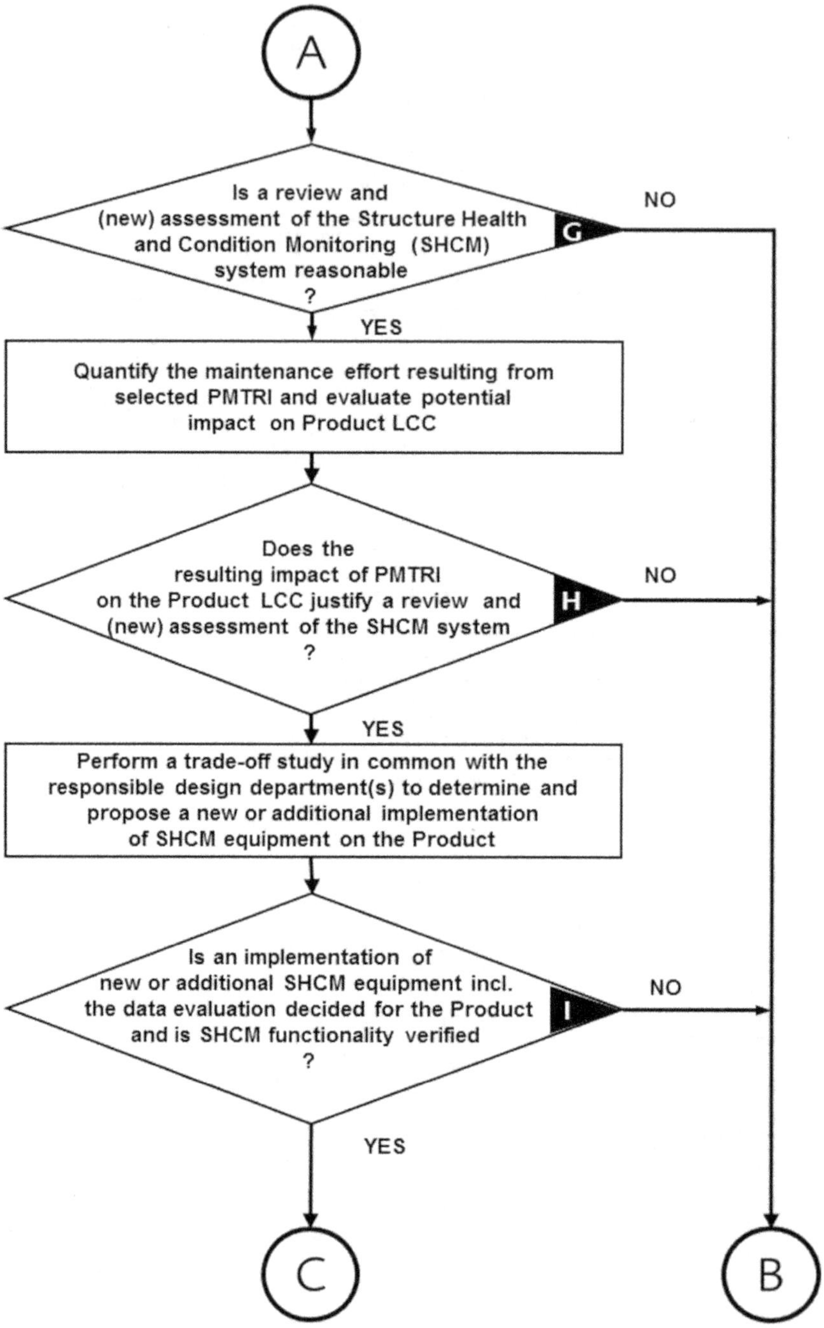

ICN-B6865-S4000P0040-001-01

Fig 7 SSI/SD PMTRI Selection including SHCM Assessment (Part 2)

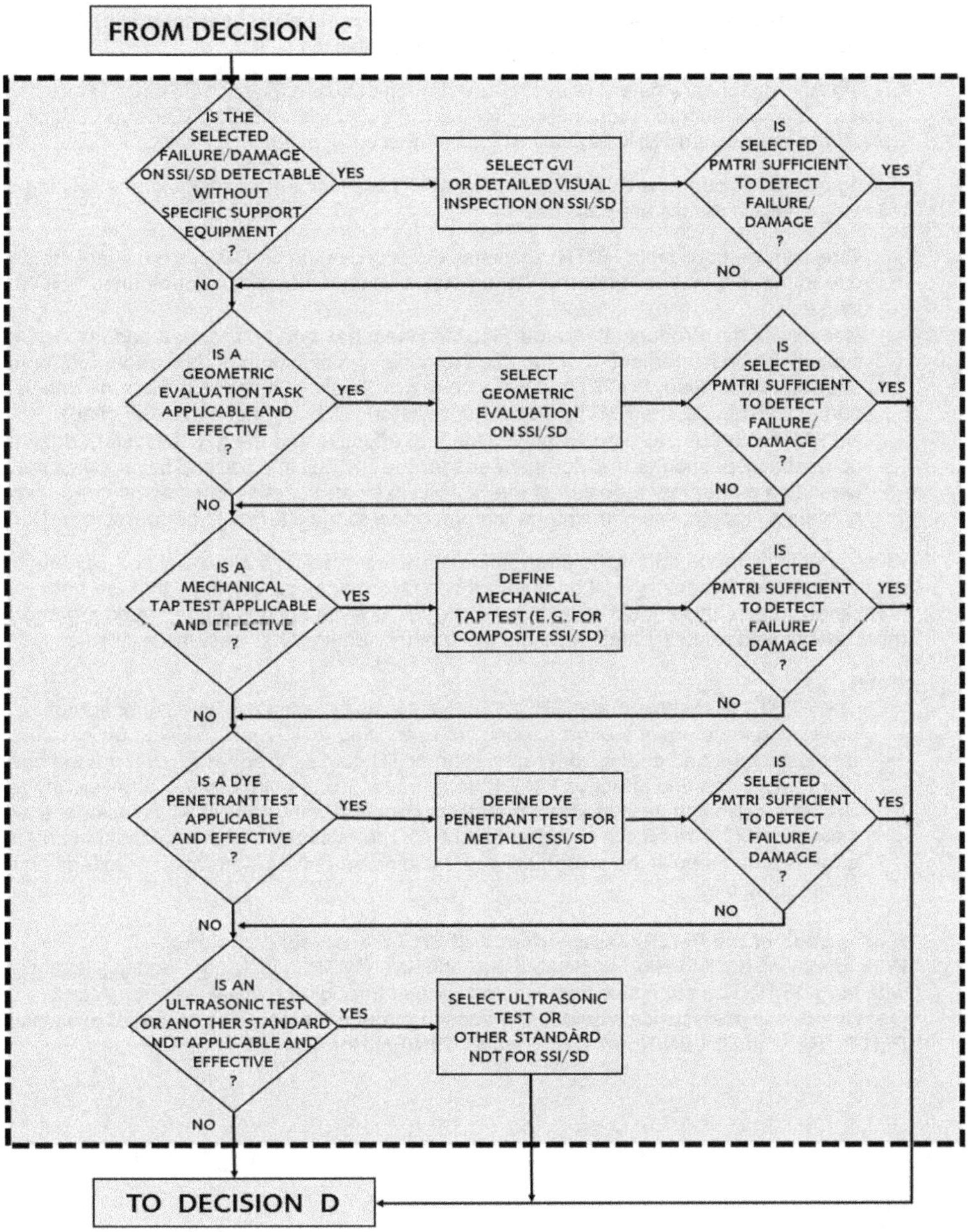

ICN-B6865-S4000P0041-001-01

Fig 8 Detailed selection Logic for Inspections or Functional Tests for SSI/SD - Example

5.3 PMTRI assessment and SHCM analysis procedure

For an individual SSI/SD either the design principle damage tolerant or safe life is selected by the Product structure design department. A potential SFF on a damage tolerant metallic SSI/SD must be detected in time and must be followed up. For this purpose, the PMTRI assessment and SHCM analysis logics must be applied. Refer to Fig 6 thru Fig 8.

In addition, each selected SSI/SD is impacted by one or more Product-specific parameters leading to ED and from AD events with different probabilities.

ED and AD impact parameters or events are damage causes for each SSI/SD. These damage causes must be detected independently for each SSI/SD from the SSI/SD design principle. The PMTRI assessment and SHCM analysis logics must be applied.

Having passed through the decisions of the PMTRI assessment and SHCM analysis logics, the following analysis results are possible:

–   One or more applicable PMTRI are selected because the SHCM system is not installed or due to missing inspection or monitoring capabilities of the existing or planned SHCM system
–   A review of the Product-integrated SHCM system has been performed and the SHCM system will be implemented or modified to cover the detection of SFF and/or damage causes. In this case, PMTRI that have been previously selected, can become obsolete or partly obsolete (ie, the PMTRI maintenance effort will be reduced in every case).
–   No PMTRI can be selected as applicable and effective and the SHCM system does not cover the inspection or monitoring needs for the SSI/SD in parallel. This analysis result leads to a mandatory redesign of the SSI/SD itself and/or of Product items or equipment preventing the access of maintenance personnel to the SSI/SD to perform the PMTRI.

All assumptions made during the analysis must be recorded for traceability and validation of decisions made. For example, if an analysis is based on design solutions that are not completely frozen, this should clearly be recorded. All assumptions made during the analysis must be checked and validated once the information required has become available.

Note:
The PMTRI assessment and SHCM analysis logic is based on the assumption of an increasing maintenance effort starting with servicing task types, followed by inspection or test task types and ending with restoration or TCI tasks. After having determined one or more applicable and effective PMTRI from the technical point of view, a review of the SHCM system can be performed directly in common with the PMTRI assessment, if the selected PMTRI results in high Product LCC. The evaluation of the potential maintenance effort in a first step is the prerequisite in deciding an SHCM integration or extension in a subsequent step.

5.3.1   Explanation of the PMTRI assessment and SHCM analysis decisions

Prior to making decisions on applicable and effective PMTRI, Decision A and Decision B clarify whether a PMTRI must be selected. Having passed through the initial Decision A and Decision B, this analysis logic guides the analyst through the whole spectrum of possible PMTRI. Refer to DIN/EN Norm 13306 and/or DIN/EN Norm 31051.

Decision A

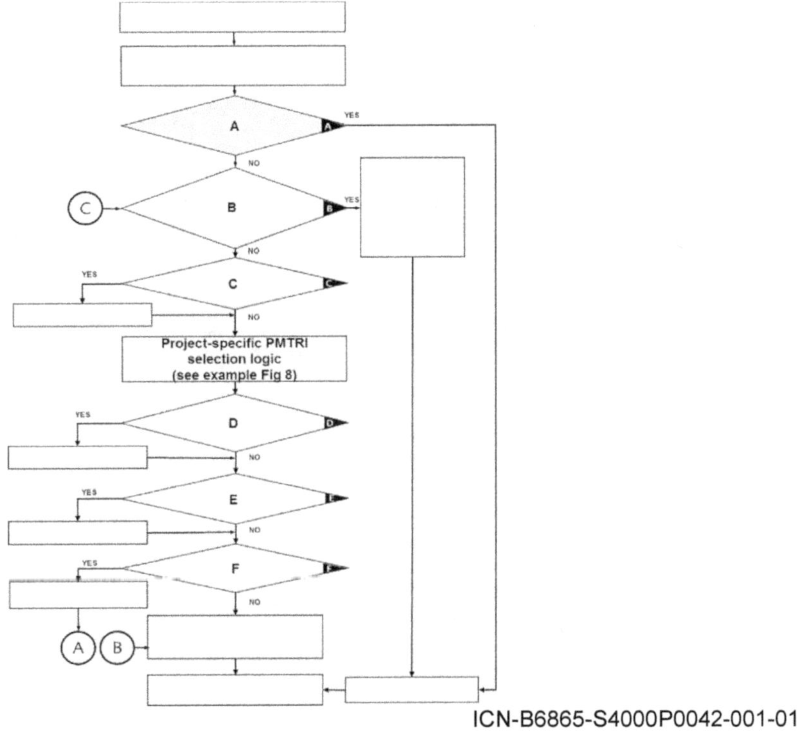

ICN-B6865-S4000P0042-001-01

Fig 9 Decision A

Is probability of occurrence of selected SFF or damage cause below a numerical threshold value (to be defined)?

Numerical values for probability thresholds for SFF and/or analysis relevant damage causes for SSI/SD are recommended to be defined in a Product-specific PPH.

The definitions of threshold values or a decision to ignore threshold values are subject to project risk management. Threshold values should take into account the safety-related criticality category of each SSI/SD.

If the probability of the appearance of an SFF and/or of the damage cause is below a predicted threshold (Answer YES), no PMTRI must be selected.

If the probability threshold of the SFF or of the damage cause under analysis exceeds the threshold or if thresholds are to be excluded for a certain Product according to a PPH (Answer NO), continue with Decision B.

Decision B

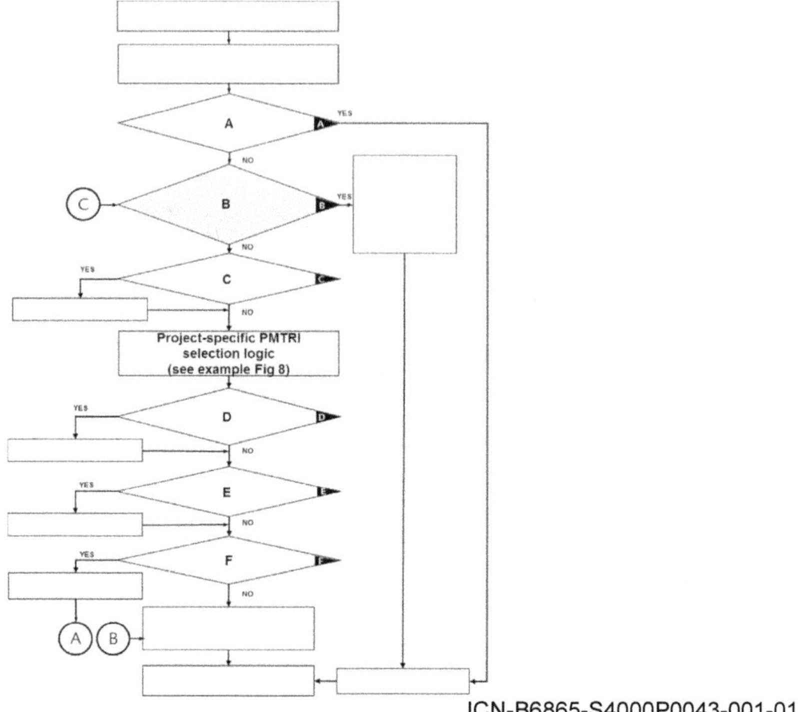

ICN-B6865-S4000P0043-001-01

Fig 10 Decision B

Is the condition and/or degradation trend of the SFF or damage cause under analysis fully detectable by SHCM equipment?

If the Product-integrated SHCM equipment or system delivers sufficient and useable data for technical interpretation necessary to clearly evaluate the status and condition of the SSI/SD under analysis (Answer YES), additional preventive maintenance based on the PMTRI selection, is not required for the SSI/SD.

Evaluate the necessity of preventive functional test tasks as an applicable and effective PMTRI for the SHCM system itself to ensure correct long-term data delivery.

If an SHCM system is not installed for the SSI/SD or if it does not deliver the required condition-based information (Answer NO), continue with Decision C.

Decision C

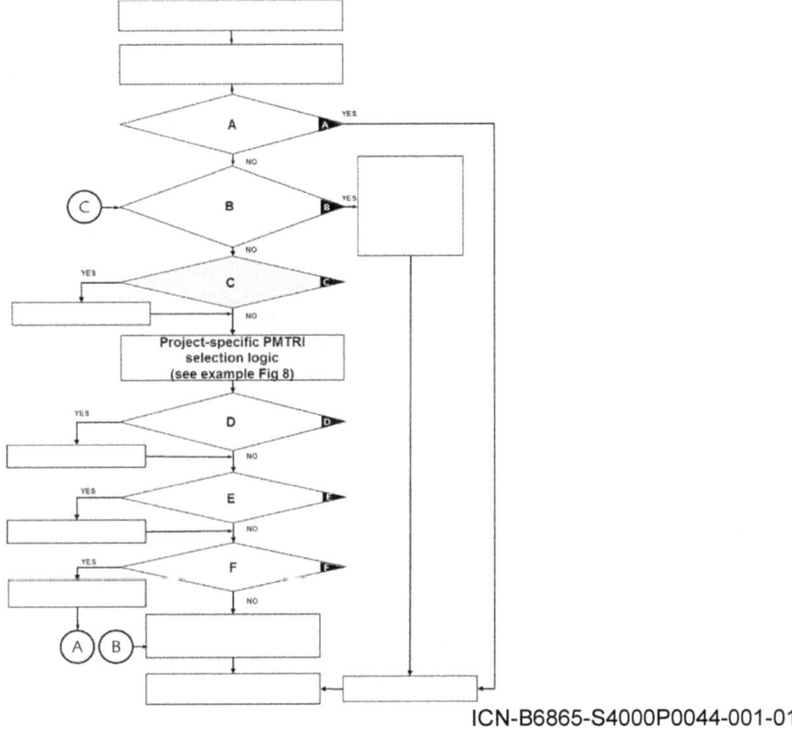

ICN-B6865-S4000P0044-001-01

Fig 11   Decision C

Are SERVICING tasks for SSI/SD applicable and effective?

A servicing task can be selected for an SSI/SD to maintain inherent design capabilities of the SSI/SD under analysis. Servicing for SSI/SD concentrates on the following maintenance task types which can be selected in parallel to other PMTRI:

– Cleaning or washing
– Conservation or preservation (corrosion protection or prevention)

Note:
It is common practice in Product maintenance for cleaning tasks to be the prerequisite for performing effective SSI/SD inspections afterwards.

If the answer to this decision is YES - select PMTRI.

If the answer is NO - continue with the project-specific selection logic for SSI/SD inspection or functional test. Refer to Fig 8.

Decision D

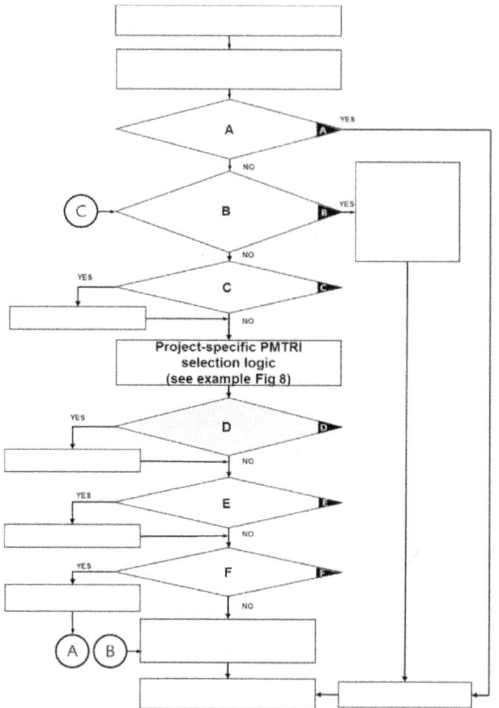

ICN-B6865-S4000P0045-001-01

Fig 12 Decision D

Is a RESTORATION or OVERHAUL task for SSI/SD applicable and effective?

The objective of this preventive maintenance task is to limit the progress of an identified SFF or to protect or improve the protection of an SSI/SD against impacting damage causes.

A restoration task is the work on the installed SS/SD on the Product so that its resistance to failure or damages can be restored to an acceptable level.

Applicable maintenance task types are:

– Surface protection or coating
– Modification (installation of a cover layer or sheet etc)

The SSI/SD restoration is accompanied by servicing tasks (eg, cleaning).

If the answer is YES- select PMTRI.

If the answer is NO - continue with <u>Decision E</u>.

Decision E

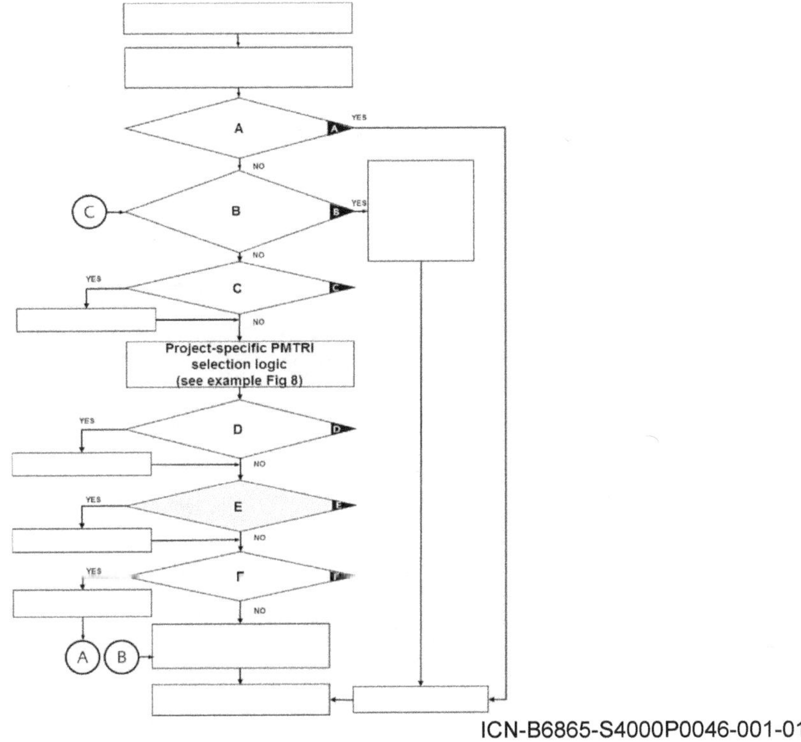

ICN-B6865-S4000P0046-001-01

Fig 13 Decision E

Is a scheduled replacement of the SSI/SD applicable and effective?

The objective of this preventive maintenance task is to avoid an SFF exceeding an acceptable tolerance level, or to limit the impact period of one or more damage causes on the SSI/SD under analysis by scheduled SSI/SD replacement.

The prerequisites for an SSI/SD replacement are:

- When a specified life limit is defined for the SSI/SD and when a restoration task is not applicable and effective
- When on-condition maintenance is not applicable or effective

If the answer is YES - select PMTRI.

If the answer is NO - continue with <u>Decision F</u>.

Decision F

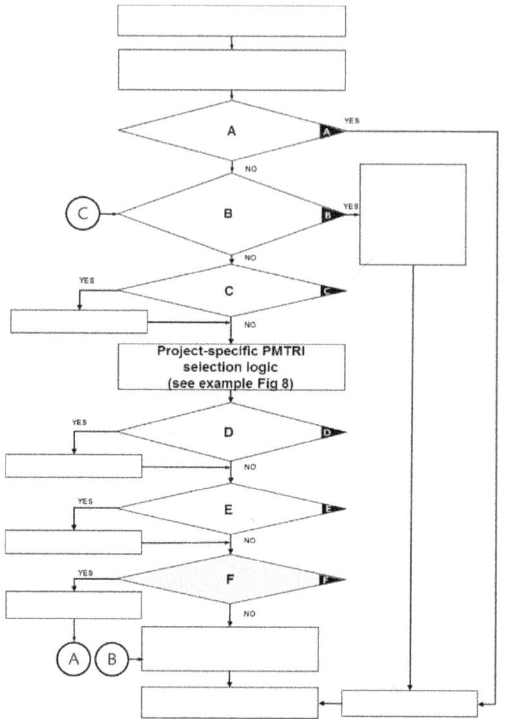

ICN-B6865-S4000P0047-001-01

Fig 14 Decision F

Is an individual PMTRI or a combination of them applicable and effective?

If the answer is YES, all PMTRI must be selected in parallel due to the safety-related criticality of each SSI/SD. Continue with Decision G.

If the answer is NO, a redesign must be assessed for the SSI/SD itself to improve the accessibility situation for SSI/SD inspection.

Decision G

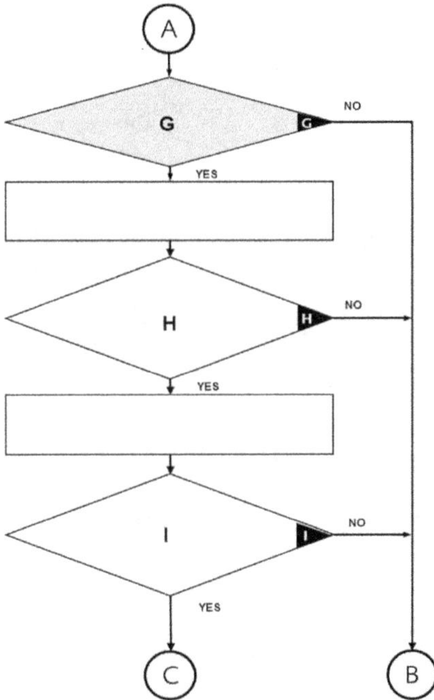

ICN-B6865-S4000P0048-001-01

Fig 15 Decision G

Is a review and (new) assessment of the SHCM system reasonable?

The result of Decision F is the selection of one or more PMTRI applicable and effective based on the present Product design (including the present SHCM layout).

If an SHCM system is implemented into the Product and if the system with the FC under analysis is monitored by the SHCM system, a review of the SHCM system can be performed.

Because the answer to Decision B was NO, the detection or avoidance of the FC is unlikely to be sufficiently covered by the present SHCM system.

The decision to perform an SHCM system review (answer YES) requires the expected maintenance effort resulting from the selected PMTRI to be quantified and an evaluation of the potential impact on the Product LCC. Continue with Decision H.

With answer NO, the assessment of the SHCM is decided to be excluded. This must be documented with justification. Redesign must be assessed for the SSI/SD itself and/or the accessibility situation for selected PMTRI must be improved.

Decision H

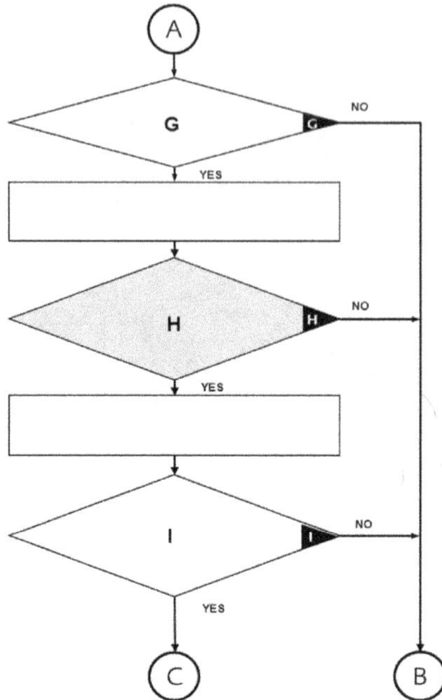

ICN-B6865-S4000P0049-001-01

Fig 16 Decision H

Does the resulting impact of PMTRI on the Product LCC justify a review and (new) assessment of the SHCM system?

With a first pass of the maintenance effort resulting from the selected PMTRI, taking into account the planned Product fleet size and the expected or specified usage profiles, the potential impact on Product LCC can be quantified.

Depending on the result, the analyst must decide whether a new assessment of the SHCM system design is required. The assessment should be performed before the CDR of the SHCM system.

The answer YES to Decision H leads to a trade-off study with the design department to determine and propose new or additional implementation of SHCM equipment into the Product design. Continue with Decision I.

If an assessment of the SHCM system is excluded (answer NO), redesign must be assessed for the SSI/SD and/or the accessibility situation for selected PMTRI must be improved.

Decision I

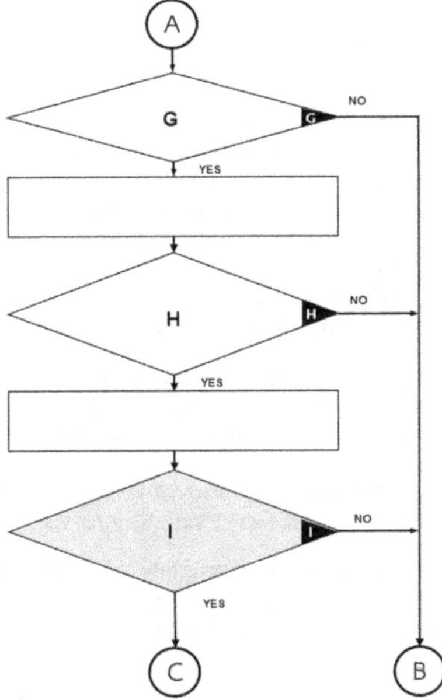

ICN-B6865-S4000P0050-001-01

Fig 17 Decision I

Is an implementation of new or additional SHCM equipment including data evaluation decided for the Product and is SHCM functionality verified?

Based on the outcome of the trade-off study, the Product manufacturer decides whether updating the SHCM system in order to reduce the Product maintenance effort by implementing further equipment and/or functionalities into the integrated SHCM system is justified.

Confidence of new SHCM functionality must be demonstrated to support the analyst to justify the answer YES and to return to <u>Decision B</u>.

If the decision after the trade-off study is, that the SHCM system cannot be integrated or improved (answer NO), a redesign must be assessed for the SSI/SD itself and/or the accessibility situation for selected PMTRI must be improved.

6 Rating systems for SSI/SD

Depending on the material type of an SSI/SD, interval rating systems must be applied to ensure the traceability of the numerical interval values that have been determined for selected PMTRI.

The development of the PMTRI interval rating system must comprise:

- manufacturers' best engineering judgments
- state-of-the-art technology knowledge
- consideration of all existing Product analysis requirements
- requirements from or conditions predicted by authorities
- operator experience

Where new preventive maintenance task types are developed in the future, the optimization of PMTRI using the ISMO process will consider these new technologies during the Product in-service phase. An updated maintenance task selection logic must be documented in the

respective ISMO PPH. Refer to Chap 3.1 thru Chap 3.4. Several interval rating examples are included in this structure analysis. Refer to Fig 19 thru Fig 22.

However, interval rating sheets or files must be individually developed for each Product under analysis and must not be transferred from one Product to another without a detailed evaluation.

Each likely source of damage to the SSI/SD, and the susceptibility of the SSI/SD to that damage must be rated. The combination of the rating results covers all deterioration impacts on the SSI/SD under analysis. Additionally, the differences between metallic, non-metallic materials and material combinations for each SSI/SD to be taken into account.

The purpose of developing structural PMTRI is to provide timely detection of potential impacts by AD, ED, and SFF. The interval rating systems used for both AD and ED must be in a suitable format that will enable comparative assessments for SSI/SD.

For metallic SSI/SD, the analysis must apply a rating table for corrosion protection. Refer to Fig 20. This table must include both the manufacturer experience and operator feedback taking into account different environmental conditions under which the Product will be operated.

When the interval ratings for all SSI/SD in the same inspection area (with common accessibility) are complete, it is recommended that the resulting intervals are harmonized.

The amount and severity of damage, accessibility and the different inspection methods are important factors when defining an interval rating system for SFF. For the final SFF interval determination the crack growth curve must be calculated by the structure design department.

Note
> PMTRE selected for special events are not based on any rating tables because any task interval determination is obsolete.

6.1 Rating structure fatigue failure

The interval rating system for SFF must lead to an inspection or test PMTRI for the Product used as specified. The applicable inspection PMTRI must be determined based on the PMTRI selection logic. Refer to Fig 6 thru Fig 8.

The inspection intervals of each selected PMTRI must provide a high probability of detecting SFF in the fleet before such failure reduces any Product's residual strength below allowable levels.

To achieve this, the interval rating system must consider:

— detection standards for applicable inspection or test methods

Note
> Estimated detectable crack lengths can be used for the SFF detection evaluations required as part of Product type certification.

— applicable inspection or test levels and methods (eg, visual, NDT, etc), directions (external, internal) and repeat intervals

The designers of structure fatigue must be provided Product-specific information about selected SSI/SD so that the appropriate PMTRI intervals can be calculated.

6.2 Rating accidental damage

The interval rating systems for AD must include evaluations of:

— the susceptibility of the SSI/SD to minor accidental damage
— the residual strength of the SSI/SD after accidental damage has occurred
— the timely detection of damage

6.2.1 Susceptibility to minor accidental damage

Susceptibility to minor AD must be based on the frequency of exposure and the location of the damage from one or more sources.

Typical examples include, but are not limited to:

- manual handling on or close to the Product
- human error resulting from errors during manufacture, maintenance, and/or operation
- foreign objects or debris
- inclement weather, including rain, hail, etc
- cargo handling or air delivery
- mission role change (military)
- air-to-air refueling (military)

6.2.2 Residual strength after damage occurrence

Residual strength after damage occurrence must be based on the probable amount and severity of the damage in relation to the critical damage criteria for the SSI/SD.

6.2.3 Timely detection of damage

Timely detection of damage must be based on the expected rate of damage growth and visibility of the SSI/SD for inspection. Account must also be taken of the damage growth associated with non-chemical interaction with an environment, such as separation of material layers or delamination growth associated with for example, freeze or thaw cycle.

6.3 Rating environmental deterioration of metallic structure

All parts of metallic structures are susceptible to ED, particularly when they are exposed to abrasive or corrosive agents that cause a localized loss of material. If the damage is not discovered at an early stage, this process reduces the load carrying capability of the affected structure, lowering the structure fatigue strength.

The occurrence of the damage is usually measured with calendar time, increasing with the age of the structure. Each metallic SSI/SD must be rated for ED for:

- the type of corrosion
- the surface protection
- the exposure to corrosion

The interval ratings for ED are based on an item's susceptibility to damage induced by the environment, and the potential effectiveness and durability of surface protection systems.

Specific examples of ED exposure are:

- exposure to a deteriorating environment (eg, pressure cabin condensation, galley spillage, toilet spillage, cleaning fluids, missile exhaust, chaff-flare operation)
- galvanic corrosion (eg, a contact between dissimilar materials with potential for galvanic activity)
- breakdown of surface protection systems (eg, deterioration of paint, primer, bonding, sealant, corrosion inhibiting compounds and cladding systems with the resulting corrosion of metallic materials or fluid incursion into permeable non-metallic materials)

Attention must be given to the Products anticipated operating environment and the likelihood of damage from contact between dissimilar metals. Generally, areas exposed to moisture, dirt and heat are the most susceptible to corrosion and must be properly maintained.

A timely detection is determined by sensitivity to relative amount and severity of damage and visibility of the SSI/SD for inspection.

6.4 Rating environmental deterioration of non-metallic structure

Environmental deterioration associated with composites includes delamination, separation of material layers, blistering and the appearance of internal voids. Interval rating systems must permit evaluation of the susceptibility to, and timely detection of any structural deterioration of the material in common with an assessment of the efficiency of the protective system, the material composition and exposure to the environment.

Typical factors that affect composite materials are:

- moisture or humidity
- heat or high temperature
- Ultra-Violet (UV) light

Specific ED examples of common composite materials are:

- Aramid Fiber Reinforced Plastic (AFRP, also known as Kevlar), for example, is sensitive to UV light, moisture and other fluids, when directly exposed
- Glass Fiber Reinforced Plastic (GFRP), for example can undergo long term degradation when directly exposed to UV light, but is judged to have a low sensitivity to the environment
- Carbon Fiber Reinforced Plastic (CFRP) is judged to have a low sensitivity to the environment

6.5 Rating of metallic and non-metallic structure material combinations

The individual interval rating sheets or files for metallic and non-metallic material are also applicable for material combinations of metallic and non-metallic materials. However, depending on the type of material combination, the location of the installation on the Product and the resulting exposure to accidents and/or deterioration, rating values of a material combination differ from a homogeneous material type rating. Rating systems for material combinations are based on the manufacturer experience and/or operator feedback.

7 Definition of interval thresholds

For definition of an initial interval threshold for a PMTRI on SSI/SD, the source of damage or the failure cause must be taken into account:

- AD. An inspection threshold is not applicable for interval rating in the frame of accidental damage analysis.
- ED. The initial inspection thresholds for all levels of inspection are based on existing relevant in-service experience, manufacturer recommendations, and/or a conservative age exploration process.
- SFF - Inspections directly related to SFF detection will occur after an interval threshold. This interval threshold must be defined by the manufacturer and approved by the appropriate regulatory authority. Thresholds are normally established as part of the damage tolerance certification requirements. These are subject to change as service experience, additional testing, and/or analysis work is obtained. The inspection thresholds and repeat intervals must also be defined. Both threshold and repeat interval definitions must be provided by the Product structure design department.

8 Definition of repeat inspection intervals

After the initial PMTRI has been conducted, the repeat interval give the periods until the next inspection becomes due:

- AD. The repeat intervals of the inspection must be based on operator and manufacturer experience with similar Product structures.

Chapter 2.5

Developing PMTR - Zonal analysis

Table of contents

Page

Developing PMTR - Zonal analysis...1

References...1

1   Product zones...2

2   Objectives of zonal analysis 2

3   Zonal analysis procedure 4

List of tables

1   References 1

List of figures

1   Zonal analysis - Main logic 5

2   Flow chart standard zonal analysis 7

3   Flow chart Enhanced Zonal Analysis 9

4   Flow chart L/HIRF analysis...11

5   Flow chart Zonal interface analysis 14

6   Interval rating sheet for standard zonal inspection, example (Sheet 1 of 2) 19

7   Interval rating sheet for standard zonal inspection, example (Sheet 2 of 2) 20

References

Table 1 References

Chap No./Document No.	Title
Chap 2.3	Developing PMTR - System analysis
Chap 2.4	Developing PMTR - Structure analysis
Chap 2.6	Developing PMTR - Consolidation of analysis results, harmonization with other preventive maintenance task requirement sources for traceability
Chap 2.7	Developing PMTR - Special event analysis
Chap 3	Optimizing PMTR
Chap 6	Terms, abbreviations and acronyms
S1000D	International specification for technical publications using a common source database
S3000L	International procedure specification for Logistic Support Analysis - LSA

1 Product zones

For analysis purposes, Product geometry must be sub-divided into two and/or three-dimensional areas, called Product zones. Each Product zone is adjacent to one or more other Product zones or is limited only by its own zonal dimensions.

A Product zone is defined based on the ability of a Product user and/or maintainer to gain access to the zone:

- with a limited accessibility from outside the Product
- with a limited accessibility from inside the Product
- with unlimited accessibility

The selection and definition of Product zones must be defined in a Product zonal plan. This document must cover all the physical Product dimensions. A zonal numbering system must be applied to each Product zone. Overlapping areas between single Product zones must be avoided.

If a Product is composed of several main Product components (eg, main system components for Unmanned Air Vehicle (UAV) systems such as air vehicle and ground stations) a component zonal plan for each Product component must be prepared. The components are physically separated from each other with their own physical dimensions, with different impact parameters during in-service phase, with different usage parameters etc.

2 Objectives of zonal analysis

Both the system analysis (refer to Chap 2.3) and the structure analysis (refer to Chap 2.4) concentrate on failure and/or damage causes and their consequences and functional effects on functional levels of a Product system or of structure. For these failure and/or damage causes, applicable and effective preventive maintenance task requirements with repetitive scheduled intervals (PMTRI) must be defined or item redesign must be required/evaluated.

These analytical methodologies, and the zonal analysis must be applied to a selected Product zone with all items from Product systems being installed inside the zones.

In developing effective and applicable PMRTI, the zonal analysis takes into account:

- zonal damage susceptibility
- density and/or complexity of equipment/item installation in the zone under analysis
- access frequency of maintenance personnel to the zone under analysis
- criticality of interfaces between equipment/items and interferences of different systems and functions with other systems with functions inside a zone under analysis
- potential interference and allocated criticalities between single zones
- external impacts on Product zones and the equipment/items installed inside (environmental and/or accidental impacts)

PMTRI for zones must be developed from the application of the zonal analysis procedure according to this specification.

The zonal analysis logic has a modular structure by intention. The selection of one or more applicable Zonal Analysis Modules (ZAM) allows a modular composition of the zonal analysis methodology necessary for different Product types and Product technologies:

- ZAM 1 - Standard zonal analysis
- ZAM 2 - Enhanced zonal analysis
- ZAM 3 - Lightning/High Intensity Radiated Field (L/HIRF) analysis
- ZAM 4 - Zonal interface analysis
- ZAM X - one or more additional Zonal Analysis Modules (ZAM) defined for a specific Product type

The set of applicable ZAM must be invented and/or composed individually for a Product under analysis.

The module ZAM 1 must be selected for every Product zonal analysis. It is limited to the selection of the maintenance task type General Visual Inspection (GVI) and evaluates the relevant standard impact parameters for an individual Product zone. The numerical interval value of the PMTRI for a zone is defined based on a specific rating sheet/table (for examples refer to Fig 6 and Fig 7).

Note
>
> Many support items such as plumbing, ducting, structure attachment items, wiring, etc, cannot be evaluated as potential Failure Cause (FC) with possible contribution to Functional Failures (FF) during system analysis (refer to Chap 2.3). In all Product zones, visible failures or damages, items without a correct attachment, foreign objects and visible degradation can occur during Product in-service usage. For these cases the preventive zonal GVI is an appropriate initial failure/damage detection method.

ZAM 2, ZAM 3, ZAM 4 and ZAM X (if applicable for the Product under analysis) give additional appropriate attention to every Product zone in terms of:

- probable sources of ignition (eg, caused by damages on electrical wiring installations) in ZAM 2
- combustible material and/or accumulation of explosive vapor in ZAM 2
- Lightning (L) impacts in ZAM 3
- impacts from High Intensity Radiated Fields (HIRF) in ZAM 3
- impacts of one or more system functions or potential malfunctions and other impact sources from one zone on another zone/on other zones in ZAM 4
- other Product-specific impact sources (if applicable) in ZAM X

ZAM 2 focuses on potential zonal hazards and can be applied on many Product types.

ZAM 3 is Product specific and has no or only a limited applicability on several Product types (eg, not for submarines or satellite analysis).

ZAM 4 takes into account potential impacts initiated in a zone on one or more other zones of the Product. ZAM 4 can be applied on most Product types.

ZAM X can be defined and composed in common with ZAM 1, ZAM 2, ZAM 3 and/or ZAM 4 for every individual Product type.

Note 1
>
> ZAM 2 and ZAM 3 have initially been developed and applied by industry for aircraft zonal analysis. For other individual Product types these ZAM might be partial applicable, might not be applicable or must be adapted.

Note 2
>
> ZAM 4 analyses for potential hazardous and/or critical (functional) interferences between single Product zones. The definition of such a zone-to-zone impact analysis in a PPH depends on the Product type under analysis.

The zonal analysis logics in ZAM 2, ZAM 3, ZAM 4 and in ZAM X are to be linked to results from Product system analysis (refer to Chap 2.3) and to Product structure analysis (refer to Chap 2.4). This is to enable a traceable selection of applicable and effective PMTRI intervals next to GVI requirements resulting from ZAM 1.

In the final work steps of the zonal analysis main logic (refer to Fig 1) identified PMTRI must be harmonized on basis of the following rules:

- If a PMTRI cannot be integrated into zonal GVI intervals (ie, stand-alone maintenance tasks), the respective PMTRI must be harmonized with PMTRI from system analysis and/or from structural analysis. For all stand-alone PMTRI, the relevant FC and the allocated

criticality category must be transferred into the analysis sheets or files sheets or files of the respective analysis. For system analysis, refer to Chap 2.3 and/or for structural analysis, refer to Chap 2.4.

- Each GVI with scheduled interval on an equipment/item identified from a system analysis (refer to Chap 2.3) and/or from a structural analysis (refer to Chap 2.4) and/or from ZAM 2, ZAM 3 and/or ZAM X, that has no stand-alone PMTRI, can be harmonized with the interval of the GVI for the zone, where that equipment/item is installed

The accessibility of maintenance personnel to a Product zone or to a limited area of a zone is taken into account in this zonal analysis procedure. If limitations or exclusions of access are identified during this zonal analysis, feedback to the responsible design departments and/or Product management must be provided (eg, during a design review meeting such as PDR, CDR). Depending on design feedback, the selection of PMTRI must be assessed again.

A zonal analysis based on this analysis methodology leads to harmonized PMTRI with original interval types and numerical interval values. To determine maintenance tasks with repetitive scheduled intervals for a Product maintenance program/OMP, follow process and rules given in in S3000L. For maintenance task packaging purpose, original PMTRI intervals can be adapted according to given rules.

The PMTRI review and optimization process is applicable and effective during the Product in-service phase, to optimize PMTRI for Product zones documented in a maintenance program/OMP based on the ISMO process. Refer to Chap 3.

3   Zonal analysis procedure

This procedure is illustrated on the process flow charts shown in Fig 1, Fig 2, Fig 3, Fig 4 and Fig 5.

The procedure overview for zonal analysis is shown in the following main structure analysis logic diagram:

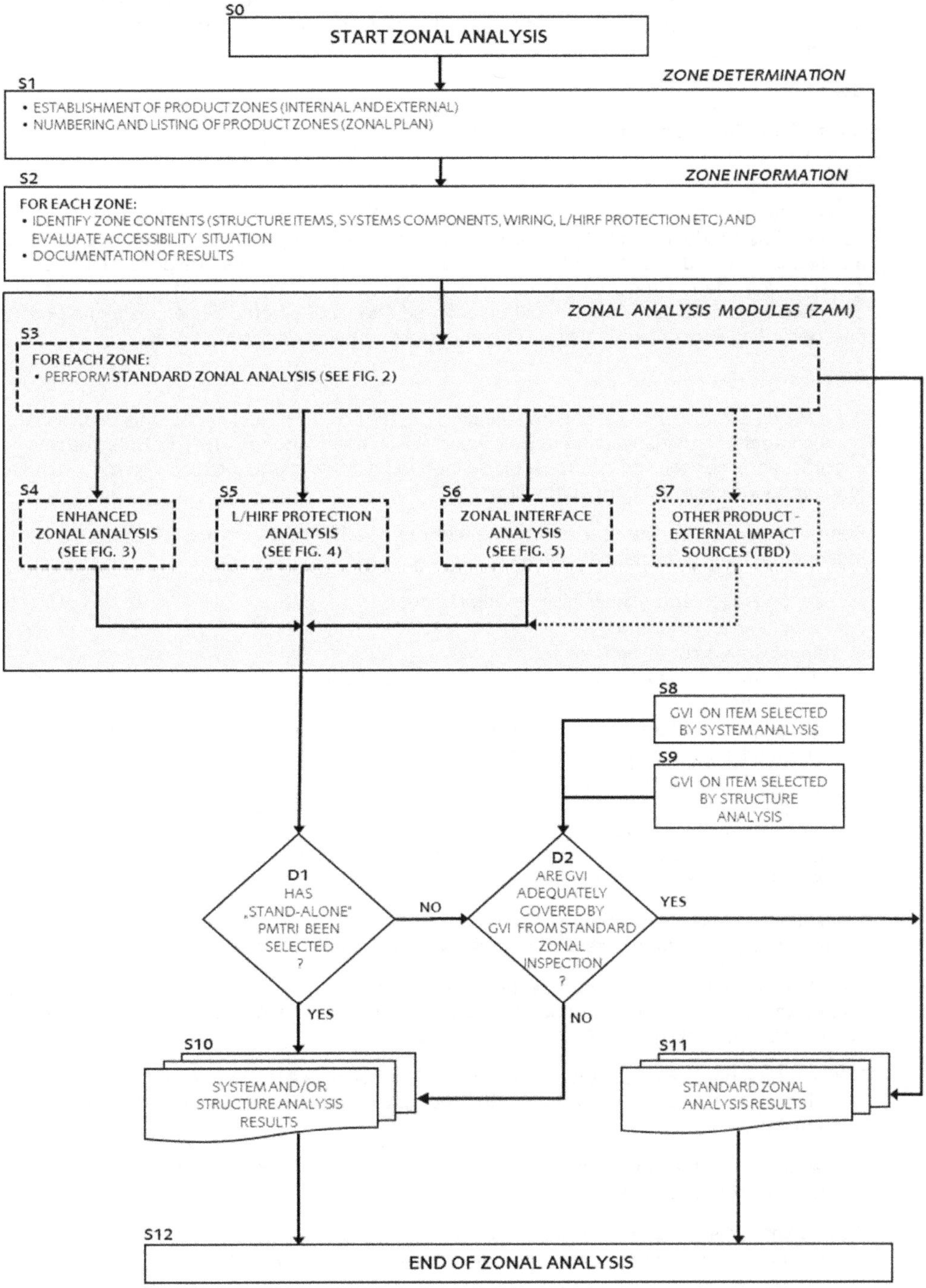

ICN-B6865-S4000P0056-001-01

Fig 1 Zonal analysis - Main logic

The process Steps S (Step S0, Step S1, Step S2, Step S3, etc) and the Decisions D (Decision D1 and Decision D2) according to this zonal analysis procedure are explained as follows:

Step S0:

Start of the Zonal analysis for the Product.

Step S1:

The Product must be divided into Product zones with precise geometric dimensions and borders. The Product zonal plan including the zone numbering for internal and/or external zones must be issued and kept current. For the definition of Product zones, the accessibility of the zones during a later Product in-service phase must be taken into account. The Product with its complete geometric dimensions must be covered and all geometric deviations in the Product fleet, including Product variants must be covered by the Product zonal plan.

Step S2:

If the Product zonal analysis can be limited to pre-selected Product zones, this information must be documented and justified in the Policy and Procedure Handbook (PPH). Selected and suppressed zones for analysis must be defined, documented and justified and made available to the responsible regulatory authorities.

For each zone under analysis, prepare one or more work sheets or files collecting zonal relevant data and information such as:

- zone location and accessibility on the Product
- directly adjoined zones
- approximate zonal dimensions
- numbers and types of technical systems and components installed, both permanent and temporary
- typical power levels in wiring bundles and wiring/cable types inside the zone
- information specific to L/HIRF protection items installed in the zone
- vibration and shock levels
- temporarily installed equipment/goods that are expected to be transported and/or stored in the zone under analysis
- expected or known impact parameters from Environmental Deterioration (ED) and/or Accidental Damage (AD)

In addition, assess the presence of combustible material, either through contamination (eg, dust) or that can occur by design (eg, potential accumulation of fuel vapor).

Identify zones that have comparable and/or identical impacts from ED, AD and a comparable zonal density. These zones can be addressed in one common interval rating sheet in the standard zonal analysis (ZAM 1).

Every enhanced zonal analysis (ZAM 2), L/HIRF analysis (ZAM 3) and/or other analysis modules (ZAM X, if decided for a specific Product type in a PPH) must be performed for each individual zone.

The analyst must take into account all configurations of each Product zone under analysis on the zonal work sheets/files.

Equipment/items installed in a zone must be documented, whether they are options or modifications and whether they are permanently or temporarily installed.

Step S3:

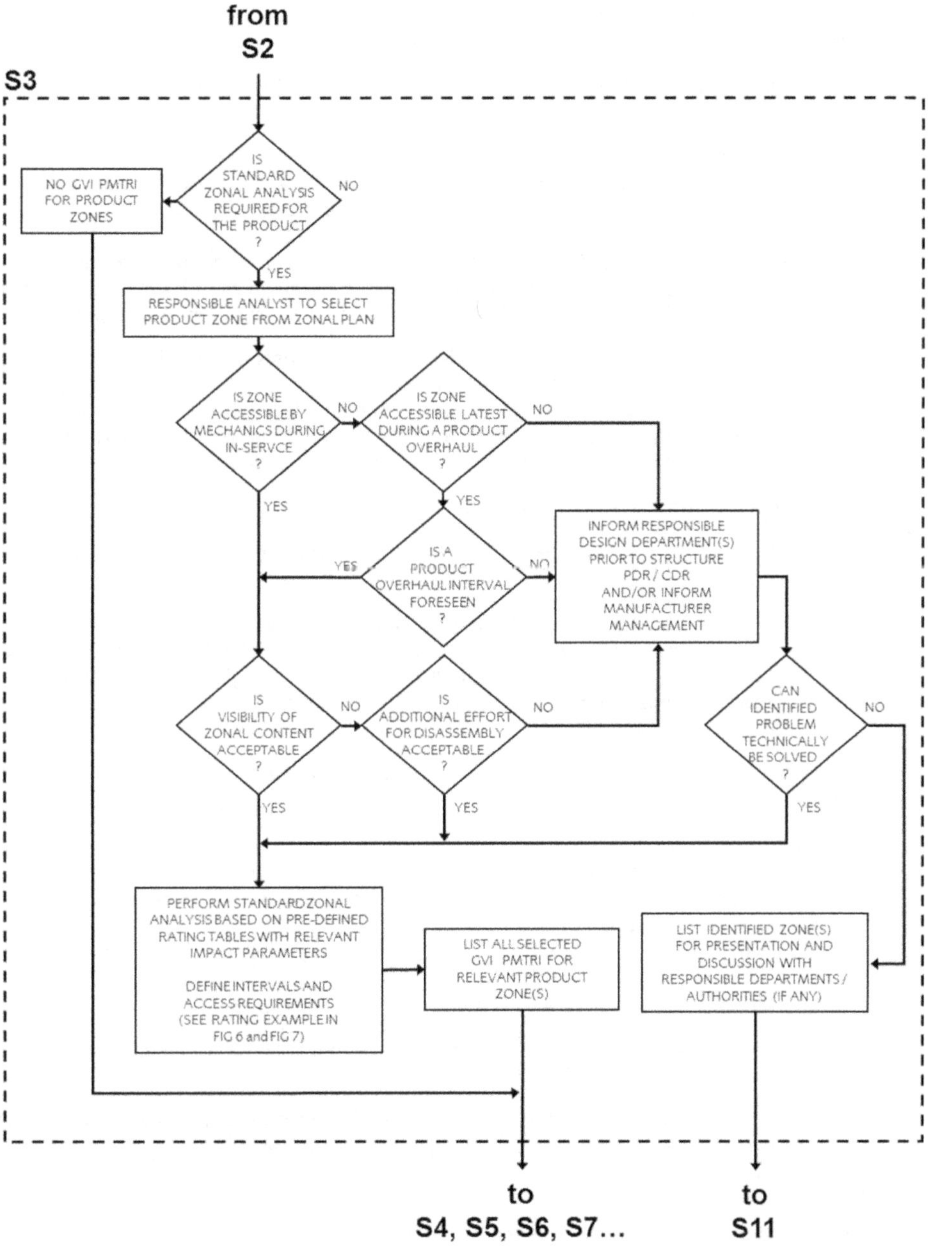

ICN-B6865-S4000P0057-001-01

Fig 2 Flow chart standard zonal analysis

The standard zonal analysis (ZAM 1) (refer to Fig 2) in general defines the maintenance task type GVI with applicable and effective scheduled intervals for the Product zones.

The zonal GVI with a repetitive scheduled interval for an individual Product zone can be defined based on the stable status of design, if personnel access to the zone is not limited (or impossible) and the visibility of equipment/items installed in the zone is sufficient for inspection purposes.

The following cases do not allow the definition of a GVI with scheduled interval for selected zones during an ongoing zonal analysis:

- An identified problem (eg, accessibility, new positioning of equipment inside a zone) must be resolved first. Communication between the analyst and the design department and/or management of the manufacturer is therefore required. The analysis of the relevant zones must be postponed.
- A GVI is not applicable for a zone under analysis because for example, accessibility will not be possible after Product assembly and the zonal design can't be changed anymore. Identified zone/zones must be documented with information and/or justifications

All numerical values of intervals for GVI determined on basis of ZAM 1 must be derived from rating sheets/tables available in the PPH (refer to Fig 6 and Fig 7). These examples show the potential likelihood of AD parameters including specific damage causes (eg, because of military weapon activation and the effect of hot gas emissions after missile launch, gunfire vibrations, ejection of chaff and flares) and of expected environmental deterioration parameters.

The selection of repetitive scheduled intervals takes into account:

- the definition of numeric interval values starting from the beginning of the in-service phase on

- the definition of initial interval thresholds with subsequent repeat intervals
- the implementation of change steps for numerical interval values during the Product in-service phase (eg, start GVI with small intervals at the begin of the life cycle, followed by extended intervals during the Product midlife phase and again followed by small intervals at the end of the Product life cycle)

When determining numerical interval values and interval types for a zonal GVI, the following must be taken into account:

- hardware susceptibility to damage
- density of equipment/items installed in the zone under analysis
- the amount of preventive and non-preventive activities and access frequency to the zone (operator, maintenance or other personnel)
- amount of equipment newly designed, developed or produced and therefore, less in-service experience exists
- operator and manufacturer experience with similar Products

If possible, intervals must correspond to those selected for targeted overall preventive maintenance.

ZAM 1, according to Step S3, is followed by one or more additional ZAM explained in further analysis steps. Refer to Step S4, Step S5, Step S6 and Step S7.

Step S4:

All Product zones with equipment, wiring, tubes, etc, installed, must be analyzed by ZAM 2, if they contain one or more sources of ignition (eg, sparks caused by a damaged electrical isolation of a power cable, hot spots on tubes/ducts/outlets) and/or contain combustible material and/or explosive vapor.

For Product zones, perform the work steps and make the decisions as shown in Fig 3.

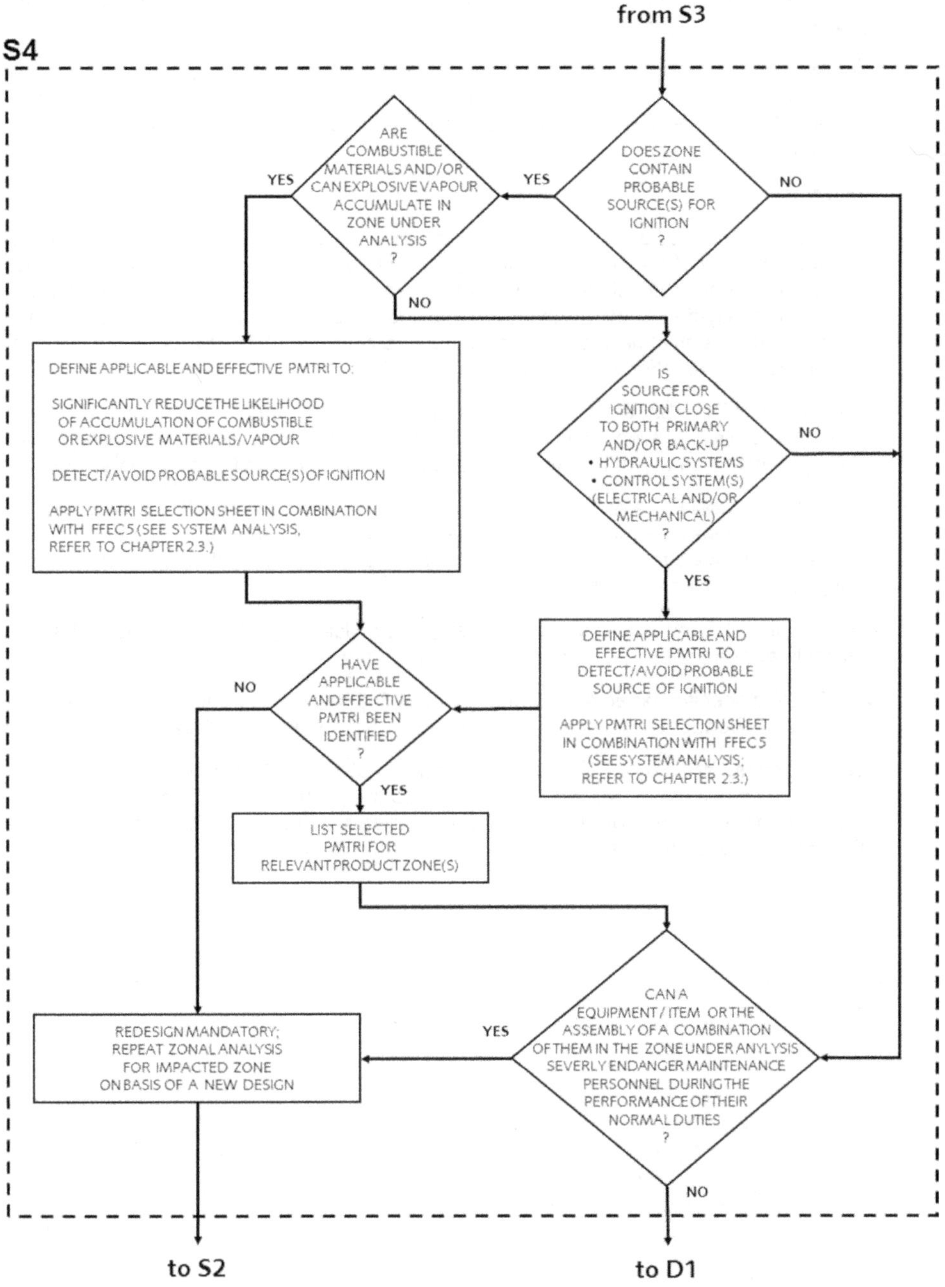

ICN-B6865-S4000P0058-001-01

Fig 3 Flow chart Enhanced Zonal Analysis

ZAM 2 is linked to the standard maintenance task type selection sheet used in the system analysis (refer to Chap 2.3), that enables identification of applicable and effective PMTRI including GVI.

All possible sources of ignition, which can lead to fire and/or explosion in the zone under analysis must be identified for all selected PMTRI.

Applicable and effective PMTRI must also be selected to minimize any contamination by an accumulation of combustible materials inside the zone. The size and layout of the zone, its accessibility and the density of installed equipment have an influence on the selection of the most effective PMTRI.

Example:

A deteriorated or damaged electrical isolation of an electric power cable, in combination with explosive fuel vapor surrounding that cable, is a probable critical scenario for a safety-relevant functional failure. A selection of a preventive high voltage test for the cable (to detect faulty/damaged spots on the cable isolation) and a preventive servicing task of the fuel vapor ventilation system (eg, scheduled cleaning of air ventilation holes) can be an applicable and effective combination of PMTRI.

Sources of ignition that are in close proximity (eg, within 2 inches or 50 mm) to both primary and back up hydraulic, mechanical or electrical controls are subject to the analysis in ZAM 2. For those potentially safety-critical failure causes, one or more PMTRI must be selected.

Examples for PMTRI selection are provided in the system analysis (refer to Chap 2.3) and structural analysis (refer to Chap 2.4). The determination of intervals (numerical value and type) for PMTRI follows analytical methodologies and rules to be identified in Product-specific interval rating sheets or files of the PPH.

When, during this enhanced zonal analysis, no applicable PMTRI can be identified for the critical interfaces, the Product redesign is mandatory.

AD, ED and specific expected damage sources (eg, as a consequence of the use of a weapon in a military Product usage scenario) must also be considered in ZAM 2.

Every zone under analysis, in its current design status, must be analyzed for unacceptable threats which can endanger maintenance personnel during the performance of their duties. Endangering equipment or item allocation or other health-threatening aspects must be highlighted to design department to enable early redesign.

Step S5:

<u>Fig 4</u> shows the process work steps and decisions necessary to perform the optional ZAM 3 for a Product zone.

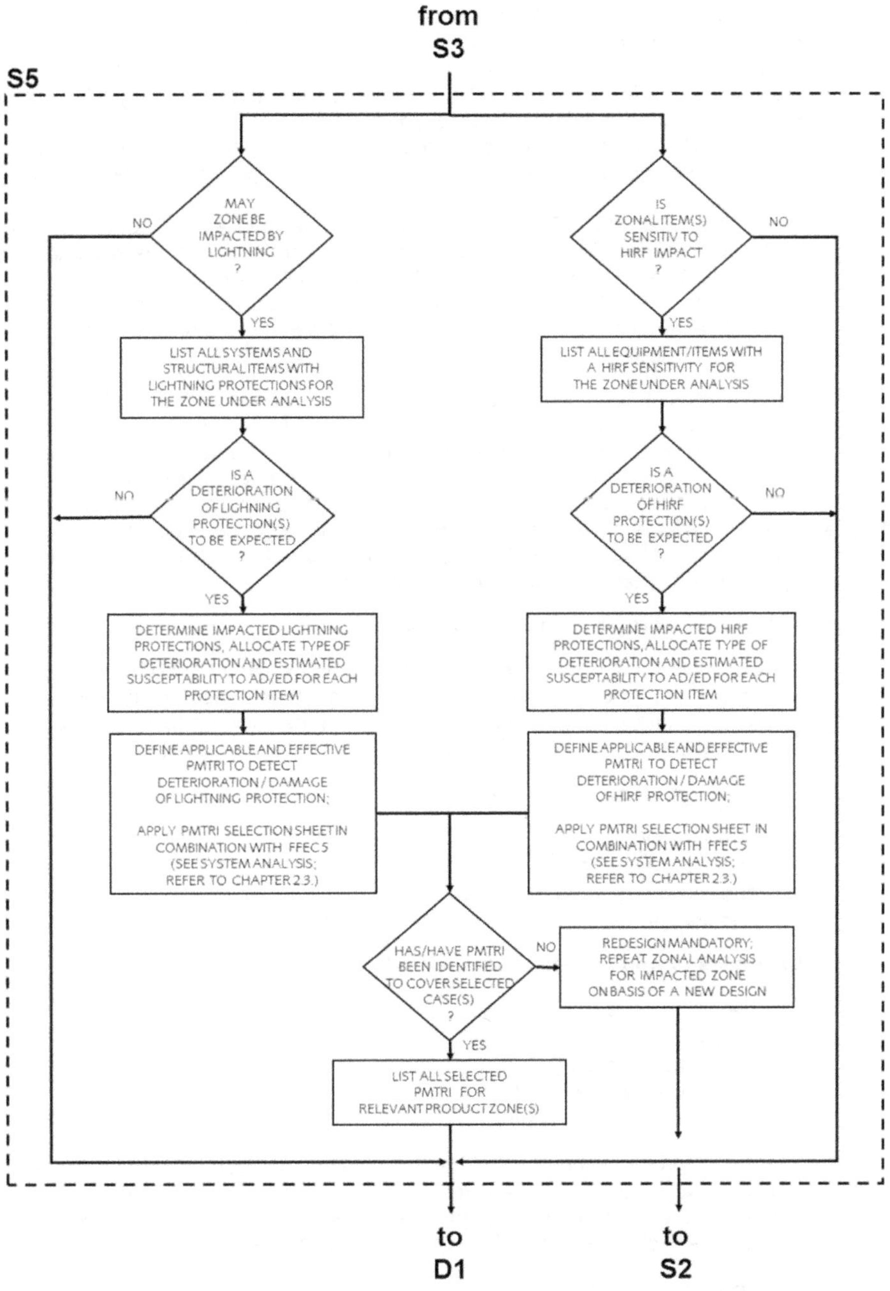

ICN-B6865-S4000P0059-001-01

Fig 4 Flow chart L/HIRF analysis

L/HIRF preventive maintenance relies on adequate protection provided by both equipment internal and equipment external L/HIRF protection components:

–   equipment internal L/HIRF protection components are those L/HIRF protection features, incorporated inside the equipment. Protection devices such as filter pin connectors, discrete filter capacitors and transient protection devices are installed within equipment on one or more of interface circuits. For equipment whose failure can have an adverse effect on safety, the Product manufacturer must confirm that the maintenance philosophy will ensure the continued effectiveness of L/HIRF protective features. This can include specific procedures or other data acceptable to regulatory authorities to ensure that the L/HIRF protection devices continue to perform their intended functions throughout the in-service phase. The equipment internal L/HIRF protection components are not subject to ZAM 3 analysis.
–   equipment external L/HIRF protection components installed on Product level (ie, any protection not installed within an equipment), whose failure can have an adverse effect on safety, must be analyzed by ZAM 3. This includes items such as shielded wires, back shells, metallic mesh raceways, bonding jumpers, connectors, composite fairings with conductive mesh, the inherent conductivity of the Product structure and specific devices such as RF gaskets.

PMTRI for the equipment external L/HIRF protection systems on the Product must be developed to support the Product type certification and to develop the Preventive Maintenance Review Board (PMRB) report. These L/HIRF protection systems must be identified for analytical development of PMTRI. The intent of this is to reduce the possibility that a single external failure cause (eg, a lightning strike) in combination with the occurrence of an AD or ED technical failure cause across redundant channels of L/HIRF protection, that can impact safety during the Product in-service phase. Each L/HIRF protection system must be evaluated in terms of its susceptibility to degradation from ED and/or AD impacts.

The analytical work required in ZAM 3 is based on:

–   a description of the L/HIRF protection system and a list of L/HIRF protection components by zone whose functional failure can have an adverse effect on safety. Protection within a given zone must include both electrical and non-electrical protection components. Create a matrix that lists the location of each component within the zone.

Examples of electrical components:

*   wire shielding
*   pigtail terminations
*   back shells
*   bonding straps

Examples of non-electrical components:

*   metallic meshes
*   raceways
*   conductive gaskets
*   conductive coatings
*   structure and substructure

–   information on the component characteristics and applicable performance data for each protection component within a zone is required. Protection component characteristics are properties that are relied upon to provide L/HIRF protection, such as resistance to corrosion, effects of environment and robustness of design. This information includes:

*   development data
*   qualification test data

- in-service predictions for the Product environment such as effects of environmental parameters surrounding the Product, corrosive effects, condensation, temperature, vibration on a protection item with respect to degradation effects
- in-service predictions for Product susceptibility to damage, such as the probability of damage during maintenance activities or the likelihood of damage during operations/missions/deployments (eg, areas where connectors can be stepped on by personnel, effects of de-icing fluid on a connector during winter operations)

The detailed and self-explanatory L/HIRF analytical process logic of ZAM 3 is shown in Fig 4. Using a logic-based analytical process and taking into account probable consequences of the protection system failures/damages, the analyst must determine the types of PMTRI that are both applicable and effective in combination with their scheduled intervals.

Both the Lightning (L) and the HIRF impacts must be analyzed in parallel.

For equipment that is installed in a zone which is sensitive to either or to both of these impacts, applicable and effective PMTRI must be determined based on the standard PMTRI selection sheet that is also used during the system analysis (refer to Chap 2.3).

The numerical value of the PMTRI interval must be defined based on either the interval rating sheets or files provided in the PPH or according to the PPH/guidelines detailed in Chap 2.3. L/HIRF protections require an analysis for functional failure effects (FFE) caused by ED and AD to determine the likelihood of component degradation based on the environment in which the component is installed.

The selection of a PMTRI or of a combination of PMTRI (if more PMTRI are applicable and effective) depends on the criticality category of the potential Functional Failure Effect Code (FFEC) that is FFEC 5 (ie, hidden safety effects) for all selected L/HIRF-related PMTRI to the FC.

If no PMTRI can be identified as applicable and effective for the equipment/item under analysis, then redesign is the resulting mandatory requirement because of the allocation of FFEC 5.

Resulting PMTRI must be harmonized with other PMTRI identified in other ZAM and/or from system- and/or structure analysis.

Step S6

<u>Fig 5</u> shows the process work steps and decisions necessary to perform the ZAM 4 for a Product.

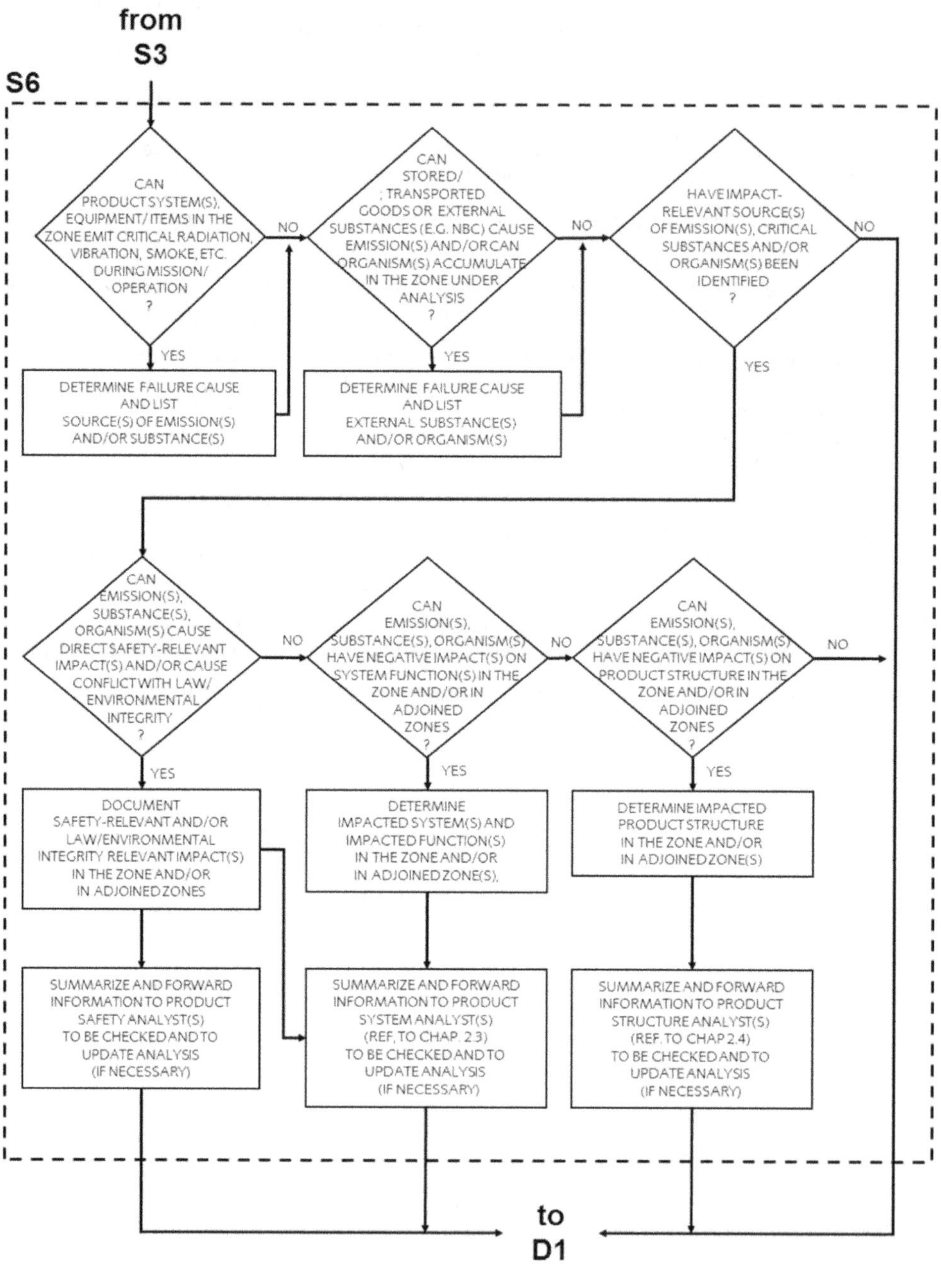

ICN-B6865-S4000P0060-001-01

Fig 5 Flow chart Zonal interface analysis

Applicable to: All

The scope of the Zonal interface analysis in ZAM 4 is to identify potential sources of critical emissions, sources for functional failures or sources for structural damages which can either be caused by:

- the Product systems themselves without functional failure or as a potential consequence of one or more functional failures
- objects or goods being stored or transported in one or more Product zones
- accumulation of substances in a zone which descend from external sources (eg, nuclear, biologic, chemical (NBC) substances)
- the growth/reproduction of biologic organisms supported by the environmental conditions in a zone a positive way

Examples:

- Cargo emitting electromagnetic radiation in a storage room of a transport ship can have influence on installed system equipment in adjoining zones
- The accumulation of fungus in a zone can impact the air supply and air-conditioning system and several other zones in a submarine or in a spacecraft

When the impact sources are determined, the analysis in ZAM 4 continues with the selection of the potential criticality of the expected impacts. Identified safety and/or law/environmental integrity relevant impact sources must be documented, and this information must be presented to the Product design and the safety departments.

If impact sources can have an influence on Product system functions and/or on SSI/SD of Product structure are identified, they must be documented and presented to the preventive maintenance analysts.

Step S7:

If required, additional ZAM X can be composed as options to cover the analysis needs of individual Product types.

The definition of additional ZAM X depends on the individual Product type and its operator-specific in-service usage. Based on experience with comparable Products and their in-service behavior, requirements, etc, a Product zonal analysis procedure must be extended by further ZAM X. All selected ZAM X must be documented together with the relevant impact sources and/or parameters.

Examples for additional ZAM X for specific Product types:

- The analysis of zones for potential impacts from underwater shockwaves on submarines
- The analysis of zones for potential impacts from radiation sources outside of the earth atmosphere on spacecraft or satellites. Collision of a satellite zones with foreign particles in the orbit.
- The analysis of zones of an aircraft due to frequent flights through air pollution

Decision D1:

The standard zonal analysis ZAM 1 is limited to selection of the maintenance task type GVI. This inspection method is not only focused on one or more equipment/items installed in a Product zone. A zonal GVI is valid and must be performed for the zone under analysis. But the numerical interval value and the interval type of the GVI for a zone is specific and depends on the rating of the zone (refer to Step S3).

ZAM 2 identifies stand-alone PMTRI such as:

- GVI for specific equipment/items in a limited area within the zone where the numerical interval value can deviate from the zonal GVI interval

- Detailed visual inspections for specific equipment/items in a limited area or on specific equipment/items installed in a zone
- Functional checks and/or tests on specific equipment/items installed in a zone
- Restoration or cleaning task requirements on specific equipment/items installed in a zone

ZAM 3 defines stand-alone PMTRI such as:

- GVI for specific L/HIRF protections in a limited area within the zone where the numerical interval value can deviate from the zonal GVI interval
- Detailed visual inspections for specific L/HIRF protections in a limited area or on specific equipment/items installed in a zone
- Functional checks and/or tests on L/HIRF protections installed in a zone

Note

Identified PMTRI from ZAM 2 and/or ZAM 3 must be stand-alone PMTRI because potential FFE are either safety-critical or can conflict with law and/or environmental integrity.

ZAM 4 can result in updates of Product safety analysis, re-design or can trigger the definition of stand-alone PMTRI and/or GVI for Zonal Inspections based on the feedback given to analysts.

The analysis in ZAM X can also define stand-alone PMTRI for specific equipment/items within the zone.

If an identified PMTRI is selected as a stand-alone task (Answer YES), continue with Step S10.

If not (Answer NO), continue with Decision D2.

Step S8:

All preventive GVI requirements with intervals determined by the system analysis and categorized with FFEC 1, 2, 5 or 6 must remain as stand-alone GVI requirements with their own intervals.

For remaining preventive GVI requirements from system analysis categorized with FFEC 3,4,7 or 8, Decision D2 becomes relevant.

Step S9:

All preventive GVI selected for SSI/SD determined by the structure analysis must remain as stand-alone PMTRI allocated to a FFE criticality category as follows:

- FFEC 1 (safety impact) or FFEC 2 (conflict with law/environmental integrity) for evident functional failures of the Product structure
- FFEC 5 (safety impact) or FFEC 6 (conflict with law/environmental integrity) for hidden functional failures of the Product structure

Preventive GVI on structural items categorized as non-SSI must be allocated to one of the following FFE criticality categories:

- FFEC 3 (mission/operation impact) or FFEC 4 (economy impact) for evident functional failures of the Product structure
- FFEC 7 (mission/operation impact) or FFEC 8 (economy impact) for hidden functional failures of the Product structure

For all GVI requirements categorized with FFEC 3, 4, 7 or 8, Decision D2 becomes relevant.

If there is any doubt when categorizing, the worst case FFEC must be selected. This ensures that the FFEC with the lower applicable numerical value must be selected for evident Functional Failures (FFEC 1 thru 4) or for hidden Functional Failures (FFEC 5 thru 8) in every case.

Decision D2:

For this decision, only those preventive GVI with intervals are relevant without categorization as a stand-alone PMTRI.

The interval of each preventive GVI requirement on equipment/item must be compared with the numerical interval value for the zonal GVI in the respective zone.

The preventive GVI requirement for the equipment/item is covered by the zonal GVI (Answer YES), if:

- the numerical value of the interval of the zonal GVI is smaller than the GVI interval for the equipment/item
- the numerical value of the interval of the zonal GVI is larger than the GVI interval for the equipment/item, but the numerical value of the interval of the zonal GVI can be reduced to the GVI interval for the equipment/item

Note

A general prerequisite for the integration of an equipment/item GVI into a zonal GVI is accessibility to and visibility of the identified equipment/item in the installed position.

If a GVI on an equipment/item cannot be integrated into a zonal GVI (Answer: NO), a stand-alone GVI with intervals must be defined for the equipment/item and listed in the PMTRI summary of the system or structure analysis.

A preventive GVI, in combination with FFEC 1, 2, 5 and 6, must lead to answer NO. These GVI must remain as stand-alone PMTRI. Only preventive GVI requirements with intervals categorized as FFEC 3, 4, 7 or 8, can lead to answer YES in this decision.

If a GVI is adequately covered by standard zonal inspection (Answer YES), continue with Step S11.

If not (Answer NO), continue with Step S10.

Step S10:

In this analysis step, the identified PMTRI must be transferred either to the results from the relevant Product system analysis (refer to Chap 2.2) or to the results from Product structural analysis (refer to Chap 2.3).

This information must include the identified failure causes and/or damage causes, the FFEC criticality categorizations per PMTRI and a consolidated PMTRI interval on the level of zonal analysis for:

- all stand-alone GVI with intervals resulting from ZAM 2, ZAM 3, ZAM 4 and/or from ZAM X

and

- all PMTRI with the maintenance task type GVI (eg, preventive detailed inspection, functional test, NDT)

All PMTRI must be identified and documented to allow traceability during future OMP reviews and/or changes. This is to prevent the later inadvertent deletion or escalation of stand-alone PMTRI without proper consideration of risks.

Step S11:

This zonal analysis step integrates preventive GVI without a stand-alone requirement from system analysis (refer to Chap 2.3) and/or from structure analysis (refer to Chap 2.4) into the standard zonal inspections.

The GVI requirements are covered by the zonal GVI with interval in that zone, where the equipment/item under analysis is installed (ZAM 1, Step S3).

If an adaption of the interval for the zonal GVI has been identified in order to allow integration of one or more identified system or structural GVI with intervals, background information and/or justifications must be documented in the ZAM 1.

Step S12:

End of the zonal analysis.

If the design of Product zones changes, the manufacturer must establish an approval process, to determine whether the zonal analysis process must be repeated for the impacted zones. If so, the analysis results must be updated accordingly.

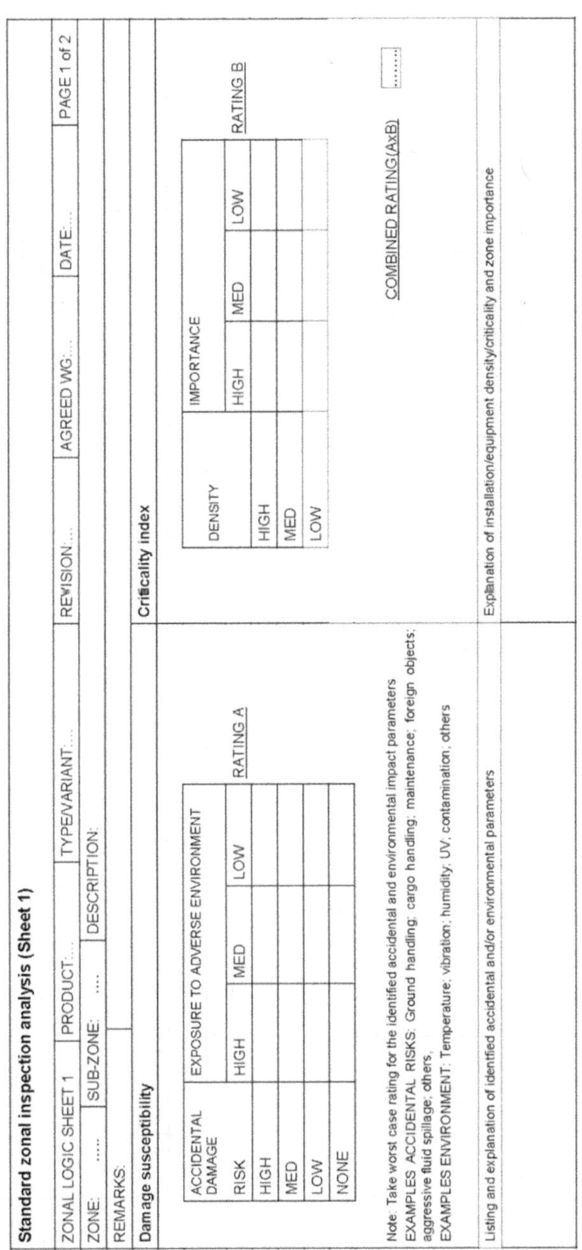

ICN-B6865-S4000P0061-001-01

Fig 6 Interval rating sheet for standard zonal inspection, example (Sheet 1 of 2)

ICN-B6865-S4000P0062-001-01

Fig 7 Interval rating sheet for standard zonal inspection, example (Sheet 2 of 2)

Chapter 2.6

Developing PMTR - Consolidation of analysis results, harmonization with other preventive maintenance task requirement sources for traceability

Table of contents

Page

Developing PMTR - Consolidation of analysis results, harmonization with other preventive maintenance task requirement sources for traceability 1

References 1

1 General 2

2 Consolidation of PMTRI resulting from S4000P analysis methodologies 4

2.1 Consolidation of analysis results 4

2.2 Initial consolidation of analysis results 5

2.3 Subsequent consolidation of analysis results from Product zonal analysis 6

3 Harmonization of PMTRI with other sources of preventive maintenance tasks 6

4 Handling impact sources on the set of consolidated and harmonized PMTRI after exchanging data from S4000P to S3000L 9

4.1 Handling impact sources prior to the start of the Product in-service phase 10

4.2 Handling of impact sources after the start of the Product in-service phase 10

5 Traceability of PMTRI and other sources of maintenance tasks with repetitive scheduled intervals 10

List of tables

1 References 1

List of figures

1 Overview on consolidation and harmonization activities of PMTRI necessary during the Product life cycle 3

2 Consolidation of PMTRI data resulting from Chap 2 analysis 4

3 Consolidation of PMTRI data resulting from Chap 3 analysis 5

4 Initial consolidation of analysis results to PMTRI 6

5 Example CCMR/CMR and harmonization with analysis results 7

6 Example PMTRI and CMR defined in parallel 8

7 Example PMTRI meeting a CCMR 9

8 Online traceability of preventive maintenance task sources with repetitive scheduled intervals 11

References

Table 1 References

Chap No./Document No.	Title
Chap 2	Developing PMTR

Chap No./Document No.	Title
Chap 2.3	Developing PMTR - System analysis
Chap 2.4	Developing PMTR - Structure analysis
Chap 2.5	Developing PMTR - Zonal analysis
Chap 3	Optimizing PMTR
Chap 4	S4000P Interfaces
Chap 5	Data model and data exchange
Chap 6	Terms, abbreviations and acronyms
S1000D	International specification for technical publications using a common source database
S3000L	International procedure specification for Logistic Support Analysis - LSA
S5000F	International specification for operational and maintenance data feedback
SX000i	International guide for the use of the S-Series Integrated Logistics Support (IPS) specifications

1 General

The S4000P analysis methodologies cover a complete Product analysis for the development of applicable and effective Preventive Maintenance Task Requirements with repetitive scheduled Intervals (PMTRI). These are:

- System analysis. Refer to Chap 2.3.
- Structure analysis. Refer to Chap 2.4.
- Zonal analysis. Refer to Chap 2.5.

Each of these analytical methodologies can develop PMTRI, which must be consolidated on a first level within the single analysis methodologies by the analysts. On the next higher level, selected PMTRI require the consolidation among the above listed analysis methodologies. Refer to Para 2.

There are necessary harmonization activities of PMTRI resulting from analysis with other sources for repetitive scheduled maintenance tasks (eg, Candidate Certification Maintenance Requirements (CCMR)). Refer to Para 3. These additional sources can impact analysis-based PMTRI. They must be known prior to finalizing the analytical results. The subsequent S4000P/S3000L data exchange based on an applicable PMTRI data exchange file triggers subsequent Logistic Support Analysis (LSA) activities. Refer to S3000L.

There must be rules and recommendations for how to deal with other unscheduled sources (eg, requirements, recommendations, change proposals, etc) that also impact the set of repetitive scheduled maintenance tasks that are being defined by the Product technical publications (refer to S1000D) after the finalization of all PMTRI consolidation and harmonization work steps. Refer to Para 4.

A permanent data traceability related to preventive Product maintenance is essential. Refer to Para 5.

Note

The wording of task requirements in the abbreviations PMTR, PMTRI and PMTRE is used by intention for preventive maintenance analysis results. Original analysis-based interval data of PMTRI can be adapted or modified later during LSA activities (refer to S3000L) and/or during the elaboration of the Product technical publication. Refer to S1000D. Therefore, the interval type and/or the numerical interval size of a scheduled maintenance task in the Product documentation must not be identical to the original PMTRI interval data that has been identified based on the analysis. Adaptations of scheduled intervals of maintenance tasks are required to allow an optimized maintenance planning during the Product in-service phase.

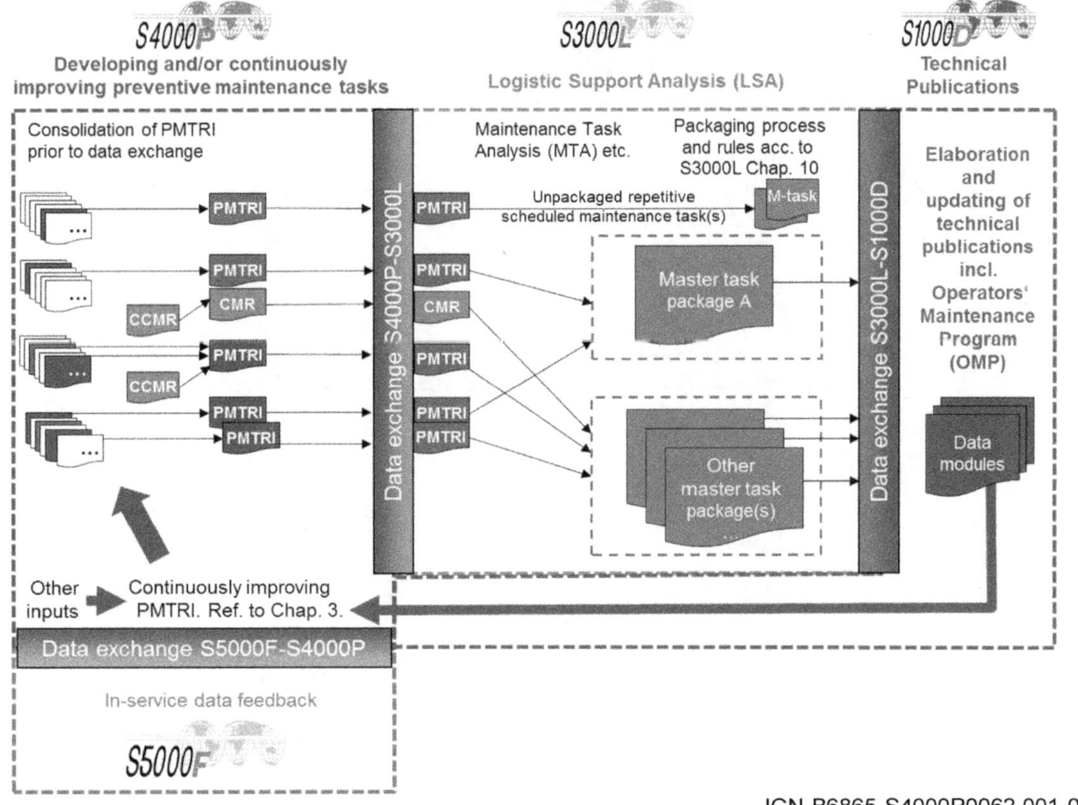

ICN-B6865-S4000P0062-001-01

Fig 1 Overview on consolidation and harmonization activities of PMTRI necessary during the Product life cycle

Fig 5 shows an overview on the PMTRI consolidation and harmonization activities covering both the Product development phase (refer to Chap 2) and the Product in-service phase (refer to Chap 3). Additional preventive maintenance task sources, which can also impact the set of repetitive scheduled maintenance tasks are not shown in Fig 5. Refer to Para 4.

The overall scope of the PMTRI consolidation and harmonization activities, is to achieve traceability and acceptance of the analysis results by authorized personnel prior to the data transfer into the S3000L database. This PMTRI data exchange is, for example, based on pre-defined data elements according to a data exchange file. Refer to Chap 4 and Chap 5.

Further data exchanges between other specifications of the S-Series IPS specifications and the S3000L data source are also shown in Fig 5. They are necessary to elaborate and update an effective Product maintenance program/Operators' Maintenance Program (OMP).

2 Consolidation of PMTRI resulting from S4000P analysis methodologies

2.1 Consolidation of analysis results

The initial development of PMTRI detailed in Chap 2, comprises an initial consolidation of the detailed analysis results as shown in Fig 5:

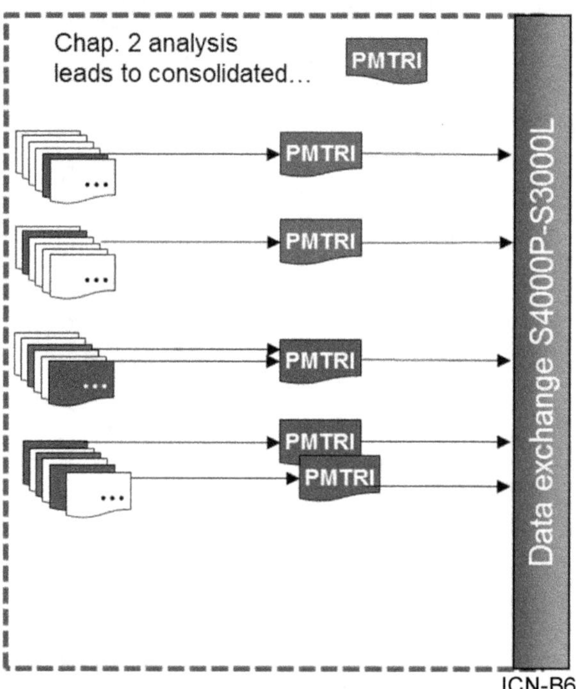

ICN-B6865-S4000P0063-001-01

Fig 2 Consolidation of PMTRI data resulting from Chap 2 analysis

In the same way as the initial development of PMTRI detailed in Chap 2, the results from the later review and optimization process of PMTRI based on Chap 3, must again be consolidated with the previous analysis results. Refer to Fig 5.

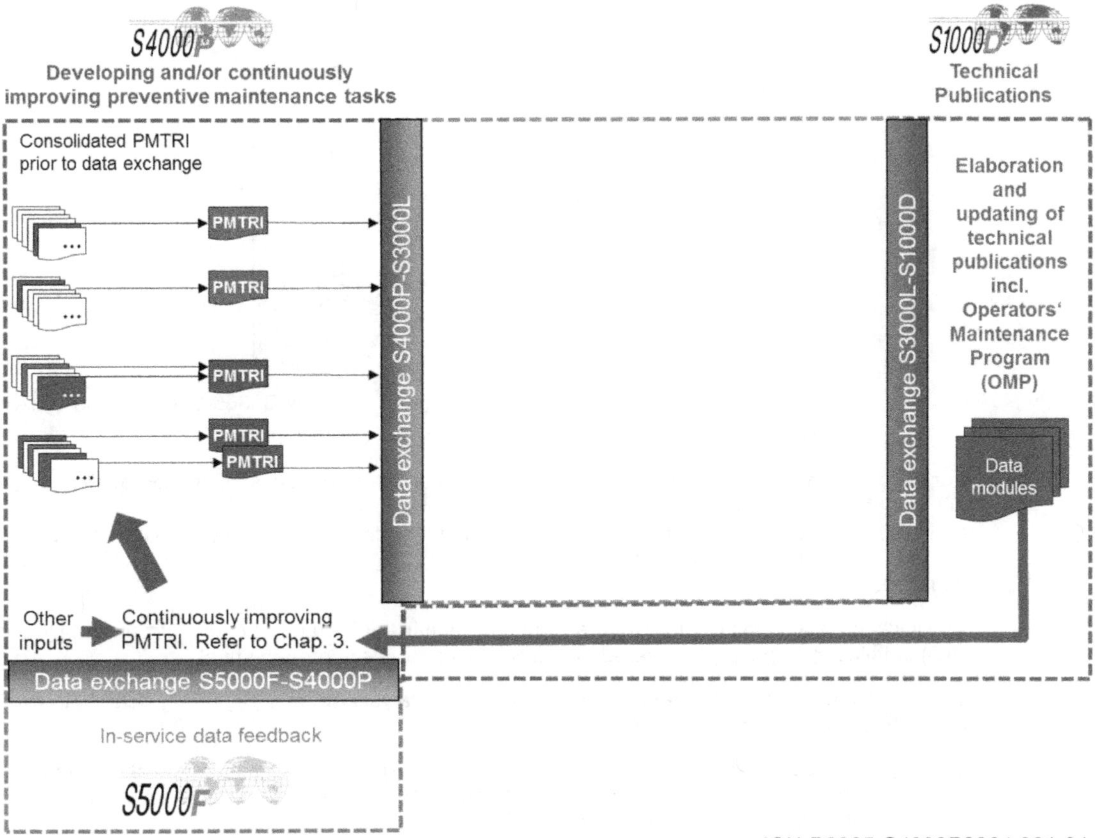

ICN-B6865-S4000P0064-001-01

Fig 3 Consolidation of PMTRI data resulting from Chap 3 analysis

The PMTRI review and optimization process during the Product in-service phase (refer to Chap 3) must be based on the content of the released and authorized technical publication of the Product at a calendar-based time that is defined in the analysis guideline/PPH.

To achieve optimization results of the complete preventive Product maintenance, reliable in-service feedback and other input(s) must be provided, evaluated and used for the harmonized analysis purpose. Refer to Chap 3 and S5000F.

2.2 Initial consolidation of analysis results

When a system analysis is completed (refer to Chap 2.3), the analyst must consolidate all identified PMTRI that are selected as applicable and effective for the identified Failure Causes (FC) that are documented in, for example, the respective system analysis reports.

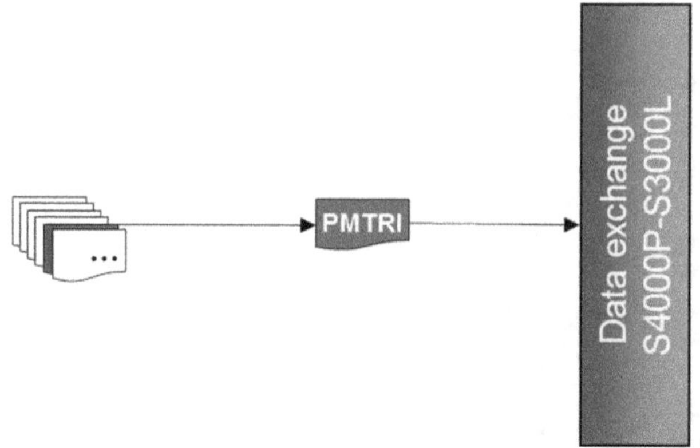

ICN-B6865-S4000P0065-001-01

Fig 4 Initial consolidation of analysis results to PMTRI

For each system analysis (refer to Chap 2.3), the initial consolidation is influenced by the number of applicable and effective PMTRI that are determined for all identified FC under analysis. The initial consolidation of PMTRI resulting from the system analysis, differs from both the PMTRI developed by structure analysis (refer to Chap 2.4) and from PMTRI developed by zonal analysis (refer to Chap 2.5).

The initial consolidation of PMTRI for a Structure Significant Item (SSI) and/or Significant Details (SD) detailed in Chap 2.4 is covered by the SSI/SD analysis summary sheet.

The consolidation of PMTRI resulting from the zonal analysis (refer to Chap 2.5) deals with two preventive maintenance task types:

1   General Visual Inspection (GVI) requirements for a Product zone as a result of the standard zonal analysis. The initial consolidation of zonal GVI is covered in the final steps and decisions of the zonal analysis process. Refer to Chap 2.5.

2   PMTRI except GVI selected during enhanced zonal analysis, the L/HIRF analysis, the zonal interface analysis and/or during other Product-specific Zonal Analysis Modules X (ZAM X). All PMTRI except GVI are subject to a subsequent consolidation work step. Refer to Para 2.3.

2.3   Subsequent consolidation of analysis results from Product zonal analysis

With the exception of the Standard Zonal Analysis (ZAM 1), all maintenance task types of PMTRI can be selected for the analysis-relevant equipment or items in the ZAM.

The zonal analyst must consolidate all PMTRI results developed on the basis of these ZAM with PMTRI, resulting from the analysis of respective Product systems, from Product structure analysis or with other predefined PMTRI. This PMTRI consolidation step must take into account any different criticalities and potential deviations of the repetitive scheduled interval (ie, interval type and/or numerical interval value) per individual PMTRI.

3   Harmonization of PMTRI with other sources of preventive maintenance tasks

As well as the consolidation activities detailed at Para 2, a harmonization of the selected PMTRI with other known sources of preventive maintenance tasks, (eg, a Functional Hazard Analysis (FHA), a Product/System Safety Hazard Analysis (SSHA), a Fault Tree Analysis (FTA), with (national) law requirements and/or with the content of other appropriate analysis documents) can be required.

When identifying other safety-relevant FC external to the Product or when identifying additional combinations of critical FC not yet covered by the analytical results from analysis methodologies, a further PMTRI harmonization and update is mandatory.

Depending on the availability of the individual impacts on PMTRI and/or other PMTRI requests, the PMTRI harmonization must be performed not only prior to the formal delivery of analysis results, and subsequently on an ongoing basis. Refer to Para 4.

Fig 5 shows an example of work steps and decisions necessary in a harmonization process between PMTRI and known CCMR.

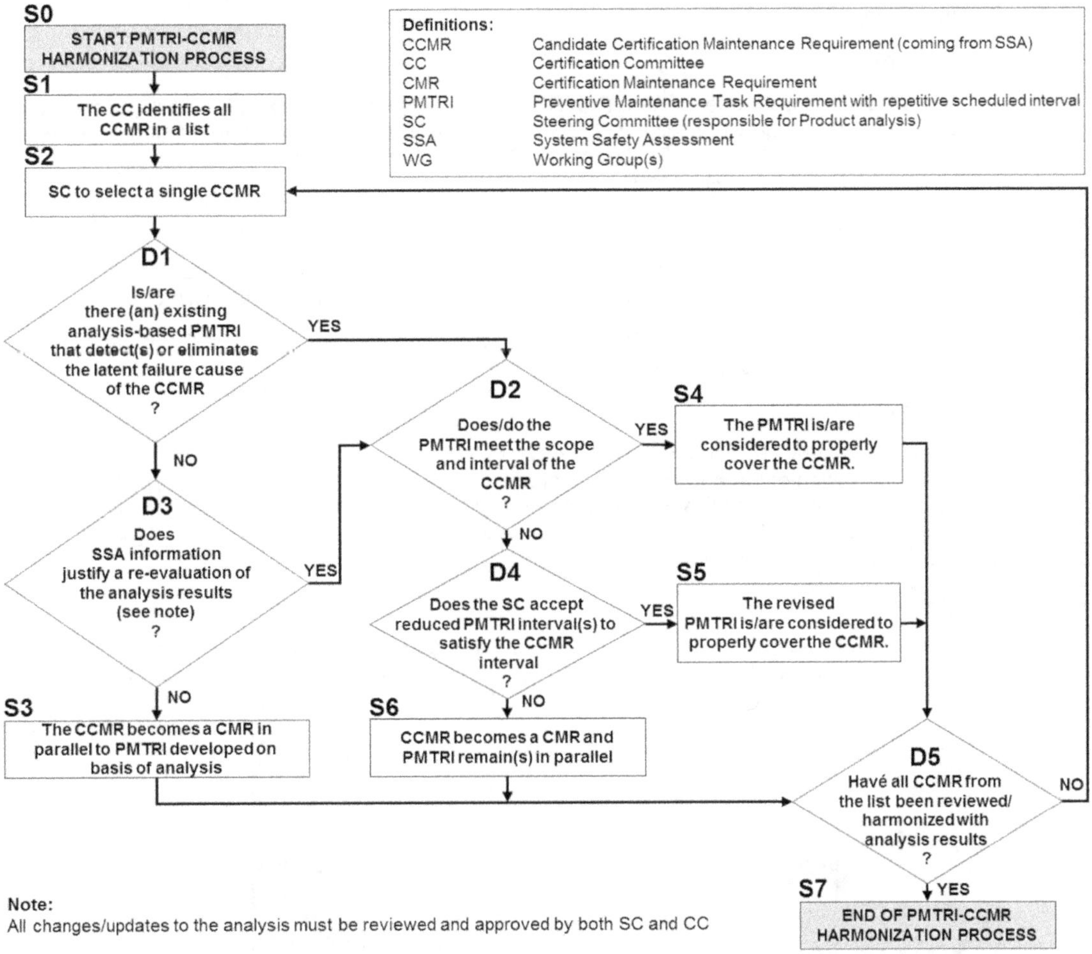

Fig 5 Example CCMR/CMR and harmonization with analysis results

The harmonization process example shown in Fig 5, can be an acceptable means to permit the use of an PMTRI in lieu of CCMR, as determined by an appropriate Certification Committee (CC). The work Steps Step S0, Step S1, Step S2, etc, together with the decisions Decision D1, Decision D2, etc, as shown in Fig 5 are:

Step S0:

The PMTRI-CCMR harmonization process starts.

Step S1:

The CC identifies all CCMR from the System Safety Assessment (SSA) or other applicable sources in a common data list and forwards the data list to the SC.

Step S2:

The Steering Committee (SC) selects a single CCMR from the list for checking by the subsequent process.

Decision D1:

The SC determines if one or more PMTRI exists, which are categorized for the impact on safety, environmental integrity or collide with law and which will detect or eliminate the latent failure identified in the SSA. If such PMTRI exists (Answer YES) continue with Decision D2. If not (Answer NO), continue with Decision D3.

Decision D2:

If the re-assessment was performed and one or more PMTRI were generated, clarification must be provided on whether the PMTRI meets both interval and scope of the CCMR.

If the PMTRI does not meet the intent of the CCMR, continue with Decision D4. If the intent is met (Answer YES), continue with Step S4.

Decision D3:

If one or more PMTRI does not exist, the CC must ask the SC/responsible Working Group (WG) if a re-evaluation of the analysis of the impacted systems, structures or zones is possible, to develop and include applicable and effective PMTRI, based on additional information provided by the SSA report. If the re-evaluation is required (Answer YES), continue with Decision D2. If not (Answer NO), continue with Step S3.

Step S3:

If the re-evaluation of the analysis was not required and therefore not performed, then the CCMR becomes a CMR in parallel to PMTRI developed on basis of an analysis. Refer to Fig 6.

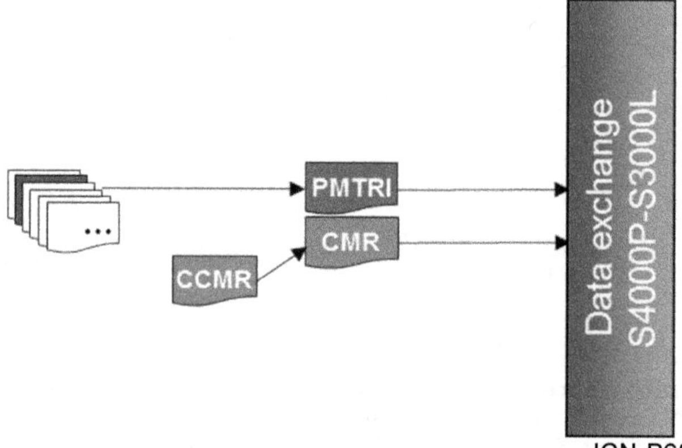

ICN-B6865-S4000P0067-001-01

Fig 6 Example PMTRI and CMR defined in parallel

Step S4:

Existing PMTRI are considered appropriate to meet the CCMR. Refer to Fig 7.

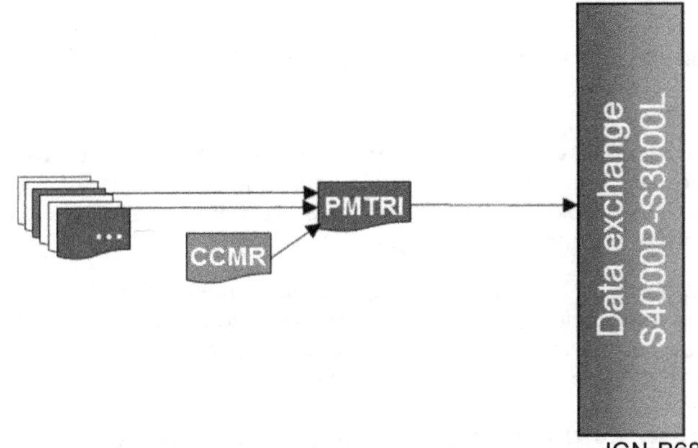

ICN-B6865-S4000P0068-001-01

Fig 7 Example PMTRI meeting a CCMR

Decision D4:

The SC, in cooperation with the analysis WG, can accept a CC proposed reduction in the PMTRI intervals in lieu of a CMR. The SC/WG must consider the advantages and disadvantages of both. If the interval reduction is decided (Answer YES), continue with Step S5. If not (Answer NO), continue with Step S6.

Step S5:

If the SC/WG accepts the CC proposed reduced scheduled intervals, the revised PMTRI are considered to meet the CCMR. The requirement for none CMR must be decided besides the PMTRI.

Step S6:

If the SC/WG does not accept the CC proposed change of the PMTRI intervals, then a CMR must be established in parallel to the analysis-based PMTRI. The CMR and PMTRI remain valid in parallel.

Decision D5:

This question clarifies if all CCMR from the list have been reviewed and/or harmonized with existing analysis results. If they have been reviewed and/or harmonized (Answer YES), the harmonization process stops with Step S7. If further CCMR must be reviewed and/or harmonized (Answer NO), continue with Step S2.

Step S7:

The PMTRI-CCMR harmonization process ends.

4   Handling impact sources on the set of consolidated and harmonized PMTRI after exchanging data from S4000P to S3000L

Rules and recommendations on how to deal with unforeseen and unscheduled impact sources (ie, requirements, recommendations, change proposals, etc) on the set of repetitive scheduled maintenance tasks defined for preventive Product maintenance must be given.

4.1 Handling impact sources prior to the start of the Product in-service phase

All new impact sources on analysis results must be reviewed by the Product analyst team or WG and/or by the SC, which is responsible for the Product analysis.

Each review of the analysis results can lead to updates and/or supplements to the set of PMTRI. In this case, the data exchange between S4000P and S3000L must be repeated. If the impacts sources are irrelevant, a justification must be documented by the analyst, WG or SC.

4.2 Handling of impact sources after the start of the Product in-service phase

The application of Chap 3 in the Product in-service phase comprises the set-up and the maintenance of traceable data from preventive maintenance analysis to the resulting technical publication for the Product. Refer to Para 5.

Each impact source on the preventive maintenance must initially be checked based on the ISMO analysis logic (refer to Chap 3.3). If the new impact source is related to a new FC that is not covered by the relevant Product analysis detailed in Chap 2, a review of affected analysis methodologies must be carried out by the analyst, WG or SC.

5 Traceability of PMTRI and other sources of maintenance tasks with repetitive scheduled intervals

The development of PMTRI, the continuous improvement of PMTRI and the harmonization with other sources of preventive maintenance tasks, require various data exchanges and data traceability between the analysis and other data sources. Analysis-relevant interfaces between the S-Series IPS specifications and between other interfaces outside the S-Series IPS specifications, are described in Chap 4. SX000i and the Data Exchange (DEX) specifications define all exchange data elements.

For traceability reasons, the original interval sources of each analysis-based PMTRI that is derived from the analytical work, each CMR and/or other sources must be documented in the LSA database. Refer to S3000L.

Fig 8 shows an overview of data sources that must be traced for all PMTRI, CCMR, CMR and/or all other sources of preventive maintenance tasks with repetitive scheduled intervals.

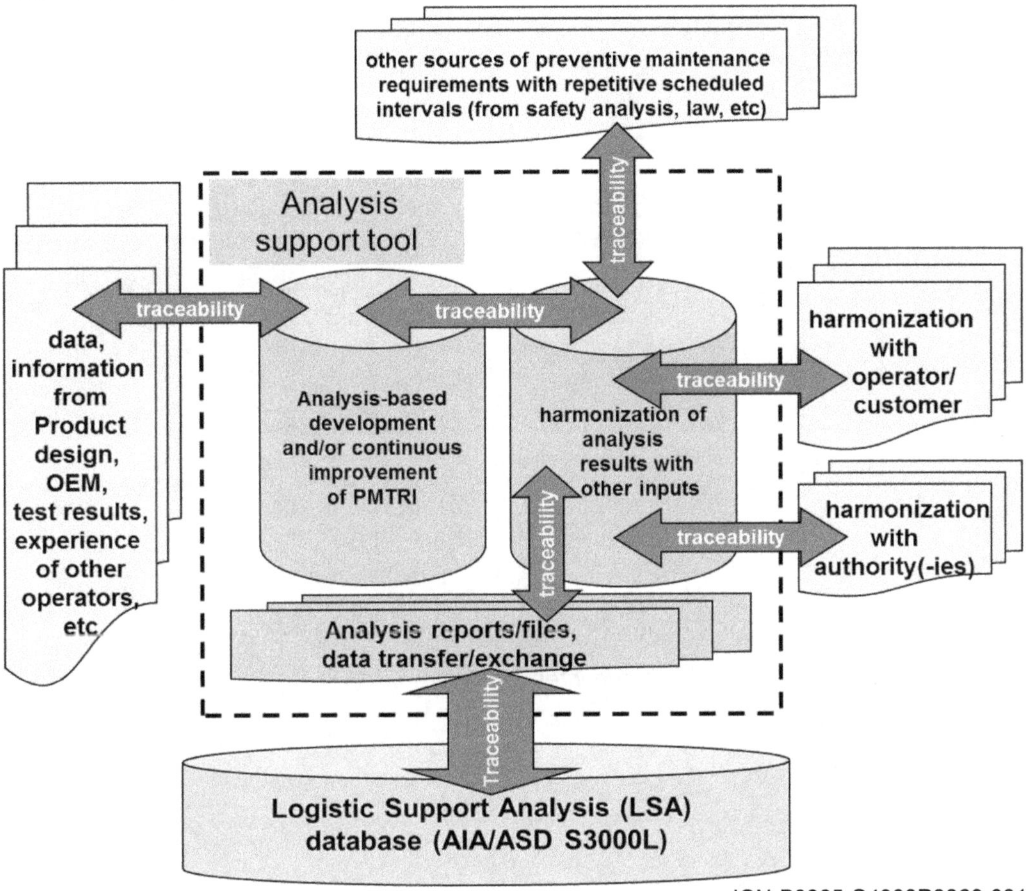

ICN-B6865-S4000P0069-001-01

Fig 8 Online traceability of preventive maintenance task sources with repetitive scheduled intervals

Page intentionally blank.

Chapter 2.7

Developing PMTR - Special event analysis

Table of contents

Page

Developing PMTR - Special event analysis 1

References 1

1   Overview 2

2   Initial identification of Product-relevant special events and probable impacts 2

3   PMTRE analysis process 4

4   PMTRE review process 6

List of tables

1   References 1

List of figures

1   Process for identifying special event data 3

2   Special event analysis (Sheet 1 of 2) 4

3   Special event analysis (Sheet 2 of 2) 5

References

Table 1 References

Chap No./Document No.	Title
Chap 2.1	Developing PMTR - General
Chap 2.3	Developing PMTR - System analysis
Chap 2.4	Developing PMTR - Structure analysis
Chap 2.5	Developing PMTR - Zonal analysis
Chap 2.6	Developing PMTR - Consolidation of analysis results, harmonization with other preventive maintenance task requirement sources for traceability
Chap 3	Optimizing PMTR
Chap 3.5	Optimizing PMTR - Review of PMTRE for special events
Chap 6	Terms, abbreviations and acronyms
S1000D	International specification for technical publications using a common source database
S3000L	International procedure specification for Logistic Support Analysis - LSA

1 Overview

The complete Product analysis for developing Preventive Maintenance Task Requirements with repetitive scheduled Intervals (PMTRI) applicable to a Products' specified in-service phase and usage conditions are:

- System analysis (refer to <u>Chap 2.3</u>)
- Structure analysis (refer to <u>Chap 2.4</u>)
- Zonal analysis (refer to <u>Chap 2.5</u>)

<u>Chap 2.6</u> describes the process for consolidating and/or harmonizing identified PMTRI.

The special event analysis must be in line with the analytical work and the results from the system, structure and zonal analysis. The PMTRI development process must ensure traceability of all related decisions/activities including a consolidation of PMTRI. The resulting PMTRI are adjoined to relevant Product systems, structure and zones.

Note:

The analysis described here can be used in conjunction with systems, structure and zonal analysis specified in other documents. If a project decides to do this, the details of the combined analysis approach must be clearly described and explained in the project's PPH.

In addition to PMTRI, single PMTRE or sets of PMTRE must be determined which are not associated with repetitive scheduled intervals but to special events that can impact a Product. These PMTRE also belong to the category of preventive maintenance tasks. The preventive maintenance tasks, resulting from a PMTRE, must be performed after the assumption or real occurrence of an unforeseeable special event.

A special event that impacts or could impact a Product can be identified, confirmed or assumed by the operating crew or maintenance personnel.

In both cases pre-defined tasks must be performed in order to detect potential failure causes and/or damages that could have or have already been caused by the special event. The Product special event analysis should always be performed based on results from Product system, structural and zonal analyses. Updates to the results of these analyses must be checked for any potential impact(s) on the sets of PMTRE selected for special events.

Note:

All PMTRE determined for special events must be presented to and discussed with the Product's design department and the customer. Requests and/or inputs from the design department and/or inputs from any available usage experience must be taken into account in the sets of PMTRE.

2 Initial identification of Product-relevant special events and probable impacts

The initial identification process for one or more special events that impact or can impact a Product is described in S3000L.

As well as the identification of one or more relevant special events, the S3000L process delivers event-specific inputs and information to the following questions:

- Can one on more Product systems be impacted by the special event under analysis?
- If there is a probable impact on systems, which systems are assumed to be impacted?
- Can the Product structure be impacted?
- If there is a probable impact on structure, which structural areas are assumed to be impacted?
- Can one or more Product's zones be impacted?
- If there is a probable impact on zones, which zones are assumed to be impacted?

Note

For all probable impacts, a detailed description must be given and documented in the PPH.

Fig 1 shows the logic for the preparation work necessary prior to the start of a special event analysis.

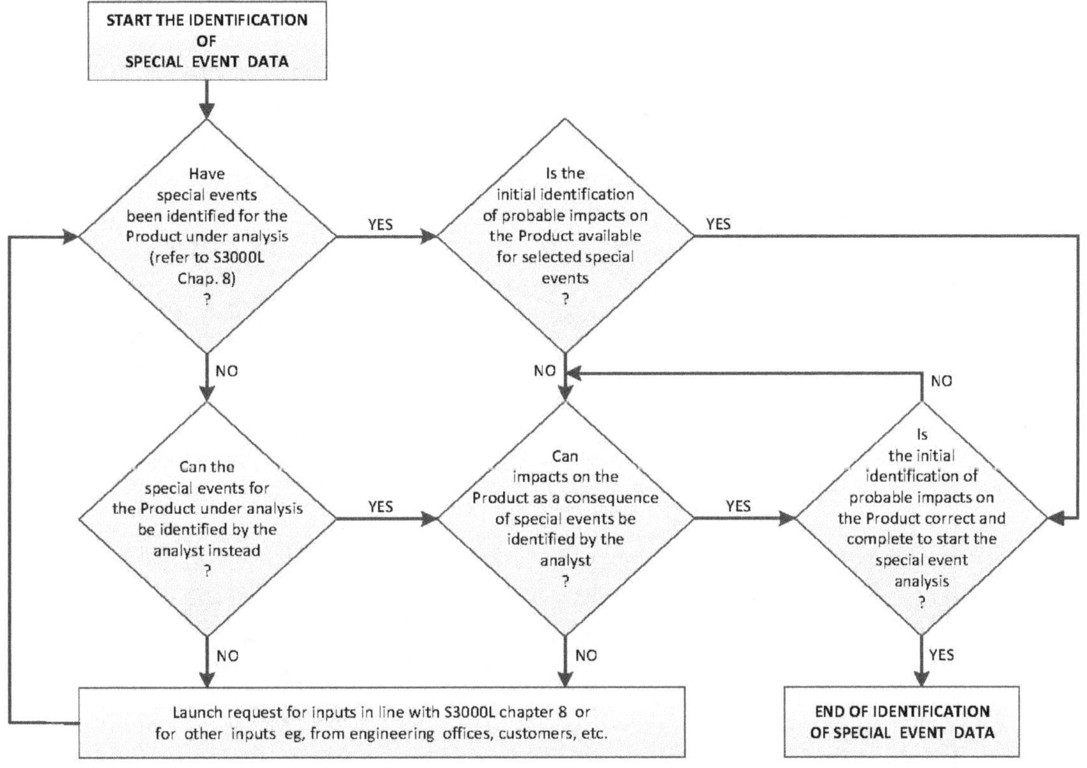

ICN-B6865-S4000P0071-001-01

Fig 1 Process for identifying special event data

3   PMTRE analysis process

Based on the process for identifying special event data (refer to Fig 1) **¡Error! No se encuentra el origen de la referencia.**the special events analysis process shown in Fig 2 and Fig 3 must be performed in order to determine the PMTRE for each special event.

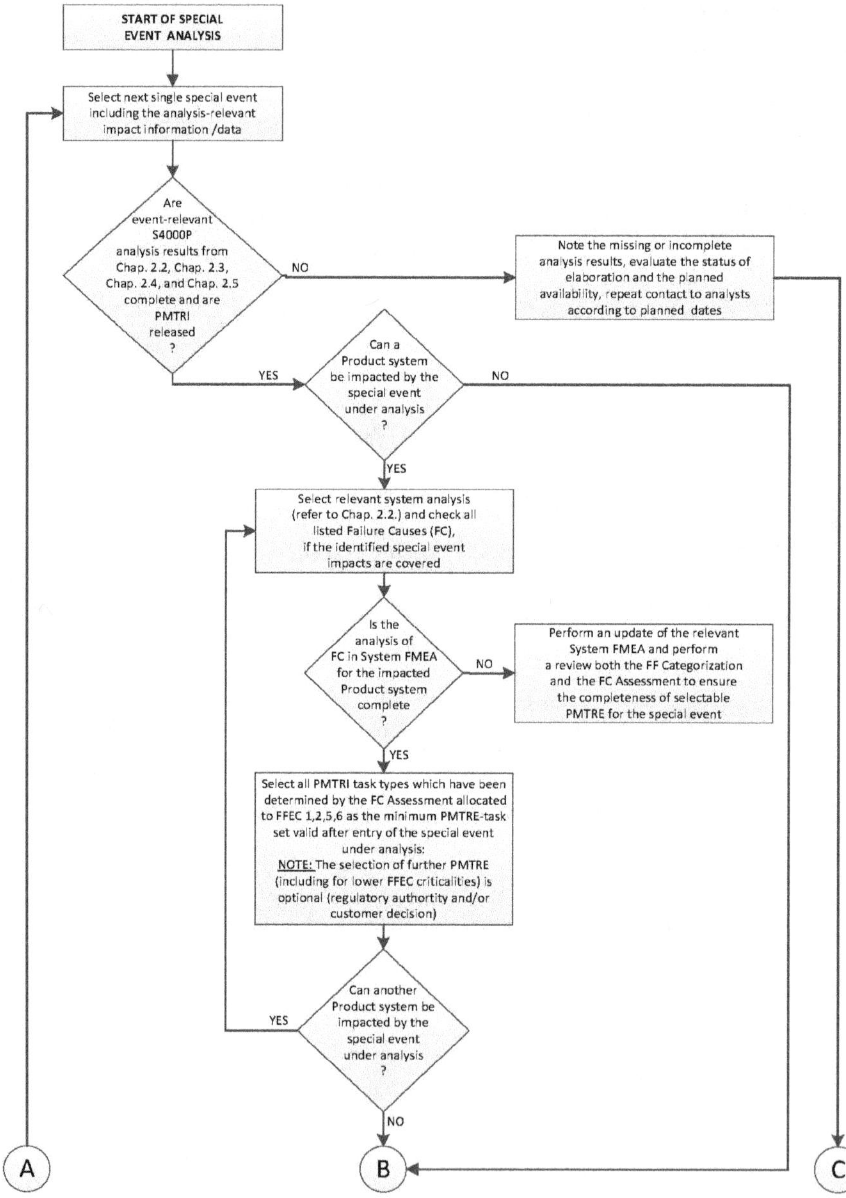

ICN-B6865-S4000P0072-001-01

Fig 2 Special event analysis (Sheet 1 of 2)

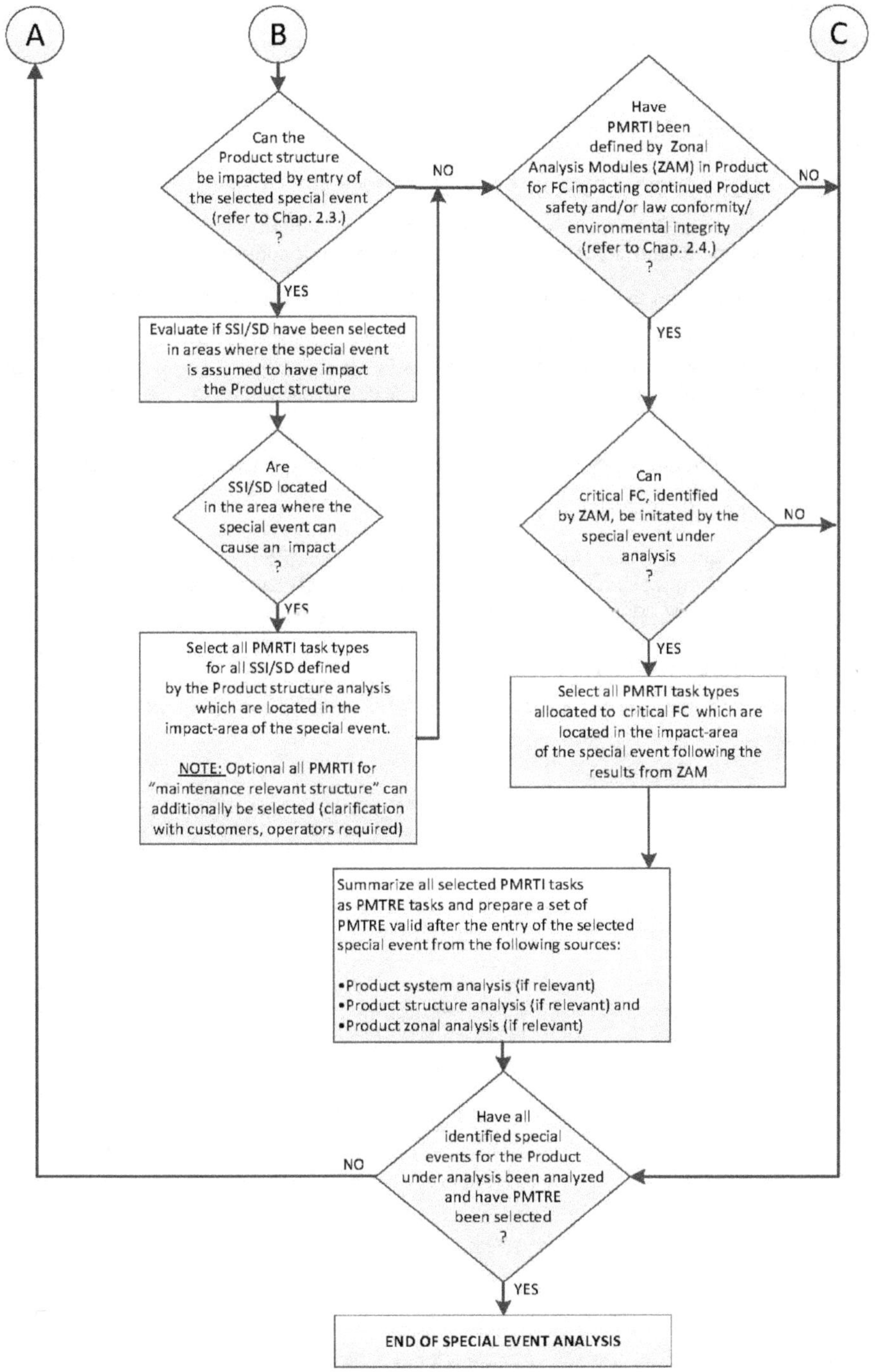

ICN-B6865-S4000P0073-001-01

Fig 3 Special event analysis (Sheet 2 of 2)

A single special event can cause:

- One or more Functional Failures (FF) on one or more Product systems
- One or more areas of damage on Product Structure
- Critical FF which are subject to the analysis in a ZAM of the Product zonal analysis methodology

Therefore, these aspects must be evaluated in sequence for each special event.

All PMTRE defined for special events are to be documented and processed in the S3000L data base to become a later input for the Product technical documentation according to S1000D.

Examples for special events and their impact on this special event analysis:

1. Collision of ship 1 into the rear section of ship 2 during a harbor maneuver. Depending on the location and intensity the incident, the forward section of ship 1 and the structure of the rear section of ship 2, can cause the propulsion system, etc, of ship 2 to become relevant for a special event analysis.

2. Impact of a volcano eruption and the air contamination on a flying jet aircraft. The Air Data System (ADS), jet engines, air condition systems, aircraft structure, etc, can become relevant for the special event analysis.

3. Mission flight of military aircraft through a contaminated environment (eg, due to nuclear particles, chemical/biological substances on air, etc). Several aircraft systems and all impacted zones can become relevant for the special event analysis.

4 PMTRE review process

The review and update process for PMTRE during the Product in-service phase is described in Chap 3.5.

End of data module

Chapter 3

Optimizing PMTR

Chapter	Data module title	Data module code	Applic
Chap 3.1	Optimizing PMTR - General	S4000P-A-03-01-0000-00A-040A-A	All
Chap 3.2	Optimizing PMTR - ISMO preparation phase	S4000P-A-03-02-0000-00A-040A-A	All
Chap 3.3	Optimizing PMTR - ISMO analysis phase	S4000P-A-03-03-0000-00A-040A-A	All
Chap 3.4	Optimizing PMTR - ISMO follow-up phase	S4000P-A-03-04-0000-00A-040A-A	All
Chap 3.5	Optimizing PMTR - Review of PMTRE for special events	S4000P-A-03-05-0000-00A-040A-A	All

Page intentionally blank.

Chapter 3.1

Optimizing PMTR - General

Table of contents

	Page
Optimizing PMTR - General	1
References	1
1 General	2
2 The ISMO process	2
3 ISMO process overview	7
4 Review of PMTRE	8

List of tables

1	References	1

List of figures

1	Development and continuous improvement of scheduled Product maintenance	3
2	Example with 2 ISMO analysis loops during the Product in-service phase	6
3	Overview on the ISMO process phases	8

References

Table 1 References

Chap No./Document No.	Title
Chap 1	Introduction to the specification
Chap 2	Developing PMTR
S1000D	International specification for technical publications using a common source database
S3000L	International procedure specification for Logistics Support Analysis - LSA
S5000F	International specification for operational and maintenance data feedback
vJAP(D) 100C-22	MILITARY AVIATION ENGINEERING - Guide To Developing And Sustaining Preventive Maintenance Programs (UK MoD)
UK DEF STAN 00-45	Using Reliability Centered Maintenance to Manage Engineering Failures Part 3: Guidance on the Application of Reliability Centered Maintenance

1 General

The optimization of Preventive Maintenance Task Requirements (PMTR) during the in-service phase of a Product is limited on the review and a subsequent optimization of PMTR (if necessary) described in this specification.

PMTR are either to be performed based on pre-defined repetitive scheduled intervals (PMTRI) or after an entry of a special event (PMTRE) that is outside the standard usage scenario of the Product and unknown when to happen.

The optimization of PMTRI is subject to the ISMO process described from Chap 3.2 thru Chap 3.4. A description and explanation of the ISMO preparation phase (Chap 3.2), followed by the ISMO analysis phase (Chap 3.3) and ends with the ISMO follow-up phase (Chap 3.4).

For the review of all PMTRE identified by the process in Chap 2.7, the process logic according to Chap 3.5 must be applied.

2 The ISMO process

The process for Product In-Service Maintenance Optimization (ISMO), described in this document, must be carried out on Products, Product systems or Product equipment with in-service experience available. The feedback from the Product in-service phase supports the improvement of existing scheduled maintenance tasks or maintenance program (Operators' Maintenance Program (OMP)) in the "as built and as maintained" Product configuration.

With an effective set of scheduled maintenance tasks and intervals documented in an operator/customer-specific OMP, unscheduled maintenance is also influenced. Therefore, the ISMO process optimizes the complete Product maintenance whether scheduled or unscheduled.

The steps in developing an OMP in accordance with Chap 2 (or another applicable specification), an ISMO Policy and Procedure Handbook (ISMO PPH) must be written for the individual Product prior to starting the analytical ISMO work. The ISMO PPH covers Product-specific needs.

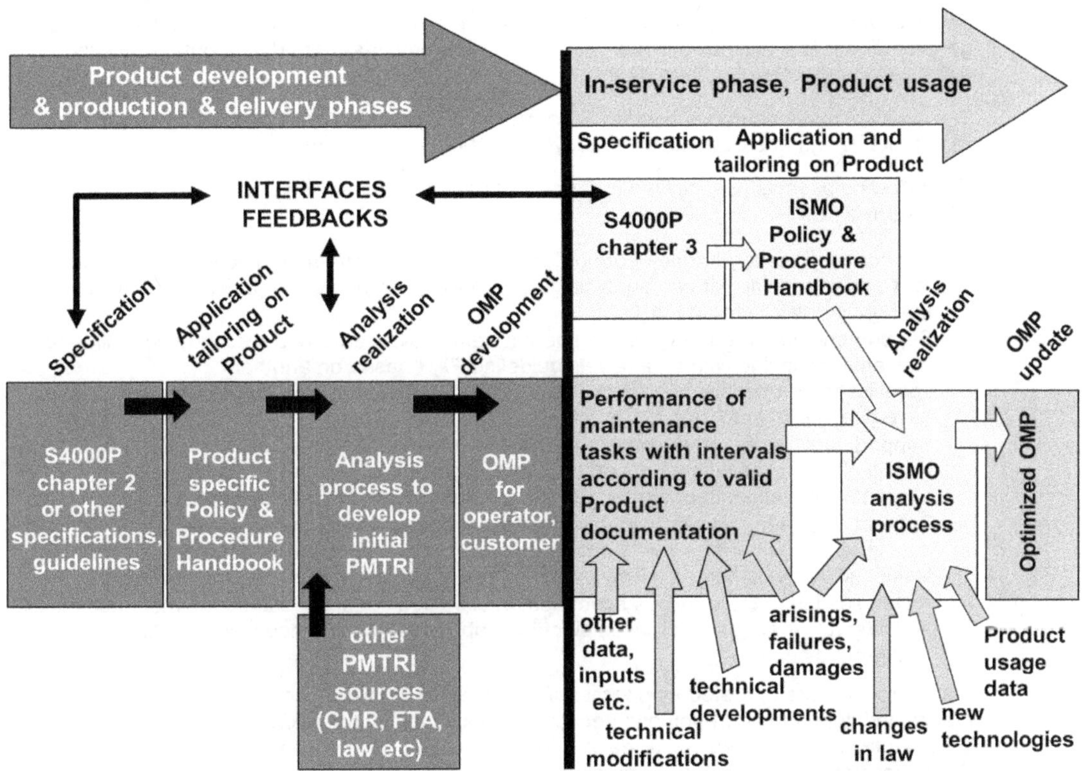

ICN-B6865-S4000P0074-001-01

Fig 1 Development and continuous improvement of scheduled Product maintenance

As shown in <u>Fig 1</u>, several information sources (technical inputs, data, experience, changes of (usage) parameters, new technologies, test results, etc.) can appear during the Product in-service phase. These sources are mainly based on in-service data/information from Product usage. These are necessary to determine, whether former analytical assumptions (eg, Best Engineering Judgement (BEJ)) and/or requirements (eg, PMTRI, Certification Maintenance Requirements (CMR)), which led to scheduled maintenance tasks or intervals in an OMP, can be confirmed, updated and/or completed. The ISMO analytical process works such as a test-bench for each single scheduled maintenance task with interval, and comprises questions and answers supported by reliable in-service experience.

This ISMO process is composed of logical sequential work steps and decisions leading to detailed recommendations on individual scheduled maintenance tasks and/or intervals. In addition to this logic, explanations and examples are provided for a better understanding of all process steps and decisions. Based on experience gained and lessons learned from several ISMO applications, a generic process variant has been introduced. This generic ISMO process is applicable on all complex technical Products but it must be extended to make it a project specific ISMO PPH.

It is recommended that a pilot ISMO process be developed after enough in-service experience is accumulated. The more maintenance task-specific in-service experience available, the higher the probability is to achieve a better ISMO result for each maintenance task under analysis. In-service data and experience from both Product usage and Product maintenance must be used.

The availability of in-service data is not a decisive prerequisite for starting an ISMO process in general. The ISMO logic also works with small or missing in-service data/inputs. However, the optimization potential can be reduced.

The ISMO process can be applied to Products with different histories and backgrounds related to Product design and development, as well as OMP developments.

The following aspects possibly led to, or had influence on scheduled maintenance tasks and intervals in an OMP:

- Support engineering or engineering departments have performed a scheduled maintenance task analysis in line with an analysis guideline/PPH given in Chap 2. Results have been kept up to date. Refer to Fig 1.
- Support engineering or engineering departments have performed a scheduled maintenance task analysis in line with an analysis guideline/PPH based on another specification/procedure handbook (eg, JAP(D) 100C-22, UK DEF STAN 00-45). Results have been kept up to date.
- Support engineering or engineering departments have performed a scheduled maintenance task analysis in line with an accepted analysis guideline/PPH but this dataset is not available, not valid, out of date and/or does not allow any traceability, etc
- Support engineering was not involved during Product development or scheduled maintenance task analysis was not performed. For example, all scheduled maintenance tasks and intervals have exclusively been determined by engineering based on BEJ.
- A combination of the previous scenarios resulted in a set of scheduled maintenance tasks and intervals that has no or insufficient traceability of maintenance task/interval backgrounds

Many Products are operated by operators/customers worldwide. These Products must be maintained during their on-going in-service phases. In all cases valid and updated documentation is the baseline for each ISMO application. This documentation can contain deviations from one operator/customer to another.

A scheduled maintenance task with intervals written in an OMP is based on at least one of the following sources:

- Requirements from authorities including law-based requirements, CMR, etc
- Predictions by equipment manufacturers sometimes interconnected with warranty-background
- PMTRI resulting from analysis activities of a Product responsible manufacturer
- BEJ by provided by Product engineering departments

Based on a Product ISMO PPH/analysis guideline, PMTRI of the following maintenance tasks types can be defined:

- Servicing (eg, wash, clean, lubricate, preserve)
- Inspection tests and/or /functional checks
- Replacement (Time Change Items (TCI) /overhaul)

The analyst defines the maintenance task type (eg, detailed inspection) and an appropriate interval type plus a numerical interval value for each PMTRI, (eg, 200 start cycles).

For analysis purposes the analyst uses all available development data, prototype test results/experience and other technical information.

PMTRI must identify and/or eliminate Failure Causes (FC) leading to potential Product Functional Failure Effects (FFE).

Potential FFE at the Product level are as follows:

1   Safety can be impaired. If there is an impact on continued Product operational safety including the involvement of personnel during maintenance activities.

2   Environmental integrity/law conformity can be impaired. If there is an impact on environmental integrity including law conformity during Product operation or mission.

3   Operational or mission availability can be impaired. If there is an impact on the specified Product operational or mission availability.

4   Economy/costs can be impaired. If there is an impact on Product economy resulting in increased Life Cycle Costs (LCC).

If PMTRI are linked to FFE allocated to items 1 and 2 above, then continued Product safety, environmental integrity and/or law conformity can be impacted. Authorities, responsible for Product certification, will review these PMTRI by preference and approve these PMTRI.

An operator/customer focuses on PMTRI allocated to items 3 and 4. Customers require or appreciate a reduction of FC to increase operational or mission availability and/or Life Cycle Costs (LCC), which can be fixed by, for example, a Performance Based Logistic (PBL) contract between individual customers and Product manufactures. In such cases the manufacturer will insist on the performance of identified PMTRI having operational or mission and/or cost impacts. Without existing PBL/contractual constraints, every Product operator/customer can adjust PMTRI allocated to items 3 and 4 within their own responsibility because Product certification is not impacted.

Having gained approval by the authorities and supplemented, where required, with further scheduled maintenance tasks with intervals (eg, maintenance tasks/intervals from safety analysis, legal requirements, manufacturer and design requirements), the resulting scheduled maintenance tasks with intervals are defined in an OMP. Refer to S1000D.

The OMP becomes valid for the customer/operator starting with the Product in-service phase.

It is recognized that, during a Product in-service phase, further scheduled maintenance tasks with intervals will be added in an OMP. For all FFE of scheduled maintenance tasks, the numerical interval values can be reduced within a limited frame by customers (eg, reduction from 14 months to 12 months). In most cases, the effort for Product maintenance increases during its in-service phase. This can have an impact on the Product's LCC.

This structured ISMO analytical process identifies various recommendations on each scheduled maintenance task with interval under analysis (eg, maintenance task deletion, interval extension, maintenance task replacement) with justification for each recommendation given. The ISMO process structure guarantees that the approach of different analysts is harmonized based on a common analysis process logic.

Industry experience is that the ISMO process results in a significant lowering of in-service maintenance effort without an increase of certification-relevant risks and without a reduction of Product availability.

By considering new analysis methodologies, new maintenance technologies, in-service experience when performing the analytical work during the Product life cycle, ISMO also contributes to lowering the certification-relevant risks and to improving the Product availability for mission/operation.

<u>Fig 2</u> shows the optimization principle of the ISMO process for a Product during its in-service phase based on two ISMO analytical-loops after starting the Product in-service phase.

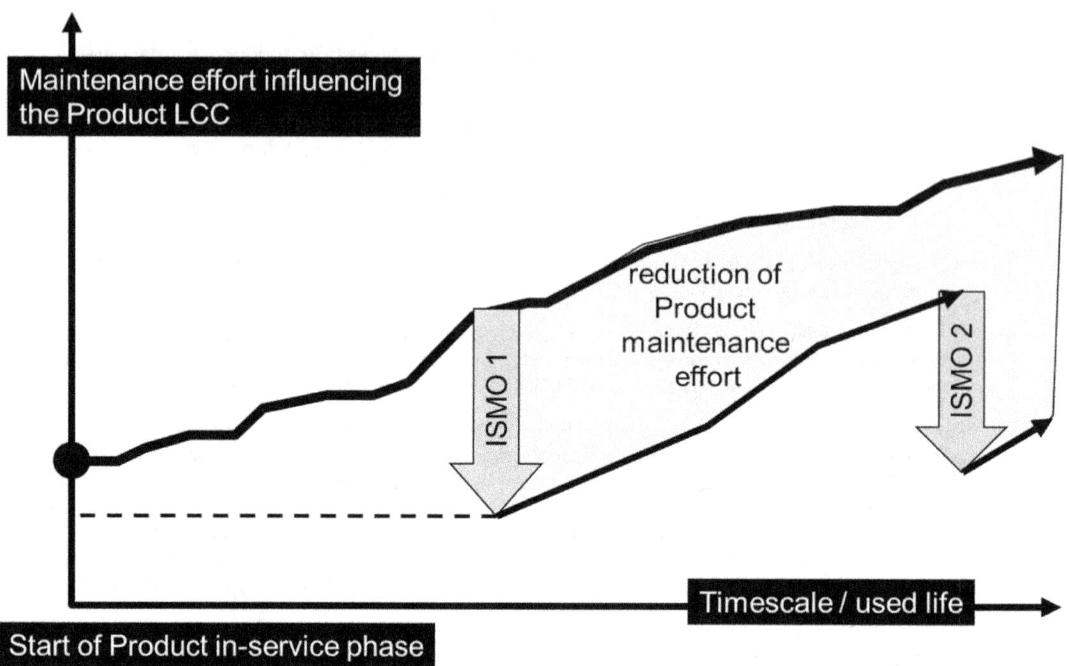

ICN-B6865-S4000P0075-001-01

Fig 2 Example with 2 ISMO analysis loops during the Product in-service phase

An ISMO process must be performed more than once during the Product in-service phase. The setup of an initial ISMO analysis loop after the start of an in-service phase consumes the major preparation and analytical effort. These initial investigations are the pre-requisite to performing later ISMO analysis loops on the whole Product or on selected parts of the Product breakdown.

Because maintenance task decisions and/or interval definitions are more conservative at the early period of Product usage, experience shows that the initial ISMO loop provides a high potential for optimization. Therefore, the resulting maintenance effort can be significantly lowered after finishing this initial ISMO loop. A second ISMO analysis as shown in Fig 2 and subsequent ISMO analyses, are based on and can refer to the initial ISMO preparation work.

Deviating from a repetitive application of ISMO analysis loops, an ongoing ISMO process provides the best case for the Product integrity management of a Product fleet. That means that every intended change of the OMP should be checked on basis of the ISMO analysis logic prior to its implementation into the OMP.

The main scope of the ISMO process includes:

- Reduction of risks that could lead to certification-relevant consequences (including Product safety)
- Ensuring that environmental integrity and the conformity with national laws are adhered to increase Product availability
- Reduction of Product LCC
- Applicability on all Products independent from their development history
- Applicability on all Products independent from in-service data/experience background

- Applicability on all Products independent from the organisational situation (eg, no contact to Product manufacturer, low manufacturer inputs or other Product user data available on demand or not)
- Applicability on all types of Products (airborne, on/under the ground, on/under sea, outer space)
- Integration and use of former analytical data (eg, from an initial preventive maintenance analysis)
- Integration and use of in-service data inputs from S5000F and other in-service information/knowledge available
- Provision of a traceability between existing analytical background data and the valid maintenance tasks documented in an OMP of a Product
- Creation of a data base prior to, and during the ISMO analytical process for optimizing all scheduled maintenance tasks with intervals which will be used throughout the remaining Product in-service life for further ISMO analysis loops
- Approval and/or compensation of missing criticality categories selected as one Functional Failure Effect Code (FFEC) per scheduled maintenance task with interval
- Evaluation of potential changes in a Product usage scenario compared to the former assumptions during design and development, to check the impacts on scheduled maintenance tasks and intervals for those changes
- Evaluation of new knowledge in scheduled maintenance task analysis methodology including a check of consequences on scheduled maintenance for the Product
- Investigation on the completeness of the preventive maintenance task analysis on Product configurations and Product variants
- Coverage of different usage scenarios in national and multinational Product development
- Coverage of customer/operator specific Product maintenance programs/OMP with different usage scenarios and/or environmental conditions
- Product design changes, configuration differences (eg, individual repairs for customer/operator)
- Provision of a clear and traceable output of all recommendations with justifications during ISMO analysis ready for approval and acceptance
- Provision of an updated PMTRI data list/file for a further data exchange/transfer with/to the Product supportability database (refer to S3000L) as data output from every ISMO analysis

3   ISMO process overview

The ISMO process consists of the following three main phases:

- Phase 1 - ISMO preparation phase
- Phase 2 - ISMO analysis phase
- Phase 3 - ISMO follow-up phase

At the end of the ISMO preparation phase, the identified set of valid scheduled maintenance tasks with intervals must be complete and sufficient background information for each single scheduled maintenance task must be collected. The data and information of the updated Master Task List (MTL) are important pre-requisites for every analyst to be able to perform the subsequent work during the ISMO analysis phase.

Note:
> The ISMO analysis phase can be started for those Product systems, structure or zones where all analysis-relevant data have been collected and completed during the ISMO preparation phase.

Phase 3 is not directly dependent on the period of performance of the ISMO analysis phase. This phase can run in parallel to the ISMO analysis phase or can be performed at a later stage. Phase 3 can be used to permanently monitor the in-service data for unscheduled anomalies on items where scheduled maintenance is not yet identified.

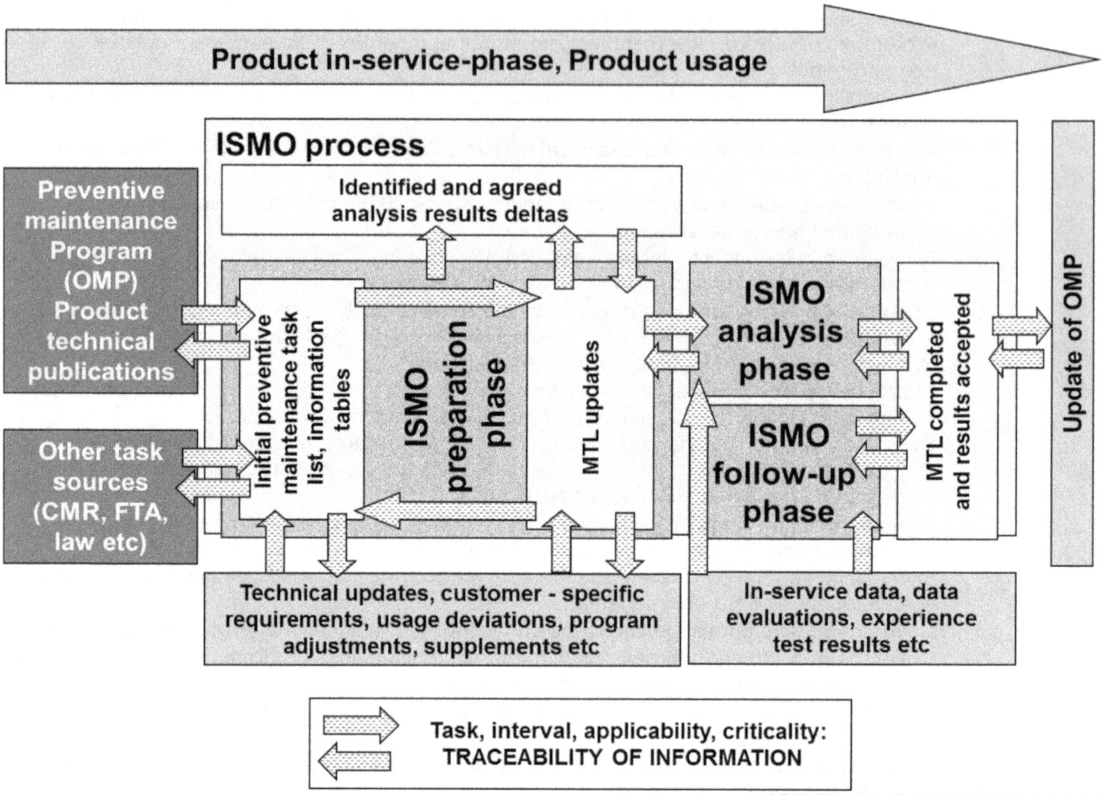

ICN-B6865-S4000P0076-001-01

Fig 3 Overview of the ISMO process phases

It is essential that a verification of every maintenance task FFEC be performed as part of the ISMO process. If there are any discrepancy between the maintenance task FFEC and the Product design safety case, appropriate actions must be taken by the Product-responsible industry.

When an FFEC is missing, not known or not allocated to a scheduled maintenance task, an applicable criticality must be defined during the ISMO analytical process.

If there is any doubt or missing knowledge, the ISMO analyst must decide for the next higher criticality level of the FFEC fail safe assumption.

4   Review of PMTRE

As described in Chap 2.7, single PMTRE or sets of PMTRE are developed on basis of the results from the different analytical methodologies described in Chap 2.3 thru Chap 2.5.

The results from the guidelines describing the PMTRI consolidation and harmonization must also be considered to determine PMTRE for special events. Refer to Chap 2.6.

PMTRE are not linked to any repetitive scheduled interval but to one or more special events where the occurrence is unknown. Before any special event, real or expected, that can impact a Product occurs, the analysis for one or more applicable and effective PMTRE must be carried out and the tasks defined and allocated accordingly. PMTRE must also be described in the OMP.

The scope of a review of selected PMTRE is:

- to check if existing PMTRE or sets of PMTRE are incomplete and must be extended by one or more additional PMTRE for an expected special event
- to check if single PMTRE can be deleted and/or replaced; because experience showed that these are not applicable and/or not effective
- to start the special event analysis for PMTRE for every new/additional special event that has appeared or can appear during the future Product in-service phase

Page intentionally blank.

Chapter 3.2

Optimizing PMTR - ISMO preparation phase

Table of contents

Page

Optimizing PMTR - ISMO preparation phase 1

References 1

1   Introduction 1

2   Process logic of ISMO preparation 2

3   Description of process logic of ISMO preparation 5

List of tables

1   References 1

2   Scheduled maintenance task check table 8

List of figures

1   ISMO analysis preparation (Sheet 1 of 3) 3

2   ISMO analysis preparation (Sheet 2 of 3) 4

3   ISMO analysis preparation (Sheet 3 of 3) 5

References

Table 1 References

Chap No./Document No.	Title
Chap 2	Developing PMTR
Chap 3.3	Optimizing PMTR - ISMO analysis phase
Chap 3.4	Optimizing PMTR - ISMO follow-up phase
Chap 6	Terms, abbreviations and acronyms
S1000D	International specification for technical publications using a common source database

1   Introduction

The process of the In-Service Maintenance Optimization (ISMO) preparation examines if an analytical basis for the valid maintenance tasks with repetitive scheduled intervals exists and if the procedural aspect of that analytical basis for PMTRI can be judged as technically correct and up to date current.

Any deficits identified in the analytical PMTRI development process lead to the determination of subsequent analysis activities where needed. Where parts of the analytical PMTRI development process do not exist or cannot be verified, subsequent analysis activities must be examined for areas of potential compensation. This can be supported by utilizing extensive operating

experience with the Product under analysis. In this context, Failure Causes (FC) with potentially safety-relevant Functional Failure Effect Code (FFEC) should be determined using the analytical approach must be considered. In these cases, it is not appropriate to wait for the Functional Failure Effect (FFE) to occur during the Product in-service phase.

All valid maintenance tasks with repetitive scheduled intervals must be identified and collected to:

1   prepare the Master Task List (MTL) which must comprise all maintenance tasks with repetitive scheduled intervals valid for the Product with additional data from manufacturer/OEM/customer/user

2   review validity of the individual scheduled maintenance tasks with respect to the present configuration of the Product fleet

3   examine the applicability of every individual scheduled maintenance task for the Product serial numbers of the Product fleet

The ISMO analysis preparation develops and creates all data and parameters necessary for the analysts to conduct the later ISMO analysis process according to this specification.

The ISMO analysis preparation comprises:

−   comparison of analysis process and the analysis methodology originally used for the Product with known scheduled maintenance task analysis standards in industry. Refer to Chap 2.
−   evaluation of additional analysis effort for functional systems, structure and/or zones of the Product
−   checking whether revised or new documents, legal requirements, etc, are relevant for analysis
−   collecting cross-reference data that enables traceability between individual maintenance tasks with repetitive scheduled intervals defined in the technical documentation and the PMTRI analyses roots or other scheduled maintenance task/interval sources
−   merging all cross-reference lists/data into an MTL that enables a complete overview of all maintenance tasks with repetitive scheduled intervals based on the Product documentation that is allocated to items/equipment of the Product systems, structure and zones including. the task/interval source/history
−   determination of analyst workshare for the ISMO analysis process taking into account the design responsibility of the system, item or zone under analysis
−   establishing working groups, meeting structures, definition and implementation of reporting structure, if necessary
−   defining and coordinating tasks to manage communication, responsibilities, etc, between Product manufacturer, equipment manufacturers and regulatory authorities, etc

2   Process logic of ISMO preparation

The logic diagrams show the individual process **Steps** (S) and the **Decisions** (D) numbered consecutively.

The process steps and decisions are detailed in Para 3.

The steps and decisions in the process logic are given an alphanumeric code **VYZZ** where:

−   **V** - gives the code for preparation
−   **Y** - gives the Step S or Decision D
−   **ZZ** - is a number, ascending from 01 to 99

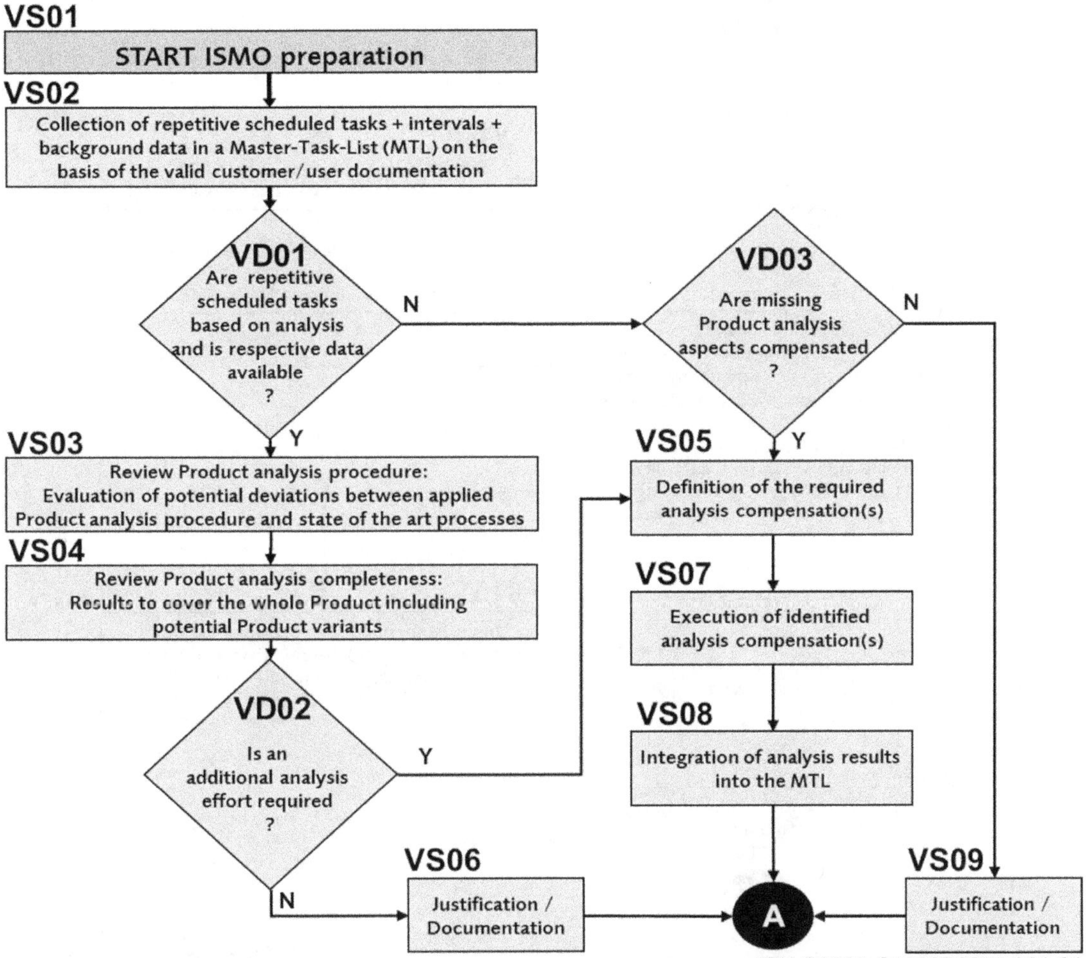

ICN-B6865-S4000P0077-001-01

Fig 1 ISMO analysis preparation (Sheet 1 of 3)

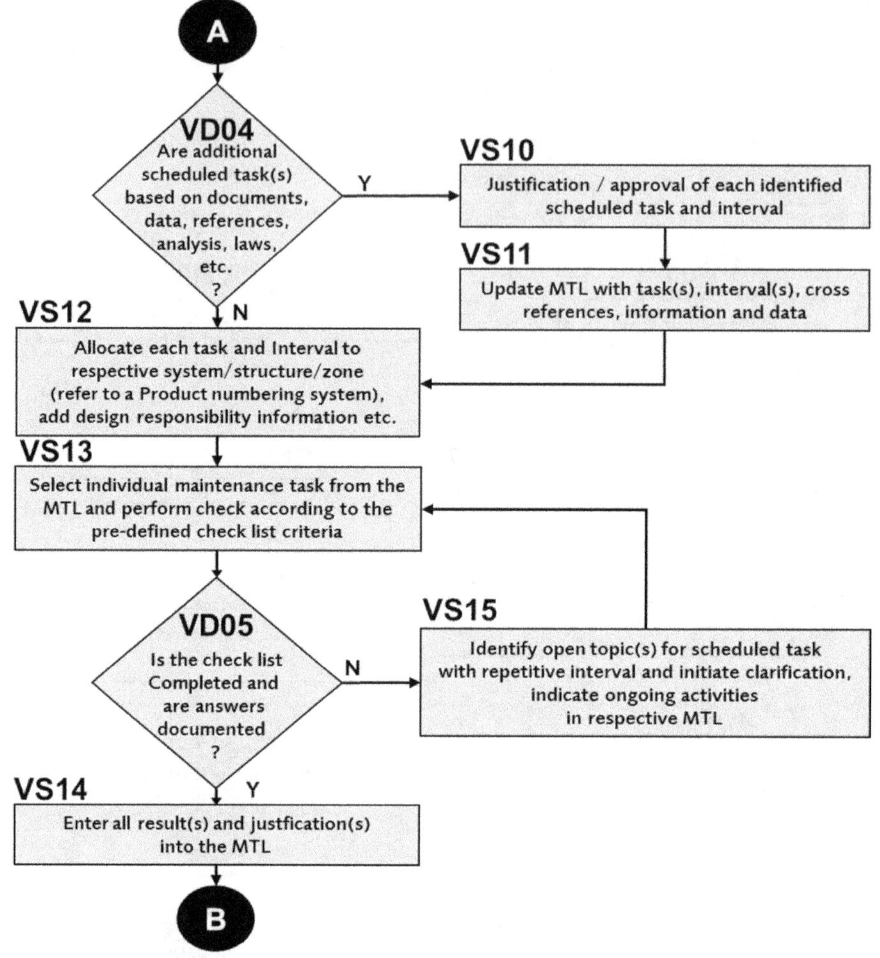

ICN-B6865-S4000P0078-001-01

Fig 2 ISMO analysis preparation (Sheet 2 of 3)

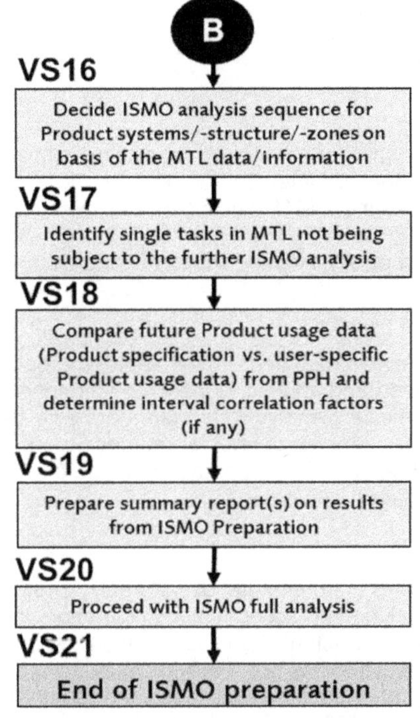

ICN-B6865-S4000P0079-001-0

Fig 3 ISMO analysis preparation (Sheet 3 of 3)

3 Description of process logic of ISMO preparation

This paragraph describes the working **Steps** (S) and the **Decisions** (D) of the logic used during the ISMO preparation.

Note

In answering decision questions, the following principle applies:

- A conservative decision must be taken if there is a lack of information/data, ambiguity or doubt. In these cases, the decision must be made in favour of greater preparation work (eg, decision in favour of conducting further analysis).

VS01:

The ISMO analysis preparation is a logic module that must be processed independently and before commencing the ISMO analysis process.

The ISMO analysis preparation is intended to ensure that all PMTRI required for the operating safety, law conformity/environmental integrity, availability and economy of technically complex Products are collected and completed with analysis relevant background information for all analysis-relevant Product systems, structure and zones.

VS02:

All maintenance tasks with their valid repetitive scheduled intervals that are predicted by the Product documentation and other sources must be listed in an MTL. It is recommended that an IT tool or software support the analytical work on basis of the MTL. All the maintenance tasks with repetitive scheduled intervals must be allocated to the functional subsystems of the Product using the Standard Numbering Systems (SNS) from S1000D. Analysis-relevant background

---

information for the single maintenance tasks must be documented in the MTL (eg, task sources such as PMTRI, Certification Maintenance Requirement (CMR), FFEC, priority level due to in-service experience, etc).

VD01:

This question clarifies, whether an analytical baseline is available for existing maintenance tasks with repetitive scheduled intervals for the Product.
If a baseline with PMTRI in the MTL exists (Answer YES), refer to Chap 2 and continue with VS03 and VS04.
If no analytical baseline exists (Answer NO), continue with VD03.

VS03:

The analysis process review examines which analysis process from which analysis methodology was defined and applied to the Product during its design and development phase. More recent issues of existing analysis standards or newly developed analysis methods can show considerable improvements over older methods, particularly with respect to certification of relevant aspects. Such advances in approach must be taken into account during the comparison of analysis methodologies.

VS04:

This process step reviews the completeness of analysis and results during the development of PMTRI for a Product, taking into account all configuration variants. All Product systems/sub-systems with equipment, Structure Significant Items (SSI) and the Product zones must either be covered by analysis or justified as non-analysis relevant system, structure and/or zone. For analysis exceptions a set of maintenance tasks and repetitive scheduled intervals can, for example be predicted by OEM, authorities, etc. Any analysis deficits must be identified and documented.

VD02:

After performing work steps VS03 and VS04 supplementary analysis can be performed.
If supplementary analyses are necessary (Answer YES), continue with VS05.
If not (Answer NO), continue with VS06.

VD03:

If no analytical justification for maintenance tasks with repetitive scheduled intervals exists (eg, defined based on Best Engineering Judgement (BEJ)), it must be determined and decided as to whether a complete or a reduced analysis compensation is required to determine PMTRI. Refer to Chap 2. If a complete analysis is required, Product systems, structure and zones are analysed, in a similar way to an initial PMTRI analysis during a Product design and development phase. Depending on the decision of involved authorities and/or manufacturer, the analysis compensation can be limited.
A reduced Product analysis, in contrast to a new and complete analysis, must cover at least all FC with an FFEC related to safety-relevant Functional Failures (FF). This procedure covers the minimum certification-relevant FFEC. PMTRI and/or redesign recommendations must be defined.
An analysis guideline or PPH for the complete or reduced analysis must be prepared by the manufacturer and approved by the responsible authorities prior to starting the analytical work.
In additional analytical effort is identified (Answer YES), continue with VS05 and VS06.
If additional analytical effort is not required (Answer NO), continue with VS09.

VS05:

If the requirement for a supplementary analysis requirement is identified, the scope and detailed approach is to be determined and documented. Involved authorities approve and release the documented analytical approach prior to the analysis work can start.

VS06:

If an analytical basis exists and is judged to be complete and in- line with the most current analysis methodologies of PMTRI development, no supplementary PMTRI analysis is necessary. The review of the decision must be documented with justifications.

VS07:

Perform identified analysis activities decided according to VS05.

VS08:

After performing the compensating analysis, the MTL for the Product is to be reviewed as to:

- Whether the PMTRI determined by analysis is already listed. If the scheduled maintenance task already exists, the previous categorisation of that maintenance task must be compared with the analysis results associated with the potential FFE and must be corrected where necessary. The higher critical FFEC must be selected by the analyst when in doubt. If a PMTRI developed by analysis is not in the list, the list must be amended to include this PMTRI along with the interval and the FFEC identified in the supplementary analytical work.
- Whether the PMTRI determined by supplementary analysis agree with the intervals of the existing scheduled maintenance tasks in the MTL. If not, the differences/deviations must be identified and noted in the MTL.

VS09:

As no analytical baseline exists and no complete or reduced analysis is required, the examination result/decision must be documented with justifications.

VD04:

Whether further PMTRI that are not included in the MTL based on step VS08 are valid, must be determined. Further relevant PMTRI can be based on for example, the operating experience of customers/users of comparable Products. Changes in legal bases (eg, new national environmental or occupational safety regulations) can lead to additional PMTRI and/or Certification Maintenance Requirements (CMR), which must be added to the MTL.
If further PMTRI/CMR become relevant or will become relevant for the Product (Answer YES), continue with VS10.
If not (Answer NO), continue with VS12.

VS10:

Identified PMTRI/CMR must be added to the respective Product breakdown element of the MTL (refer to S1000D). The sources of PMTRI/CMR must be determined and documented in the MTL.

VS11:

The PMTRI/CMR identified in the previous step VS10 must be documented in the MTL for the affected Product system, structure or zone including all background information available. When potential differences concerning legislation from one customer or user to another occur, be aware that deviations of identified maintenance tasks with repetitive scheduled intervals can occur.

VS12:

At this step, the MTL contains all maintenance tasks with their repetitive scheduled intervals plus any interval threshold from valid Product documentation and the task source or history (ie, PMTRI) for analysis during the subsequent ISMO analysis process.
The MTL clarifies which individual scheduled maintenance task is valid for which configurations of the Product system, subsystem, equipment and/or item.
Additionally, information about the design responsibility, the ISMO analysis relevance or exclusion and the analyst responsibility is allocated to each scheduled maintenance task in accordance to the System Breakdown Code (SBC) in the MTL.

VS13:

Single scheduled maintenance tasks listed in the MTL are not always prepared for being an ISMO analysis task in the ISMO analysis process.

In these cases, questions Q1 thru Q6 must be answered for each scheduled maintenance task to clarify its availability for analysis. Table 2 contains these questions which, together with their answers must be documented in the project-specific ISMO guideline/PPH.

Table 2 Scheduled maintenance task check table

No	Question	Remark
Q1	Is the scheduled maintenance task still applicable for the Product fleet operated by the customer/user or is this maintenance task limited to a subset of the fleet? For example, performed on single Product serial numbers only.	Check whether the maintenance task is valid and applicable in terms of the valid configuration- and build standard. Individual maintenance task that do not apply to the configuration of the Product fleet must be documented in the MTL. This individual maintenance task is to be marked for exclusion from the further maintenance task analysis.
Q2	Is the scheduled maintenance task listed as a single maintenance task available for later analysis or is it part of, for example, a maintenance task combination or a maintenance task mixture?	For example, the combination of a wash task and a lubrication task at a certain scheduled interval is a maintenance task mixture that can be separated into a wash task and a lubricate task.
Q3	Does a scheduled maintenance task package (eg, a Zonal Inspection) contain safety-relevant subtasks, or have such maintenance tasks been transferred into that maintenance task package?	Maintenance task packages that comprise a set of individual maintenance tasks, must be separated according to the following basic rule: Every safety, law or environmental integrity-relevant maintenance task within a maintenance task package must be taken out of that package and included in the MTL as a standalone maintenance task with its own interval under the corresponding functional Product system, structure, or zone and with correct FFEC allocation.
Q4	Does the maintenance task under analysis have a repetitive scheduled interval?	Maintenance tasks without repetitive scheduled intervals are not subjected to the ISMO analysis process (eg, a maintenance task that becomes relevant only at one time when a Product is modified.

No	Question	Remark
Q5	Is the interval for the scheduled maintenance task without limitations or thresholds?	It is known that selected scheduled maintenance tasks have been introduced, for example, by engineering departments specifically to gain additional experience during the initial Product in-service phase only. Structural items can be inspected after a certain interval threshold for the first time. Any inspection before the threshold is expected to be not effective. Knowledge of these issues support the later ISMO analysis process and contribute to the reduction of maintenance effort.
Q6	Has the scheduled maintenance task been determined based on a CMR Safety/Fault-Tree Analysis (FTA) or has the maintenance task been dictated by law, etc?	Information about the maintenance task source (eg, from safety, law, etc) supports the correct categorization of the maintenance task criticality with a correct FFEC allocation.

The questions in Table 2 are not always answered immediately for each scheduled maintenance task listed in an MTL.
Open questions or unclear aspects must be highlighted in the MTL and can be answered at a later stage in the ISMO process.
Question 1 thru Question 4 must be answered prior to the maintenance task and/or interval analysis in the subsequent ISMO analysis process.
Question 5 and Question 6 can be answered if the information is available.
If a task is not a maintenance task (eg, an organisational task), the ISMO analysis process is not applicable and stops for that task under analysis.

VD05:

If, at least Question 1 thru Question 4 according to VS13 have been checked and answered, the individual maintenance task with repetitive scheduled interval is available for the ISMO analysis process.
In this case (Answer YES), continue with VS14.
If not (Answer NO), continue with VS15.

VS14:

The results of all analyses carried out in VD05 must be documented in the MTL.

VS15:

When ongoing clarifications related to Question 1 thru Question 4 in VD05 are required the scheduled maintenance task is not available for the ISMO analysis phase and if the task is a system-related scheduled maintenance task, the analysis of the allocated Product system must be postponed. This status must be tracked in the MTL.

VS16:

When the analyst indicates that the MTL is completed for the Product system under analysis, the Product structure or the Product zone, commencement of the ISMO analysis phase can be decided. To support the selection-sequence of Product systems for ISMO analysis, the MTL must contain information about the level of impact on individual Product systems, the overall Product availability and/or on Life Cycle Cost (LCC). Depending on the Product maintenance philosophy, a distinction at least between high impact, medium impact and low impact is recommended.

VS17:

All maintenance tasks with or without repetitive scheduled intervals which do not fulfill the criteria for the ISMO analysis phase must be clearly marked in the MTL. Those maintenance tasks are later candidates for deletion or documentation in separate Product documentation. Hence, the ISMO preparation reduces the effort for ISMO analysis in advance.

VS18:

The determination of PMTRI for the initial maintenance program/OMP is based on the original Product use study giving information about the planned usage scenario. This scenario was specified for the Product design with its subsystems, equipment components, structural items and zones.

The customer usage of the Product in its future in-service phase can deviate from the original development assumptions. This information must be documented in the ISMO PPH.

In this step, differences must be determined and potential impacts on an individual scheduled maintenance task must be documented in the MTL. Based on this, decisions must be made during the ISMO analysis phase in respect of the retention or change of intervals and interval relations at least for the safety-relevant and law/environmental integrity related individual maintenance tasks, depending on the Product's usage.

VS19:

To document all decisions and results collected during the ISMO analysis preparation a common report must be prepared and made available.

VS20:

For this step, the detailed ISMO analysis process for PMTRI with the analysis sequence determined in VS16 is started. In the ISMO analysis process, individual scheduled maintenance tasks based on the validity of the Product documentation and/or other relevant sources are subjected to a detailed analysis.

VS21:

The ISMO preparation has been conducted.

If PMTRI are identified and are not listed in the MTL at the end of this ISMO preparation, those maintenance tasks must be analyzed at a later project stage.

Note

If the analysis methodology for developing PMTRI changes, a part of this process shown in the logic decisions VD01 to VD03 with the related works steps VS03 to VS09 must be reviewed.

Chapter 3.3

Optimizing PMTR - ISMO analysis phase

Table of contents

Page

Optimizing PMTR - ISMO analysis phase 1

References...1

1   Introduction 1

2   Process logic overview ISMO analysis..2

3   Process logic of ISMO analysis 3

4   Description of the generic process logic for ISMO analysis 10

List of tables

1   References 1

List of figures

1   Overview/links of analysis modules for the ISMO analysis process 3

2   ISMO maintenance task criticality and applicability analysis 4

3   ISMO servicing task analysis..5

4   ISMO inspection or functional test task analysis (SSI-inspections and zonal inspections excluded) 6

5   ISMO time change item or overhaul task analysis 7

6   ISMO SSI/SD task analysis 8

7   ISMO zonal inspection task analysis..9

8   ISMO interval and trend leader analysis 10

References

Table 1 References

Chap No./Document No.	Title
Chap 3.2	Optimizing PMTR - ISMO preparation phase
DIN Norm 31 051/(DIN/EN 13306)	Maintenance Terminology

1   Introduction

The In-Service Maintenance Optimization (ISMO) analysis process contains a detailed analysis for individual maintenance tasks with repetitive scheduled intervals based on a valid Product documentation. These maintenance tasks must be identified with information completed in the Master Task List (MTL) during the ISMO preparation.

The methodology of this ISMO analytical logic supports the detailed analysis of every repetitive scheduled maintenance task from valid documents of the Product under analysis. These tasks

can be based on Preventive Maintenance Task Requirements with repetitive scheduled Intervals (PMTRI), CMR or on other sources such as Best Engineering Judgement (BEJ).

To satisfy the requirements from Product certification this methodology therefore covers the detailed analysis of:

- certification-relevant scheduled servicing tasks
- certification-relevant scheduled inspections and functional tests
- certification-relevant scheduled replacements (Time Change Items (TCI)) or overhauls
- Scheduled inspections on each Structural Significant Item (SSI) or on every Significant Detail (SD) on an SSI

The ISMO analysis process follows a uniform, comprehensible decision logic which introduces or validates the following aspects for each individual repetitive scheduled maintenance task:

- Criticality categorization (Functional Failure Effect (FFE)) of the Failure Cause (FC) to which a scheduled maintenance task (including each BEJ task) is related
- Remove safety-relevant individual General Visual Inspections (GVI) on items/equipment from zonal inspections. Standalone scheduled maintenance tasks must be created
- Detailed analysis of the different types of scheduled maintenance tasks including inspections or functional tests on SSI/SD and zonal inspections
- Determination of any interval threshold per scheduled maintenance task that the Product documentation does not take into account
- Harmonization of interval types in accordance with international specifications (refer to DIN Norm 31 051 (DIN/EN 13306))
- Integration of current in-service experience from Product maintenance including the effectiveness of the individual scheduled maintenance tasks
- Integration of further sources related to applicable in-service- and test-feedback
- Integration of the fleet-leader concept for single scheduled maintenance tasks
- Integration of sampling principles for single scheduled maintenance tasks

The approval of the Product-specific analysis guideline/PPH including the ISMO process logic by responsible authorities is decisive for the subsequent acceptance and implementation of the ISMO analysis results.

Note:
Approval by the responsible authorities is to be sought before the start of the actual ISMO analysis.

2   Process logic overview ISMO analysis

During the ISMO analysis process every repetitive scheduled maintenance task must be checked by a set of questions and decisions accompanied by activities/work steps that are required from the responsible analyst.

The analysis logic of this ISMO analysis process is composed of logic modules which are linked with each other as shown in Fig 1.

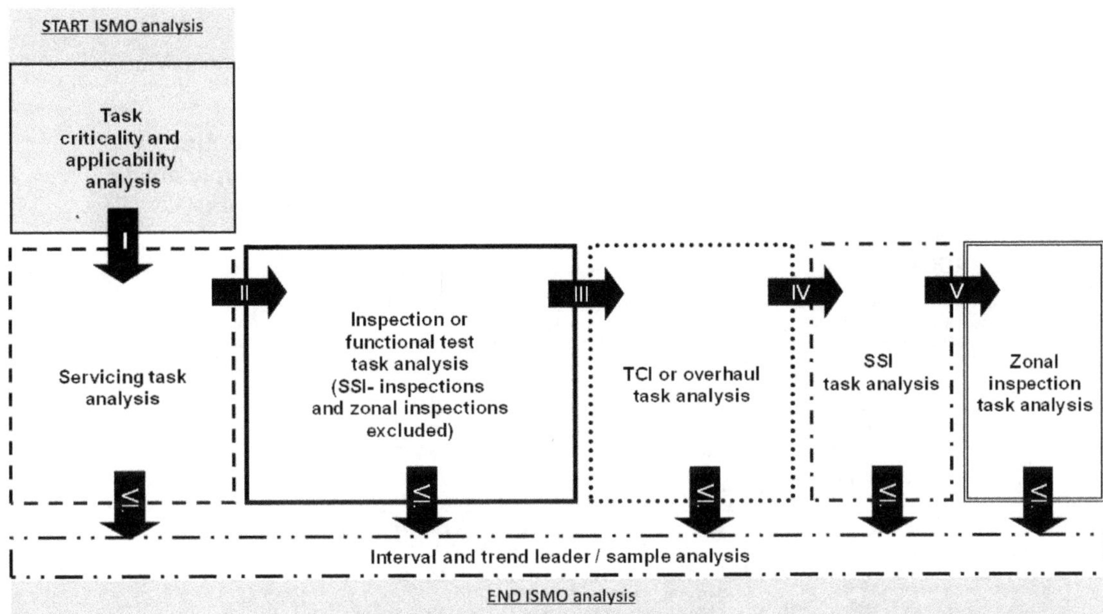

ICN-B6865-S4000P0080-001-01

Fig 1 Overview/links of analysis modules for the ISMO analysis process

The modules cover the analysis of all scheduled maintenance task types. Depending on the maintenance task type, logic questions must be answered in respect to servicing tasks, inspections/functional tests, TCI/scheduled overhaul, SSI or for zonal inspections. Each analytical module comprises detailed questions, evaluations and/or investigations which must be determined in the analysis guideline/PPH.

Note

After one of the first questions in the individual query blocks, the analysis can terminate leading to one or more recommendations. This lowers the analytical effort for each analysis task.

Trend leader and sampling analysis is only performed when the maintenance task under analysis cannot be deleted based on the queries in the previous analysis modules.

For more detailed information about the content of the analysis modules, refer to Chap 3.

Note

It is recommended to implement the detailed analysis logic, including the description of the individual analysis steps, decisions and recommendations, in an electronic analytical tool to be used by all analysts. Such a tool will support the analysts, reduce inconsistent data entries and lower the analytical effort.

3 Process logic of ISMO analysis

The logic diagrams show the individual process **Steps** (S), the **Decisions** (D) and the **Recommendations** (R), numbered consecutively. Refer to Para 4.

All steps, decisions and recommendations in the process logic are given an alphanumeric code **2YZZ** where:

-   — "**2**" - gives the code for ISMO analysis phase
-   — "**Y**" - gives the Step S, Decision D or Recommendation R

— "**ZZ**" - is a number, ascending from 01 to 99

The following analysis logic is a generic version of a detailed analysis logic that must be elaborated and defined in the analysis guideline/PPH.

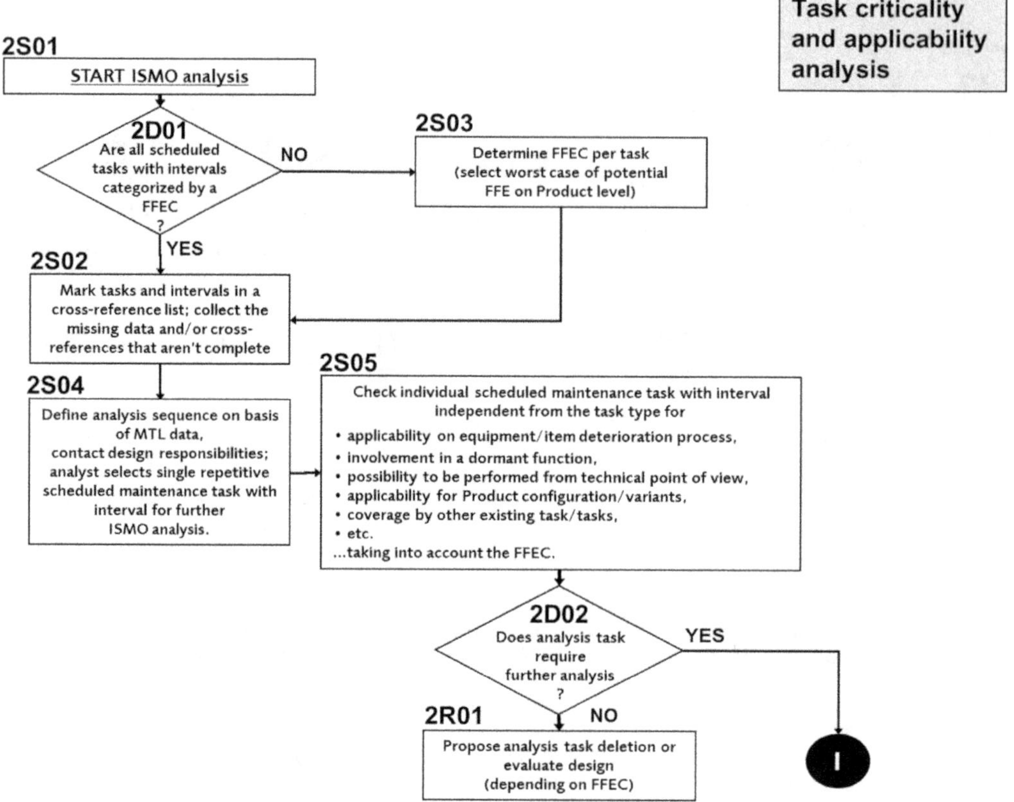

ICN-B6865-S4000P0081-001-01

Fig 2 ISMO maintenance task criticality and applicability analysis

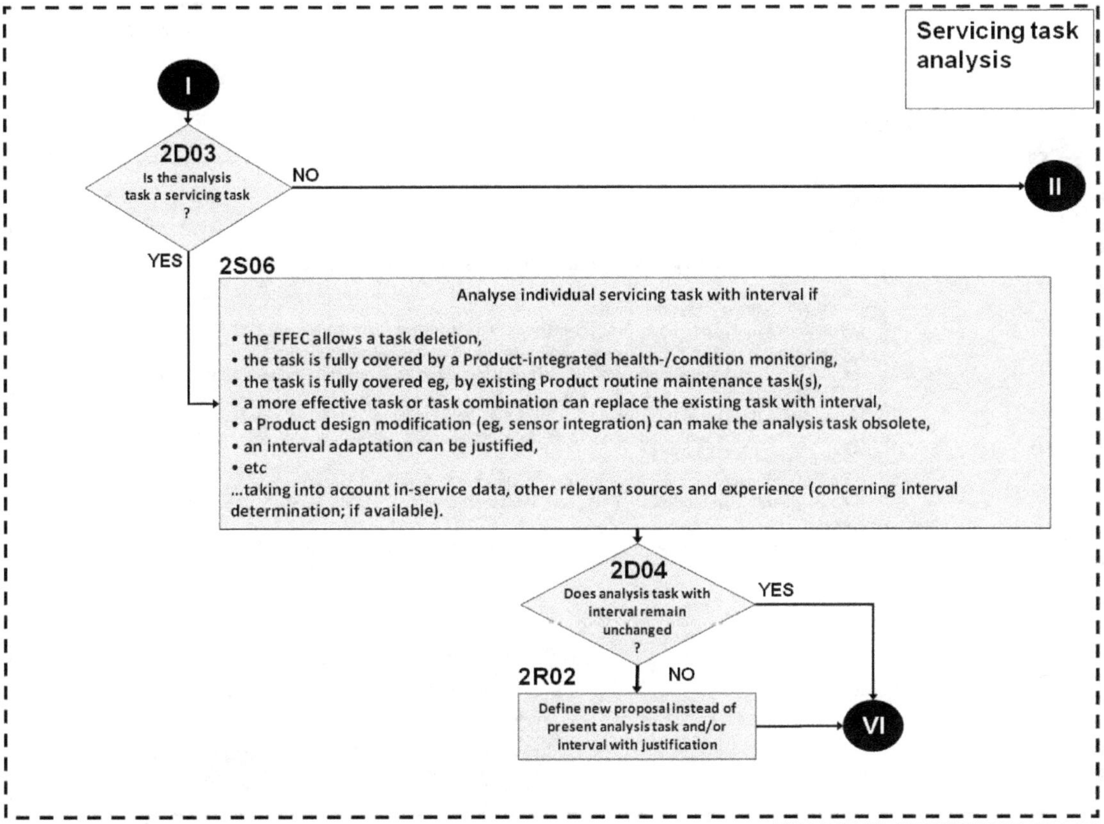

ICN-B6865-S4000P0082-001-01

Fig 3 ISMO servicing task analysis

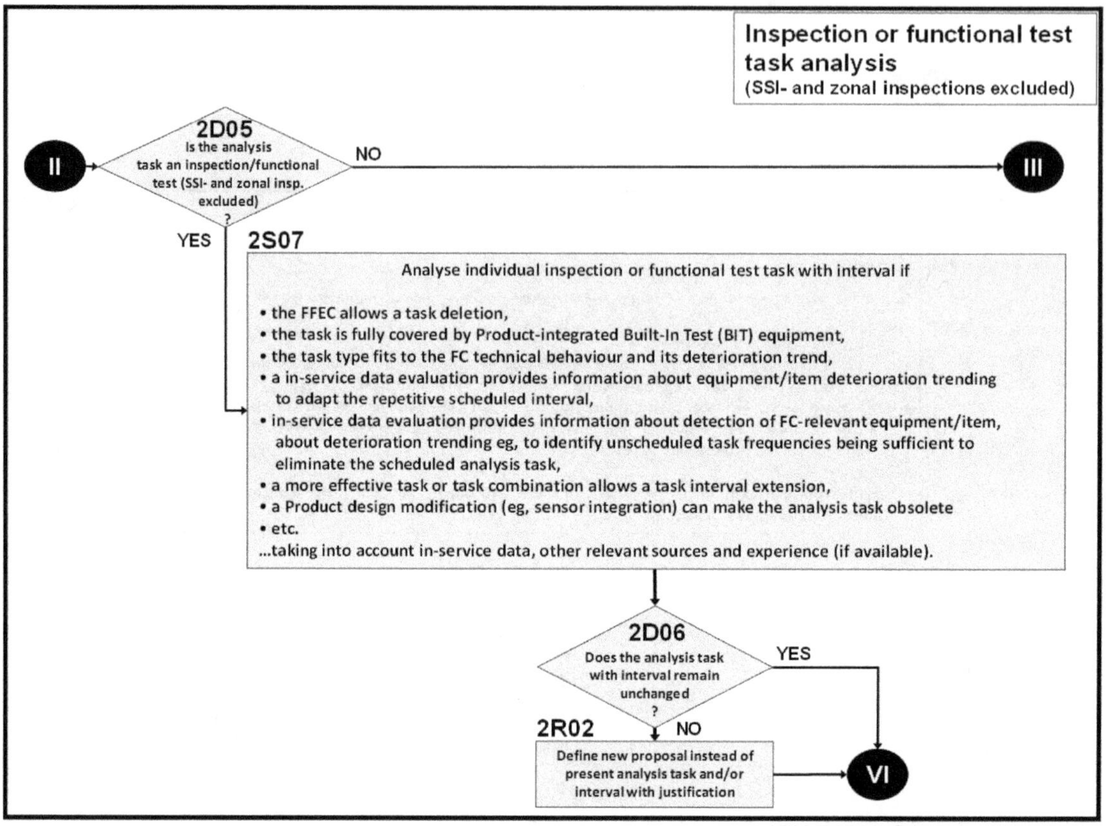

ICN-B6865-S4000P0083-001-01

Fig 4   ISMO inspection or functional test task analysis (SSI-inspections and zonal inspections excluded)

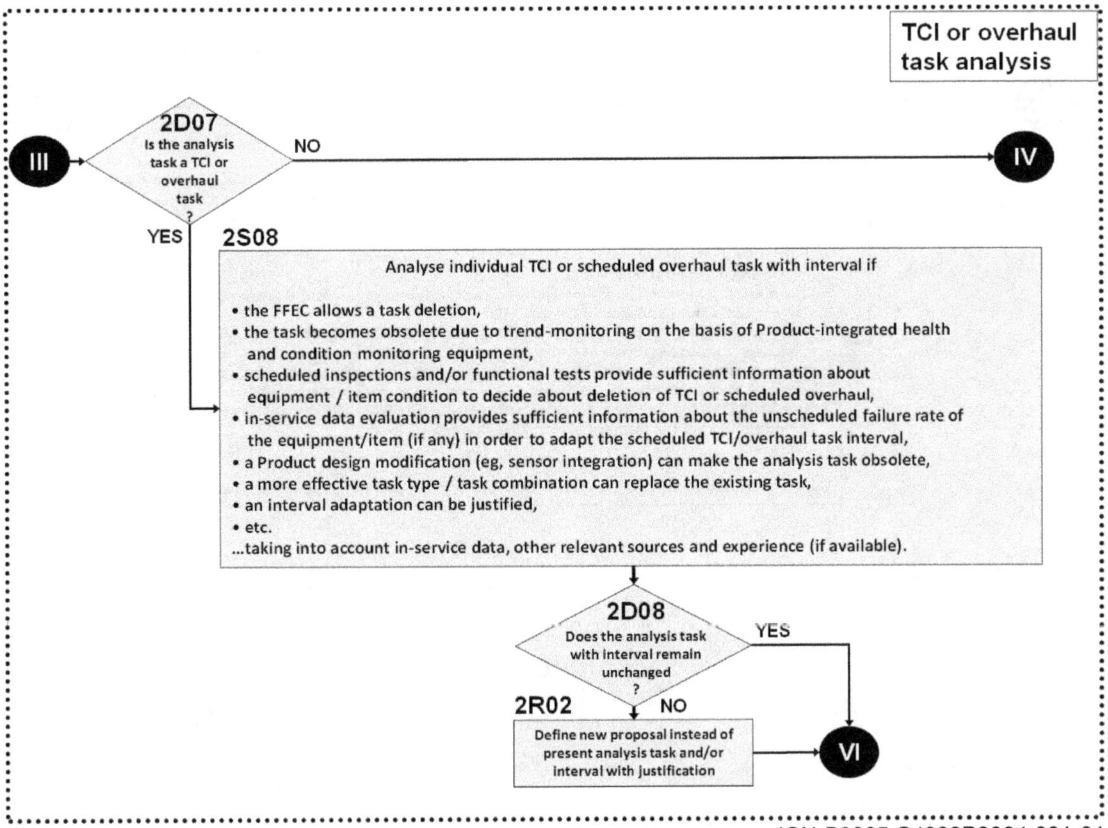

ICN-B6865-S4000P0084-001-01

Fig 5 ISMO time change item or overhaul task analysis

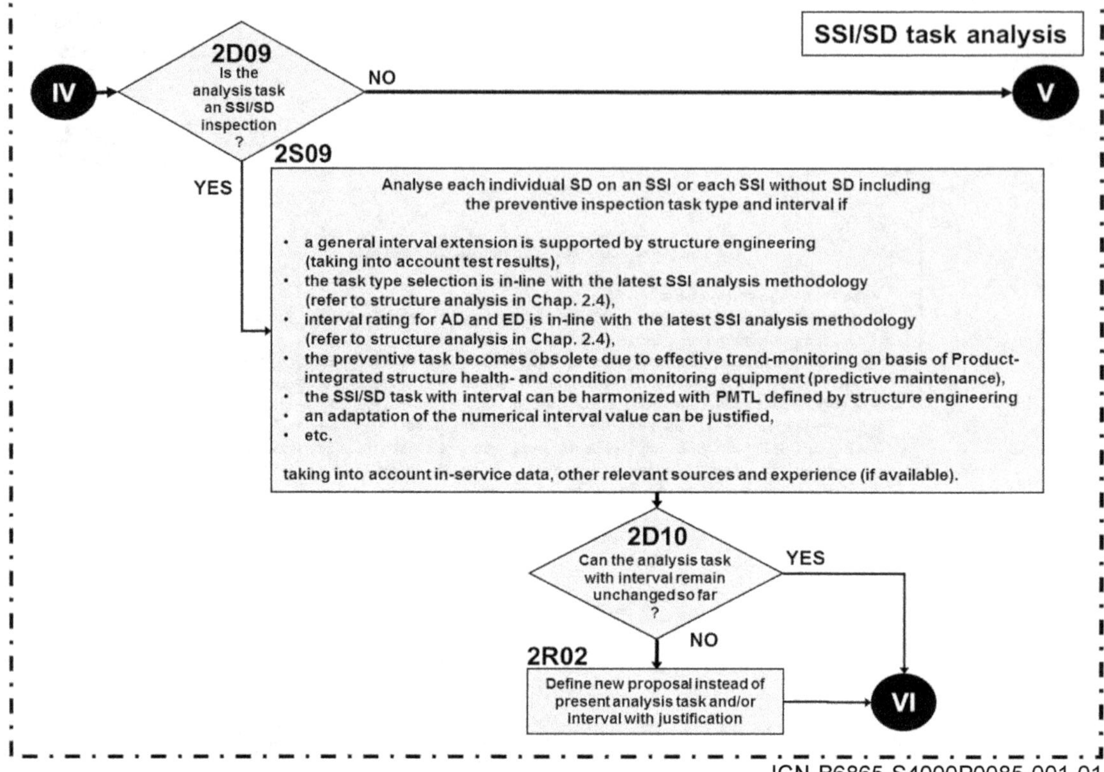

ICN-B6865-S4000P0085-001-01

Fig 6 ISMO SSI/SD task analysis

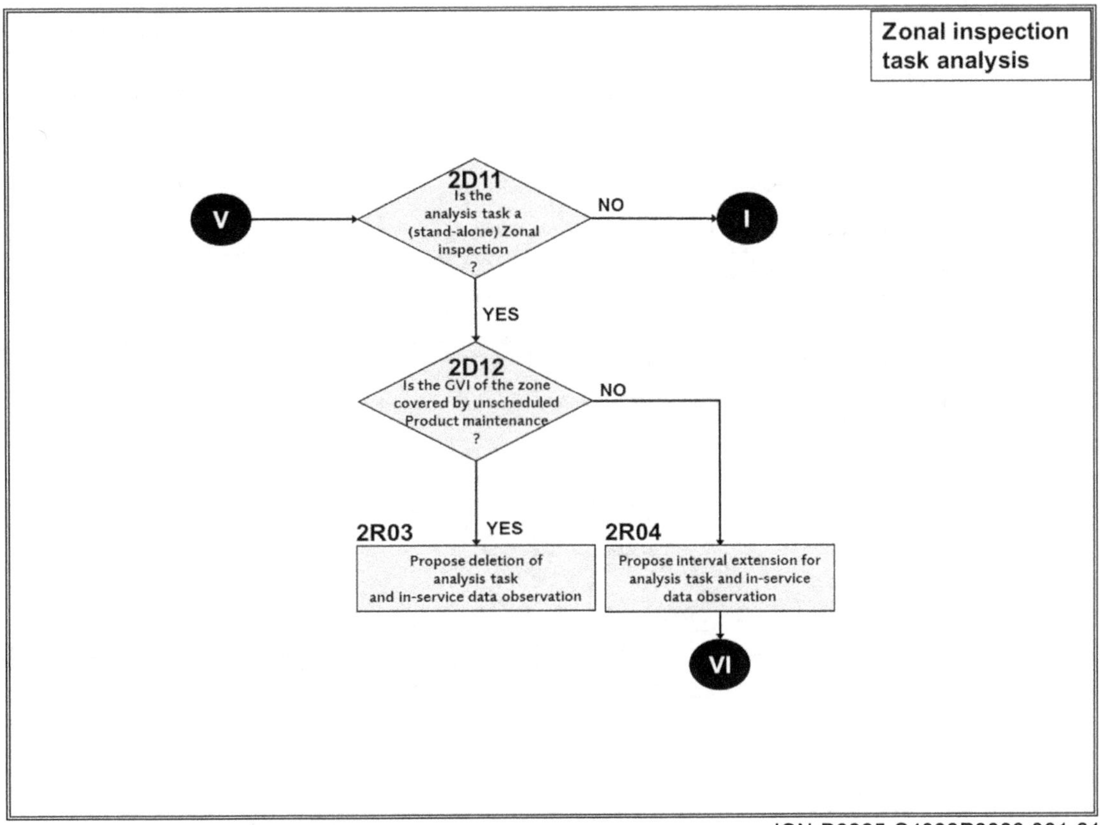

Fig 7 ISMO zonal inspection task analysis

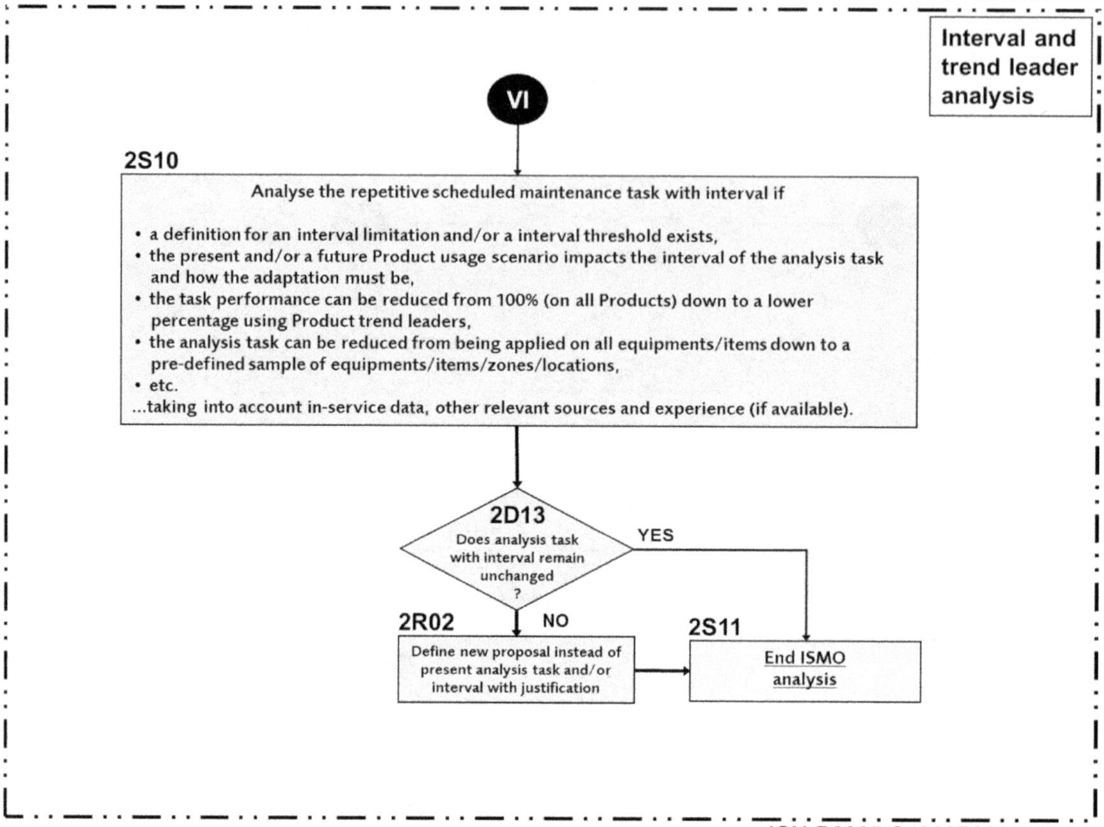

VI

2S10

ICN-B6865-S4000P0087-001-01

Fig 8 ISMO interval and trend leader analysis

4 Description of the generic process logic for ISMO analysis

This paragraph describes the working **Steps** (S), **Decisions** (D) and **Recommendations** (R) of the generic logic used during the ISMO analysis process.

With the view on a Product-specific analysis guideline/PPH, specific the working steps 2S05, 2S06, 2S07, 2S08, 2S09, 2S10 must be detailed in decision logics.

The generic analysis logic on the following pages comprises 2R01, 2R02, 2R03 and 2R04 as general recommendations. In a project-specific analysis guideline/PPH these must be extended to detailed recommendations.

Note

In answering decision questions, the following rule applies:

– A conservative decision must be made in the event of lack of information or data, and/or when there is ambiguity or doubt.

2S01:

The performance of the ISMO preparation is the prerequisite for starting the ISMO analysis process. Refer to Chap 3.2.

A suitable ISMO analysis team requires not only professional knowledge regarding maintenance in general, but also particular specialized knowledge of both the technology of the Product under analysis and the field of support engineering including IPS concepts.

To assist and support the analyst, it is recommended that a software tool that guides each analyst through the detailed query logic, be provided and explained in the Product-specific analysis guideline or PPH. Decisions on questions with justification information, work steps as well as recommendations must be documented in this tool so that all answers are traceable.

2D01:

For a system under analysis and all repetitive scheduled maintenance tasks, the MTL must comprise all analysis relevant data (ie, FFEC, background information, traceability of maintenance task roots, maintenance importance rating, etc). This is the prerequisite for starting the ISMO analysis process for the system, structure or zone under analysis and the single scheduled maintenance tasks allocated to.

The Answer is YES if:

— analysis relevant information per system is completed

or

— the SSI/SD selection is checked, and the task criticality is categorized

or

— the Zonal inspection is checked to be free from stand-alone task(s) and task criticality is categorized.

In these cases (Answer is YES), continue with 2S02. In other cases (Answer is NO), continue with 2S03.

2S02:

Indicate Product systems, structure and zones completed with analysis-relevant background data ready for being analyzed in the ISMO analysis process.

2S03:

Where information for the ISMO analysis (specific the criticality categorization) is missing, the lack of data must be compensated by the analyst. If in any doubt, the responsible analyst must select a certification-relevant FFEC for the analysis task.

2S04:

The analysis must be enabled at a functional subsystem or item level to detect optimization potential in the set of scheduled maintenance tasks per subsystem, equipment, item or zone. For example, multiple functional tests or inspections at different intervals can be identified and deleted.

To start the analysis on functional subsystems, different selection criteria must be taken into consideration, and include but not be limited to:

— Analysis relevant data and information (including in-service data) should be available,
— A subsystem, equipment or item that significantly contributes to mission availability/Life Cycle Cost (LCC) must be analyzed with the highest priority (using data from logistic support analysis databases, operating data (if available) or alternatively an analyst's estimation about the maintenance effort per individual maintenance task)

The analyst selects an individual scheduled maintenance task according to his analysis responsibility from the MTL and proceeds with the further analysis steps.

2S05:

Independent of the maintenance task type answers must first be given to the general questions related, but not limited to:

- How is deterioration process of one or more relevant FC?
- Is the FC involved in a dormant or emergency function?
- Are the prerequisites for maintenance task realization positive?
- Is the analysis task applicable for all or for limited Product configuration/variants?

The FFEC allocated to the maintenance task supports a decision if the maintenance task can or cannot be deleted.

2D02:

The output from 2S05 must either be a confirmation of the analysis task (Answer is YES, continue with 2D03), or leads to a recommendation that the maintenance task type is not applicable (Answer is NO, continue with 2R01).

2D03:

This question asks for a scheduled maintenance task type servicing. Scheduled servicing tasks are, for example:

- Cleaning
- Replenishment or supplement consumables
- Preservation
- Lubrication, greasing
- Adjustment, calibration

If this question is answered YES, continue with 2S06. If not (Answer NO), continue with 2D05.

2S06:

For the maintenance task type servicing, specific technical prerequisites must exist. Alternative solutions to compensate the analysis task depend on the maintenance task type and the failure cause/the failure causes related.

The evaluation of the analysis task must answer the questions, which must be defined in an applicable logic sequence in the analysis guideline/PPH. These questions include but are not limited to:

- How is the FFEC categorized?
- Can the criticality category be used for optimizing decisions?
- Is health and/or condition monitoring equipment installed on the Product that provides the condition status?
- Does a comparable routine maintenance task exist in parallel to the analysis task?
- Can alternative maintenance tasks with extended intervals substitute the analysis task?
- Can the current design effectively be modified?
- How is the experience from the in-service phase?
- Can the interval of the analysis task be extended?

Depending on the FC and the related analysis task criticality a detailed recommendation must be developed and justified according to the analysis guideline/PPH.

2D04:

If the analysis task with interval remains unchanged (Answer YES), continue with 2S10. If the ISMO analysis leads to a new proposal or recommendation (Answer NO), continue with 2R02.

2D05:

As the analysis task is not a servicing task, this question asks for a scheduled inspection or functional test. Scheduled inspections/functional tests comprise:

– GVI
– Detailed visual inspection
– Measurement (of dimensions)
– Material testing (destructive or non-destructive)
– Condition/functional test (with or without testing device/equipment)

If the analysis task can be assigned to one of these maintenance task types above (Answer YES), continue with 2S07. If not (Answer NO), continue with 2D07.

2S07:

For the inspection or functional test specified technical prerequisites must exist. Alternative solutions to compensate the analysis task depend on the maintenance task types and the failure causes behind.

The evaluation of the analysis task must take into account the questions, which must be defined in an applicable logic sequence in the analysis guideline/PPH. These questions include but are not limited to:

– How is the FFEC categorized?
– Can the criticality category be used for optimizing decisions?
– Is effective Built-In Test (BIT) equipment for health-/condition monitoring installed on/in the Product that provides the condition status?
– Can the FC be attributed to deterioration process or its fault trending (taking into account in-service data output and evaluation)?
– Can one or more alternative maintenance tasks with extended intervals substitute the analysis task?
– Can the current design effectively be modified/adapted?

Depending on the FC and the related analysis task criticality, a detailed recommendation must be made and justified, and recorded in the analysis guideline/PPH.

2D06:

If the maintenance task with interval remains unchanged (Answer YES) continue with 2S10. If the analysis leads to a new proposal concerning maintenance task and/or the interval (Answer NO), continue with 2R02.

2D07:

As this analysis task is neither a servicing task nor an inspection or functional test (except for SSI inspection and zonal inspection), it must be determined as to whether this is one of the following scheduled maintenance tasks types:

– Equipment, item, part or replacement TCI
– Overhaul of the item, part, module or equipment

If the maintenance task type belongs to one of these maintenance task types (Answer: YES), continue with 2S08. If not (Answer NO), continue with 2D09.

2S08:

For a scheduled replacement task, TCI or overhaul task, specific technical prerequisites must exist.

Alternative solutions to compensate the analysis task depend on the maintenance task type and the FC related to it.

The evaluation of the analysis task must take into account the questions, which must be defined in an applicable logic sequence in the analysis guideline/PPH. These questions include but are not limited to:

- How is the FFEC categorized?
- Can the criticality category be used for optimizing decisions?
- Is health and/or condition monitoring equipment installed on/in the Product that provides the condition status?
- Does other maintenance task-based information and/or sources allow for condition monitoring?
- Is the analysis task effective, based on evaluating unscheduled failures/faults?
- Can one or more alternative maintenance tasks with extended intervals substitute the analysis task?
- Can the interval of the analysis task be adapted to make it more effective?
- Can present design effectively be modified?

Depending on the FC and the related analysis task criticality a detailed recommendation must be developed and justified according to the analysis guideline/PPH.

2D08:

If the analysis task with interval remains unchanged (Answer YES) continue with 2S10. If the analysis leads to a new proposal or recommendation concerning maintenance task and/or the interval (Answer NO), continue with 2R02.

2D09:

The analysis task is not a servicing task, not an inspection/functional test (except SSI inspection or zonal inspection) and not a TCI or overhaul task.

This question asks for a SSI/SD inspection. If the answer is YES, continue with 2S09. If the answer is NO, continue with 2D11.

2S09:

If the analysis task is a SSI/SD inspection/test a specific analysis process is required. The individual SSI/SD task with interval must be checked to ensure that:

- a general interval extension is supported by the design department
- the maintenance task type selection is in line with a valid SSI/SD analysis methodology referred in the analysis guideline/PPH
- the analysis task interval is correctly rated in line with the referred SSI/SD analysis methodology and harmonized with other maintenance task/interval sources
- an interval adaptation can be justified, etc

Depending on the analysis result a detailed recommendation must be developed and justified according to the analysis guideline/PPH.

2D10:

If the analysis task with interval remains unchanged (Answer YES) continue with 2S10. If the analysis leads to a new proposal concerning maintenance task type and/or the repetitive scheduled intervals (Answer NO), continue with 2R02.

2D11:

As the analysis task is neither a servicing task, no inspection/functional test (except SSI inspection and zonal inspection), no scheduled replacement/overhaul, nor an SSI inspection, the analysis task must be a zonal inspection as it is the only remaining maintenance task type.

Stand-alone zonal inspections without critical subtasks must be categorized as non-certification-relevant GVI. Subtasks with a higher criticality must have been extracted from Zonal analysis during the ISMO preparation prior to starting the ISMO analysis process.

If answer on zonal inspection is YES, continue with 2D12. If answer is NO, go back to 2D03 for renewed querying of the maintenance task type.

2D12:

If operating crew or maintenance personnel have access to a zone frequently, the scheduled GVI of the zone can be omitted because of high frequency of unscheduled GVI activities (eg, due to high fault frequency and failure elimination or to other frequent activities within the zone).

Note

The criterion for a minimum unscheduled access and inspection frequency to a zone must be determined jointly with the responsible authorities and/or manufacturers.

The prerequisites for deleting a scheduled zonal inspection are:

1   The responsible maintenance personnel are well trained and instructed to perform a GVI in this zone after every unscheduled access and work

2   No additional dismantling/removal is required in the zone under analysis

If answer on this question is YES, continue with 2R03. If answer is NO, continue with 2R04.

2S10:

This analysis step must prove that the analysis task can be limited on certain time periods only (eg, an upper interval limit, or a threshold).

In addition, whether the maintenance task with interval can be limited on a Product sample or on a sample of equipment, items, zones, locations, etc, on the Product must be clarified.

Depending on the analysis result a recommendation must be developed and justified.

2D13:

If the analysis task with interval remains unchanged (Answer is YES) continue with 2S11. If the analysis leads to a new proposal concerning applicable and effective maintenance task type and/or the interval (Answer is NO), continue with 2R02.

2S11:

End of ISMO analysis process.

The results must be documented and a final report with all analysis results and substantiation must be submitted to customers, users and authorities.

Following final authorization and approval by the responsible authorities, the report is used as the basis for updating the technical documentation.

General recommendations:

2R01:
Depending on the FFEC, propose analysis task deletion or evaluate design.

2R02:
Define a new proposal instead of present analysis task and/or interval with justification.

2R03:
Propose an analysis task deletion and in-service data observation.

2R04:

Propose an interval extension for analysis task and in-service data observation.

Note

General recommendations 2R01 thru 2R04 must be extended to detailed recommendations in the Product-specific analysis guideline/PPH like the following:

- Delete maintenance task with interval
- Propose new or additional maintenance task with interval
- Keep maintenance task type and reduce interval
- Keep maintenance task interval as an upper limit
- Extend maintenance task interval
- Reduce maintenance task interval permanently
- Reduce maintenance task interval temporarily
- Design change proposed
- Detailed analysis is mandatory
- Define upper interval limit
- Define interval threshold
- Define product sample for maintenance task with interval
- Define reduction of maintenance task application on equipment and/or items.

The logic of ISMO analysis process must lead to at least one of these recommendations or to combinations of them.

Chapter 3.4

Optimizing PMTR - ISMO follow-up phase

Table of contents

Page

Optimizing PMTR - ISMO follow-up phase 1

References 1

1   Introduction 1

2   Process logic of ISMO follow-up analysis 2

3   Description of process and decision steps of ISMO follow-up analysis 3

4   Recommendations from the ISMO follow-up analysis: 5

List of tables

1   References 1

List of figures

1   ISMO follow-up analysis (Sheet 1 of 2) 2

2   ISMO follow-up analysis (Sheet 2 of 2) 3

References

Table 1 References

Chap No./Document No.	Title
Chap 2	Developing PMTR

1   Introduction

There are various reasons for deviations between initial assumptions during the development of Preventive Maintenance Task Requirements with repetitive scheduled intervals (PMTRI) and the subsequent elaboration of a Product maintenance program/OMP and maintenance experience accumulated during the usage of a Product.

Therefore, it is essential to identify unscheduled failure and/or damage messages from events which have not been taken into account in the initial approach while determining and improving scheduled maintenance tasks predicted and/or recommended by a maintenance program/OMP for a Product.

Events that have been identified as safety-critical or events that may have conflicted with law/environmental integrity, applicable decisions have already been initiated during the running Product in-service phase using regulatory mechanisms established per Nation/customer etc. In-between Product users, the exchange of Product-important information should be established and co-ordinated as well.

To improve or eliminate serious impacts on mission availability of the Product, and/or on Product Life Cycle Cost (LCC) (eg, because unscheduled maintenance activities result in high costs), selectable improvement mechanisms depend on the individual use and the maintenance strategy for a Product.

This ISMO follow-up analysis takes into account these aspects using process and logics according to this document.

For improvement purpose new PMTRI might be determined, which have not been taken into account in the respective maintenance program/OMP of the customer/user before.

The application of the ISMO follow-up analysis ensures that newly identified PMTRI are in line with the remaining scheduled maintenance tasks of the single item/equipment maintenance concepts. In addition, full traceability of all maintenance task-related decisions is required which can be used during the remaining Product in-service phases. This ensures in-service experience-oriented and an on-going development of the maintenance programs/OMP of different customers.

If scheduled maintenance cannot reduce or eliminate unscheduled maintenance resulting from events, the evaluation of design improvements can be recommended by analysts. To support these evaluations and decisions, in-service data will be collected, filtered, evaluated and calculated as inputs for support cost trade-offs.

2 Process logic of ISMO follow-up analysis

The logic diagrams show the individual process **Steps** (S), the **Decisions** (D) and the **Recommendations** (R) numbered consecutively.

The process steps, decisions and recommendations are detailed and explained in Para 3.

The process steps, decisions and recommendations in the process logic are given an alphanumeric code **NYZZ** where:

- **N** - gives the code for ISMO follow-up analysis,
- **Y** - gives the Step S, Decision D or Recommendation R,
- **ZZ** - is a number, ascending from 01 to 99.

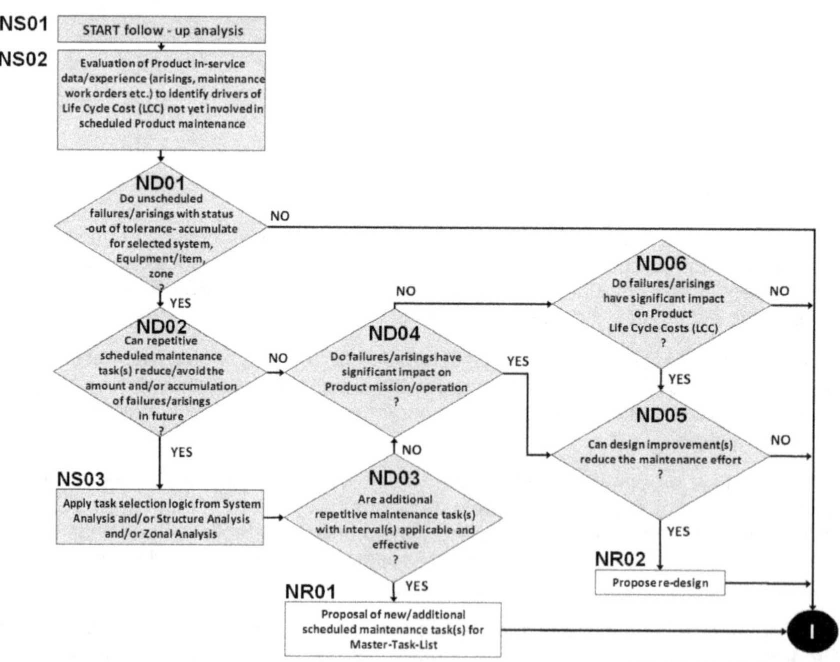

ICN-B6865-S4000P0088-001-01

Fig 1 ISMO follow-up analysis (Sheet 1 of 2)

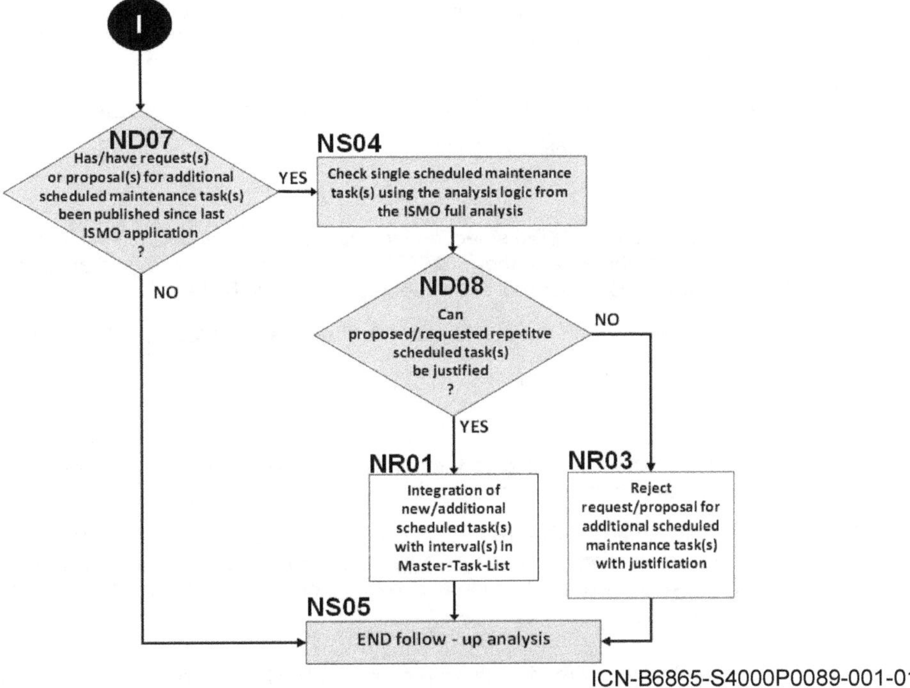

Fig 2 ISMO follow-up analysis (Sheet 2 of 2)

3 Description of process and decision steps of ISMO follow-up analysis

The working **Steps** (S), the **Decisions** (D) and the **Recommendations** (R) of the ISMO follow-up analysis are explained hereafter.

Note

In answering decision questions, the following principle and rule applies:
A conservative decision is to be taken in the event of lacking information or data, ambiguity or doubt.

NS01:

The ISMO follow-up analysis can be started before, in parallel to the ISMO analysis process or later. After complete ISMO process, no scheduled maintenance task with repetitive scheduled interval should remain within the Product maintenance program/OMP that is not applicable, not effective or without any technical justification.

NS02:

In support of the ISMO analysis process, the Product in-service data evaluation is focused on systems, equipment, items and zones for which repetitive scheduled maintenance tasks have already been determined and performed. The data from this evaluation is used by the analyst when answering logic questions and in justifying the answers in the single analysis logics.

This work step identifies potential events and the resulting unscheduled maintenance effort that has significantly impacted Product availability and/or Product LCC, where repetitive scheduled maintenance was not established in the past.

ND01:

This question determines whether there are failures/events and resulting unscheduled maintenance activities documented for selected items/equipment which significantly exceeds the assumptions made during the Product design and development phase.

If such cases have been identified (Answer YES), continue with ND02.

If not (Answer NO), continue with ND07.

ND02:

Prior to applying the PMTRI selection including the interval determination process, the analyst determines whether one or more PMTRI are probably applicable and effective for the identified Failure Cause (FC). That probability should be 50% or higher.

If the probability is high enough to justify further analysis (Answer YES), continue with NS03.

If not (Answer NO), continue with ND04.

NS03:

Depending on the item/equipment that has been identified for further analysis, the analyst defines which analysis methodology is required. Refer to Chap 2.

To determine effective PMTRI for a mission and/or economical relevant FC without any contractual restrictions between manufacturer and customer, decisions can be made by the customer/user only (based on in-service experience and/or future Product usage plans).

ND03:

Having applied the agreed analysis process for PMTRI determination, either one or more repetitive scheduled maintenance tasks have been identified or no scheduled maintenance tasks were found.

If PMTRI have been defined (Answer YES), continue with NR01.

If not (Answer NO), continue with ND04.

ND04:

If PMTRI are not applicable or effective a technical improvement or a change of the design must be evaluated. Reductions in mission/operational availability are assumed to be more important than economic aspects.

If mission/operational availability is severely impacted (Answer YES), continue with ND05.

If not (Answer NO), continue with ND06.

ND05:

The answer to this question is obtained using the analysts best engineering judgement. The concurrence of the design department with the answer cannot be guaranteed.

If Product design improvement can reduce the unscheduled maintenance effort in future (Answer YES), continue with ND02 and ND07.

If not (Answer NO), continue with ND06.

ND06:

Unscheduled maintenance activities which lead to high costs during a Product in-service phase must be reduced to a minimum. A reduction of related costs automatically influences the Product LCC in a positive manner.

If LCC can be reduced significantly by design (Answer YES), continue with ND05.

If not (Answer NO), continue with ND07.

ND07:

In parallel to an on-going ISMO analysis process, requests or recommendations for additional PMTRI might be raised by users/customers. All new requests or recommendations must be answered using the questions in line with the ISMO analysis process.

If new requests or recommendations for PMTRI exist (Answer YES), continue with NS04.

If not (Answer NO), close the ISMO follow-up analysis with NS05.

NS04:

Perform the analysis process of the ISMO analysis phase with each new PMTRI. Answer the questions taking into account all relevant in-service experience/data.

ND08:

After having the ISMO analysis process applied, a decision can be made as to whether an additional PMTRI can be justified and if the proposed repetitive scheduled interval is correct or must be adapted. Each new PMTRI must be added to the MTL for the respective system, structure or zone of the Product under analysis.

With approved new PMTRI (Answer YES), continue with NR01.

In case of new PMTRI cannot be justified (Answer NO), continue with NR03.

NS05:

The ISMO follow-up process is closed within the ISMO analytical process. Summarize and explain the results from the ISMO follow-up analysis.

4 Recommendations from the ISMO follow-up analysis:

NR01:

Propose new and/or additional PMTRI which were not previously predicted by the Product technical publication before.

NR02:

An investigation must be proposed and initiated into whether a design improvement could reduce the documented accumulation of events resulting in unscheduled maintenance.

NR03:

If the PMTRI cannot be justified, a rejection statement with a suitable justification must be prepared for the originator of each request.

Page intentionally blank.

Chapter 3.5

Optimizing PMTR - Review of PMTRE for special events

Table of contents

Page

Optimizing PMTR - Review of PMTRE for special events 1

References...1

1   Introduction 1

2   PMTRE review process 2

3   PMTRE review process logic...3

List of tables

1   References 1

List of figures

1   Review of PMTRE for special events 2

References

Table 1 References

Chap No./Document No.	Title
Chap 2.7	Developing PMTR - Special event analysis
Chap 3.2	Optimizing PMTR - ISMO preparation phase
Chap 3.3	Optimizing PMTR - ISMO analysis phase
Chap 3.4	Optimizing PMTR - ISMO follow-up phase
S3000L	International procedure specification for Logistics Support Analysis - LSA

1   Introduction

The process for developing PMTRE is given in Chap 2.7. However, for each PMTRE, it is highly recommended that, during the Product in-service phase, the PMTRE be reviewed as part of an ISMO analysis loop. The ISMO analysis is described from Chap 3.2 thru Chap 3.4.

2 PMTRE review process

The review process of PMTRE selected for special events is shown in Fig 1.

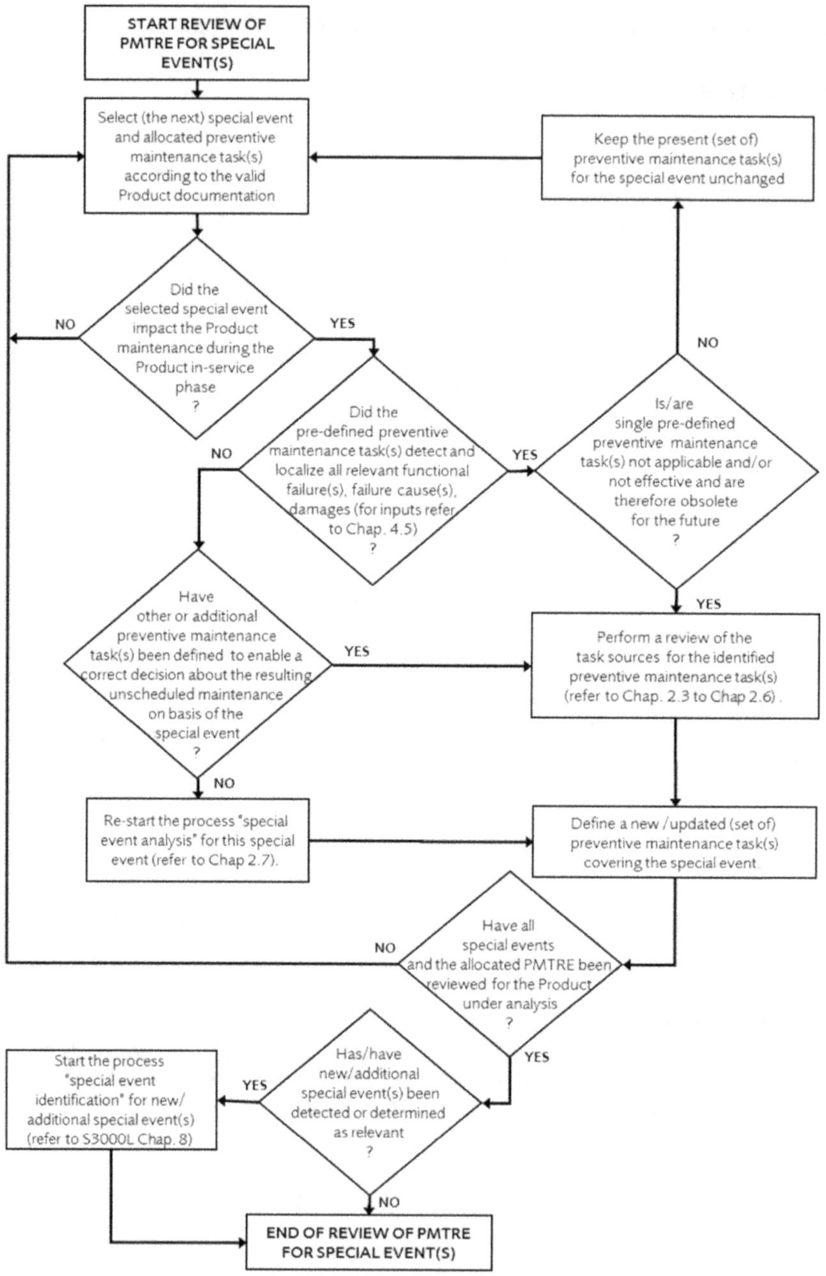

ICN-B6865-S4000P0090-001-01

Fig 1 Review of PMTRE for special events

3 PMTRE review process logic

The process logic starts with the selection of one special event and the allocated preventive maintenance tasks according to the valid Product documentation. If in-service data and experience with this special event is available for the Product, the correctness and completeness of these tasks and the initiating PMTRE is evaluated. This process is applicable for each known special event.

Note

If in-service experience for the Product or for other comparable Products (if experience can be transferred), detects new/additional special events, the special event analysis must be repeated. Refer to Chap 2.7.

Page intentionally blank.

Chapter 4

S4000P Interfaces

Chapter	Data module title	Data module code	Applic
Chap 4.1	S4000P Interfaces - General	S4000P-A-04-01-0000-00A-040A-A	All
Chap 4.2	S4000P Interfaces - S4000P interfaces outside the S-Series IPS specifications	S4000P-A-04-02-0000-00A-040A-A	All
Chap 4.3	S4000P Interfaces - S1000D	S4000P-A-04-03-0000-00A-040A-A	All
Chap 4.4	S4000P Interfaces - S3000L	S4000P-A-04-04-0000-00A-040A-A	All
Chap 4.5	S4000P Interfaces - S5000F	S4000P-A-04-05-0000-00A-040A-A	All
Chap 4.6	S4000P Interfaces - SX000i	S4000P-A-04-06-0000-00A-040A-A	All

Page intentionally blank.

Chapter 4.1

S4000P Interfaces - General

Table of contents
Page

S4000P Interfaces - General 1

References...1

1   General 2

List of tables

1   References 1

References

Table 1 References

Chap No./Document No.	Title
Chap 1	Introduction to the specification
Chap 2	Developing PMTR
Chap 3	Optimizing PMTR
Chap 4.2	S4000P Interfaces - S4000P interfaces outside the S-Series IPS specifications
Chap 4.3	S4000P Interfaces - S1000D
Chap 4.4	S4000P Interfaces - S3000L
Chap 4.5	S4000P Interfaces - S5000F
Chap 4.6	S4000P Interfaces - SX000i
Chap 5	Data model and data exchange
S1000D	International specification for technical publications using a common source database
S2000M	International specification for material management - Integrated data processing
S3000L	International procedure specification for Logistic Support Analysis - LSA
S5000F	International specification for operational and maintenance data feedback
SX000i	International guide for the use of the S-Series Integrated Product Support (IPS) specifications

1 General

As described in Chap 1, the S4000P is one of the integrated S-Series IPS specifications and has several interfaces.

The analysis activities described, depend on information and data necessary about the Product. Inputs are required from both the S-Series IPS specifications and other specifications.

Detailed data or data-element definitions are given in SX000i. A common data model is developed by the Data Model and Exchange Working Group (DMEWG). The information about the data model and data exchange is given in Chap 5.

Chap 4.2 deals with the S-Series-external interfaces of S4000P mainly to design department(s) of the Product manufacturer and involved suppliers/Original Equipment Manufacturers (OEM). Further interfaces to internal manufacturer management and departments are excluded. S4000P has interfaces to regulatory authorities that support Product certification and to Product customers/users for Product qualification, based on project requirements.

The overall philosophy of the S-Series IPS specifications reflects the idea of a central database containing data from Logistic Support Analysis (LSA) based on S3000L. These logistic core data are essential for planning and management of all IPS resources required during the Product in-service phase. The interface between S4000P and S3000L is described in Chap 4.4. With a S3000L database in place, no direct interfaces from ASD S4000P to other S-Series IPS specifications such as S1000D and S2000M, are required (refer to SX000i).

During the Product life cycle, a direct data feedback from the S-Series IPS specifications to S4000P is expected. These feedback interfaces are described in Chap 4.3 (interface with S1000D) and in Chap 4.5 (interface with S5000F).

Chap 4.6 describes which S4000P analysis activities should be focused toward specific phases of the Product life cycle. Depending on the Product life cycle phases the interfaces to and from S4000P and the intensity of data-exchange vary. The experience of these variations is based on project-implementations of S4000P during Product design and development phases (refer to Chap 2) and PMTR reviews and optimizations during Product in-service phases (refer to Chap 3).

Chapter 4.2

S4000P Interfaces - S4000P interfaces outside the S-Series IPS Specifications

Table of contents

Page

S4000P Interfaces - S4000P interfaces outside the S-Series IPS Specifications 1

References 1

1   Introduction 1

2   S4000P interfaces outside the S-Series Interfaces during Product design and development 2

2.1   Required inputs to a Policy and Procedure Handbook describing a chapter 2 analysis.3

2.2   Inputs for and outputs from a Chap 2 analysis 4

3   S4000P interfaces to outside the S-Series during the review and optimization of preventive maintenance 4

3.1   Required inputs for the Policy and Procedure Handbook describing the review and optimization of preventive maintenance 5

3.2   Inputs for and outputs from a review and optimization of preventive maintenance 6

List of tables

1   References 1

List of figures

1   Required inputs for a chapter 2 PPH...3

2   Inputs to and outputs from a chapter 2 analysis..4

3   Required inputs for a chapter 3 PPH...5

4   Inputs to and outputs from a chapter 3 analysis..6

References

Table 1 References

Chap No./Document No.	Title
Chap 1	Introduction to the specification
Chap 2	Developing PMTR
Chap 3	Optimizing PMTR
Chap 5	Data model and data exchange

1   Introduction

There are interfaces to and from S4000P which are outside the S-Series IPS Specifications. These interfaces are essential to correctly perform the S4000P analysis activities.

2   S4000P interfaces outside the S-Series Interfaces during Product design and development

In a Product life cycle the major Product design and development activities take place prior to Product manufacturing, Product delivery and before the Product in-service phase starts.

Design and development activities for complete technical Products or for selected Product systems, structure and/or zones can continue during the in-service phase. Therefore, the interfaces identified and described in this chapter also continue during the Product in-service phase.

Fig 1 shows the necessary inputs to S4000P from interfaces outside the S-Series IPS Specifications that are necessary to prepare and perform the Chap 2 analysis. In addition, the recipients of the outputs/results of the Chap 2 analyses are shown.

2.1 Required inputs to a Policy and Procedure Handbook describing a chapter 2 analysis

Before starting a Chap 2 analysis for an individual Product a Policy and Procedure Handbook (PPH) must be elaborated. For preparation of a PPH that will gain acceptance, signatures and authorization the inputs shown in Fig 1 are required.

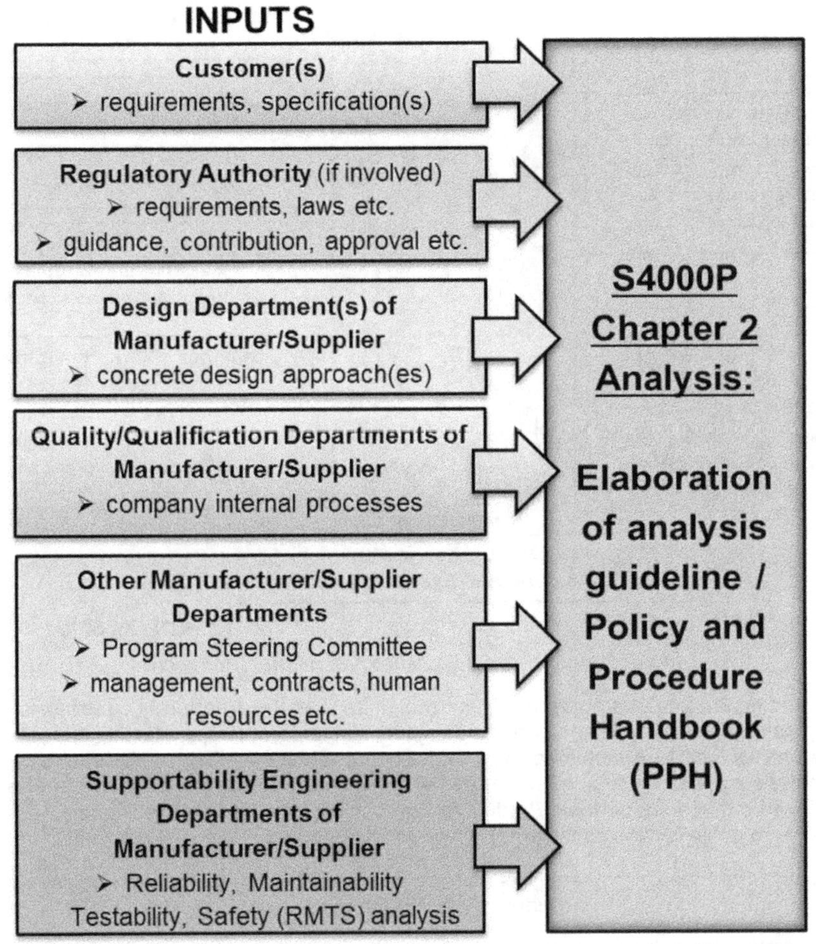

ICN-B6865-S4000P0091-002-01

Fig 1 Required inputs for a chapter 2 PPH

2.2 Inputs for and outputs from a Chap 2 analysis

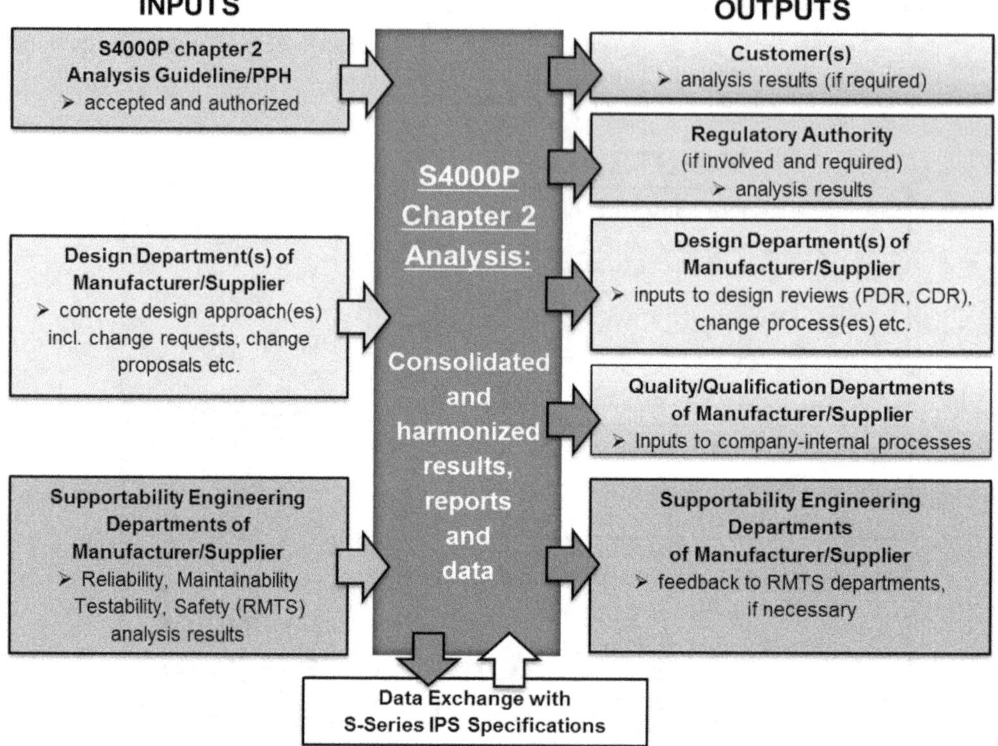

ICN-B6865-S4000P0092-001-01

Fig 2 Inputs to and outputs from a chapter 2 analysis

Based on the analysis guideline/PPH each Chap 2 analysis depends on reliable and concrete inputs from involved design departments and from different supportability analysis sources (mainly Reliability, Maintainability, Testability and Safety (RMTS) analysis results). These single analysis sources must be interchanged and harmonized between project supportability experts to ensure that a supportable Product design can be achieved as specified by the customer. The aim is to achieve data consistency between all supportability analysis results.

Results from the Chap 2 analysis must be delivered in a timely manner. Delivery dates and contents depend on the individual project planning.

Fig 2 also shows inputs from manufacturer/supplier due to change proposals and change requests after a Chap 2 analysis has been started. These impacts on the Product built standard must be checked by analysts to identify potential influences on existing analysis results (eg, PMTRI updates/changes).

3 S4000P interfaces to outside the S-Series during the review and optimization of preventive maintenance

During the in-service phase the Product must be maintained in accordance with pre-defined preventive maintenance tasks for Product systems, structure and zones documented in a Product maintenance program/Operators' Maintenance Program (OMP).

Preventive maintenance tasks documented in an OMP are either based on PMTRI having been developed and kept up to date in accordance with Chap 2.3 to Chap 2.6, on PMTRE

determined for special events based on Chap 2.7, or on further preventive maintenance task sources (eg, CMR predicted by involved regulatory authorities and/or by laws).

Preventive maintenance tasks defined by an OMP should be reviewed periodically to review and optimize the single task sources (PMTRI, PMTRE, CMR, etc) first and the resulting sets of preventive maintenance tasks in an updated OMP afterwards. The in-service review and the optimization of the task sources of the preventive maintenance is described in Chap 3.

The following illustrations in Fig 3 and Fig 4 show necessary inputs from interfaces outside the S-Series IPS Specifications necessary for the optimization of preventive maintenance. Recipients of the analysis outputs are shown on Fig 4.

3.1 Required inputs for the Policy and Procedure Handbook describing the review and optimization of preventive maintenance

The prerequisite for the review and optimization of preventive maintenance according to Chap 3 is an accepted, signed and authorized analysis guideline/ PPH that must be elaborated based on the inputs specific for an individual Product before starting the analysis.

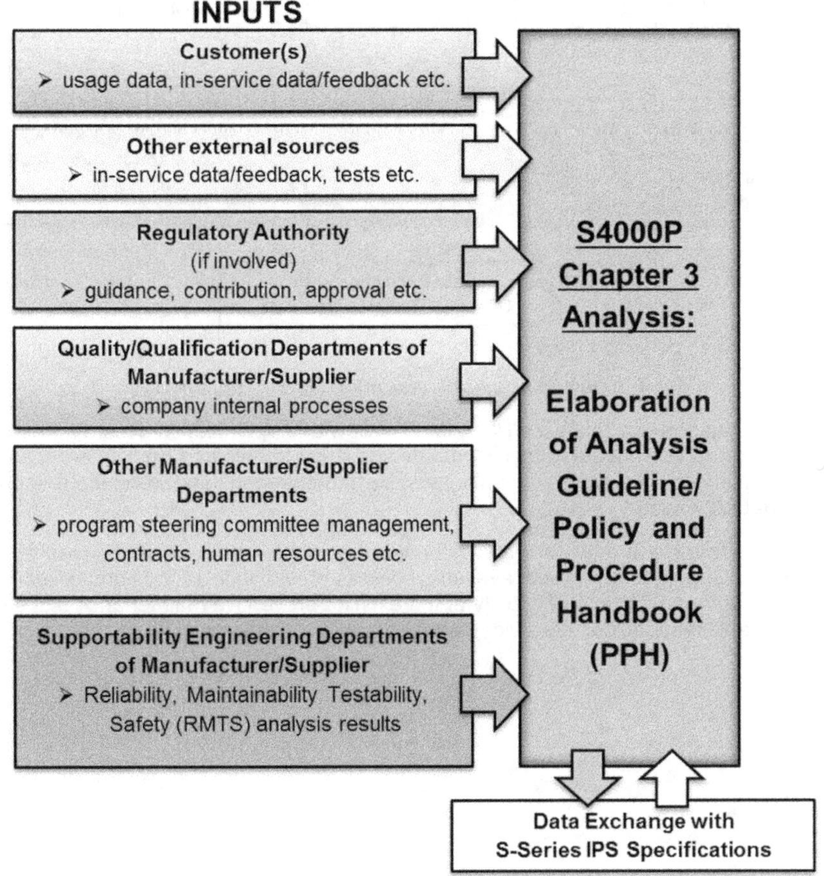

ICN-B6865-S4000P0093-001-01

Fig 3 Required inputs for a chapter 3 PPH

3.2 Inputs for and outputs from a review and optimization of preventive maintenance

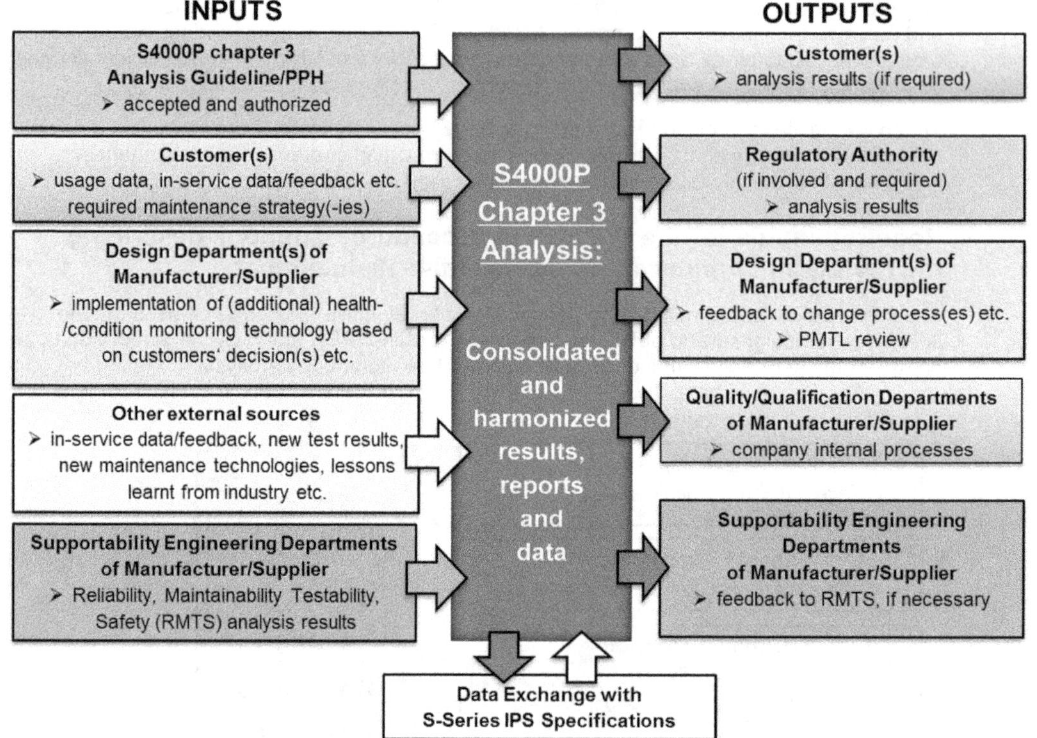

ICN-B6865-S4000P0094-001-01

Fig 4 Inputs to and outputs from a chapter 3 analysis

Based on the analysis guideline/PPH, each review and optimization according to Chap 3 depends on reliable inputs from involved design departments and from different supportability analysis sources. The analysis results must be interchanged in between the responsible supportability experts.

The aim is to achieve data consistency between all supportability analysis results. Fig 4 shows inputs to a Chap 3 analysis with available sources providing in-service and/or test feedback. To check the applicability and effectivity of the existing preventive maintenance tasks from the valid OMP reliable feedback of in-service data/information is essential.

Chapter 4.3

S4000P Interfaces - S1000D

Table of contents

Page

S4000P Interfaces - S1000D 1

References 1

1   Introduction 2

2   Data transfer from S1000D to S4000P for Chap 3 analysis 2

3   Special cases requiring a direct interface between S4000P and S1000D 3

List of tables

1   References 1

List of figures

1   Temporary interface between S4000P chapter 3 and S1000D 3

2   Special cases requiring a direct transfer of S4000P analysis results to S1000D 4

References

Table 1 References

Chap No./Document No.	Title
Chap 2	Developing PMTR
Chap 3	Optimizing PMTR
Chap 3.2	Optimizing PMTR - ISMO preparation phase
Chap 3.4	Optimizing PMTR - ISMO follow-up phase
Chap 3.5	Optimizing PMTR - Review of PMTRE for special events
S1000D	International specification for technical publications using a common source database
S3000L	International procedure specification for Logistic Support Analysis - LSA
SX000i	International guide for the use of the S-Series Integrated Logistics Support (IPS) specifications

1 Introduction

Direct interfaces between S4000P and S1000D are not described as standard interfaces in accordance with SX000i. Interfaces between S4000P and S1000D, are described herein.

2 Data transfer from S1000D to S4000P for Chap 3 analysis

Chap 3 describes the review and optimization processes for preventive Product maintenance that is subdivided into the following two main processes:

- Optimization of PMTRI using the In-Service Maintenance Optimization (ISMO) process (refer Chap 3.2 to Chap 3.4)
- Optimization of PMTRE (refer to Chap 3.5)

During the ISMO preparation phase all valid and authorized repetitive scheduled maintenance tasks from a Product Operators' Maintenance Program (OMP) and from other task sources must be collected, put in a numbering sequence according to a Product Breakdown Structure (PBS) and prepared for the subsequent ISMO analysis process at a defined project milestone.

In a Product Technical Documentation, selected preventive maintenance tasks are combined in applicable task packages with a common repetitive scheduled (master) interval to support Product maintenance in a positive manner (refer to S3000L). To elaborate the Master Task List (MTL) as input for the Chap 3 analysis it is required to re-allocate single preventive maintenance tasks from the OMP to the relevant Product systems, structure and zones of the PBS for PMTR overview purpose. In addition, the task sources (PMTRI, PMTRE, CMR, etc) must be allocated to the valid preventive maintenance tasks.

The Product Technical Publication/documentation (refer to S1000D) must continuously be kept up-to-date as the baseline for creating Maintenance Work Orders (MWO) for Product maintenance during the In-Service Phase. With this process all Service Bulletins (SB), Candidate Certification Maintenance Requirements (CCMR), CMR or other comparable sources impacting preventive Product maintenance must be taken into account in the Product Technical Publication/documentation in line with an update process of the Product maintenance program/OMP accepted between manufacturer, supplier and customer/user and involved authorities. For the Chap 3 analysis, it is essential to identify the baseline date, on which the set of preventive maintenance tasks were extracted from the valid scheduled maintenance tasks from the valid Technical Publication, for traceability. All updates, changes and supplements of the Product maintenance program/OMP decided after that date must separately be analyzed after the Chap 3 analysis process.

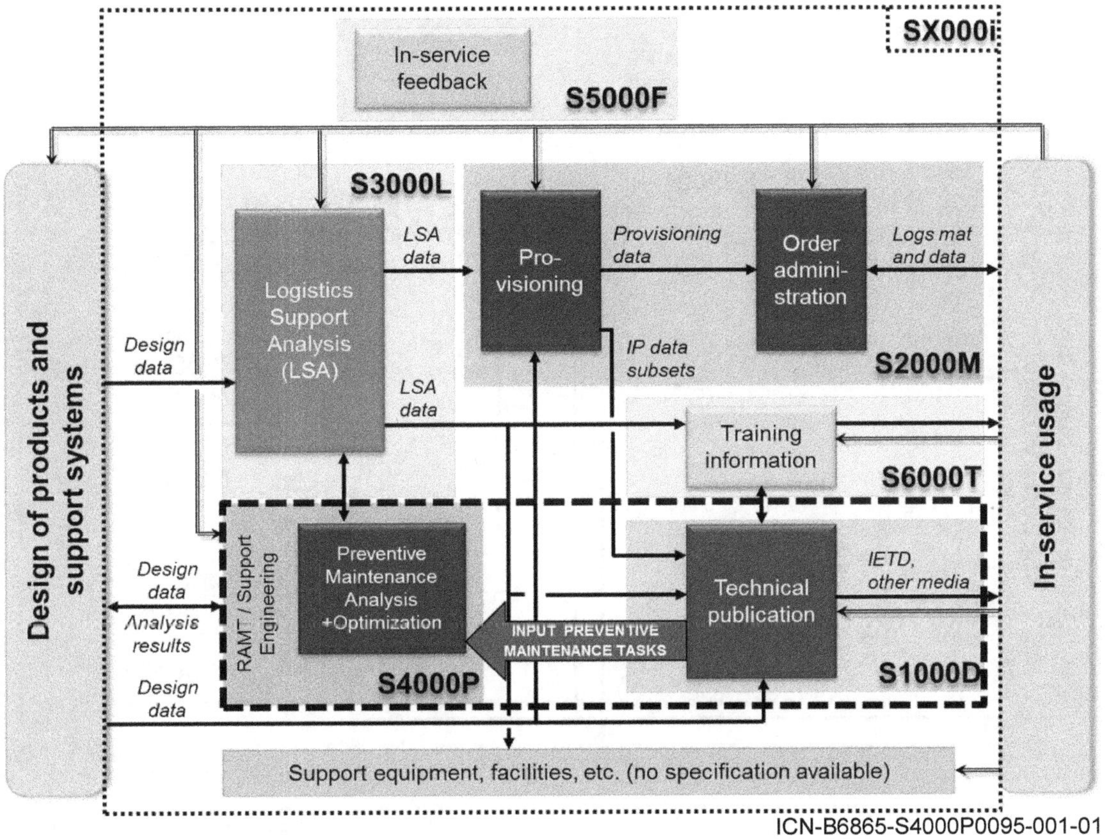

Fig 1 Temporary interface between S4000P chapter 3 and S1000D

3 Special cases requiring a direct interface between S4000P and S1000D

There are special cases when a direct transfer of limited analysis results from S4000P to S1000Dcan be required. These include, but are not limited to:

- Elaboration of a Product Technical Publication/documentation, in accordance with S1000D, for a single prototype Product and for Product test purpose assuming Logistic Support Analysis (LSA) data is not available
- Performance of S4000P analysis compensations for legacy Products, where for example, no analysis methodologies or obsolete analysis methodologies have been applied. PMTRI, PMTRE results from additional analysis activities must be cross-checked with the existing content of the Technical Documentation produced using S1000D.
- An LSA database is not established (eg, for legacy Products that are still in-service)
- Small projects with low budget and/or a short time schedule which does not allow the full application of the S-Series of IPS Specifications

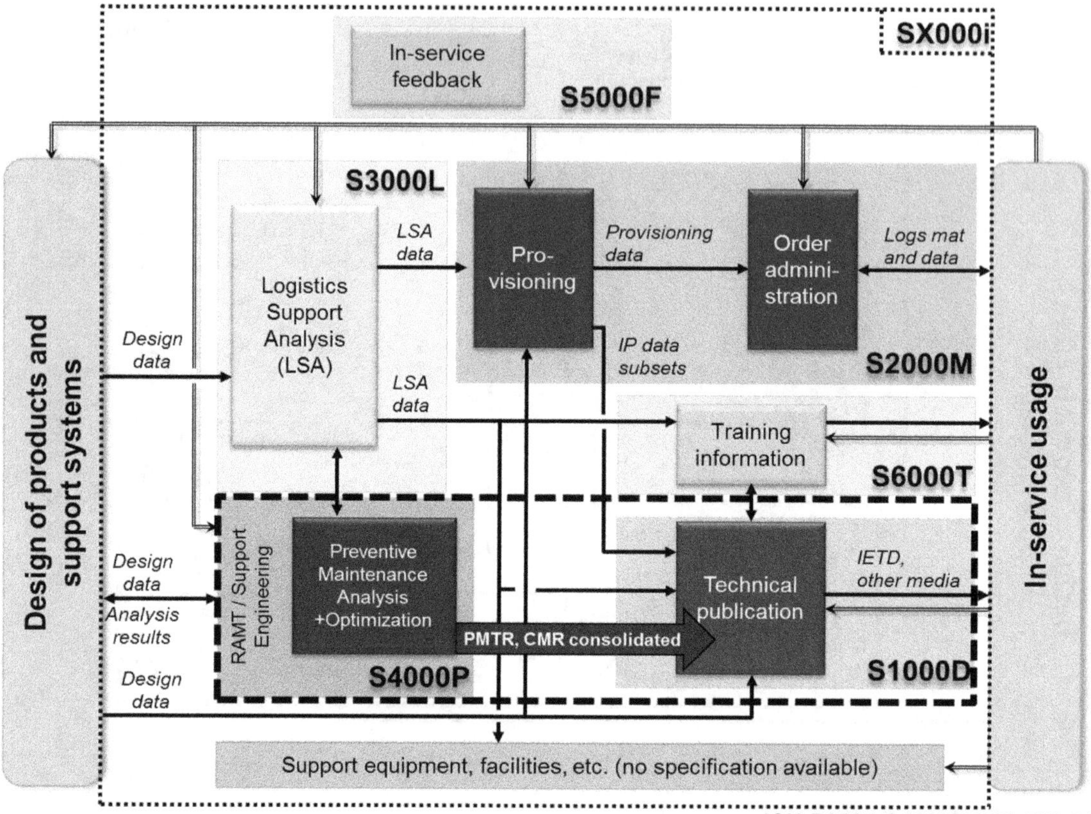

ICN-B6865-S4000P0096-001-01

Fig 2 Special cases requiring a direct transfer of S4000P analysis results to S1000D

Note

The results from a PMTR obtained from the S4000P analysis require a Maintenance Tasks Analysis (MTA) to be performed first followed by a packaging process in accordance with S3000L, to adequately transfer information about preventive Product maintenance as input for the Technical Publication/documentation for the Product.

If a database according toS3000L or any other comparable specification/standard was/is not established, both MTA and packaging process must be compensated. In addition, the interfaces to and the data exchange with other ASD specifications are disconnected or interrupted (ie, there is no effective Integrated Logistic Support (IPS) process).

Chapter 4.4

S4000P Interface - S3000L

Table of contents

Page

S4000P Interface - S3000L 1

References 1

1   Introduction 2

2   Overview of the interface between S4000P and S3000L 3

3   S4000P/S3000L data exchange after PMTRI development 4

4   S4000P/S3000L data exchange after PMTRI, CMR review and optimization 5

5   S4000P/S3000L data exchange after PMTRE development 7

6   S4000P/S3000L data exchange after PMTRE, CMR review and optimization 7

List of tables

1   References 1

List of figures

1   Interface between S4000P and S3000L 3

2   Data exchange between S4000P and S3000L after PMTRI development 4

3   Data exchange between S4000P and S3000L after PMTRI, CMR review and
optimization 6

References

Table 1 References

Chap No./Document No.	Title
Chap 1	Introduction to the specification
Chap 2	Developing PMTR
Chap 2.3	Developing PMTR - System analysis
Chap 2.4	Developing PMTR - Structure analysis
Chap 2.5	Developing PMTR - Zonal analysis
Chap 2.6	Developing PMTR - Consolidation of analysis results, harmonization with other preventive maintenance task requirement sources for traceability
Chap 2.7	Developing PMTR - Special event analysis
Chap 3	Optimizing PMTR
Chap 3.5	Optimizing PMTR - Review of PMTRE for special events
Chap 5	Data model and data exchange

Applicable to: All

S4000P-A-04-04-0000-00A-040A-A

Chap 4.4

Chap No./Document No.	Title
Chap 7	Examples
S1000D	International specification for technical publications using a common source database
S3000L	International procedure specification for Logistic Support Analysis - LSA
SX000i	International guide for the use of the S-Series Integrated Logistics Support (IPS) specifications

1 Introduction

The interface between S4000P and S3000L is an essential interface inside the S-Series IPS Specifications. S4000P is the task generator of Preventive Maintenance Task Requirements (PMTR) followed by S3000L analysis activities.

Data exchanges between both specifications must be possible during the complete Product life cycle (if necessary). If the interface between both specifications is not established or incorrectly established, (eg, in legacy projects), an effective Integrated Product Support (IPS) for a Product is at least negatively impacted.

Note

This chapter gives general information on the S4000P/S3000L data exchange during a Product life cycle. It doesn't describe or summarize scope and/or content of S3000L in order not to duplicate and mismatch other information sources inside the S-Series IPS Specifications.

The S4000P analytical methodologies (refer to Chap 2 and Chap 3) define the PMTRI, Certification Maintenance Requirement (CMR) and PMTRE output data at the interface between S4000P and S3000L that is forwarded to the Logistic Support Analysis (LSA) database (refer to S3000L). The content and amount of data for the data exchange must be defined in a project-specific preventive maintenance data exchange list. The content of the data exchange list deviates between output data resulting from a Chap 2 analysis and output data resulting from a Chap 3 analysis. This chapter explains these deviations and differences.

The main scope of an effective IPS for a Product is to establish online and on condition data exchanges during the whole Product life cycle. Correct and current PMTR data enable current maintenance concepts to be defined for Product systems, equipment, structural items and zones in LSA. Therefore, PMTR data triggers the definition, provision and modification (if necessary) of IPS elements necessary for the Product's in-service phase.

The data model and data exchange covering the interface between S4000P and S3000L is described in Chap 5. The information related to the definitions of single data elements involved in Data EXchanges (DEX) are described in the DEX specifications given in SX000i.

2 Overview of the interface between S4000P and S3000L

Fig 1 shows the interface between S4000P and S3000L.

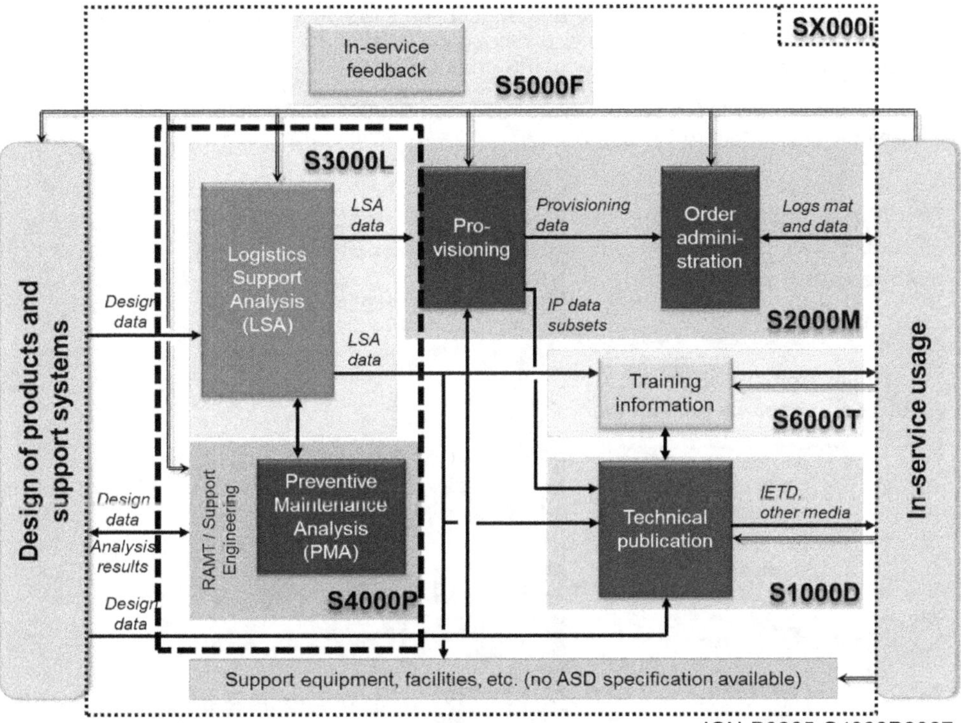

ICN-B6865-S4000P0097-001-01

Fig 1 Interface between S4000P and S3000L

Depending on the individual project management and the time schedule defined, the starting point of an analysis and the status of the LSA activities can differ.

An analysis (refer to Chap 2) should be started at an early project phase period in parallel to Product design and development activities for selected Product systems, structure and zones. In this project phase, it is possible that a logistic support oriented Product Breakdown Structure (PBS) as described in the Standard Numbering System (SNS) in S1000D is not fully defined an S3000L database. For early analysis activities - design data that is as complete as possible is essential (eg, drawings, functional descriptions, etc).

Starting this analysis early ensures maintainability feedback to the Product design departments prior to finalizing the Product design approach. It is essential that to identify any potential mandated redesign requirements, resulting from analysis, are identified as soon as possible. A request for a change to the Product design can be an outcome of the analysis if neither health or condition monitoring, or a preventive Product maintenance is not applicable and/or effective.

The early Chap 2 analysis work is based on data and information provided by the Product design department(s) and/or by the supplier/Original Equipment Manufacturer (OEM). The allocation of PMTRI, CMR or PMTRE to Breakdown Element Identifier(s) (BEI), defined by S3000L must be performed after the S4000P/S3000L data exchange at the latest.

If applicable BEI are already defined in the LSA database, every analysis result must refer to them in the data exchange lists used for S4000P/S3000L data exchanges. Identified data gaps,

---

incorrect BEI coding, etc, concerning the Product breakdown structure must be harmonized between S3000L and S4000P data.

3 S4000P/S3000L data exchange after PMTRI development

At the interface between S4000P and S3000L, an effective and dynamic data exchange must be realized. PMTRI related data and information must be forwarded to S3000L to initiate the planning, production and delivery of IPS products.

Fig 2 shows the PMTRI data exchange between S4000P and S3000L after PMTRI development (refer to Chap 2.3 thru Chap 2.6).

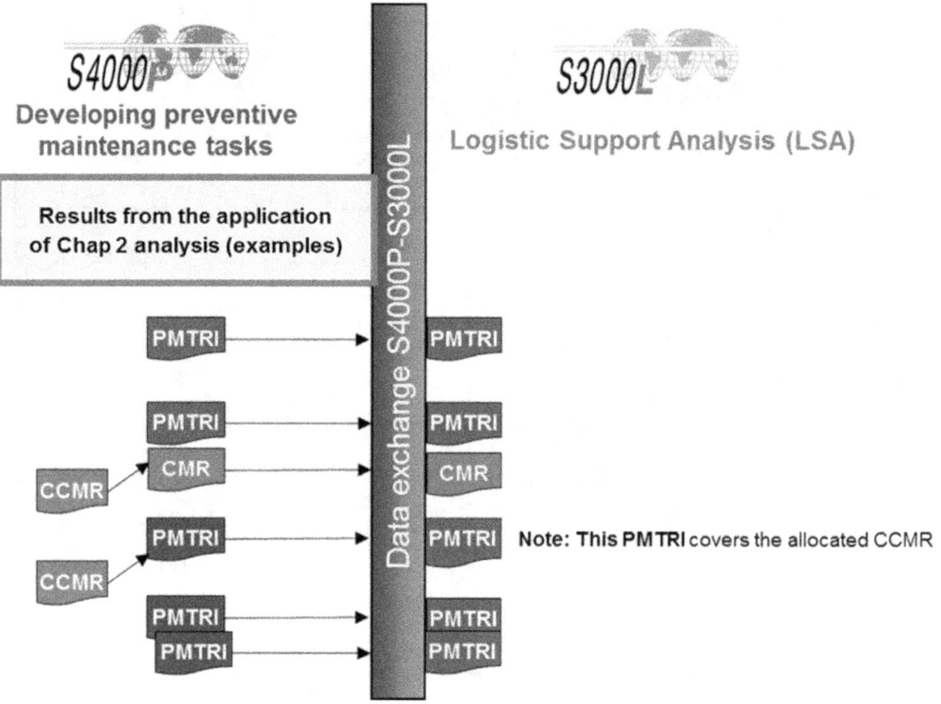

ICN-B6865-S4000P0098-001-01

Fig 2 Data exchange between S4000P and S3000L after PMTRI development

The PMTRI, CMR data exchange list, used for the data exchange after PMTRI development, must at least contain the following data/information elements:

- Line sequence number for each listed PMTRI, CMR in the preventive maintenance data exchange list
- BEI (if exists)
- BEI info/input (if necessary)
- BEI revision (issue number)
- Pre-selection of analysis candidate (yes/no)
- Justification for the analysis candidate pre-selection
- Part number/drawing number (to define the built standard/configuration status under analysis)
- Name of the subsystem, equipment, item affected by the PMTRI, CMR
- PMTRI, CMR applicability on Product variants (if existing and/or foreseen)
- PMTRI, CMR task type identification/name
- PMTRI, CMR numerical interval value 1

- PMTRI, CMR interval type 1
- PMTRI, CMR interval threshold 1 (if defined)
- PMTRI, CMR numerical interval value 2 (if applicable)
- PMTRI, CMR interval type 2 (if applicable)
- PMTRI, CMR interval threshold 2 (if applicable and defined)
- PMTRI, CMR source (S4000P, national law, CCMR, etc)
- PMTRI, CMR issue number for system, subsystem, equipment, item, Structural Significant Item (SSI), zone
- PMTRI, CMR criticality (the worst case Functional Failure Effect Code (FFEC) must be selected)
- PMTRI, CMR development status (on hold, approved, released, etc)
- Chap 2 analysis progress status (eg, on hold, approved, released)
- Remark(s) related to PMTRI, CMR

Note 1

Chap 7 provides an example of a PMTRI, CMR data exchange list after the Chap 2 analysis of a mountain bike has been performed.

Note 2

If it is necessary to select both a calendar-based interval and a usage parameter-based interval in the PMTRI, CMR data exchange list in parallel, it is assumed that two different interval types will cover the analyst needs. This requires the selection of the parameter that has the most severe impact.

4   S4000P/S3000L data exchange after PMTRI, CMR review and optimization

When Product sub-systems, equipment and/or items become subject to PMTRI, CMR review, and optimization activities PMTRI have initially been developed based on the Chap 2 analysis process or a comparable analysis methodology during the Product development phase or during later Product life cycle phases. After having performed the PMTRI, CMR review and optimization process (refer to Chap 3) for a Product, the previous data-set in the data-transfer process between S4000P and S3000L must be updated. Refer to Fig 3.

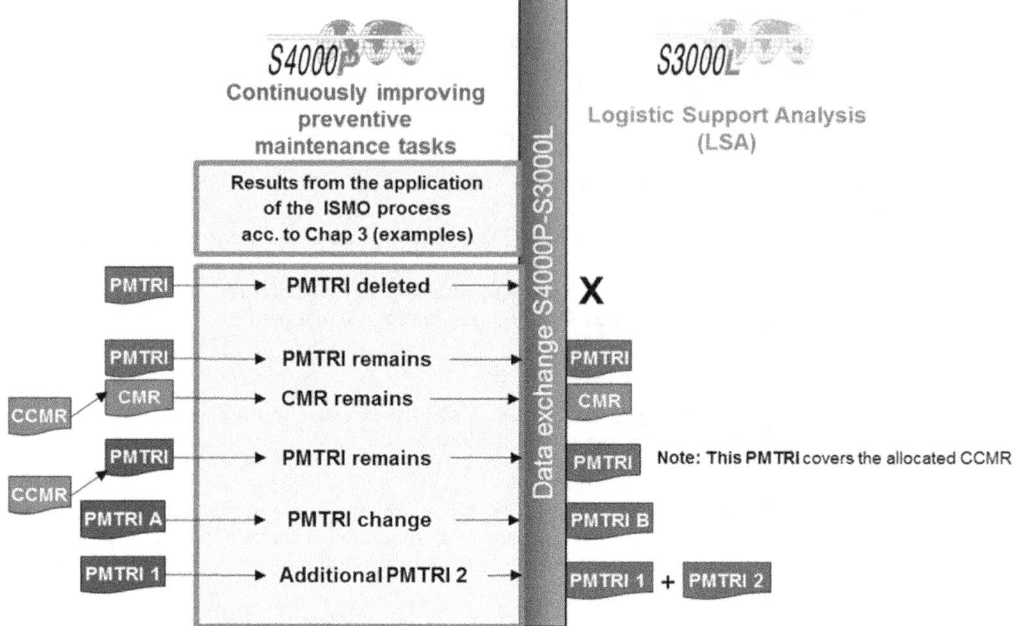

ICN-B6865-S4000P0099-001-01

Fig 3 Data exchange between S4000P and S3000L after PMTRI, CMR review and optimization

The PMTRI, CMR data exchange list used for the data exchange after the PMTRI, CMR review and optimization process requires further data/information fields in comparison to the PMTRI, CMR data exchange list used after the Chap 2 analysis (refer to Para 3).

Examples for additional data / information fields in an extended PMTRI, CMR data exchange list after finalization of a Product analysis based on Chap 3 are:

- Importance/in-service impact rating (related to impact on Product in-service phase, if selected according to the analysis guideline/PPH)
- Chap 3.3 ISMO analysis status (eg, on hold, approved, released, accepted)
- Chap 3.2 thru Chap 3.4 ISMO analysis result summary
- Design change requested, recommended or desired
- Detailed analysis required
- Result for PMTRI, CMR task type
- Result for PMTRI, CMR new task type (if another PMTRI is selected)
- Result for PMTRI, CMR numerical interval value 1
- Result for PMTRI, CMR interval type 1
- Result for PMTRI, CMR interval threshold 1 (if applicable)
- Result for PMTRI, CMR numerical interval value 2 (if applicable in addition to interval value 1)
- Result for PMTRI, CMR interval type 2 (if applicable in addition to interval value 1)
- Result on PMTRI, CMR interval threshold 2 (if applicable)
- PMTRI, CMR temporary interval adaptation (if selected)
- PMTRI, CMR criticality update (if necessary)
- Selection of trend leader(s) for PMTRI, CMR
- Selection of pilot area(s) for PMTRI, CMR
- Result for PMTRI, CMR additional task type (if an additional PMTRI is selected)
- Result for additional PMTRI, CMR numerical interval value 1
- Result for additional PMTRI, CMR interval type 1

- Result for additional PMTRI, CMR interval threshold 1 (if applicable)
- Result for additional PMTRI, CMR numerical interval value 2 (if applicable in addition to interval value 1)
- Result for additional PMTRI, CMR interval type 2 (if applicable in addition to interval value 1)
- Result on additional PMTRI, CMR interval threshold 2 (if applicable)
- PMTRI, CMR criticality for additional PMTRI (the worst case FFEC is to be selected)
- Selection of trend leader(s) for additional PMTRI, CMR
- Selection of pilot area(s) for additional PMTRI, CMR

5 S4000P/S3000L data exchange after PMTRE development

Sets of PMTRE (refer to Chap 2.7), are developed for identified special events which can be allocated to one or more of a Product's systems, structural items and zones.

Therefore, PMTRE must be allocated to a general BEI of the Product Breakdown Structure (PBS) representing the special event under analysis.

The S4000P/S3000L data exchange of these BEI data can take place earliest in the final phase of the PMTR development because of:

- The PMTRE development depends on the PMTRI development being performed before
- The identified set of PMTRE must be reviewed by the design department(s)
- Each request from design departments for potential supplements and/or changes in a set of PMTRE must be incorporated prior to any data exchange

6 S4000P/S3000L data exchange after PMTRE, CMR review and optimization

Chap 3.5 defines the review and optimization process applicable for PMTRE. Similar to the initial development of PMTRE (refer to Para 5), the related S4000P/S3000L data exchange can take place earliest in the final phase of the PMTR optimization because of the following reasons:

- The PMTRE optimization depends on the PMTRI optimization being performed before
- The reviewed and optimized set of PMTRE must be cross-checked by the design department(s) again
- Each request from design departments for potential supplements and/or changes in a set of PMTRE must be incorporated prior to any data exchange

Page intentionally blank.

Chapter 4.5

S4000P Interfaces - S5000F

Table of contents

Page

S4000P Interfaces - S5000F 1
References 1
1   Introduction 2
2   Overview on the S4000P - S5000F interface 2
3   S5000F data feedback to S4000P 3
3.1   Feedback to the ISMO analysis phase 3
3.1.1   Feedback to the ISMO analysis process for scheduled servicing tasks 4
3.1.2   Feedback to the ISMO analysis process for scheduled inspections or functional test tasks 4
3.1.3   Feedback to the ISMO analysis process for scheduled replacements of equipment/item (TCI) or scheduled overhaul 5
3.1.4   Feedback to the ISMO analysis process for scheduled SSI/SD inspections 5
3.1.5   Feedback to the ISMO analysis process for scheduled Zonal inspections 5
3.2   Feedback to the ISMO follow-up phase 6
3.3   Feedback to reviews of PMTRE for special events 6

List of tables

1   References 1

List of figures

1   Interface between S4000P and S5000F in the S-Series IPS Specifications 2

References

Table 1 References

Chap No./Document No.	Title
Chap 2	Developing PMTR
Chap 2.7	Developing PMTR - Special event analysis
Chap 3	Optimizing PMTR
Chap 3.3	Optimizing PMTR - ISMO analysis phase
Chap 3.4	Optimizing PMTR - ISMO follow-up phase
Chap 5	Data model and data exchange
S5000F	International specification for operational and maintenance data feedback

1 Introduction

The interface between S4000P and S5000F is an important internal interface of the S-Series IPS Specifications. Analysis based on S4000P Chap 2 and/or Chap 3 requires data inputs and provide data outputs during the whole Product life cycle whether using the S-Series IPS Specifications or not.

The data model and information related to Data EXchange (DEX) between both specifications is defined in Chap 5.

2 Overview on the S4000P - S5000F interface

ICN-B6865-S4000P0100-001-01

Fig 1 shows the interface between S4000P and S5000F as fully integrated elements in the S-Series IPS Specifications.

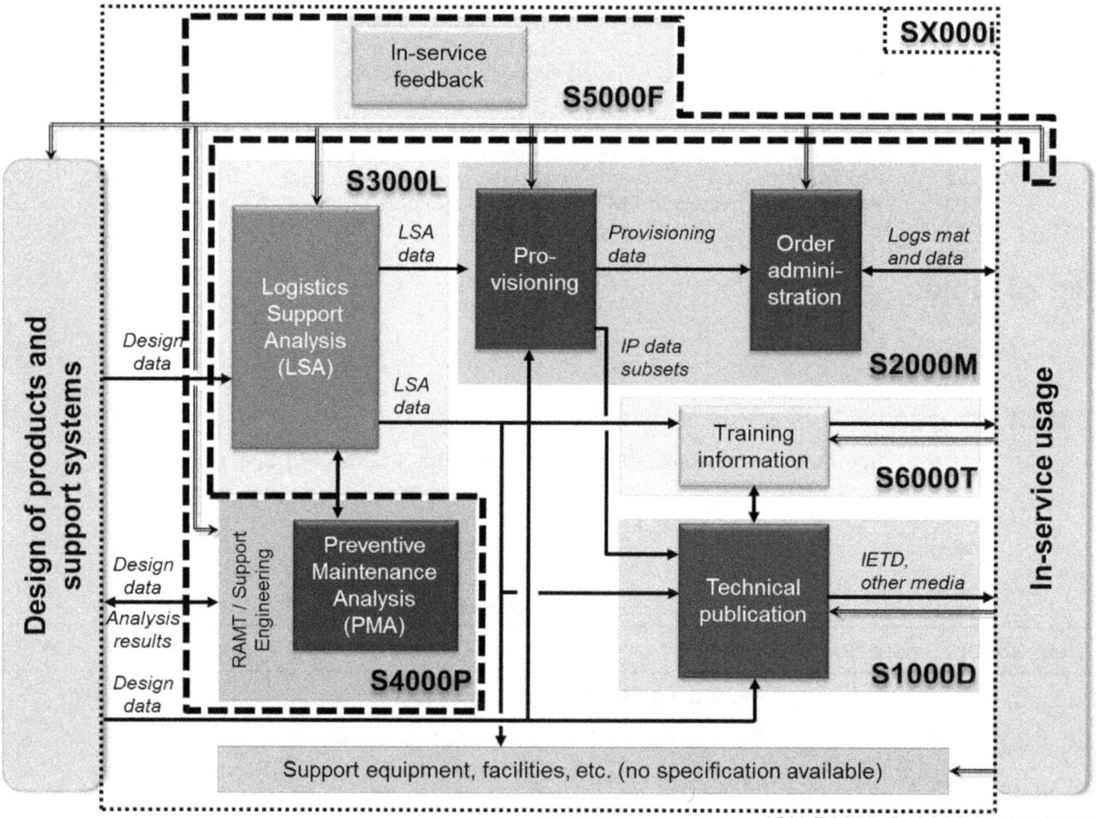

ICN-B6865-S4000P0100-001-01

Fig 1 Interface between S4000P and S5000F in the S-Series IPS Specifications

To perform the analytical work in accordance with S4000P Chap 2 during a Product design and development phase, in-service feedback from the Product under analysis isn't available because the complete Product has not yet been produced, delivered and brought into service.

Note

For selected sub-systems, equipment and/or items not newly developed for the Product under analysis, it is recommended to take in-service data feedback from other Products into account.

During the Product design and development phase feedback sources from Product design and/or suppliers, from S4000P analysts and other receivers of such data are essential.

The scope of S5000F is to handle feedback data collected from the Product in-service operation and missions. The processes in S5000F focus on operational and maintenance feedback information and the Product-related activities that take place in the operational phase of the Product life cycle. The operation phase is broken down into 5 phases. In-service and Disposal are the last two phases of a Product life-cycle that are within the scope of the current S5000F.

Therefore, the essential early Product life cycle feedback is not yet focused in that specification. Requirements for data and experience feedback to Product development, engineering support and suppliers should be raised. Once produced, delivered and brought into service, the efficiency and applicability of Product maintenance must be proved, taking into account the in-service feedback. For that purpose, the Optimization of preventive Product maintenance according to Chap 3 expects data and experience feedback on all valid preventive maintenance tasks defined in a Product maintenance program or Operators' Maintenance Program (OMP). This feedback includes a review and optimization of PMTRI and PMTRE.

For all valid preventive maintenance tasks with scheduled intervals and with PMTRI data, a detailed logic of the ISMO Analysis process logic must be defined in a project-specific analysis guideline of Policy and Procedure Handbook (PPH). ISMO analysts must work through the project-specific ISMO logic and must perform ISMO work steps using S5000F in the following main ISMO analyses modules:

- Maintenance task criticality and applicability analysis
- Servicing task analysis
- Inspection or functional test task analysis (excluding SSI-inspections and zonal inspections)
- Time Change Item (TCI) or overhaul task analysis
- SSI task analysis
- Zonal inspection task analysis
- Interval and trend leader or sample analysis

The information in this chapter supports the definition of data-elements documented and exchanged during a Product in-service phase (refer to Chap 5).

Prior to using any in-service data or any other feedback from a Product in-service phase, the analyst must confirm that the data can:

- fulfil data security and quality requirements
- ensure data completeness
- include a data supplementation
- provide filtered and clustered data
- comprise combined and trustable data (including links in between the data or data-sets)

Each scheduled maintenance task, that becomes due during the in-service phase of a Product must be initiated, be performed and the results be documented on basis of a Maintenance Work Order (MWO). The MWO can be based of paper-based document or - as it is the state of the art for complex technical Products today - in an electronic format. The same documentation-principles can cover unscheduled arisings and/or maintenance work documentation such as, for example, the results from scheduled or unscheduled functional tests.

3 S5000F data feedback to S4000P

3.1 Feedback to the ISMO analysis phase

For the ISMO analysis process (refer to Chap 3.3), in-service data and in-service feedback must be accurate, reliable and free of misleading content or conclusions. It is not possible for an analyst to perform data evaluations and to generate statements based on raw and unchecked data. It is essential for an analyst to receive collated in-service data to be able to correctly combine data, data-sets and other feedback.

Example:

An equipment that was designed and calculated to fail a maximum of 10 times per calendar year, but it fails 100 times per calendar year in a whole Product fleet. Without additional knowledge about the customers' operational or mission scenario, a hasty and wrong analysis can lead to the conclusion that the supplier hasn't met the reliability requirements.

However,

Further customer in-service feedback shows a fault distribution with 2 significant accumulation peaks of equipment failures at two months per year with 95 failures of the whole fleet documented only during these two-time periods. Further data clarifies that during these two months the Product was deployed for specific missions in usage scenarios that are outside the specified design parameters. For the remaining 10 months, with mission usage parameters as specified, the Product performed per the requirements. Consequently, the supplier must concentrate on solving the deviations during the deployment periods and not for the remaining time periods of the year.

During the ISMO analysis process, whatever feedback data, including operational and mission data, is available must be used. This data includes, but is not limited to:

- Product configuration data, built-standard data, life cycle monitoring data
- Simulation and test data of Product prototypes, equipment and items that is accumulating in parallel to a Product in-service phase
- transferable in-service data of the same Product type from other customers
- transferable in-service data of selected equipment or items that are installed on other Products

Note

Even if in-service or feedback data missing or of poor quality, analysis tasks can still be analyzed in the ISMO analysis process. However, the overall effectivity of the ISMO analysis process could be lowered.

3.1.1 Feedback to the ISMO analysis process for scheduled servicing tasks

The feedback of in-service data and experience gained for the ISMO analysis process, depends on the maintenance task type under analysis.

The efficiency of a repetitive scheduled servicing task on an equipment or item of the Product can be reviewed based on of unscheduled events being documented for the related equipment or item. These events must show where and when acceptable tolerance levels are exceeded and must not be confused or associated with the number of removal and install tasks, which may be required for accessibility or other maintenance reasons. Configuration and life cycle data of the impacted equipment or item must be traceable and clearly associated with every technical event in parallel.

If a repetitive scheduled servicing task with intervals is judged to be effective, then failures and/or damages documented by an event impacting the equipment or item should not exist or, at least, the number and severity of the events should remain at an acceptable low and stable level. Any increase of unscheduled events whether linear or exponential over time should lead to a review of the task under analysis because its efficiency is in doubt.

3.1.2 Feedback to the ISMO analysis process for scheduled inspections or functional test tasks

With the exception of Structure Significant Items/ Significant Details (SSI/SD), repetitive scheduled inspections or functional tests must be initiated with an MWO in the normal way. For these maintenance task types, it is essential to document the results from the inspection or functional test and must include a traceable link to the initiating MWO.

The scope of the S5000F feedback enables a trend analysis of the deterioration of the equipment or item, which focusses on the maintenance task under analysis by following up the results of all inspections or functional tests performed.

The schedule interval of the task can be effectively optimized depending on the deterioration trend, including the probability of whether the deterioration is stable, moderately increasing or exponentially increasing etc.

In addition, in-service data/feedback should confirm or otherwise that the condition of the equipment or item was mainly accumulated by scheduled inspections and/or functional tests or by unscheduled inspections and/or functional tests.

3.1.3 Feedback to the ISMO analysis process for scheduled replacements of equipment/item (TCI) or scheduled overhaul

The efficiency of a repetitive scheduled replacement or overhaul task on a Product TCI can be reviewed and proved by checking all unscheduled failures and/or damages being documented for the equipment or item under analysis. Unscheduled failures of the equipment or item must show where and when acceptable tolerance levels are exceeded and must not be confused with documented removal and install tasks, required for accessibility or other maintenance purpose. Configuration and life cycle data of the impacted equipment or item must be traceable and must be clearly associated with every technical event in parallel.

If a repetitive scheduled replacement or overhaul task with intervals is judged to be effective, then unscheduled events and replacements of the equipment or item should not be documented in between the maturity of the scheduled replacement/overhaul tasks. With an unacceptably high number of unscheduled events, the efficiency of the scheduled replacement or overhaul task is in doubt and a review of the analysis task must be performed.

3.1.4 Feedback to the ISMO analysis process for scheduled SSI/SD inspections

SSI with or without SD require repetitive scheduled inspections and/or tests to examine the structural item for potential Structure Fatigue Failures (SFF) and/or to monitor the status of different types of potential damage impacts. Damages on an SSI/SD can be caused by impacts of Environmental Deterioration (ED) and/or from Accidental Damage (AD). The aim is to prove whether relevant damage impacts and potential SSI/SD deterioration remain within a pre-assumed limit or not and whether they could have been prevented.

The repetitive scheduled inspections or tests on SSI/SD are launched by MWO in the same way as for all other scheduled maintenance tasks. Every discovery of an individual SSI/SD must be documented and allocated to the initiating MWO. Precise descriptions of each discovery (including pictures, measurement data from the damaged SSI/SD, etc) must be documented and reference the initiating MWO. Inspection and/or test results such as no SSI/SD discovered, status unchanged and within the tolerance limits etc, must also be documented.

3.1.5 Feedback to the ISMO analysis process for scheduled Zonal inspections

Repetitive scheduled zonal inspections are General Visual Inspections (GVI) in a Product zone. These maintenance tasks are also launched by MWO. Every GVI-based discovery in a zone must be associated with the initiating MWO and data of each discovery (including pictures and precise measurement data from identified failures, damages, Foreign Objects (FO) etc), must be documented.

To evaluate the effectivity of an individual zonal inspection analysis task, it is important to receive feedback from Product in-service phase, if the discoveries in a zone have been predominantly detected based on unscheduled maintenance tasks or based on the scheduled zonal GVI.

3.2 Feedback to the ISMO follow-up phase

For the ISMO Follow-up Phase (refer to Chap 3.4), an evaluation of the complete Product in-service data is necessary to identify reasons giving rise to the Product in-service maintenance effort, which have not been covered by preventive maintenance before.

Documented events and the allocated unscheduled maintenance effort must be evaluated for Product systems, structure or zones for their significant negative impact on Product availability and/or Product Life Cycle Cost (LCC).

3.3 Feedback to reviews of PMTRE for special events

In-service feedback is required to check if pre-defined PMTRE or sets of PMTRE can be judged to be complete and correctly selected when they have been applied after the occurrence of an expected special event.

If a new and unexpected special event has been documented during the Product in-service phase, this must be taken into account when defining appropriate PMTRE for these events. Based on the results of the PMTRE development (refer to Chap 2.7), a future update of the Logistic Support Analysis (LSA) database and of IPS elements (including technical publication) is required.

Chapter 4.6

S4000P Interfaces - SX000i

Table of contents
Page

S4000P Interfaces - SX000i..1

References..1

1   Introduction 2

2   The Product life cycle phases..2

3   Activities during the project preparation phase 3

4   Activities during the Product development phase 4

5   Activities during the Product production phase 5

6   Activities during the Product in-service phase..5

7   Activities during the Product disposal phase..6

List of tables

1   References 1

List of figures

1   Product life cycle phases..2

2   Activities during the project preparation phase 3

3   Activities during the Product development phase 4

4   Activities during the Product production phase 5

5   Activities during the Product in-service phase..5

6   Activities during the Product disposal phase..6

References

Table 1 References

Chap No./Document No.	Title
Chap 2	Developing PMTR
Chap 2.3	Developing PMTR - System analysis
Chap 2.6	Developing PMTR - Consolidation of analysis results, harmonization with other preventive maintenance task requirement sources for traceability
Chap 3	Optimizing PMTR
Chap 3.2	Optimizing PMTR - ISMO preparation phase
Chap 3.3	Optimizing PMTR - ISMO analysis phase
Chap 3.4	Optimizing PMTR - ISMO follow-up phase

Chap No./Document No.	Title
Chap 4.4	S4000P Interfaces - S3000L
Chap 5	Data model and data exchange
Chap 7	Examples
S1000D	International specification for technical publications using a common source database
S3000L	International procedure specification for Logistic Support Analysis - LSA
S5000F	International specification for operational and maintenance data feedback
SX000i	International guide for the use of the S-Series Integrated Logistics Support (IPS) specifications

1 Introduction

SX000i is the overall specification of the S-Series IPS Specifications defining processes and rules valid for all individual specifications of the S-Series. This paragraph does neither describe nor summarize the scope and/or the content of SX000i in order not to duplicate or mismatch with related information inside the S-Series IPS Specifications.

Analytical activities based on Chap 2 and Chap 3 take place at different times throughout a Product life cycle.

Therefore, this is not an interface chapter dealing with data-exchange or having other direct functional interrelations, such as the interfaces S4000P - S3000L and S4000P - S5000F.

The S4000P data model and data exchange with interface to SX000i is described in Chap 5.

2 The Product life cycle phases

SX000i defines the following 5 phases in a Product life cycle:

- Preparation Phase
- Development Phase
- Production Phase
- In-Service Phase
- Disposal

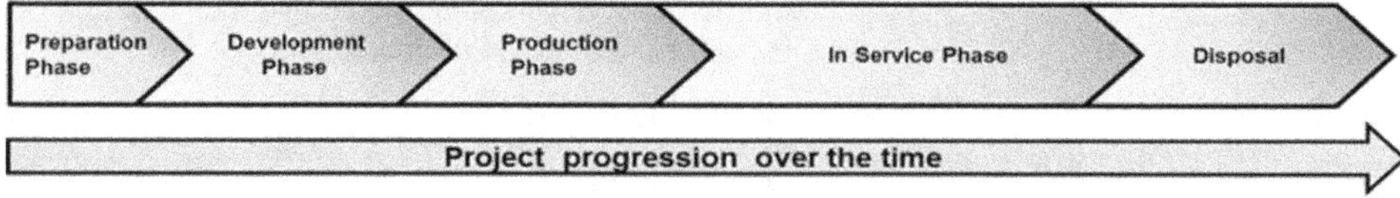

ICN-B6865-S4000P0101-002-01

Fig 1 Product life cycle phases

Depending on the phase in the Product life cycle, different activities are necessary to be focused on. The subsequent paragraph recommends S4000P-related activities and allocates them to the single Product life cycle phases.

Note
> Fig 1 shows a simplified version of the sequence of the single Product life cycle phases. The experience-based overlapping of single phases must be managed.

3 Activities during the project preparation phase

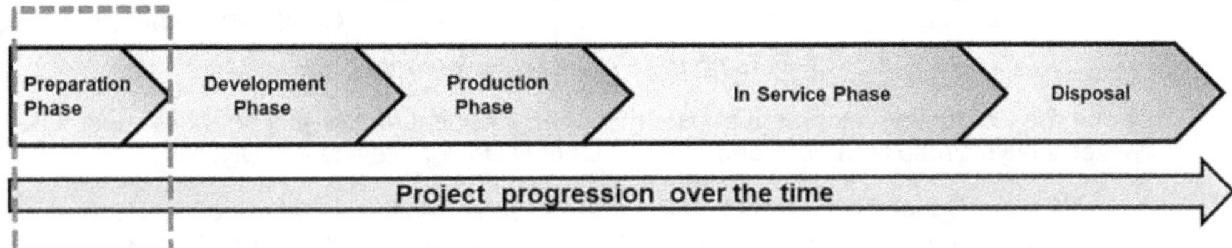

ICN-B6865-S4000P0102-001-01

Fig 2 Activities during the project preparation phase

To define the Product specific analysis amount and methodology precisely, an analysis guideline or Policy and Procedure Handbook (PPH) must be prepared during the project preparation phase.

It is essential that both the customer and regulatory authority are involved.

The PPH should be prepared in the project preparation phase prior to the start of the Product development phase.

When the PPH is prepared, including customer input (eg, planned usage scenario), regulatory authorities must prove and authorize the PPH before the analytical work is started.

A PPH for a Chap 2 analysis that is applicable for the project preparation phase must include, but not be limited to:

- Scope and background information relevant for analysis. Refer to Chap 2.
- Operational and/or mission parameters describing the intended Product use during its later in-service phase as part of a Use Study and, any deviations and/or variants
- Framework information on the planned or actual Product maintenance philosophy
- Overview on the analysis-relevant Product subsystems and areas (eg, because of a pre-selection of ARC, SSI/SD and Product zones
- Specifications, requirements and laws imposed by responsible regulatory authorities and/or by individual nations
- Assignment of responsibilities to perform the analysis work especially for complex projects with several nations involving and/or suppliers
- Organizational, administrational regulations or definitions for analysis responsibilities
- Provisions of analysis tools and/or analyzing logic
- Process logics and descriptions including a review and update process
- Planning guidelines including milestone definitions

Chap 7 of this specification also provides examples for PPH contents based on Chap 2.

4 Activities during the Product development phase

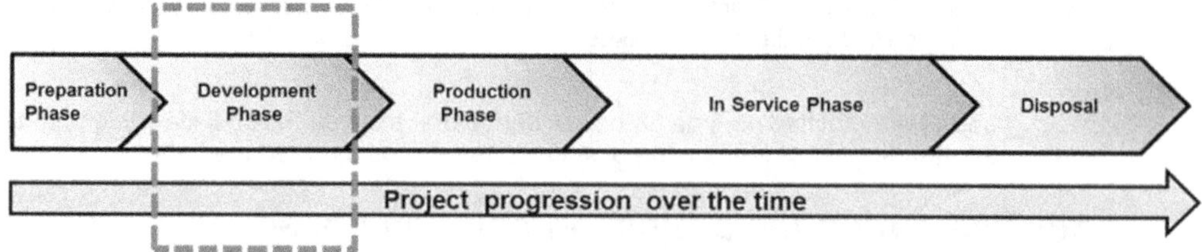

ICN-B6865-S4000P0103-001-01

Fig 3 Activities during the Product development phase

During the Product development phase, the Chap 2 minimum analysis activities must at least deliver analysis results prior to one or more Critical Design Reviews (CDR) for:

- all Failure Causes (FC) identified in Product system analysis that are allocated to Functional Failures (FF) and Functional Failure Effect Categories (FFEC) 1,2, 5 and 6 because these FFEC are certification-relevant. Refer to Chap 3.
- all Structure Significant Items/Structural Details (SSI/SD) identified for the Product structure
- the Enhanced Zonal Analysis
- the Lightning/High Intensity Radiation Field (L/HIRF) Analysis
- additional Zonal Analysis Modules (ZAM) which become relevant for a Product certification process

It is essential that the Chap 2 analysis of these aspects is performed prior to project CDR milestones because of any resulting mandatory re-design requirements, if effective PMTRI cannot be determined.

After the Product design freeze, the development of remaining PMTRI can be performed for:

- FC allocated to FF and the remaining FFEC in Product Systems (means for FFEC 3,4,7 and 8). Refer to Chap 2.3.
- the Maintenance Relevant Structure
- the Standard Zonal Analysis

Based on the PMTRI development, PMTRE can be defined.

After the project CDR, the initial acquisition of logistics-relevant data is mostly completed. However, the analysis activities performed at this stage must be reviewed continuously to keep aligned with the latest Product built-standards and configurations defined in design or by suppliers. A robust Product development process minimizes the risk of the analysis effort.

Note

When defining preventive maintenance tasks for Product prototypes, one or more Product prototypes are designed, produced, assembled and tested in parallel to a Product development process. Also, for the Product prototypes preventive and corrective maintenance tasks must be defined prior to the start of the prototype test activities. In early project stages, Best Engineering Judgement (BEJ) is essential to compensate for any missing analysis results. All experiences from legacy Product variants must be taken into account.

To determine preventive maintenance tasks for the Product prototypes, inputs from Product engineering, suppliers and support engineering must be collected and documented. If analysis results for the serial Product version become available at a later stage and if the analytical results are transferable, they must be implemented into the Product prototype documentation.

The preventive maintenance effort on Product prototypes can be significantly higher in comparison to the preventive maintenance effort on a later serial Product. This is acceptable

because it helps to accumulate experience and technical knowledge about the Product as soon as possible.

5 Activities during the Product production phase

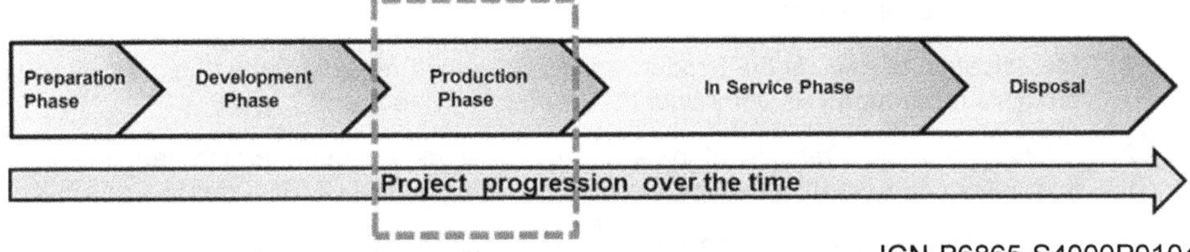

ICN-B6865-S4000P0104-001-01

Fig 4 Activities during the Product production phase

Having successfully passed the project PDR/CDR milestones, the production of the serial Product and its equipment and/or components can commence. Based on the production of equipment at the Product manufacturer and/or at suppliers, the assembly of the Product begins. After final assembly and test, the Product can be delivered.

During the Product production phase all necessary IPS elements must be defined and the IPS products delivered.

Design changes to the Product or its equipment after a CDR milestone, and during the Product production phase, can occur. Analysts must therefore be fully involved in the change processes. PMTR, resulting from Chap 2 analysis, must be checked for validity and kept technically current. The PMTR development must be reviewed, if a design change is required after the PDR/CDR milestones.

The current valid set of PMTR resulting from the Chap 2 analysis forms the input dataset for the Logistic Support Analysis (LSA) according to S3000L and all subsequent IPS activities Refer to Chap 2.6 and Chap 4.4.

6 Activities during the Product in-service phase

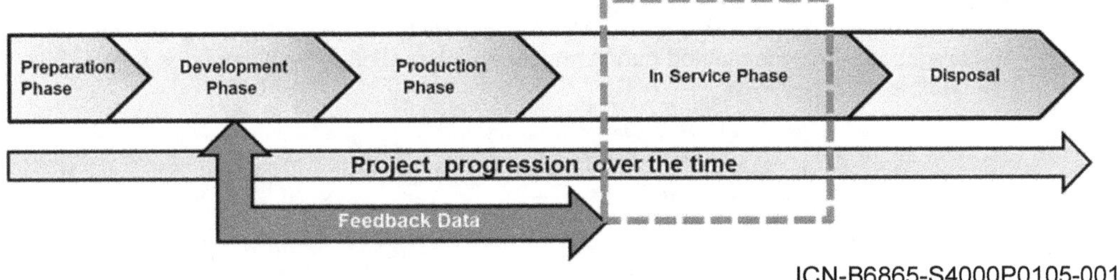

ICN-B6865-S4000P0105-001-01

Fig 5 Activities during the Product in-service phase

Several factors can impact a Product and its IPS elements during a Product in-service phase. Refer to Chap 3. These impacts can even change Product maintenance concepts and can, therefore, impact preventive maintenance tasks previously developed as PMTRI and/or PMTRE. For the evaluation of the effectivity of the preventive maintenance tasks documented in a Product maintenance program or OMP, the review and optimization processes become essential. Refer to Chap 3. The Product maintenance program or OMP is part of the Product's Technical Publications. Refer to S1000D.

An analysis guideline or PPH must also be prepared prior to the start of the review and optimization analysis. Refer to Chap 3. The analysis guideline or PPH also needs approval and authorization by regulatory authorities. An example of a PPH is given at Chap 7.

The Product In-Service Maintenance Optimization (ISMO) process (refer Chap 3.2 thru Chap 3.4) covers three functions:

1   Identification of gaps in the Product analysis and identification of a minimum Product analysis for an analysis compensation. Refer to Chap 2 and Chap 3.2.

2   Evaluation of the effectivity of the existing repetitive scheduled maintenance tasks with intervals documented, including the initiating PMTRI and CMR. Refer to Chap 3.3.

3   Evaluation of frequent unscheduled maintenance tasks for Product systems, structure and or zone resulting in a high maintenance effort that was not preventively maintained due to the Product maintenance program or OMP before. The options to be evaluated are to extend the set of PMTRI and/or to propose re-design. Refer to Chap 3.4.

The PMTRE review and/or optimization completes activities during the Product in-service phase. Refer to Chap 3.5.

7   Activities during the Product disposal phase

ICN-B6865-S4000P0106-001-01

Fig 6   Activities during the Product disposal phase

In general, this analysis is not foreseen during the Product disposal phase. Product disposal is subject to S3000L.

Note

This analysis can become applicable, particularly for complex Products that must be (partly) operational and maintained during a disposal phase, eg to be dismantled safely. This must be defined in the PPH.

Chapter 5

Data model and data exchange

Chapter	Data module title	Data module code	Applic
Chap 5.1	Data model and data exchange - General	S4000P-A-05-01-0000-00A-040A-A	All
Chap 5.2	Data model and data exchange - Data model	S4000P-A-05-02-0000-00A-040A-A	All
Chap 5.3	Data model and data exchange - Data exchange	S4000P-A-05-03-0000-00A-040A-A	All

Page intentionally blank.

Chapter 5.1

Data model and data exchange - General

Table of contents   Page

1   General 1

List of tables

1   References 1

References

Table 1 References

Chap No./Document No.	Title
None	

1   General

To achieve a quick, correct and current exchange of information of analytical work based on S4000P, the data exchange process and data model with applicable data elements must be defined.

The objective of the data model is described in Chap 5.2.

The data exchange is described in Chap 5.3.

Page intentionally blank.

Chapter 5.2

Data model and data exchange - Data model

Table of contents

Page

Data model and data exchange - Data model 1

References..1

1   Introduction 1

2   Objective 2

List of tables

1   References 1

References

Table 1 References

Chap No./Document No.	Title
Chap 3	Optimizing PMTR
S1000D	International specification for technical publications using a common source database
S3000L	International procedure specification for Logistic Support Analysis - LSA
SX000i	International guide for the use of the S-Series Integrated Product Support (IPS) specifications
www.uml.org	Unified Modelling Language (UML) Version 2

1   Introduction

A coherent data model for the data that can be exchanged between the analyses defined in S4000P and the S-Series IPS specifications and business processes is described herein. Related business processes can be either business processes that are dependent upon data being produced as a result from an S4000P analysis, or business processes that provide inputs to an analysis.

The S4000P data model is described using the UML (Unified Modeling Language) Version 2, class model (www.uml.org), and will be exchanged through an XML schema.

The S4000P data model must be harmonized with S3000L and is aligned in the Data Model and Exchange Working Group (DMEWG) of SX000i. Updates to the S3000L data model will be reflected in the S4000P data model as required. Direct interfaces with S1000D are possible through the flexibility in the S3000L/S4000P data model with the possibility of supporting multiple Breakdown Element Identifiers (BEI) in the Product Breakdown Structure (PBS). This is important for the review and optimization process of preventive Product maintenance. Refer to Chap 3.

2 Objective

The objective of the S4000P data model is to create a data-set that:

- can hold all relevant information that is required for certification purposes or other legal reasons
- gives traceability of the decisions made, including the justifications and the results of the analysis
- preserves data for later reference and re-use
- supports the creation of an XML schema for exchanging data between instances
- enables project tailoring of data requirements

Chapter 5.3

Data model and data exchange - Data exchange

Table of contents

Page

Data model and data exchange - Data exchange 1

References...1

1   General 1

List of tables

1   References 1

References

Table 1 References

Chap No./Document No.	Title
Chap 2	Developing PMTR
Chap 3	Optimizing PMTR

1   General

The data exchange mechanism for S4000P is the exchange of an XML file and associated schema or set of schemas. Every project applying S4000P, tailors the schema using a Guidance Document, which is discussed and agreed upon in the Guidance Conference. The default S4000P data schema can be, but must not be, tailored through the embedded schemas for valid values.

The exchange of data will always be a full data set. If required, intermediate updates will be agreed by the project.

The initial development of PMTR (refer to Chap 2) and the continuously improvement of preventive Product maintenance with PMTR review and optimization according (refer to Chap 3) can both use the same data model and exchange schemas. One is not dependent on the other.

Page intentionally blank.

Chapter 6

Terms, abbreviations and acronyms

Chapter	Data module title	Data module code	Applic
Chap 6	Terms, abbreviations and acronyms	S4000P-A-06-00-0000-00A-009A-A	All
Chap 6.1	Terms, abbreviations and acronyms - General	S4000P-A-06-01-0000-00A-040A-A	All
Chap 6.2	Terms, abbreviations and acronyms - Glossary of terms	S4000P-A-06-02-0000-00A-040A-A	All
Chap 6.3	Terms, abbreviations and acronyms - Abbreviations and acronyms	S4000P-A-06-03-0000-00A-040A-A	All

Page intentionally blank.

Chapter 6.1

Terms, abbreviations and acronyms - General

Table of contents
Page

Terms, abbreviations and acronyms - General...1

References..1

1   General 1

List of tables

1   References 1

References

Table 1 References

Chap No./Document No.	Title
Chap 6.2	Terms, abbreviations and acronyms - Glossary of terms
Chap 6.3	Terms, abbreviations and acronyms - Abbreviations and acronyms

1   General

For the glossary of terms (refer to Chap 6.2) and a list of acronyms and abbreviations (refer to Chap 6.3).

Page intentionally blank.

Chapter 6.2

Terms, abbreviations and acronyms - Glossary of terms

Table of contents
Page

1   Glossary of terms..1

List of tables

1   References 1

References

Table 1 References

Chap No./Document No.	Title
None	

1   Glossary of terms

Term	Definition
acceptable corrosion level	A corrosion damage that does not require structural reinforcement or replacement or corrosion occurring between successive inspections exceeds allowable limit but is local and can be attributed to an event not typical of operator usage of other Products in the same Product fleet, (eg, Corrosion Level 1).
Accidental Damage (AD)	A physical deterioration of an item caused by contact or impact with an object or influence which is not a part of the Product, or by human error during manufacturing, assembly, operation of the Product, and/or maintenance practices.
Analysis Relevant Candidate (ARC)	An item in the Product breakdown structure identified by the manufacturer on highest manageable level in the frame of system analysis, whose Functional Failure (FF): – could affect Product safety – could conflict with law and/or could have significant impact on environmental integrity (ie, ecological damage) – could have an impact on mission/operational capability – could have a significant economic impact
conditional probability of failure	The probability that a failure will occur in a specific period provided that the item concerned has survived to the beginning of that period.

contingency period	A phase to continue to operate the Product in safe conditions while operating conditions allow as many maintenance tasks, detailed in the standard Product maintenance program/Operator's Maintenance Program (OMP), as possible to be accomplished. During this period, only minimum maintenance tasks required for safety, law conformity (including environmental integrity) and mission or operation will be performed.
Corrosion Prevention and Control Program (CPCP)	Selected maintenance tasks implemented at an interval threshold to control and protect a Product structure not to exceed an acceptable corrosion level. Applicable maintenance tasks are composed of both preventive servicing and inspection tasks.
crisis time	A sequence of interactions between the governments of two or more sovereign states in severe conflict, short of actual war, but involving the perception of a dangerously high probability of war. In this crucial, unstable situation action might be taken associated with or performed by armed services.
damage tolerant Product structure	Product structure in which the FF of a single structural member will result in only a small reduction in the residual strength of the whole. The design allows for alternative load paths to mitigate the effect of a structural failure. Damage tolerant Product structures require preventive inspection or functional test. They are designed so that any cracks occurring will grow in an expected process being detectable before attaining critical length.
delamination/separation of material layers	A separation of material layers of a non-metallic structural material or cracking that occurs at or in one or more material bond planes, caused by accidental damage, environmental impact parameters and/or cyclic loading.
deployment	The distribution of a military unit, weapon systems, resources or similar systematically or strategically to perform operations/missions temporarily dislocated from the normally assigned duty area.

direct adverse effect on operating safety

Direct

– To be direct, the FF or resulting secondary damage must achieve its effect by itself, not in combination with other functional failures (no redundancy exists).

Adverse effect on safety

– If the consequence of the FF cause injury to or death of one or more human beings, safety is adversely affected.

Operating

– The time interval or period during which the Product is activated or operated or in a usage condition and one or more human beings are or can be impacted by the Product.

economic Functional Failure Effects (FFE)	All Functional Failure Effects (FFE), which have no impact on safety, do not conflict with law/environmental integrity, do not prevent from Product operation/mission, but having an economic impact on Product Life Cycle Cost (LCC) due to the resulting maintenance effort.

environment	The effects of the atmosphere, corrosive materials, condensation, temperature, and vibration on the protection, with respect to Product degradation.
Environmental Deterioration (ED)	The physical deterioration of an item's strength or resistance to failure, because of chemical interaction with its climate or environment.
exploration operation safety	A systematic evaluation of an item based on analysis of collected information from in-service experience. It verifies the item's resistance to a deterioration process with respect to increasing age.
Failure Cause	The reason for an FF.
fatigue related sampling inspection	The inspections on specific Product selected from those which have the highest operating age or usage to identify the first evidence of deterioration in their condition caused by fatigue damage.
failure	Termination of the ability of an item to perform a required function.
fault	An identifiable technical condition in which one element of a redundant system design has failed (ie, no longer available) without impact on the required function output of the Product system. At the system level, a fault is not considered to lead to an FF.
fault-tolerant system	A Product system design with redundant elements to ensure systems function properly even in case of one or more faults. Single faults are not acceptable to impact safety, to lead to a collision with law/environmental integrity, to reduce Product availability for mission/operation or to cause unacceptable high Life Cycle Costs (LCC).
Function (F)	The normal characteristic actions and/or performance of an item.
Functional Failure (FF)	The system, subsystem, equipment or item (including hardware with or without software) fails to perform its designed function to an expected level of performance.
Functional Failure Effect (FFE)	The end effect of a Functional Failure on the Product level.
Functional failure Effect collides with law	The FF causes the Product to be temporarily or permanently - not in accordance with released national and/or international legal regulations. Refer to FFE.
Functional failure Effect impacts ecological integrity	The FF causes a reversible or irreversible pollution/poisoning of the environment with temporary and/or permanent consequences for the ecosystem. Refer to FFE.
functional test	A quantitative test to determine if one or more functions of an item or a system performs within specified limits. The maintenance task must be able to detect degradation (eg, wear, leakage, etc) and not just the complete failure.
hard time	The removal from service of an item at a specified life limit when no repair task is effective or applicable.

hidden function	Active hidden function
	– A function which is normally active and whose cessation will not be evident to the operating crew/personnel during performance of normal duties.
	Inactive hidden function
	– A function which is normally inactive and whose readiness to perform, prior to it being needed, will not be evident to the operating crew/personnel during performance of normal duties.
inherent level of reliability and safety	The level which is built into the unit and, therefore, inherent in its design. This is the highest level of reliability and safety that can be expected from a Product if it receives effective maintenance to achieve higher levels of reliability generally requires modification or redesign.
inspection - DETailed (DET)	An intensive visual examination of Product hardware to detect damage, failure or any visible irregularity. Additional lightning support can be selected and further inspection aids (eg, mirrors, magnifying lenses, etc) can be necessary. Surface cleaning and elaborate access procedures can additionally be required.
Inspection - General Visual Inspection (GVI)	A visual surveillance inspection of an interior or exterior area of the Product, of hardware installation/assembly to detect obvious damage, failure or other visible irregularity (eg, foreign object impact). A mirror or available consumables can be necessary to support this inspection task without using specific support equipment and/or consumables. The removal or opening of access panels/doors, the use of stands, ladders or platforms can be required to gain adequate access.
inspection - Special Detailed Inspection (SDI)	An intensive visual examination concentrated on a specific item, hardware installation/assembly to detect damage, failure or other visible irregularity. The extensive use of specialized inspection techniques and/or support equipment can be appropriate. Extensive cleaning and enhanced effort related to access/disassembly can be required.
inspection - routine	A dedicated package of inspection tasks which must be performed, for example, before, between and after the use/operation/mission of a Product. (eg, before flight, after flight or at a turnaround inspection, etc).
inspection - simple	An inspection that can be performed by a human being without the use of any further technical support means (support and test equipment). GVI, DETailed inspections (DET) and Routine inspections are simple inspections.
inspection - zonal	Refer to GVI
interval (initial - repeat)	Initial interval or threshold
	– The interval between the start of Product service-life and the first time the selected scheduled maintenance task is performed.
	Repeat interval
	– The repetitive scheduled interval being valid for the same maintenance task after having passed the initial interval/threshold.

item	Any level of hardware assembly (system, subsystem, part, module, component, unit, tool, accessory, etc).
Item - Structure Significant Item (SSI)	A structural item or assembly, which is judged significantly due to carrying aerodynamic, ground, pressure or control loads and whose failure could affect the structural integrity necessary for the operating safety of the Product and/or could impact human safety and/or could impact law and/or environmental integrity.
Life Cycle (LC)	Series of stages through which an item goes, from its conception to disposal.
limitations	A section of the Instructions for Continued Operation Safety that contains each mandatory replacement time, structural inspection interval, and related structural inspection task. This section can also be used to define a threshold for the fatigue related inspections and the need to control corrosion to Level 1 or better. The information contained in the section with Item Life Limitations can be changed to reflect service and/or test experience or new analysis methods.
maintenance relevant structure	A structural item or assembly of the Product which can cause high maintenance effort and/or can have significant impact on the Product availability in case of fatigue failure and/or damage.
maintenance task	An action or a set of actions required to achieve a desired outcome, which identifies the condition of an item, restores an item to and/or maintains an item in serviceable condition.
maintenance task applicability	The technical requirements must be fulfilled, required conditions and prerequisites must be appropriate to select the maintenance task type in order to identify and/or to eliminate the FC under analysis.
maintenance task effectiveness	The economic requirements must be fulfilled from the Life Cycle Cost (LCC) perspective, the conditions and prerequisites must be appropriate to select the maintenance task type with scheduled intervals that is previously selected as technical applicable.
maintenance task type	A maintenance task type is part of the main preventive maintenance task categories servicing, inspection/functional test and TCI/overhaul (eg, a lubrication task as part of the maintenance task category servicing).
missions (military or civil)	The specific Product operations performed in the frame of Product usage. Examples from aeronautic industry: – Medical transport or evacuation flights (eg, MEDEVAC) – External cargo/load transport on helicopters – Firefighting flights – Air-to-air refueling – Boarder control flights – Approach and landing on unpaved runways – Autonomous approach – Formation flight – Low/high level flight

mission capability	The Product must be capable to carry out the pre-planned mission. That includes the functionality of the mission-specific equipment. The mission capability is more focused on the military use of a Product. Refer to operational capability.
non-ARC	An item from the Product breakdown structure, which is not relevant to a deeper system analytical effort after having finished the ARC and non-ARC selection.
non-critical structure	Refer to uncritical structure.
non-metallic	Any structural material without metallic components composed of components such as graphite, fiberglass or Kevlar layers, acrylics bonded together by a medium. An applicable adhesive is used as a bonding medium to permanently join these kinds of components.
normal duties	Those duties associated with the operation of the Product, on a daily basis (or every time the Product is used), to include the following: – Procedures and checks performed during Product operation in accordance with the Product maintenance and operating publications. – Recognition of abnormalities or failures by the operating crew or personnel using normal physical senses (noise, vibration, temperature, visual observation of damage or failure, changes in physical input force requirements, etc). Refer to operating crew/personnel.
operational capability	The Product must be capable to carry out the pre-planned operation. The operational capability is more focused on the civil use of a Product. Refer to mission capability.
operating crew/personnel	The trained and qualified personnel who are on duty to operate the Product. In most cases, the maintenance crew is not part of operating crew. Refer to normal duties.
operational check	An operational check is a maintenance task to determine that an item is fulfilling its intended purpose. Does not require quantitative tolerances. This is a failure finding maintenance task.
Operational/mission effect	The effect of an FF on the intended Product operation and/or mission. The related FF can cause delay, cancellation, interruption, restriction, derogation, etc, of the intended Product operation/mission.
other structure	Refer to uncritical structure.
Partner Company (PC)	A company, which is responsible to design structure parts, equipment or systems of the technical Product in line with an agreed Product work share.
potential failure (detectable)	An identifiable condition of an item under analysis that indicates an FF will occur if no preventive maintenance will be performed.

preventive maintenance task	A maintenance activity to timely identify and/or eliminate a potential FC or consequence of a damage prior to an FF of the affected item or zone. The scope is to avoid the occurrence of a FFE for the Product related to the following FFE categories: – safety – conflict with law / environmental integrity – mission/operational availability – economy For a preventive maintenance task all IPS elements have been defined to perform the task. Preventive maintenance includes scheduled activities with numerical interval values and interval types and activities following special events (eg, after a lightning strike on an aircraft). For these events scheduled intervals or interval thresholds cannot be defined. For example, typical interval types are based on calendar time (ie, days, months, years, etc) and usage-oriented parameters such as operating cycles or operating hours. Therefore, scheduled maintenance is a subset of preventive maintenance. For scheduled maintenance tasks the final interval types and numerical interval values are defined in a Product maintenance program/OMP (eg, after task packaging).
Preventive Maintenance Task Requirements (PMTR)	A preventive maintenance task requirement (PMTR) is the result from a project-specific analytical work based on a Policy and Procedure Handbook (PPH). Every PPH details one or more applicable analysis methodologies for developing and/or improving PMTR. PMTR can be subdivided into PMTRI (ie, PMTR with repetitive scheduled intervals) and PMTRE (ie, PMTR which are to be performed after special events). The determination of each PMTRI must be traceable on basis of data from a related Product system analysis, structure analysis and/or zonal analysis. The traceability comprises the allocation of each PMTRI to a worst-case Functional Failure Effect Code (FFEC). Single numerical interval values or interval types of PMTRI can be adapted prior the definition of final preventive maintenance tasks in the Product Technical Publication (eg, an adaption of numerical interval values can be required. Refer to S3000L. The determinations of PMTRE take into account the results from PMTRI analysis.
Preventive Maintenance Task Requirements Event (PMTRE)	One or more PMTR which has/have to be performed after an assumption/detection of the entry of a special event. These PMTR have no scheduled interval.
Preventive Maintenance Task Requirements Interval (PMTRI)	One or more PMTR with one or more repetitive scheduled intervals each. A scheduled interval is composed of a numerical interval value plus an interval type.
Preventive Maintenance Review Board (PMRB)	A board of maintenance experts taking part in regular meetings to discuss both procedural steps and analysis results.
prime manufacturer	A manufacturer responsible for the complete Product.
Product	Any technical platform, system, equipment, vehicle, facility, etc, be it air, sea, land, space, civil or military eg, aerial ropeway systems, trains, ships, submarines, wind energy production plants, etc.

Product Breakdown Structure (PBS)	The Product Breakdown Structure provides an exhaustive, hierarchical tree structure of items that make up the Product, arranged in whole-part relationship.
project	The task spectrum to develop, maintain and dispose of the Product.
protection device	Technical system, equipment or item installed to avoid, eliminate or reduce the consequences of a special event or of other functional impacts.
P to F interval	Interval between the point at which a potential failure becomes detectable and the point at which it causes an FF.
restoration	The work on or off the Product required so that its resistance to failure can be restored to an acceptable level.
routine inspection	A line maintenance activity on Product. Example from aeronautics industry: daily, preflight, turnaround/transit, post flight inspections.
safe life structure	A Product structure designed such that its inherent strength combined with the imposition of a Safe Life prevents failure from fatigue maximum during Product service life. Safe life structure with a limited service life can be selected as Time Change Item (TCI).
safety effect	An effect on safety implies that the consequences of the FC is extremely serious or possible catastrophic and could cause: – injury to human beings – the loss of the Product itself or related Products – extensive damage to equipment
safety/emergency systems or equipment	A device or system that: – enhances the evacuation of the Product in an emergency or if it does not function when required – results in a failure condition that might have an adverse effect on safety
scheduled maintenance task	Refer to preventive maintenance task.
Significant Detail (SD)	A limited area of an SSI or a local spot being also part of the whole SSI.
servicing	Any act of lubricating or other servicing tasks such as washing, replenishment of consumables, etc, for maintaining inherent design capabilities.
special event	A special event occurs unexpected during the in-service phase of a Product. For example, irregular environmental impacts, unforeseen accidental impacts, the usage of a Product outside specified parameters are special events. If a special event has appeared or is assumed to have appeared, potential failures and/or damages must be detected and maintained (if necessary) prior to an FF. Regular impacts on the Product and Product usage parameters do not lead to special events. These impacts and parameters have been taken into account for both the Product design and for the definition of the repetitive scheduled Product maintenance.

stand-alone maintenance task	A maintenance task selected either in the enhanced zonal analysis in the L/HIRF protection analysis or by another certification relevant Zonal Analysis Module (ZAM) during the zonal analysis process. Each stand-alone maintenance task with an interval must prevent at least probable safety relevant failure effects. Due to the critical background of this maintenance task any merging with other maintenance tasks, such as with a GVI of a zone, is therefore not allowed. For traceability all stand-alone maintenance tasks must be separately listed in a Product maintenance program/OMP to be carried out during the Product in-service phase.
structural assembly	Several structural items, which together provide a basic structural function.
structural function	The mode of action of Product structure. It includes acceptance and transfer of specified loads in items (eg, details, elements, assemblies) and provides consistently adequate Product response and operation characteristics.
Structure Fatigue Failure (SFF)	The loss of a structural function occasioned by the application of cyclic, tensile stresses to an element of structure. The nature of the material, imposed stress levels and the method of fabrication determine the number of cycles required to induce cracks with subsequent propagation.
Structural Significant Item (SSI)	A structural item or assembly of the Product, which contributes significantly to carrying loads (eg, flight, ground, pressure or control loads on an aircraft). The fatigue failure and/or damage could affect the structural integrity necessary for the operating safety of the Product and/or could impact human safety and/or could collide with law, including environmental integrity.
susceptibility to damage	The likelihood of damage during maintenance or during operations or missions.
Time Change Item (TCI)	An equipment/item on the Product which must be replaced prior to a predefined replacement interval is exceeded.
Temporary Protection System (TPS)	A single servicing task or servicing task packages, which are suitable to protect metallic SSI/SD from a negative corrosion impact during a certain period of time. After a deadline has passed the temporary protection task must be performed again or if the environmental impact on the Product changes.
uncritical structure	A Product structure which is judged neither to be a Structure Significant Item (SSI) nor a maintenance relevant structure. The loss of the item function has no significant impact during the Product in-service phase.
Zonal Analysis Module (ZAM)	A part of the Product zonal analysis that covers either general analysis aspects (standard zonal analysis) or Product-specific analysis aspects. ZAM must be defined in a PPH individually for a Product.

Page intentionally blank.

Chapter 6.3

Terms, abbreviations and acronyms - Abbreviations and acronyms

Table of contents
Page

1 Abbreviations and acronyms 1
1.1 General 1
1.2 Word combination - Acronym 1
1.3 Tense and number 1
1.4 Abbreviation and acronym list 1

List of tables

1 References 1

References

Table 1 References

Chap No./Document No.	Title
None	

1 Abbreviations and acronyms

1.1 General

When there is doubt that an abbreviation or acronym will be understood or whenever there is ample space to write in full, the term must be written out rather than abbreviated. Abbreviations and acronyms listed reflect their use in S4000P and not in other documents.

1.2 Word combination - Acronym

Abbreviations for word combinations, acronyms, must be used as such and not separated for use singly, unless authorized singly.

Single abbreviations can be combined when necessary if there is no abbreviation listed for the combination.

1.3 Tense and number

The same abbreviation must be used for all tenses, possessive cases, singular and plural forms of a given word.

1.4 Abbreviation and acronym list

Abbreviation/acronym	Definition
AD	Accidental Damage
ADR	Alternative Dispute Resolution
AECMA	Association européenne des constructeurs de matériel aérospatial

AFRP	Aramid Fiber Reinforced Plastic (Kevlar)
AIA	Aerospace Industries Association
ARC	Analysis Relevant Candidate
ASD	Aerospace and Defense Industries association of Europe
ATA	Air Transport Association (of America)
A4A	Airlines for America
BEI	Breakdown Element Identifier(s)
BIT	Built-In Test
CC	Certification Committee
CCMR	Candidate Certification Maintenance Requirement
CDR	Critical Design Review
CFRP	Carbon Fiber Reinforced Plastic
CMR	Certification Maintenance Requirement
CPCP	Corrosion Prevention and Control Program
CPSC	(ASD) Customer Product Support Committee (from 2011: PSG - Product Support Group)
DEF-STAN	DEFence STANdard
DET	DETailed inspection
DMC	Data Module Code (see AIA/ASD S1000D)
DMEWG	Data Model and Exchange Working Group
D&D	Design and Development
ED	Environmental Deterioration
EIS	Entry Into Service
EWIS	Electrical Wiring Interconnection System
EZAP	Enhanced Zonal Analysis Procedure
F	Function(al)
FC	Failure Cause
FF	Functional Failure
FFE	Functional Failure Effect
FFEC	Functional Failure Effect Code
FHA	Functional Hazard Analysis
FMEA	Failure Mode and Effects Analysis
FMECA	Failure Mode and Effects Criticality Analysis
FTA	Fault Tree Analysis

GFRP	Glass Fiber Reinforced Plastic
GVI	General Visual Inspection
ICC	International Chamber of Commerce
ILS	Integrated Logistic Support
IPR	Intellectual Property Rights
IPS	Integrated Product Support
ISMO	In-Service Maintenance Optimization
IT	Information Technology
LC	Life Cycle
LCC	Life Cycle Costs
LCN	Logistic Control Number
L/HIRF	Lightning/High Intensity Radiated Field
LIL	Lifed Item List
LSA	Logistic Support Analysis
MSG-3	Maintenance Steering Group 3
MTA	Maintenance Task Analysis
MTL	Master Task List
N/A	Not Applicable
NBC	Nuclear, Biological, Chemical
NDT	Non Destructive Test(ing)
OEM	Original Equipment Manufacturer
OH	Operating Hours
OMP	Operators' Maintenance Program
OMR	Other Maintenance Requirement
PBL	Performance Based Logistics
PBS	Product Breakdown Structure
PC	Partner Company
PDR	Preliminary Design Review
PHCM	Product Health and Condition Monitoring
PMRB	Preventive Maintenance Review Board
PMRBR	Preventive Maintenance Review Board Record
PMTR	Preventive Maintenance Task Requirement
PMTRE	Preventive Maintenance Task Requirement for a special Event

PMTRI	Preventive Maintenance Task Requirement with repetitive scheduled Interval(s)
P/N	Part Number
PPH	Policy and Procedure Handbook (product-specific)
PSSG	Product Services Specification Group (within ASD)
PZP	Product Zonal Plan
RCM	Reliability Centered Maintenance
RMTS	Reliability, Maintainability, Testability, Safety
SBC	System Breakdown Code
SC	Steering Committee
SD	Significant Detail (on an SSI)
SDI	Special Detailed Inspection
SFF	Structure Fatigue Failure
SHA	System Hazard Analysis
SHCM	Structure Health and Condition Monitoring
SSA	System Safety Assessment
SSHA	System Safety Hazard Analysis
SSI	Structural Significant Item
TCI	Time Change Item - listed in Lifed Item List (LIL)
TPS	Temporary Protection System
UV	Ultra-Violet light
ZAM	Zonal Analysis Module
ZHA	Zonal Hazard Analysis

Chapter 7

Examples

Chapter	Data module title	Data module code	Applic
Chap 7.1	Examples - General	S4000P-A-07-01-0000-00A-040A-A	All
Chap 7.2	Examples - Product system analysis	S4000P-A-07-02-0000-00A-040A-A	All
Chap 7.3	Examples - Policy and Procedure Handbook content	S4000P-A-07-03-0000-00A-040A-A	All

Page intentionally blank.

Chapter 7.1

Examples - General

Table of contents

Page

Examples - General 1
References 1
1   General 1

List of tables

1   References 1

References

Table 1 References

Chap No./Document No.	Title
Chap 2	Developing PMTR
Chap 3	Optimizing PMTR
Chap 7.2	Examples - Product system analysis
Chap 7.3	Examples - Policy and Procedure Handbook content

1   General

Depending on the needs of Product users/customers and/or Product manufacturers/suppliers this chapter will be updated/supplemented with further examples (eg, structure analysis, zonal analysis modules (ZAM), PMTRE development, PMTR review and optimization processes) in future document issues.

A detailed example of an implementation of a system analysis is given in Chap 7.2.

Examples of the content for Product analysis, using the Chap 2 and Chap 3 of this specification, is given in Chap 7.3.

Page intentionally blank.

Chapter 7.2

Examples - Product system analysis

Table of contents

Page

Examples - Product system analysis 1
References 2
1 Example for a Product system analysis in accordance with Chapter 2.3 2
1.1 Introduction 2
2 Design overview on the analysis example Mountain Bike 2
3 Functional description of the Mountain Bike brake system 4
4 System analysis Mountain Bike front brake 4
4.1 Step 1: ARC/non-ARC determination 5
4.2 Step 2: ARC System FMEA 6
4.3 Step 3: FF Categorization 7
4.4 Step 4: FC + PHCM Assessment 7
4.5 PMTRI task type selection criteria 10
4.6 PMTRI interval definition 11
4.7 Result summary from Mountain Bike system analysis example 14
4.8 PMTRI data transfer to S3000L via PMTRI data list 14

List of tables

1 References 2

List of figures

1 Mountain Bike design overview 1 2
2 Mountain Bike design overview 2 3
3 Mountain Bike front brake sub-system: Design details (Sheet 1 of 2) 3
4 Mountain Bike front brake sub-system: Design details (Sheet 2 of 2) 4
5 System analysis Mountain Bike - Step 1 5
6 System analysis Mountain Bike - Step 2 6
7 System analysis Mountain Bike - Step 3 7
8 System analysis Mountain Bike - Step 4 (Part 1) 8
9 System analysis Mountain Bike - Step 4 (Part 2) 9
10 System analysis Mountain Bike - Step 4 (Part 3) 9
11 PMTRI task type selection criteria 10
12 PMTRI interval definition logic (PMTRI 1) 11
13 PMTRI interval definition logic (PMTRI 2) 12
14 PMTRI interval definition logic (PMTRI 3) 13
15 Results from Mountain Bike system analysis example 14
16 PMTRI data transfer to S3000L via PMTRI data list 14

References

Table 1 References

Chap No./Document No.	Title
Chap 2.3	Developing PMTR - System analysis

1 Example for a Product system analysis in accordance with Chapter 2.3

1.1 Introduction

After a short design overview and a functional description of the Mountain Bike selected for this system analysis example. Refer to Para 2 and Para 3, respectively.

The four steps of the system analysis in accordance with Chap 2.3 are performed on the Mountain Bike sub system front brake. Refer to Para 4.

- ARC/non-ARC Determination
- ARC System FMEA
- FF Categorization
- FC + PHCM Assessment

The detailed knowledge about the individual technical Product design and its functional layout is the prerequisite to correctly perform the analytical work.

2 Design overview on the analysis example Mountain Bike

Both the design and all functions of the Product under analysis must be defined by responsible design departments and/or by OEMs. Analysis-relevant data and information must be available at the analyst.

Fig 1, Fig 2, Fig 3, and Fig 4 give an overview on the design of the analysis-relevant Mountain Bike.

ICN-B6865-S4000P0107-001-01

Fig 1 Mountain Bike design overview 1

From the Product Mountain Bike shown in Fig 1 the brake system (Pos. 2) is selected for this system analysis example.

			PARTNUMBER	NCAGE	DESCRIPTION
000	1		MTB-2000M	B6865	MOUNTAIN BIKE
001	2		MTB-WHS800	B6865	WHEELS
002	2		MTB-BRS800	B6865	BRAKE SYSTEM (REF TO FIG 02)
003	2		MTB-STS800	B6865	STEERING SYSTEM
004	2		MTB-FRS800	B6895	FRAME SYSTEM
005	2		MTB-DTS800	B6865	DRIVE TRAIN SYSTEM
006			MTB-GES800	B6865	GEAR SYSTEM

ICN-B6865-S4000P0108-001-01

Fig 2 Mountain Bike design overview 2

ICN-B6865-S4000P0109-001-01

Fig 3 Mountain Bike front brake sub-system: Design details (Sheet 1 of 2)

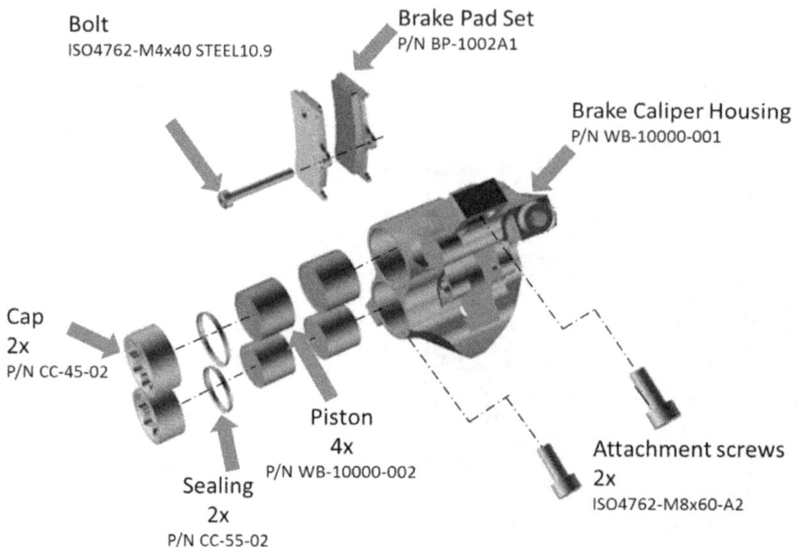

ICN-B6865-S4000P0110-001-01

Fig 4 Mountain Bike front brake sub-system: Design details (Sheet 2 of 2)

3 Functional description of the Mountain Bike brake system

The Mountain Bike brake system is composed of a forward and a rear brake subsystem which work independently from each other.

Each of these subsystems is composed of a hydraulic brake following the same design principle.

The power from a manual activation of a brake lever generates an increasing oil pressure in the oil-filled hydraulic line of the corresponding brake subsystem. The front and/or rear hydraulic line transfers the oil pressure to the forward and/or to the rear brake caliper housing.

A brake pad set is installed on each brake caliper housing. When a brake lever is manually activated, the hydraulic oil pressure moves the brake pistons, which are installed in the brake caliper housing.

Depending on the oil pressure the brake pistons move against the brake pad set (installed on each side of the metallic brake disk) and press them towards the brake disk. This causes friction between the material surfaces of the brake pads and the brake disk.

This leads to a deceleration of the Mountain Bike wheel when the brake is activated.

The Mountain Biker can vary the manual power at the brake levers to adapt the intensity of the friction in the front and/or rear brake subsystem. In this way the resulting deceleration of the Mountain Bike can be controlled.

Each of both brake lever assemblies comprises a non-metallic hydraulic oil reservoir. This oil reservoir can be opened and closed by screws using a specific rubber sealing. The oil reservoir design allows oil refilling and/or a change of the hydraulic oil.

4 System analysis Mountain Bike front brake

The Mountain Bike front brake is analyzed in accordance with the four analysis steps described in Chap 2.3. All decisions on the logic questions taken in the analysis Step 3 (refer to Para 4.3)

and Step 4 (refer to Para 4.4) are indicated by lines showing where decisions YES or NO have been selected.

The analytical process applied on this Mountain Bike example leads to the definition of three Preventive Maintenance Task Requirements with intervals (PMTRI), which must be selected in parallel in accordance with PMTRI task type selection criteria. Refer to Para 4.5.

The traceable selection of both the interval type and the numerical interval value the system analysis is shown for each of the selected PMTRI as part of Step 4 (refer to Para 4.6). All decisions on these logic questions are indicated by path lines showing where decisions YES or NO have been selected in this analysis example.

4.1 Step 1: ARC/non-ARC determination

		Product System Analysis ARC / non-ARC determination							
				DETERMINATION QUESTIONS					
S4000P CODE	Design Identi- fication Drawing- No Part-No etc	S1000D SNS DMC S3000L LCN / PBI / etc ...	ITEM NAME	Could a Functional Failure (FF) affect Product safety, including safety/ emergency systems and/or emergency equipment ?	Could a FF conflict with law and/or could the FF have a significant impact on environmental integrity (ecological damage) ?	Could a FF have an impact on mission/ operational capability ?	Could a FF of the selected item have significant economic impact ?	ARC ?	REMARKS
F4	MTB-BRS800-801	DA1-10	**Front Brake**	YES	NO	YES	NO	YES	Worst case: FF has a safety impact during the downhill period

In this analysis example the Brake System of the Mountain Bike is selected as an Analysis Relevant Candidate (ARC) already with one YES answer

ICN-B6865-S4000P0111-001-01

Fig 5 System analysis Mountain Bike - Step 1

4.2 Step 2: ARC System FMEA

ASD S4000P SYSTEM ANALYSIS AIA/ASD Mountain Bike			ARC Logistic Control Number (LCN) or a similar Product identification number	**BEI:** DA1-10 **P/N:** MTB-BRS800-801			
ARC FUNCTION AND FAILURE DATA SHEET / TABLE			ARC nomenclature	Front Brake			
Date		Analyst					
REF. no. F	FUNCTION (F) Function(s) of the ARC under analysis	REF. no. FF	FUNCTIONAL FAILURE (FF) One or more Functional Failure(s) identified for each ARC function	REF. no. FFE	FUNCTIONAL FAILURE EFFECT (FFE) Description of the potential "worst-case" end effect of each single FF on Product level	REF. No. FFC	Functional Failure Cause (FFC) One or more Failure Cause(s) allocated to each FF with FFE	Probability ranking of single FFC (optional) Estimation of a probability of each FFC occurence in relation to the other idendified per FF	Remarks update information etc.
...	...	...	...	...	...	...	...	...	...
F41	Front brake to produce friction for deceleration	FF41-1	No friction for deceleration	FFE 41-1-1	Potential crash in case of braking event; safety impact	FFC 41-1-1 -1	Hydraulic leakage oil reservoir front brake lever;	60%	P/N MTB-BRS800-401
						FFC 41-1-1 -2	Front brake tube damaged	40%	P/N MTB-BRS800-403
		FF41-2	Friction for deceleration is reduced	FFE 41-2-1	Extended braking distance- safety impact	FFC 41-2-1 -1	Front brake pads deteriorated	50%	P/N BP-1002A1
...	...	...	...	...	...	...	...	...	...

ICN-B6865-S4000P0112-001-01

Fig 6 System analysis Mountain Bike - Step 2

4.3 Step 3: FF Categorization

The Functional Failure (FF) categorization logic shown in Fig 7 must be applied to each FF identified in Step 2 (refer to Para 4.2).

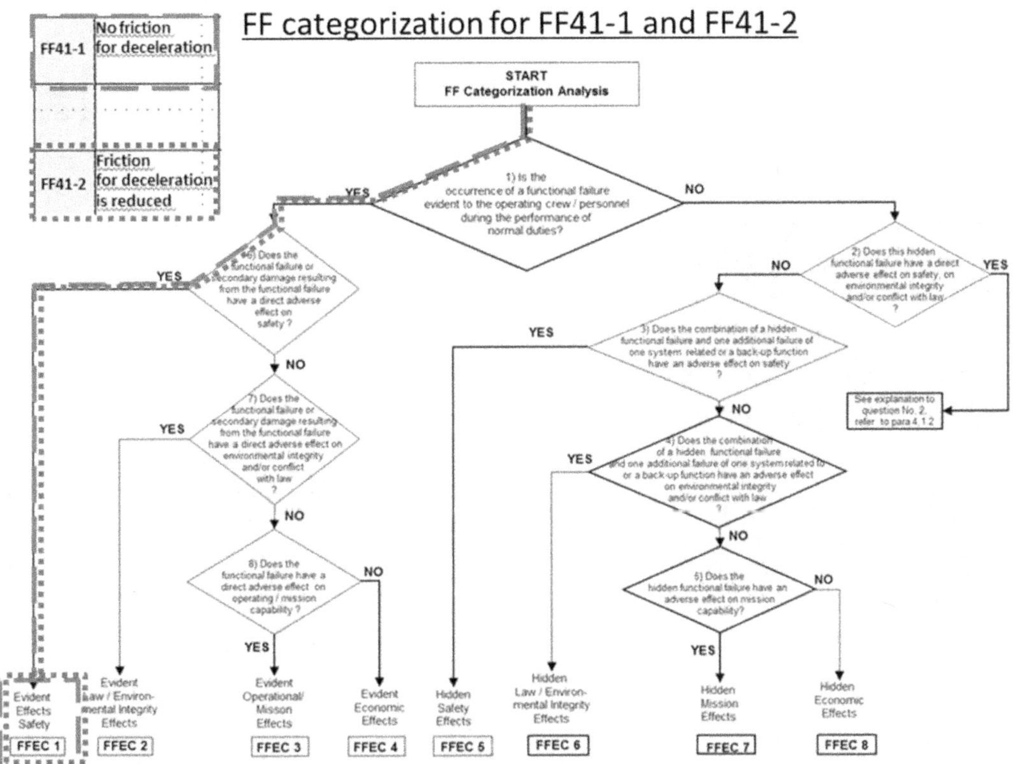

RESULT OF FF CATEGORIZATION:

Both Functional Failures FF41-1 and FF41-2 are to be allocated to FFEC1 („Evident Effects Safety")

ICN-B6865-S4000P0113-001-01

Fig 7 System analysis Mountain Bike - Step 3

4.4 Step 4: FC + PHCM Assessment

The Failure Cause (FC) + PHCM assessment logic shown in Fig 8 must be applied to each FC determined in Step 2 (refer to Para 4.2). In this analysis example, FFC 41-1-1-1 is selected for further analysis.

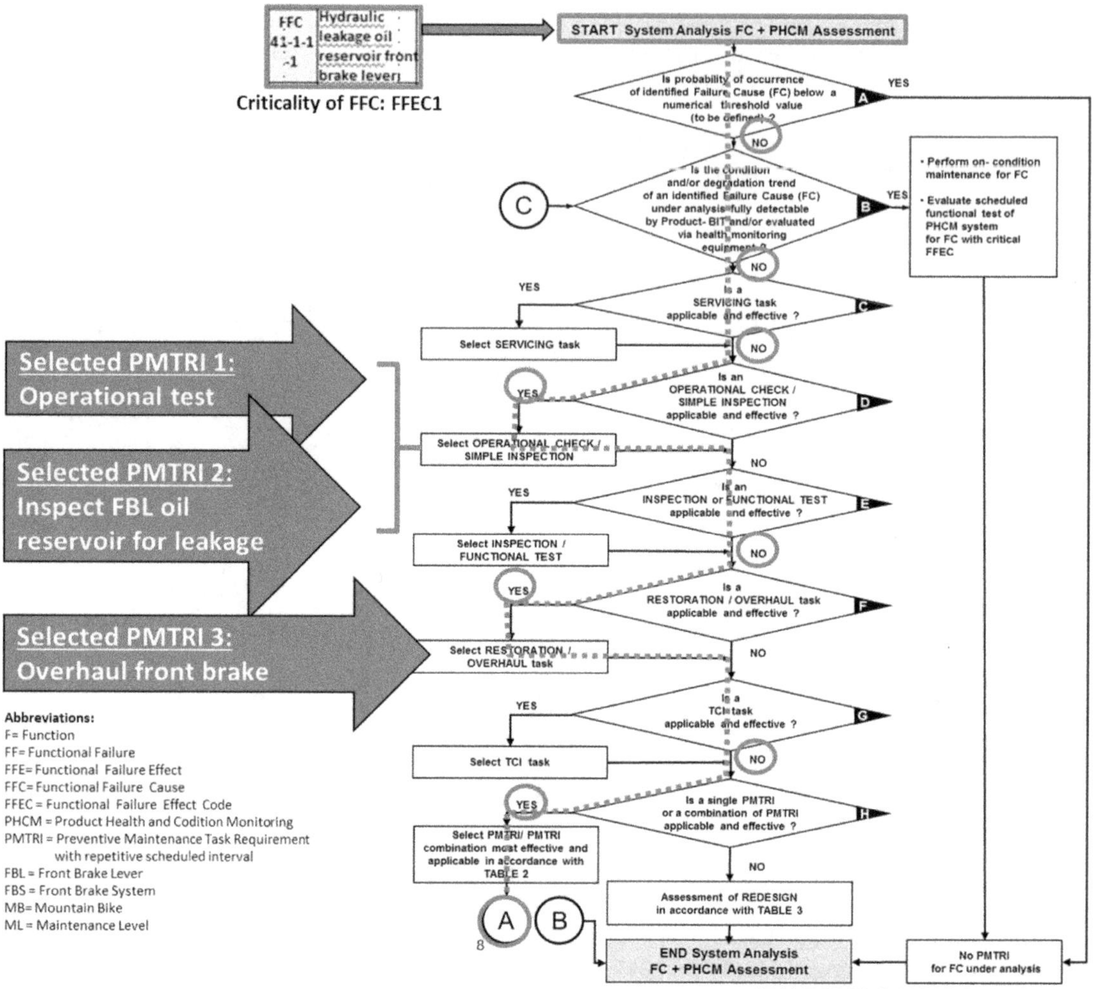

Fig 8 System analysis Mountain Bike - Step 4 (Part 1)

The review and re-assessment of the PHCM system is obsolete for the Mountain Bike analysis example. Therefore, answer NO is selected on Decision I. This leads to the End of FC + PHCM assessment as shown in Fig 10.

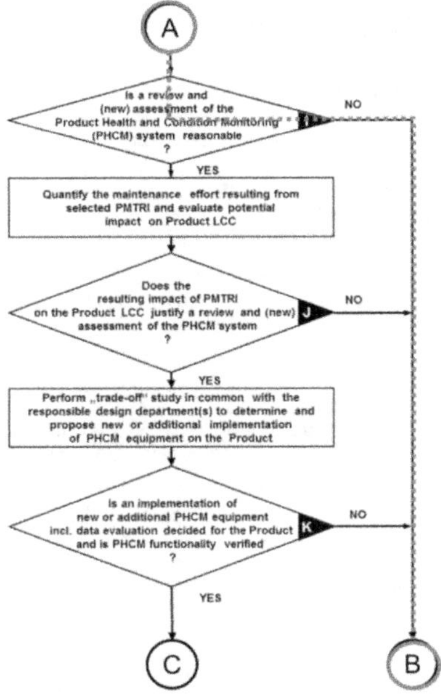

ICN-B6865-S4000P0115-001-01

Fig 9   System analysis Mountain Bike - Step 4 (Part 2)

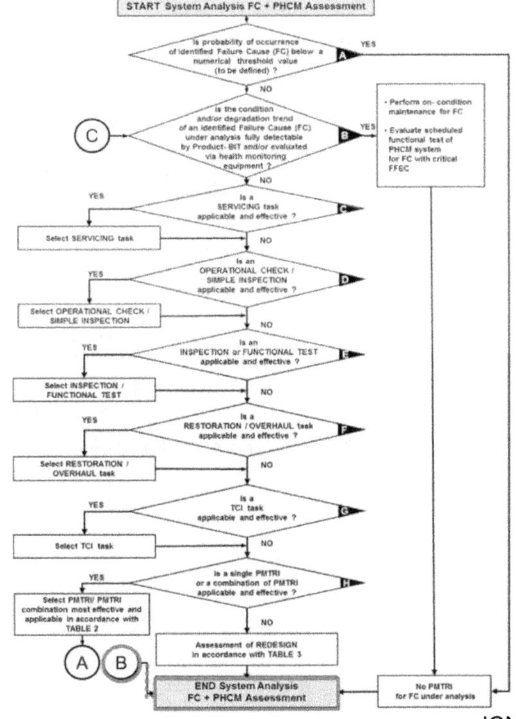

ICN-B6865-S4000P0116-001-01

Fig 10   System analysis Mountain Bike - Step 4 (Part 3)

4.5 PMTRI task type selection criteria

Application of Chapter 2.3, TABLE 2

FFEC	Selection of maintenance task type or a combination of them	Remark
1 Evident - Safety	Select the applicable and effective PMTRI or an appropriate combination of them	PMTRI interval to be defined for each maintenance task type (refer to Paragraph°5)
2 Evident - Law/ Environmental integrity	Select the most effective PMTRI or a combination of them	Harmonization of PMTRI intervals is recommended
3 Evident - Operation/Mission	Select a maximum of two applicable and effective PMTRI	PMTRI interval to be defined for each maintenance task type (refer to Paragraph°5) . Harmonization of PMTRI intervals is recommended
4 Evident - Economic	Select the most applicable and effective PMTRI	None
5 Hidden - Safety	Select the applicable and effective PMTRI or an appropriate combination of them	PMTRI interval to be defined for each maintenance task type (refer to Paragraph°5). Harmonization of PMTRI intervals is recommended
6 Hidden - Law/ Environmental integrity	Select the most effective PMTRI or a combination of them	Harmonization of PMTRI intervals is recommended
7 Hidden - Mission	Select a maximum of two applicable and effective PMTRI	PMTRI interval to be defined for each maintenance task type (refer to Paragraph°5). Harmonization of PMTRI intervals is recommended
8 Hidden - Economic	Select the most applicable and effective PMTRI	None

ICN-B6865-S4000P0117-001-01

Fig 11 PMTRI task type selection criteria

Applicable to: All

DMC-S4000P-A-07-02-0000-00A-040A-A_002-00_EN-US.docx

4.6 PMTRI interval definition

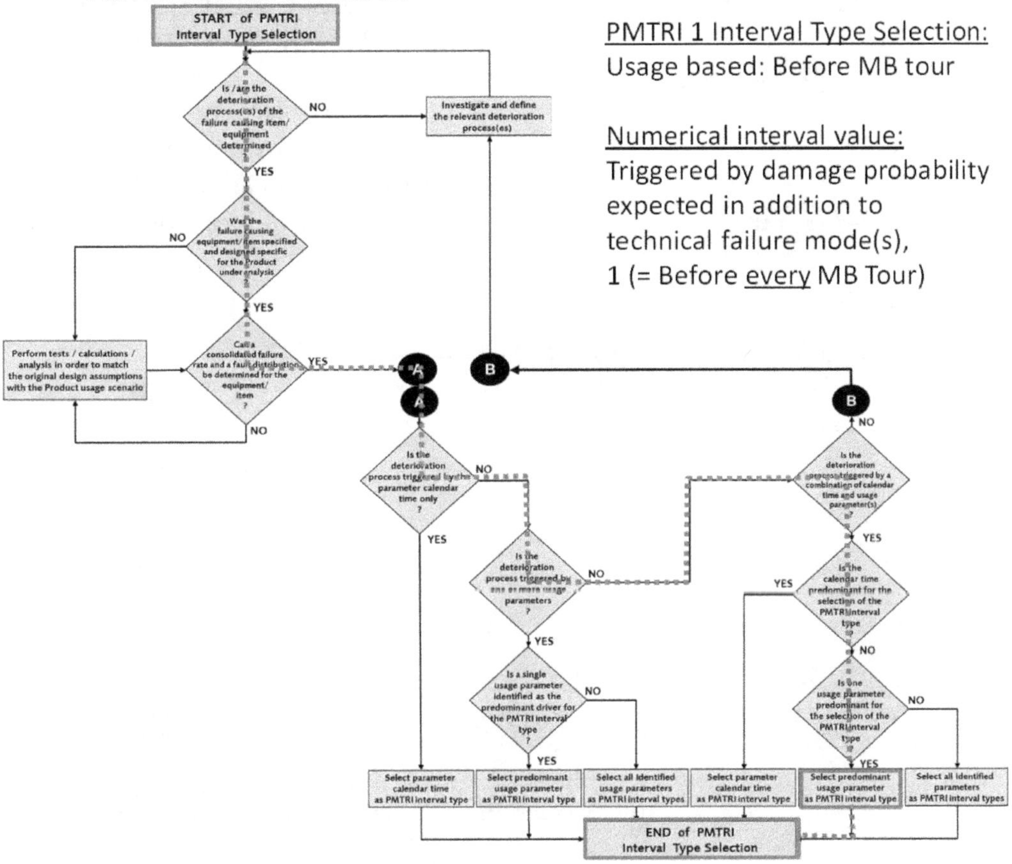

ICN-B6865-S4000P0118-001-01

Fig 12 PMTRI interval definition logic (PMTRI 1)

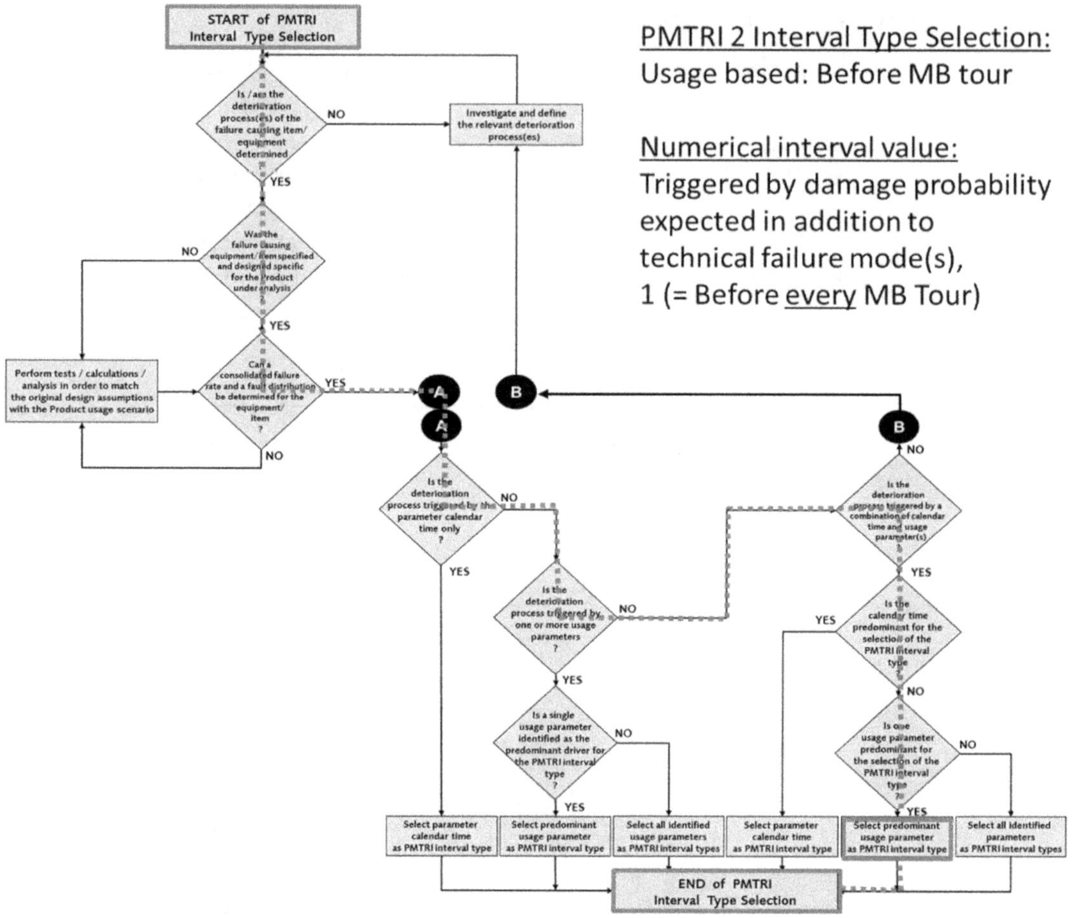

ICN-B6865-S4000P0119-001-01

Fig 13 PMTRI interval definition logic (PMTRI 2)

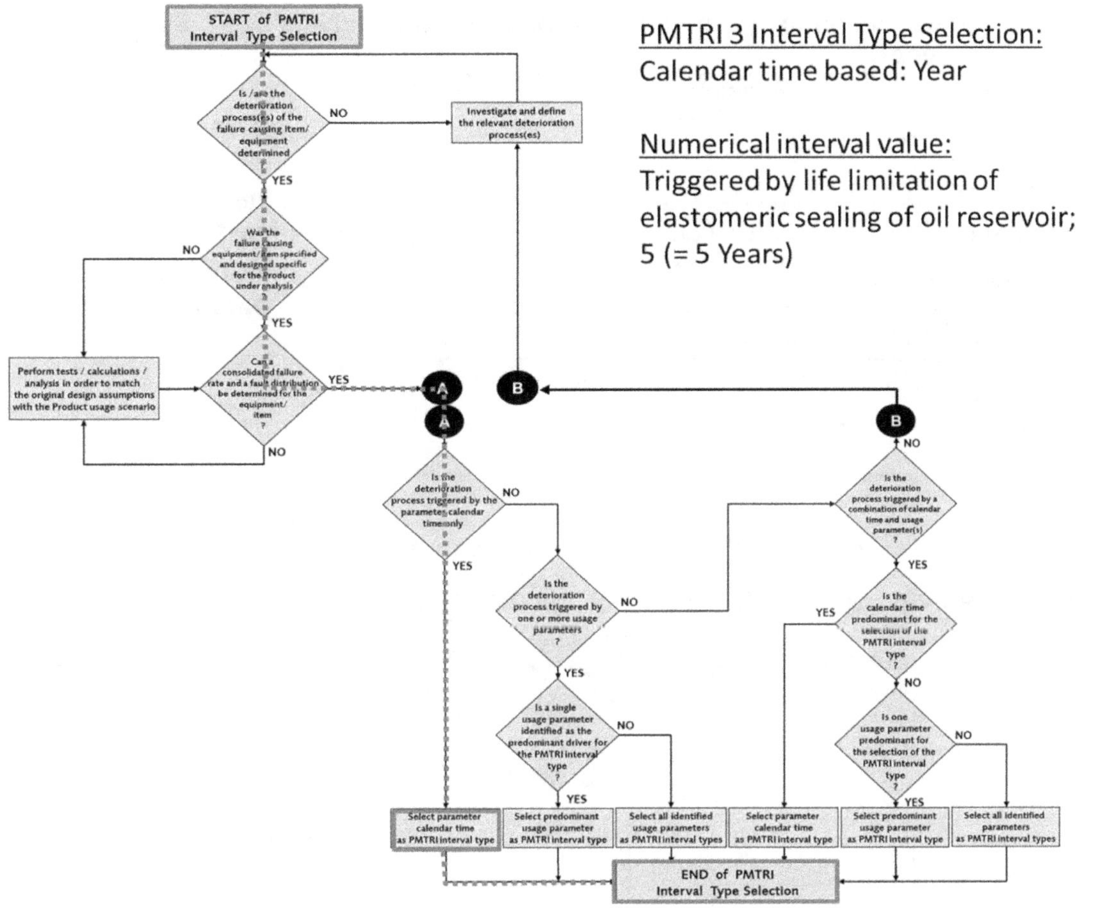

PMTRI 3 Interval Type Selection:
Calendar time based: Year

Numerical interval value:
Triggered by life limitation of elastomeric sealing of oil reservoir; 5 (= 5 Years)

ICN-B6865-S4000P0120-001-01

Fig 14 PMTRI interval definition logic (PMTRI 3)

4.7 Result summary from Mountain Bike system analysis example

PMTRI 1:	Operational test of FBS by activation of FBL
Interval type:	Before MB Tour
Numerical interval value:	1
Criticality code:	FFEC1
Supportability information:	ML User

PMTRI 2:	Inspect FBL oil reservoir for oil leakage
Interval type:	Before MB Tour
Numerical interval value:	1
Criticality code:	FFEC1
Supportability information:	ML User

PMTRI 3:	Replace sealing of FBL oil reservior (overhaul)
Interval type:	Year
Numerical interval value:	5
Criticality code:	FFEC1
Supportability information:	ML Authorized workshop

Data transfer of PMTRI 1,2 and 3 via PMTRI data list into S3000L Database

ICN-B6865-S4000P0121-001-01

Fig 15 Results from Mountain Bike system analysis example

4.8 PMTRI data transfer to S3000L via PMTRI data list

Breakdown Element Identifier (BEI)	Breakdown Element (BE) revision	BE name	Part identifier	Part name	S3000L candidate	Task-requirement ID	Task req. revision	PMTRI criticality	Task requirement type	Description of task requirement	Numerical interval value	Interval type	Status of task requirement	Supportability information
DA1-10	1.0	Front Brake	MTB-BRS800-801	Front Brake	Full	PMTRI 1	1.0	FFEC1	PMTRI	Operational test	1	Before MB tour	released	ML User
DA1-10	1.0	Front Brake	MTB-BRS800-801	Front Brake	Full	PMTRI 2	1.0	FFEC1	PMTRI	Visual inspection of FBL oil reservoir for oil leakage	1	Before MB tour	released	ML User
DA1-10	1.0	Front Brake	MTB-BRS800-801	Front Brake	Full	PMTRI 3	1.0	FFEC1	PMTRI	Replace sealing of FBL oil reservoir during overhaul	5	Year	released	ML Authorized workshop

ICN-B6865-S4000P0122-001-01

Fig 16 PMTRI data transfer to S3000L via PMTRI data list

Applicable to: All

End of data module

DMC-S4000P-A-07-02-0000-00A-040A-A_002-00_EN-US.docx

Chapter 7.3

Example - Policy and Procedure Handbook content

Table of contents

Page

Example - Policy and Procedure Handbook content 1

References 1

1 General 1

2 PPH content example for developing preventive Product maintenance 2

3 PPH content example for optimizing preventive Product maintenance 4

4 PPH content example for developing and optimizing preventive Product maintenance. 7

List of tables

1 References 1

References

Table 1 References

Chap No./Document No.	Title
Chap 2	Developing PMTR
Chap 2.3	Developing PMTR - System analysis
Chap 2.4	Developing PMTR - Structure analysis
Chap 2.5	Developing PMTR - Zonal analysis
Chap 2.7	Developing PMTR - Special event analysis
Chap 3	Optimizing PMTR
Chap 3.2	Optimizing PMTR - ISMO preparation phase
Chap 3.3	Optimizing PMTR - ISMO analysis phase
Chap 3.4	Optimizing PMTR - ISMO follow-up phase
Chap 3.5	Optimizing PMTR - Review of PMTRE for special events

1 General

Each project must develop a Policy and Procedure Handbook (PPH). Three examples are given:

- PPH content example for a Product analysis from Chap 2. Refer to Para 2.
- PPH content example for a Product analysis from Chap 3. Refer to Para 3.
- PPH content example for a Product analysis from a combined application of Chap 2 and Chap 3. Refer to Para 4.

2 PPH content example for developing preventive Product maintenance

2.1 Front matter

History of document changes

Table of contents

Figures and tables

Referenced documents

2.2 CHAPTER 1: INTRODUCTION GENERAL

1.1. Basics about product maintenance and maintenance program

1.2. Chap 2 analysis background and history

1.3. Chap 2 analysis scope

1.4. Revision applied

1.5. Requirements from regulatory authorities

2.3 CHAPTER 2: PROJECT ORGANIZATION AND ADMINISTRATION

2.1. General

2.2. Contractual background

2.3. Organization and project team

2.4. Analyst selection and training

2.5. Use of IT analysis support tools

2.6. Communication and interface management

2.7. Meeting organization and meeting reports

2.8. Involvement of in-service feedback, test feedback

2.9. PPH approval

2.10. Analysis report revisions

2.4 CHAPTER 3: PRODUCT USAGE AND MAINTENANCE FRAMEWORK

3.1. Introduction

3.2. Objectives

3.3. Scope

3.4. Product XY in-service utilization assumptions

3.5. Scheduled interval framework for PMTRI

2.5 CHAPTER 4: PRODUCT-SPECIFIC ANALYSIS PRE-SELECTIONS AND LIMITATIONS

4.1. Introduction

4.2. Product Breakdown Structure (PBS)

4.3. Product Zonal Plan (PZP)

4.4. Allocation of analysis pre-selections and limitations in PBS and PZP

2.6   CHAPTER 5: SYSTEM ANALYSIS BASED ON CHAP 2.3

5.1. Introduction

5.2. Principles

5.3. System analysis process and procedure

5.4. Detailed process description

5.5. Supplementary methodologies

5.6. Analysis administration

5.7. Review procedure of analysis results

5.8. MWG meetings and interfaces with product type certification process

2.7   CHAPTER 6: STRUCTURE ANALYSIS BASED ON CHAP 2.4

6.1. Introduction

6.2. Principles

6.3. Structure analysis process and procedure

6.4. Detailed process description

6.5. SSI/SD and MRS configuration management

6.6. SSI/SD PMTRI consolidation and summary

6.7. Analysis administration

6.8. Review procedure of analysis results

6.9. MWG meetings and analysis review procedure

2.8   CHAPTER 7: ZONAL ANALYSIS BASED ON CHAP 2.5

7.1. Introduction

7.2. Zonal analysis process and procedure

7.3. Detailed process description

7.4. Zonal analysis procedure

7.5. Consolidation of requirements

7.6. Interfaces to system and/or structure analysis results

7.7. PMTRI output data

2.9   CHAPTER 8: SPECIAL EVENT ANALYSIS BASED ON CHAP 2.7

8.1. Introduction

8.2. Developing PMTRE: process and procedure

8.3. Detailed process description

2.10   CHAPTER 9: ANALYSIS ACCEPTANCE/PRODUCT TYPE CERTIFICATION

9.1. General

9.2. Certification maintenance requirements

9.3. Life limited items

9.4. Requirements from safety analysis

9.5. Consolidation of <u>Chap 2</u> analysis results with other PMTRI sources

2.11 APPENDIX A: S4000P ANALYSIS <u>CHAP 2</u> WORK SHEETS/TABLES
A.1. System analysis: ARC-selection

A.2. System analysis: ARC system FMEA

A.3. System analysis: FF categorization

A.4. System analysis: FC assessment

A.5. SSI/SD, MRS selection and location

A.6. Structure analysis: PMTRI selection sheet

A.7. Structure analysis: interval rating sheets

A.8. Structure analysis: PMTRI summary sheets

A.9. Standard zonal analysis: form sheets

A.10. Zonal analysis: PMTRI transfer documentation sheet

A.11. Special event analysis: PMTRE summary sheet

A.12. Preventive maintenance analysis: status table

2.12 APPENDIX B: GLOSSARY, ACRONYMS AND ABBREVIATIONS
B.1. Glossary

B.2. Acronyms and abbreviations

2.13 APPENDIX C: PROJECT PLAN AND MILESTONES

2.14 APPENDIX D: PROJECT ORGANIZATION CHART

2.15 APPENDIX E: MEETING REPORT FORMS

3 PPH content example for optimizing preventive Product maintenance

3.1 Front matter
History of document changes

Table of contents

Figures and tables

Referenced documents

3.2 CHAPTER 1: INTRODUCTION GENERAL
1.1 Basics about product maintenance and maintenance program

1.2. <u>Chap 2</u> analysis background and history

    1.3. Chap 3 analysis purpose

    1.4. Revision applied

    1.5. Requirements from regulatory authorities

3.3   **CHAPTER 2: PROJECT ORGANIZATION AND ADMINISTRATION**

    2.1. General

    2.2. Contractual background

    2.3. Organization and project team

    2.4. Analyst selection and training

    2.5. Use of IT analysis support tools

    2.6. Communication and interface management

    2.7. Meeting organization and meeting reports

    2.8. Involvement of in-service feedback, test feedback

    2.9. ISMO PPH approval

    2.10. ISMO analysis revisions

3.4   **CHAPTER 3: PRODUCT USAGE AND MAINTENANCE FRAMEWORK**

    3.1. Introduction

    3.2. Objectives

    3.3. Scope

    3.4. Product XY in-service utilization assumptions

    3.5. Scheduled interval framework for PMTRI

3.5   **CHAPTER 4: PRODUCT-SPECIFIC ANALYSIS PRE-SELECTIONS AND LIMITATIONS**

    4.1. Introduction

    4.2. Product Breakdown Structure (PBS)

    4.3. Product Zonal Plan (PZP)

    4.4. Allocation of analysis pre-selections and limitations in PBS and PZP

3.6   **CHAPTER 5: ISMO ANALYSIS PREPARATION BASED ON CHAP 3.2**

    5.1. Introduction

    5.2. Process logic

    5.3. Detailed process description

    5.4. Requirements and results from safety analysis

    5.5. Inputs from responsible design departments

    5.6. Handling of resulting activities from ISMO analysis preparation

3.7   CHAPTER 6: ISMO ANALYSIS PROCESS BASED ON CHAP 3.3
6.1. Introduction

6.2. Process logic

6.3. Detailed process description

6.4. Definition of input-and output data for an it analysis support tool

6.5. Data processing of IT analysis support tool

6.6. Preparation of an IT analysis support tool

6.7. Definition of acceptance process of analysis results

6.8. Update process for ISMO analysis process

Note
Items 6.2 and 6.3 can be added as attachments, if required.

3.8   CHAPTER 7: ISMO FOLLOW-UP ANALYSIS BASED ON CHAP 3.4
7.1. Introduction

7.2. Process logic

7.3. Detailed process description

7.4. Delivery of ISMO follow-up analysis results

3.9   CHAPTER 8: REVIEW AND OPTIMIZATION OF PMTRE FOR SPECIAL EVENTS BASED ON CHAP 3.5
8.1. Introduction

8.2. Review and optimization of PMTRE: process and procedure

8.3. Detailed process description

3.10   CHAPTER 9: ANALYSIS ACCEPTANCE/PRODUCT TYPE CERTIFICATION
9.1. General

9.2. Certification Maintenance Requirements (CMR)

9.3. Life limited items

9.4. Requirements from safety analysis

9.5. Consolidation of Chap 3 analysis results with other PMTRI sources

3.11   APPENDIX A: ANALYSIS CHAP 3 WORK SHEETS/TABLES
A.1. ISMO analysis preparation: summary sheet

A.2. ISMO analysis process: PMTRI output table

A.3. ISMO follow-up analysis: summary sheet

A.4. Special event PMTRE review and optimization: PMTRE summary

3.12   APPENDIX B: GLOSSARY, ACRONYMS AND ABBREVIATIONS
B.1. Glossary

B.2. Acronyms and abbreviations

3.13   **APPENDIX C: PROJECT PLAN AND MILESTONES**

3.14   **APPENDIX D: PROJECT ORGANIZATION CHART**

3.15   **APPENDIX E: MEETING REPORT FORMS**

4   **PPH content example for developing and optimizing preventive Product maintenance**

4.1   **Front matter**

History of document changes

Table of contents

Figures and tables

Referenced documents

4.2   **CHAPTER 1: INTRODUCTION GENERAL**

1.1. Basics about product maintenance and maintenance program

1.2. Analysis background and history

1.3. Analysis scope

1.4. Revision applied

1.5. Requirements from regulatory authorities

4.3   **CHAPTER 2: PROJECT ORGANIZATION AND ADMINISTRATION**

2.1. General

2.2. Contractual background

2.3. Organization and project team

2.4. Analyst selection and training

2.5. Use of IT analysis support tools

2.6. Communication and interface management

2.7. Meeting organization and meeting reports

2.8. Involvement of in-service feedback, test feedback

2.9. PPH approval

2.10. Analysis report revisions

4.4   **CHAPTER 3: PRODUCT USAGE AND MAINTENANCE FRAMEWORK**

3.1. Introduction

3.2. Objectives

3.3. Scope

3.4. Product XY in-service utilization assumptions

3.5. Scheduled interval framework for PMTRI

4.5 **CHAPTER 4: PRODUCT-SPECIFIC ANALYSIS PRE-SELECTIONS AND LIMITATIONS**

4.1. Introduction

4.2. Product Breakdown Structure (PBS)

4.3. Product Zonal Plan (PZP)

4.4. Allocation of S4000P analysis pre-selections and limitations in PBS and PZP

4.5. Identification of Chap 2 analysis relevant PBS/PZP segments

4.6. Identification of Chap 3 analysis relevant PBS/PZP segments

4.7. Coordination of analysis activities related to Chap 2 and to Chap 3

Note
Items 4.5 and 4.6 must be in line with the results from safety analysis, CMR, customer requests, etc.

4.6 **CHAPTER 5: SYSTEM ANALYSIS BASED ON CHAP 2.3**

5.1. Introduction

5.2. Principles

5.3. System analysis process and procedure

5.4. Detailed process description

5.5. Supplementary methodologies

5.6. Analysis administration

5.7. Review procedure of analysis results

5.8. MWG meetings and interfaces with product type certification process

4.7 **CHAPTER 6: STRUCTURE ANALYSIS BASED ON CHAP 2.4**

6.1. Introduction

6.2. Principles

6.3. Structure analysis process and procedure

6.4. Detailed process description

6.5. SSI/SD and MRS configuration management

6.6. SSI/SD PMTRI consolidation and summary

6.7. Analysis administration

6.8. Review procedure of analysis results

6.9. MWG meetings and analysis review procedure

4.8 **CHAPTER 7: ZONAL ANALYSIS BASED ON CHAP 2.5**

7.1. Introduction

7.2. Zonal analysis process and procedure

7.3. Detailed process description

7.4. Zonal analysis procedure

7.5. Consolidation of requirements

7.6. Interfaces to system and/or structure analysis results

7.7. PMTRI output data

4.9   **CHAPTER 8: SPECIAL EVENT ANALYSIS BASED ON CHAP 2.7**

8.1. Introduction

8.2. Developing PMTRE: process and procedure

8.3. Detailed process description

4.10   **CHAPTER 9: ISMO ANALYSIS PREPARATION BASED ON CHAP 3.2**

9.1. Introduction

9.2. Process logic

9.3. Detailed process description

9.4. Requirements/results from safety analysis

9.5. Inputs from responsible design departments

9.6. Handling of resulting activities from ISMO analysis preparation

4.11   **CHAPTER 10: ISMO ANALYSIS PROCESS BASED ON CHAP 3.3**

10.1. Introduction

10.2. Process logic

10.3. Detailed process description

10.4. Definition of input-and output data for an IT analysis support tool

10.5. Data processing of IT analysis support tool

10.6. Preparation of an IT analysis support tool

10.7. Handling and acceptance of ISMO analysis results

10.8. Update process for ISMO analysis process

Note
    Items 10.2 and 10.3 can be added as attachments, if required.

4.12   **CHAPTER 11: ISMO FOLLOW-UP ANALYSIS BASED ON CHAP 3.4**

11.1. Introduction

11.2. Process logic

11.3. Detailed process description

11.4. Handling and acceptance of ISMO follow-up analysis results

4.13   **CHAPTER 12: REVIEW AND OPTIMIZATION OF PMTRE FOR SPECIAL EVENTS BASED ON CHAP 3.5**

12.1. Introduction

12.2. Review and optimization of PMTRE: process and procedure

12.3. etailed process description

4.14   CHAPTER 13: ANALYSIS ACCEPTANCE/PRODUCT TYPE CERTIFICATION
13.1. General

13.2. Certification Maintenance Requirements (CMR)

13.3. Life limited items

13.4. Requirements from safety analysis

13.5 Consolidation of Chap 2 and Chap 3 analysis results with other PMTRI sources

4.15   APPENDIX A: CHAP 2 ANALYSIS WORK SHEETS/TABLES
A.1   System analysis: ARC-selection

A.2. System analysis: ARC system FMEA

A.3 System analysis: FF categorization

A.4. System analysis: FC assessment

A.5. SSI/SD, MRS selection and location

A.6. Structure analysis: PMTRI selection sheet

A.7. Structure analysis: interval rating sheets

A.8. Structure analysis: PMTRI summary sheets

A.9. Standard zonal analysis: form sheets

A.10. Zonal analysis: PMTRI transfer documentation sheet

A.11. Special event analysis: PMTRE summary sheet

A.12. Preventive maintenance analysis: status table

4.16   APPENDIX B: CHAP 3 ANALYSIS WORK SHEETS/TABLES
B.1. ISMO analysis preparation: summary sheet

B.2. ISMO analysis process: PMTRI output table

B.3. ISMO follow-up analysis: summary sheet

B.4. Special event PMTRE review and optimization: PMTRE summary table

4.17   APPENDIX C: GLOSSARY, ACRONYMS AND ABBREVIATIONS
C.1. Glossary

C.2. Acronyms and abbreviations

4.18   APPENDIX D: PROJECT PLAN AND MILESTONES

4.19   APPENDIX E: PROJECT ORGANIZATION CHART

4.20   APPENDIX F: MEETING REPORT FORMS

Check out the different specifications in print:

SX000H, *Handbook for the S-Series Integrated Product Support (IPS) Specifications*, Issue 1.0,
ISBN 978-84-19125-18-7

SX000i, *International specification for integrated product support (IPS)*, Issue 3.0, ISBN 978-84-19125-19-4

S1000D, *International specification for technical publications using a common source database*, Issue 5.0,
(3 volumes), ISBN 978-84-19125-31-6, 978-84-19125-32-3 and 978-84-19125-33-0

S2000M, *International specification for material management - Integrated data processing* Issue 7.0 (2
volumes), ISBN 978-84-19125-29-3 and 978-84-19125-30-9

S3000L, *International specification for Logistics Support Analysis – LSA*, Issue 2.0,
ISBN 978-84-19125-20-0

S4000P, *International specification for developing and continuously improving preventive maintenance*,
Issue 2.1, ISBN 978-84-19125-21-7

S5000F, *International specification for in-service data feedback*, Issue 3.0 (2 volumes),
ISBNs 978-84-19125-27-9 and 978-84-19125-28-6

S6000, *International specification for training analysis and design*, Issue 2.0, ISBN 978-84-19125-22-4

SX001G, *Glossary for the S-Series IPS specifications*, Issue 3.0, ISBN 978-84-19125-23-1

SX002D, *Common data model for the S-Series IPS specifications*, Issue 2.1, ISBN 978-84-19125-24-8

SX004G, *UML model reader's guide*, Issue 2.0, ISBN 978-84-19125-25-5

SX005G, *S-Series IPS specifications XML schema implementation guide*, Issue 2.0,
ISBN 978-84-19125-26-2

Further books on the S-Series to be published by Editorial Dragon:

An introduction to the S-Series IPS specifications by Ramón Somoza, ISBN 978-84-19125-16-3

S-Series data models and XML schemas by Ramón Somoza, ISBN 978-84-19125-17-0